AF759984

Peter Schneck
Rhetoric and Evidence

Law & Literature

Edited by
Daniela Carpi · Klaus Stierstorfer

Volume 1

De Gruyter

Peter Schneck

Rhetoric and Evidence

Legal Conflict and Literary Representation in U.S. American Culture

De Gruyter

ISBN 978-3-11-025376-4
e-ISBN 978-3-11-025377-1
ISSN 2191-8457

Library of Congress Cataloging-in-Publication Data

Schneck, Peter, 1960–
Rhetoric and evidence : legal conflict and literary representation in U.S. American culture / by Peter Schneck.
p. cm. – (Law & literature ; 1)
Includes bibliographical references.
ISBN 978-3-11-025376-4 (alk. paper)
1. American literature – History and criticism. 2. Law in literature. 3. Law and literature – United States – History. 4. Law in mass media. I. Title.
PS169.L37S35 2011
810.9'3554–dc22
2011015390

Bibliographic information published by the Deutsche Nationalbibliothek

The Deutsche Nationalbibliothek lists this publication in the Deutsche Nationalbibliografie; detailed bibliographic data are available in the Internet at http://dnb.d-nb.de.

© 2011 Walter de Gruyter GmbH & Co. KG, Berlin/Boston

Printing: Hubert & Co. GmbH & Co. KG, Göttingen
∞ Printed on acid-free paper

Printed in Germany

www.degruyter.com

Acknowledgements

Over the past years that it took to conceive and develop, as well as to revise and refine the ideas and arguments which eventually made it into this book, I have been rather fortunate to receive substantial support and encouragement from various individuals and institutions.

My colleagues at the Amerika Institut at the Ludwig-Maximilians Universität in Munich helped immensely to move the project past its initial phases by their active intellectual involvement and their constructive criticism. In particular, I want to thank Ulla Haselstein for her unflagging endorsement, her critical inspiration, as well as her wise counseling without which the major parts of this book would never have seen the light of day. Berndt Ostendorf, Christof Decker, Randi Gunzenhäuser, and Ralph Poole offered helpful comments and crucial advice at numerous points, in the same spirit of congeniality that also characterized the various graduate colloquia and seminars that helped me to further develop my ideas. I am grateful to the German Research Foundation (DFG) for funding an extended research stay at the University of California at Irvine which for many reasons has had a lasting impact on the project. Above all, it allowed me to work with Brook Thomas and John Carlos Rowe from whose scholarly expertise and guidance I have benefitted immensely and in numerous ways. Finally, this book would never have been completed without the help and support of my colleagues at the University of Osnabrück, especially Devin Zuber, whose patient and precise comments have allowed me to clarify and correct many inconsistencies and errors and whose continuous willingness to discuss and debate has been both encouraging and energizing. Elena Bomm, Robert Murphy, Christopher Schuller, and Stefanie Krüger have offered invaluable support in preparing the final manuscript. Special thanks to Sabine N. Meyer for vital suggestions and corrections. I am also grateful to the series' editors, Daniela Carpi and Klaus Stierstorfer, and the people at de Gruyter, especially Manuela Gerlof, for their patient encouragement and assistance.

While the continuous encouragement and support from all my colleagues and friends have thus certainly made this a better book, the flaws and mistakes it still contains are completely my own.

Thanks most of all to Alex, Carlo, and Louisa for providing continuous emotional support and helping me to maintain a sense for the truly essential things.

Table of Contents

Chapter 1
Law, Literature, and the Predicament of Representation

The following introductory chapter is meant to delineate what I consider a fundamental challenge facing the portrayal of law in literary fiction. In order to do so, I will take several related steps. Since the complex relation between the legal and the literary has become the focus of various critical approaches in the context of the so-called law-and-literature movement, I will give a first, provisional outlook on the basic divisions of the field in order to better position my own perspective. A more in-depth discussion of central debates and concepts that have developed within the law-and-literature movement is reserved for the second chapter. For now, my aim is to describe the specific interest of my approach in reference to the increased general attention given to the law and literature relation in the United States. I will regard this interest as one expression of a more general debate, which I take to be most obvious in American culture, though not exclusive to it: a debate concerning the stability and the nature of evidence in relation to the rhetorical struggles of the democratic public sphere. The intense cultural and literary interest in the law, I will argue, must be interpreted as a symptom of the functional relation, or correlation, of legal and literary concepts of evidence and rhetoric.

This is why in the United States the courtroom trial has become the dominant form and focus of cultural representations of the law, including the trials and tribunals presented in literary fictions. In these representations, the trial situation emerges as a paradigmatic situation in which the truth and evidence established by rhetorical strife are meant to serve the advancement or restoration of justice — yet also often fail to do so. That the legal process of a public trial involves the potential for drama and that failures and inequities are part of it, may be taken as one of the most obvious reasons for literature's critical engagement with the law. However, the notion of justice also implies certain exigencies in regard to the legitimacy of representation that concerns both law and literature. Starting out from Jacques Derrida's discussion of the 'mystical foundation' of legal authority and his remarks on the relation between law and literature, I attempt to describe what can be called the *predicament of representation* that challenges the literary representation of the law.

One central moment of this challenge concerns the status of linguistic representations as evidence, that is, as legitimate and appropriate representations of truth or reality. As I will discuss in more detail below, evidence must be understood as an essentially rhetorical concept. This does not simply imply that evidence is a rhetorical construction but, rather, that rhetoric makes evidence necessary as a concept: on the one hand, in order to reflect upon the relation between reality and its representation, and, on the other, to form judgments about rhetorical truth claims. The difference between legal and literary discourse finds its origin in the distinction between rhetorical and poetical practices of proof. However, as the example of Aristotle demonstrates, this distinction had already implied the similarity, or rather the complementarity, of law and literature as related yet competing rhetorics of evidence.

The predicament of representation must thus become most intense where the literary depiction of the law critically focuses on the rhetorical grounding of legal evidence in order to replace it with its own evidence. These observations will finally lead to a general thesis about the legal moment in literary fictions of law and justice, that is, the unacknowledged self-reflective and self-critical dimension of literature's portrayal of the law.

I

From the perspective of academic study and criticism in the United States, the relation between law and literature appears to be both intense and somewhat enigmatic. Of course, the intensity of the relationship has become more obvious for the contemporary observer after the emergence of the so-called law-and-literature movement in the late 1970s and its rapid development over the last four decades into a veritable interpretive and theoretical enterprise. Even though the interdisciplinary thrust of law and literature scholarship has been criticized by Julie Stone Peters and others as merely an empty gesture and its institutional standing in terms of joint programs and degrees is far from impressive, law and literature approaches and the work that results from them have spread conspicuously in reach and number, especially in the humanities. In addition, the increasing international scope and the further extension of the critical interchange between law and the humanities in general has become rather obvious over the last fifteen years, particularly in areas like literature and human rights or literature and property law.[1] The "border between law and literature has become a bridge," Kieran Dolin ob-

---

[1] See, for instance, Slaughter, *Human Rights Inc.*; Schmidgen, *Eigtheenth-Century Fiction and the Law of Property*; Porsdam, *From Civil to Human Rights;* Weitin, *Zeugenschaft: Das Recht der Literatur.*

served in 2007, "which will enable even more connections to be discerned" and most likely "produce further transformations in both fields."[2]

And yet, the enigmatic dimension of this academic success story lies in the fact that there is still no and most likely never was or will be a discernible common program, approach, or methodology that would give the comparative study of law and literature the more decisive contours of a conventional discipline or field of scientific inquiry and theoretical speculation. There is no "central programmatic thrust, whether positive or normative, to the law-and-literature movement," Richard Posner has stated, leading to "a rich but confusing array of potential links."[3] between the two fields. In a similar vein, Guyora Binder and Robert Weisberg, in their comprehensive approach to the literary criticism of law, conclude that, since there is no single theory, the diverse critical endeavors centered around the law and literature relation should

> be understood as a series of genres — discrete, historically specific social practices of criticism, organized by recurrent purposes and interests, canonical texts, problems and themes, and characteristic rhetorical tropes, voices and forensic strategies.[4]

The two genres that have become so generally recognized as to almost assume a status similar to full-grown scholarly approaches are called, respectively, *law in literature* and *law as literature*. As these appellations indicate, the former looks at the literary representation of legal issues and processes, including the study of various thematic, topical, and symbolic aspects of law in literature, as well as the role of certain legal personnel in literary fictions, like the lawyer or the judge. The latter perspective is generally understood as the criticism of legal documents, acts, records, and practices with the help of concepts and methods derived from literary and cultural theories. The law as literature perspective thus focuses on the law as text, narrative, story, performance, or rhetoric.

This approach is less easily defined by the conventional practices and objectives of literary theory, however. Those who look at the law as literature are often not only literary but also legal scholars, and indeed this approach has found resonance both with post-structuralist textual criticism in general and with the Critical Legal Studies movement specifically, with their common emphasis on the "discursive context in which law and its effects are

---

2 Dolin, *Critical Introduction,* 11.

3 Posner, *Law and Literature*, 1.

4 Binder/Weisberg, *Literary Criticisms*, 20.

created, presented, interpreted, and assessed."[5] Whatever aspect of legal discourse and practice scholars are focused on, 'law as literature' is something of a misnomer: it embraces interpretations that treat law as literature for heuristic reasons only, not because they assume that law actually is or was literature. In fact, there is every reason to call this perspective 'literature in law' since its particular interest is the use of literary means in legal discourse, that is, the literariness of the law: its stories, its metaphors, its rhetoric, and its fictions.

Even though Binder and Weisberg are almost exclusively interested in the literary criticism of law which looks at law as literature, their observations can also be made useful for an approach that, like the one I will present in this introduction, is instead concerned with the function of the law in (and for) literature. In their view, both the study of law in literature and of law as literature are characterized more by certain presumptions about the relationship between the two parts of the equation and less by strict differences in critical theory and practice on either side. Accordingly, the "analogical relation" between law and literature, for instance, which forms the basis of most literary criticisms of the law, must be regarded as a trope that hinges on rather different "images of literary activity." Law and literature, in turn, can be considered as a master trope, or, in Weisberg and Binder's words, a "fertile rhetorical figure," which is shared by a highly diversified set of critical practices and approaches, all resting on specific conceptualizations of law and of literature.[6]

What distinguishes each approach from the next, more precisely, is how these concepts are conceived of in relation to each other, and how this relation is eventually turned into a foundation for the specific analytical and interpretive strategies employed. For example, both 'law' and 'literature' are employed as metaphors or tropes in most works that discuss their relation — including my own, for now at least. Indeed, it could be argued that only through the metaphorical use of the terms a more extended comparison seems possible in the first place. There is a certain downside, though, especially when the relation features a definite article: literature and *the* law — where it is never quite clear what *the* law would entail — and when a certain understanding of one part is projected onto the other, e.g. when (the) law is reduced to text or speech. I address some of these difficulties in Chapter Four.

---

[5] Bauman, *Critical Legal Studies*, 247.
[6] Binder/Weisberg, *Literary Criticisms*, 20.

Given these conditions, it appears mandatory that, in order to introduce my own approach, I should first describe more clearly the intellectual concerns implied and the basic questions that inform these concerns. I do not deny that my approach also relies on a certain image of literary activity, as indeed my attention will be very much on literature as a critical activity or practice, a disposition which fundamentally defines its relation to the law. In this regard, the differentiation between the 'law in literature' perspective and its correlate approach, 'law as literature,' has turned from a convenient gradation signaling the advance of literary concepts within the realm of legal hermeneutics into a rather unfortunate dividing line for the development of a more advanced investigation of the representation of law in literature by literary criticism and theory.

Such an advanced investigation appears especially necessary if one considers the importance and cultural prominence which the literary (or, more generally, the symbolic) representation of legal procedures and practices has maintained in American culture from colonial times until today. Even before Independence, there was a noticeable interest in the public representation and discussion of trials which reached well beyond the immediate audience of tribunals or public executions. The publication of execution sermons, conversion narratives, and the extensive records and commentaries on accusations and trials of witchcraft demonstrate that the Puritans viewed this kind of 'literature' as exemplary in its didactic and moral function.[7] Traditional interpretations of such representations of law in literature often proceed from a somewhat limited understanding of a basic mimetic function, simply assuming that the literary portrayal of legal discourse and practice could or should be read in a rather straight-forward fashion. Another variant of this approach takes the literary representation of the law as a metaphorical or allegorical device to express and negotiate more universal notions, like justice, morality, or the necessity of normative institutions.[8]

In contrast, more recent investigations in the wake of the law-and-literature movement place heavy emphasis on the similarities of rhetorical and narrative strategies used both in legal and in literary 'stories' or 'fictions.' The more these similarities are emphasized, however, the more the relation between law and literature comes to rest on something like a conceptual essentialism. The relation between law and literature is then solely based on some

---

[7] For Puritan narratives, see Bosco, "Lectures at the Pillory;" Williams, "Criminal Conversion Narrative" and for later developments Halttunen, "The Birth of Horror" and Wiltenburg, "True Crime."

[8] See, for instance, Browne, *Law and Lawyers*, and Smith, *Law and American Literature*.

common universal disposition, such as the rhetoricity of literary and legal speech acts or the fundamental role of story-telling in legal and literary reconstructions of reality and experience. From the more radical vantage points offered by such interpretations, the representation of the law in literature must appear as just another, albeit more obvious, variant of the inherent literariness or rhetoricity of the law. To put it polemically, in the radical readings of law as literature, law itself becomes a sort of literature, or more precisely, it becomes the only literary subject worth studying for the law and literature enterprise.

This position is in a way complemented by the literary exceptionalism of interpretations that take literary texts as the better law, whose office it is to remind its readers of the moral and human failures of legalistic practice and to appeal to a sense of justice that cannot be satisfied by rules and legal reasoning alone. Hence Binder and Weisberg's warning against the "characteristic risk of the law as literature trope":

> First, a *sentimentalism,* in which passion is never cruel or self-indulgent or muddle-headed, invention is never destructive or dishonest, and civility is always inclusive and never elitist. Second, a facile sophistication that mistakes *skepticism* for criticism and dishonors good causes with bad arguments. Third, a genteel *authoritarianism* that restricts the aesthetic to the role of ornamenting institutionalized power and becalming the spirit of discontent.[9]

The question is how the literary criticisms of law that fall under the "law as literature" category could contribute to an advanced understanding of the intense interest of literature in the law — a question I will subsequently specify to investigate the particular engagement with legal matters in American fiction. That includes the question of how the models of relation on which the "law as literature" trope hinges could be made useful for the revision of the conventional "law in literature" approach.

Neither conceptual essentialism nor literary exceptionalism are particularly satisfying for an attempt to come to terms with the functional correlation of law and literature within the larger context of American history and culture. As I will discuss in detail in the next chapter, this difference and its specific cultural and historical formation have to be kept in view for a thorough understanding of the interdependence between literary and legal concepts of rhetoric and evidence in a democratic culture. In face of this interdependence of law and letters in American culture, the persisting preoccupation with the law cannot be reduced simply to a matter of mimetic and ideological reproduction. Nor can it be relegated exclusively to the artistic

[9] Binder/Weisberg, *Literary Criticisms,* 16–17.

(and economic) exploitation of the law's dramatic potential. And it certainly would be all too simplistic to interpret the obsessive interest in courtroom drama in all forms as a contemptible symptom of the inherent sensationalism of American popular culture.

On the contrary, the American obsession with the law signifies an extreme answer to the fundamental insecurity and instability of evidence established by, but also constantly defied by, the adversarial differences and the resulting rhetorical struggles between factional interests and opinions in a democratic public sphere. Also, in this way, the law-and-literature movement and the debates that surround it can be said to reflect a more general cultural struggle for evidence fought with rhetorical means. Finally, the particular confrontation between law and literature is characterized by the fact that the assertion of their respective evidence relies on very similar rhetorical strategies while their status as "truth" is often considered mutually exclusive.

A closer look at the important discussion of rhetoric in the law-and-literature movement will reveal that the debate over the rhetorical — and, by extension, the literary — dimension of the law always implies a concept about the possibility or impossibility of evidence as a consensual form of truth. Put in a more consciously rhetorical fashion, the argument about rhetoric in law and literature might be said to center around an unspoken — and probably unsolvable — question: whether rhetoric can be just without being just rhetoric.

Even though literature has responded to this question in obvious ways, the critical concern which informs most literary representations of the law cannot not be reduced to an exclusively literary perspective on legal rhetoric, just as the literary and the legal cannot simply be reduced to their institutionalized manifestations. Binder and Weisberg, for example, point to the distinction between law as the "work of a particular profession" versus law as "an ordering function, a process of identifying, allocating and testing authority that pervades all spheres of social life"; so too between literature in the narrow sense and literature as "imagination, complexity of perception, density of meaning, and the qualities of dramatic and aesthetic interest."[10]

Instead, the examination of legal rhetoric and evidence in literary fictions touches upon the performative power and interpretative violence which grounds the law and its fictions of justice, as Jacques Derrida has argued in his seminal essay, "Force of Law: 'The Mystical Foundation of Authority'" (1992). I will discuss the essay above all in regard to the relation between law and literature — a relation which occupies a prominent role in other texts by

---

10 Binder/Weisberg, *Literary Criticisms,* 5.

Derrida as well. This is meant to sharpen the contours of my own argument and to formulate a basic thesis about the nature of literature's critical engagement with the law.

II

Derrida's far-reaching speculations in "Force of Law" are based on a passage from Pascal, in which the latter asserts that the "essence of justice" does not reside in the laws themselves but in the "mystical foundation"[11] of received customs. As Derrida shows, Pascal's remark in fact presents a gloss on an (unacknowledged) passage from Montaigne which runs as follows:

> And so laws keep up their good standing, not because they are just, but because they are laws: that is the mystical foundation of their authority, they have no other. … Anyone who obeys them because they are just is not obeying them the way he ought to.[12]

At first sight, Montaigne is simply making a distinction between justice and laws because, as Derrida comments, the "justice of law, justice as law is not justice. Laws are not just as laws."[13] Yet, this distinction must be read as an open question about the real source of the law's authority, an authority which, as Pascal revises Montaigne's paradoxical observation, cannot exist without force: "and so it is necessary to put justice and force together … to make sure that what is just be strong, or what is strong be just."[14] Pascal's and Montaigne's formulations point to the same inherent problem or paradox of legal authority which refers to the necessary, but also completely arbitrary, relation between law, justice, and power (or force, as Derrida insists). If justice does not reside in the law, where, then, does it reside, and how can it serve as a foundation for the law's authority? In what way can the law realize the adjustment of justice and force?

In order to characterize the "mystical foundation" of the law's authority more clearly, Derrida refers to another of Montaigne's passages about the law, which apparently argues that this source of authority may reside in the fictions of the law: "even our law, it is said, has legitimate fictions on which it founds the truth of its justice." Again, this description does not solve but, rather, further defers the initial question of the law's authority to another in-

11 Derrida, "Force of Law," 11–12.
12 Qtd. in Derrida, "Force of Law," 12.
13 Derrida, "Force of Law," 12.
14 Pascal, *Pensées*, frag. 298, Brunschvicq edition; qtd. in Derrida, "Force of Law," 11.

quiry — one that is also central to my own discussion: "What is a legitimate fiction? What does it mean to establish the truth of justice" with the help of fictions? As Derrida suggests, there is more than one way to approach these questions. The most obvious one would be to refer to the "functional mechanism" inherent in both Montaigne's meditation on the necessity of fiction and Pascal's comments on the necessary conjunction of force and justice, and simply read — and criticize — the fictions of the law as a symbolic masking of the real (political, economic) sources of its power.[15]

More important, however, Derrida continues to insist, is Pascal's and Montaigne's common concern for an "intrinsic structure," which "a critique of juridical ideology should never overlook."[16] This concern points to a source of the law's authority which resides in its very origination and which therefore cannot be related to or grounded in either force or fiction, and yet always implies both in its performative power:

> The very emergence of justice and law, the founding and justifying moment that institutes law implies a performative force, which is always an interpretative force: this time not in the sense of law in the service of force … but rather in the sense of law that would maintain a more internal, more complex relation with what one calls force, power or violence. …
>
> Its very moment of foundation or institution …, the operation that amounts to founding, inaugurating, justifying law (droit), making law, would consist of a coup de force, of a performative and therefore interpretative violence that in itself is neither just nor unjust and that no justice and no previous law with its founding anterior moment could guarantee or contradict or invalidate.[17]

Even this elaborate attempt to describe the moment of the performative institution of law and justice inevitably involves a paradox, as Derrida concedes: "Here the discourse comes up against its limits: in itself, in its performative power itself. Here a silence is walled up in the violent structure of the founding act."[18] The original foundation of the law's authority and therefore the legitimate force of its fictions are indeed "mystical" in the sense that they defy their justification by another discourse, another fiction: "No justificatory discourse could or should insure the role of metalanguage in relation to the performativity of institutive language or its dominant interpretation."[19]

---

15 Derrida, "Force of Law," 12.
16 Derrida, "Force of Law," 13.
17 Derrida, "Force of Law," 13.
18 Derrida, "Force of Law," 13–14.
19 Derrida, "Force of Law," 13.

One reason for the difficulty these statements may present to the unwary reader is that Derrida is trying to describe a moment of institution that is outside, or before, the law, yet which nevertheless draws its justification from the very law it attempts to institute. It is of course not a concrete, localized event Derrida is talking about, but the logical underpinning of certain acts or discourses of legitimation. The question that drives these hypothetical assumptions is "what justifies the justification of the law?" That is, specifically, how can the authority of the law be justified or challenged in regard to the act that instituted it. One answer is given by Pascal, who states that the authority is based on certain customs whose authority goes back in time. The notion that the law developed out of ancient customs has always been a conventional way of giving existing laws a history or a point of origin. Derrida argues, however, that legal history in this sense presents a retrospective narrative of origin and emergence, that is, it is another fiction of the law that ultimately cannot explain how and why the law's authority should or could be grounded in justice. That is why Derrida is much more interested in the conclusion of Pascal's enigmatic remarks: "Custom is the sole basis for equity, for the simple reason that it is received; it is the mystical foundation of its authority. Whoever traces it to its source annihilates it."[20]

Derrida consequently reads Pascal's warning as another indication of the paradoxical structure of the institution of legal authority in reference to justice. In another way, it also points to a necessary form of repression or denial without which the law, or any other form of self-authorized juridical power, would demolish the foundation of its legitimacy. In this sense, literature, when it attempts to speak (for) the law, and to judge the law by tracing the sources of its authority, may find itself threatened by the annihilation of its own 'mystical' foundation.

The central compelling motivation for Derrida's argument is to speak about the possibility of justice, which he links precisely to the impossibility of its representative institution or definition. As he insists, the "mystical" dimension of the foundation of law and justice presents an "experience of aporia" that can be understood in two ways. One would emphasize the impossibility of the experience of aporia, which means that "justice would be the experience that we are not able to experience."[21] Given this impossibility, it follows that "there is never a moment that we can say in the present that a decision is just …, or that someone is a just man — even less, "I am just."[22] From a

---

20 Qtd. in Derrida, "Force of Law," 12.
21 Derrida, "Force of Law," 16.
22 Derrida, "Force of Law," 23, original emphasis.

slightly different angle, or rather by saying the same thing in a slightly different manner, aporia names an inevitable or necessary condition of justice:

> there is no justice without this experience, however impossible it may be, of aporia. Justice is an experience of the impossible. A will, a desire, a demand for justice whose structure wouldn't be an experience of aporia, would have no chance to be what it is, namely, a call for justice.[23]

Here, then, Derrida sees another reason why the law cannot be justice, or in any way guarantee that it will be justice, since according to his definition, this would require the law to acknowledge the paradoxical, aporetic experience of justice. Yet paradox and aporia are anathema to any legal system, and the procedures and practices it considers to be appropriate or just. In other words, the law is a system that attempts to drive out the paradoxical dimension of justice, and it is precisely this tendency which further contributes to the denial or repression of its original foundation in an act of performative self-authorization. This denial is already alluded to by Pascal in his conclusion to the passage discussed by Derrida (though he does not quote it). "We must not see the fact of usurpation," writes Pascal. "[L]aw was once introduced without reason, and has become reasonable. We must make it regarded as authoritative, eternal, and conceal its origin, if we do not wish that it should soon come to an end."[24]

My aim in discussing these passages is less to burden or infuse my interpretations of literary fiction with a fundamental philosophical inquiry into the essence of justice, law, or evidence. Neither would I claim that the condensed reading of some of Derrida's remarks can do more than scant justice to the complex argument they are meant to support. What I want to suggest, though, is that the description of the founding moment of law and Derrida's emphasis on what could be termed the linguistic or rhetorical defiance of this act — the impossibility of its description, justification, or criticism by any other language than that of its own performativity — also presents the essential attraction and ultimate challenge for any literary representation of the law.

One reason is that the performative power and interpretative violence of "institutive language"[25] are not unknown to literature; in fact, the claims of literature to the truth (and the authority) of its own fictions may be said to rely on similar acts of performative authorization. In other words, literature's interest in the law hinges on the same question: 'what is a legitimate fic-

23 Derrida, "Force of Law," 16.
24 Pascal, *Thoughts*, frag. 294.
25 Derrida, "Force of Law," 13.

tion?' — yet its own interest by necessity extends and translates the question 'how does one establish the truth of justice?' into another: 'how does one establish the justice of truth?' — the truth, precisely, of literary fiction. Thus, what Derrida is trying to describe I take to be the central representational predicament or paradox inherent in any notion of a legitimate fiction, that is, of a fiction of justice.

This paradox appears to be more obvious in regard to the law and its fictions than in regard to literary fictions. The legitimacy of the law may be said to rest on two conflicting notions of representation. In one sense, the law pretends to be an accurate, or at least reasonably accurate, realization of the ideal of justice, i.e. justice is realized through the form of the law, its formal process and procedure. In another sense, the law also insists on its legitimacy through its actualization of justice, i.e. justice is produced as the effect of the law, its process and procedures. Either way, the law is a legitimate representation of justice because without it there would be no justice at all, neither as a form nor as a result of representation. The problem of legal legitimacy, however, is not that the law can never really be just in its forms or its outcomes, nor that its forms and effects will never become perfectly adjusted. The deeper problem is rather that the law's legitimacy as a just representation comes to rest precisely on its being incapable of ever representing justice fully in both ways. This makes the moment of institutive self-authorization a mystical one because it assumes (or by necessity must assume) precisely that: the realization and actualization of justice as law and law as justice.

Since it grounds both justice in law and law in justice, the source of legal authority can only be a "performative force" that brings the law into being as the indispensable and, at the same time, impossible representation of justice. The predicament of representation that must beset the notion of a legitimate fiction is thus due to the inherently antagonistic structure of representational legitimacy versus performative self-authorization. In order to operate, any legal or literary fiction whose claims to legitimacy rest on the justice of its forms and effects must inevitably feel both attracted to and threatened by the performative force of self-authorization. While it is the source of its authority, it can neither be contained by its forms alone, nor reproduced in full by its effects.

As I will show in more detail in my interpretations of different representations of the law in American fiction, approaching the law with questions like 'what is a legitimate fiction?', 'when is rhetoric just?', or 'what are the rhetorical conditions of evidence?' might also result in a challenge to literature's own legitimacy as a 'just' fiction of the law. In other words, critically exploring the mystical source of legal authority with the help of literature also forces the literary text to confront the representational predicament implied in its own performative self-authorization. Like the law it sets out to criticize, literature's legitimacy as a rhetoric of evidence rests on the specific legality of literary fiction, a law of literature, to which the text and its readers must comply. To put it simply, literature can become evidence only if it presumes, and if its readers accept the presumption of, a literary jurisdiction and juridical authority existing prior to literature itself and regulating its representation of truth and justice.

The close affinity between the paradoxical structure of legal and literary self-authorization on the one hand and the problem of representation on the other has also been suggested by Derrida, who has repeatedly addressed questions of legality and jurisdiction in reference to literature, for instance, in "The Law of Genre" (1980), or in his reading of Kafka's parable "Before the Law" (1982). In the latter, Derrida described the paradoxical effects of a "juridical performative," both in literature and law, which Kafka's text attempts to exemplify in similar ways as in "Force of Law." What makes Kafka's text exemplary for Derrida is that it allows for an essential question about the relation of law to literature and vice versa: "what if the law, without being itself transfixed by literature, shared the conditions of its possibility with the literary object?"[26] Kafka's short parable opens another perspective on the performative force that Derrida characterized as the mystical source of legal authority. What the text in its most obvious reading offers as a representation of the law is in fact the common logic of legal and literary self-institution, the declaration of an appearance (of the law, of justice, of truth) that is endlessly deferred. Consequently, the law in Kafka's story is represented, or personified, by the doorkeeper or guardian, who both restricts access to the law and stands in its place because he speaks the "discourse of the law." This discourse "does not say 'no' but 'not yet,' indefinitely."[27] Thus, Derrida states, "what is deferred forever" in Kafka's story

> is entry into the law itself, which is nothing other than that which dictates the delay. … What must not and cannot be approached is the origin of *différance*: it must not be presented or represented. … That is the law of the law. …[28]

For Derrida, Kafka's story points at a fundamental problem involved in the investigation of the essence or foundation of the law. This problem is linked to the more general problems of linguistic signification and meaning, as the

---

26 Derrida, "Before the Law," 191.
27 Derrida, "Before the Law," 204.
28 Derrida, "Before the Law," 205, original emphasis.

term *différance* emphasizes: the term denotes a central concept (or rather strategy) in Derrida's critical deconstruction of Western philosophy and its dependence on linguistic logocentrism. It may be understood roughly as a radicalization of the theory of Ferdinand de Saussure that words attain their meaning due to the (phonetic) difference to other words within a linguistic system of verbal utterances. It is itself meant to demonstrate that writing may introduce differences that are unacknowledged by spoken, sensible language, which consequently suggests that linguistic difference is not simply a reaction of language to the field of sensible experience, but a requirement for the constantly changing order of the field of the sensible. Thus, the 'origin of *différance*,' that Derrida alludes to in his remark about the law, can never be found in a sensible difference or presence, and neither can it be conceived of within the same structured order of differences which *différance* sets into play. Approaching the intrinsic structure of the law's authority and power means approaching the elemental structure of signification, which in turn means that legal power in the final analysis must come to rest on a speech or rhetoric that denies or represses its origin in *différance*.

The law of the law, the "being-law of these laws,"[29] is therefore an impossible representation, or rather a representation that is denied, prohibited, or repressed in the very act of representing the law. Appearing before the law, all one ever meets are "the representatives or guardians of the law"; "the law in person, so to speak, is never present," one is always "in front of the law without ever facing it," one "never confronts" the law.[30]

This paradox is already captured in the inextricable double meaning of Kafka's title, "Before the Law," which announces and promises the summoning before the law as a being-in-the-presence of the law. At the same time, the title also maintains a topological and temporal distance to the law that can never be overcome and yet results in an endless repetition of acts of representation that must stand in for the unapproachable law. The title therefore projects an impossible representational space in which the law may appear before itself only never as itself.

The figure at the center of Derrida's reading of "Before the Law" thus explicates an aporia which obviously corresponds to the impossible experience of justice described in "Force of Law." And, indeed, the 'law of the law' appears in Kafka's story only as an experience that cannot be had, as Derrida writes:

---

[29] Derrida, "Before the Law," 192.
[30] Derrida, "Before the Law," 201.

> the story, as a kind of relation, is linked to the law that it relates, appearing, in so doing, before that law, which appears before it. And yet … nothing really presents itself in this appearance; and just because this is given to us to be read does not mean that we shall have proof or experience of it. … Kafka's story operates across the naively referential framework of its narration which leads us past a portal that it comports, an internal boundary opening on nothing, before nothing, the object of no possible experience.[31]

It is important to focus both on the resonance and the difference expressed in Derrida's correspondent descriptions of the law as the "object of no possible experience," and of justice as the "experience of the impossible." In a way, the latter phrase attempts a more positive reformulation of the first experience. While Derrida sets out to specify in "Force of Law" the relation between the law's authority and the possibility of justice, in "Before the Law" he describes the inherently contradictory conditions of the critical representation of law in (or as) literature. These conditions are characterized by a mixture, or, rather, a dialectic of desire and denial. What makes the law the law and what gives it its authority as the law, cannot be represented, that is, made present in form of a story, or a history. Such narrative undertakings must always remain extrinsic to the law's authority and its foundation:

> the law as such should never give rise to any story. To be invested with its categorical authority, the law must be without history, genesis, or any possible derivation. That would be the law of the law. … And when one tells stories on this subject, they can concern only circumstances, events external to the law and, at best, the modes of its revelation. … [N]arrative accounts would try to approach the law, to enter into a relation with it, to … become intrinsic to it, but none of these things can be accomplished. The story of these maneuvers would be merely an account of that which escapes the story and which remains finally inaccessible to it.[32]

The stories which can be told about the law are always representations of those agents, phenomena, processes, and practices that are themselves merely representative appearances of the law, but which are endowed with an authority that springs from another inaccessible source, namely the 'mystical' source of authority. And yet, as Derrida adds, the law's denial does not frustrate the investigation of its authority; it encourages it:

> … the inaccessible incites from its place of hiding. One cannot be concerned with the law, or with the law of laws, either at close range or at a distance, without ask-

---

31 Derrida, "Before the Law," 191, 212, emphasis mine.
32 Derrida, "Before the Law," 191.

> ing where it has its place and whence it comes. … The question and the quest are ineluctable, rendering irresistible the journey towards the place and the origin of law.[33]

It is certainly possible to relate these remarks from "Before the Law" to those in "Force of Law" with regard to the mystical source of legal authority. The difference is that here, in his discussion of a literary representation of the law, Derrida focuses on the paradoxical structure which informs Kafka's attempt to explore the foundations of legal authority, the 'law of the law,' with the help of narrative fiction. Taken together, the two essays thus most explicitly meet in their interest in the question of legitimate (or justified) representation. In "Force of Law," the question is how and why the law can present itself as a legitimate representation of justice; in "Before the Law," the question is asked in a similar way about literature. Consequently, we have to shift our perspective on Kafka's text and ask how the literary text is able to present to its readers a more or less convincing portrayal of the law, or, more precisely, a 'true' representation of certain characteristic features of the law that make the law what it is and that assure its 'mystical' authority.

It is essential in this regard to notice, as Derrida points out, that the doorkeeper not only stands in as the "I" of the law, but also as "that of the text."[34] While the guardian speaks in the first person singular: "Ich bin mächtig …," the country man never uses the first-person pronoun. The one instance in which he refers to himself is in his last question to the doorkeeper, and it is a rather oblique reference: "'how does it happen that for all these many years no one but myself has ever begged for admittance?'"[35] The representative of the law in the text is the representative of the text as the representative of the law. From this perspective, Derrida observes, Kafka's parable speaks only for itself as literature: it "guards itself, maintains itself … like the law," which means that the text "is the law, makes the law and leaves the reader before the law."[36] The persuasive effect of "Before the Law," the capacity of a fictional representation to claim the status of a true, appropriate, and non-trivial statement about the law, must be understood as the "effect of a juridical performative" which "proposes a text that lays down the law, and in the first place with respect to itself."[37] The dialectical structure of the relation be-

---

33 Derrida, "Before the Law," 191, 192.
34 Derrida, "Before the Law," 211.
35 Derrida, "Before the Law," 184.
36 Derrida, "Before the Law," 211.
37 Derrida, "Before the Law," 212.

tween the legal and the literary is crucial: the literary text exposes the paradoxical foundation of the law — its structure of endless deferral — in posing or proposing itself for the law, making its own structure stand in for the law. The complexity of this dialectic is fully rendered by Derrida in the following summary:

> Perhaps literature has come to occupy, under historical conditions that are not merely linguistic, a position that is always open to a kind of subversive juridicity. … This subversive juridicity requires that self-identity never be assured, nor reassuring; and it supposes also a power to produce performatively the statements of the law, of the law that literature can be, and not just of the law to which literature submits. Thus literature itself makes law, emerging in that place where the law is made … it can exercise the legislative power of linguistic performativity to sidestep existing law from which, however it derives protection and receives its conditions of emergence. This is owing to the referential equivocation of certain linguistic structures. Under these conditions, literature can play the law, repeating it while diverting and circumventing it. … In the fleeting moment when it plays the law, a literature passes literature.[38]

Again, the parallels between these remarks and the delineation of the mystical force of legal authority are rather obvious. Only now the emphasis is on the structural affinities between legal and literary self-institution, which allows literature to 'play the law' in the first place. To be sure, the law that literature makes is not 'legal' law; and the juridical power of literary authority only lasts for a 'fleeting moment.' Yet despite its transient and non-binding character, literature can only present (and criticize) the law if it successfully demands or enforces compliance to its own laws — the laws of literary representation.

Martin Kayman made some cogent comments on the converging interests developed in Derrida's writings on law and on literature. Kayman concludes his observations with a pertinent question which stresses once again the predicament of critical representations of the law. Referring to the impossibility to "enunciate a law of genre" without falling back "into the genre of legalism," Kayman asks, "[w]here can this vicious circle be broken, so that one might say something in the law?"[39] In reference to what I called the predicament of literary representations of the law, the question would be similar: How can literature enunciate and criticize the fictions of the law without exposing the quasi-juridical self-authorization of its own fictions?

There can hardly be any doubt that what is implied by a just or legitimate representation of justice or truth is a matter of power and authority. The fic-

---

[38] Derrida, "Before the Law," 216, original emphasis.
[39] Kayman, "Law-and-Literature," 12.

tional assimilation of law and literature effectuates an imaginary delegation of legal authority to literary rhetoric: the law in fiction is spoken and performed by another. This also means that the literary assumes the power of jurisdiction over the legal; in representing the law, literature claims the authority of judging the law. In this sense, representations of law in literature have been read more often than not as attempts at criticizing the law by unmasking its inequities, by revealing the misuse of legal power and authority, and, finally, by exposing the deficiency and inhumanity of legal truth and justice. I do not wish to challenge the critical value of such readings; still, my own readings will focus on a different critical aspect implied by the presence of the law in literature. The basic assumption that informs this change in focus is that the literary representation of the law inevitably involves a self-critical, or self-reflective, dimension, particularly when literature tries to critically challenge the law's authority and legitimacy as a discourse on truth and justice. Although the two can hardly be kept separate when talking about law in literature, my interest will be more in the distinct truth claims associated with legal and literary discourse, respectively, and much less in the discussion of legal and literary notions of justice. Nevertheless, in a very specific sense, the notion of justice as the foundation of the law's authority will have to be addressed again and again in order to identify the specific predicament of the literary representation of the law.

One major aspect of literature's challenge to the authority of the law is the critical unmasking of the rhetorical foundation of legal truth. In doing so, however, literature is forced to acknowledge that its own rhetorical condition is similar to that of the law. Literary representations of law therefore touch on the fundamental rhetorical nature of both legal and literary evidence. That the truth of literature and the truth of law must ultimately come to rest on the evidence of their rhetoric, is precisely what has made literature such an able critic of the law; yet it has also forced literature to continuously assert its own evidence in its confrontation with the law. The trials of literature invariably imply and involve the self-assertion of literary evidence over and against legal evidence.

This does not mean to say that any depiction of the law in literature is deliberately aiming at a description of the 'mystical' moment of performative self-authorization; the literary representation of courtroom scenes, of the testimony and cross examination of witnesses, or of the exhibition of pieces of evidence, etc. are all representations of the law as process and practice, which may or may not be sufficient to convey the injustice or justice of the law precisely as process and practice. However, reading the law in literature in this way only and interpreting its representation merely as either the criticism or justification of what is depicted is to underestimate literature's fundamental concern for and engagement with the problematic intrinsic structure of institutive language that makes its relation to the law such an intense one.

To put it simply: what I am interested in is less how, whether, and why literature proclaims the law's injustice and exposes the misconstruction of legal evidence. The much more conspicuous questions for me are how, whether, and why literary fictions employ such expositions and proclamations about the law in order to realize their own claims to truth and justice. In short, the representation of law in literature inevitably involves an interpretation of the law's founding authority, which in turn serves as the basis for literature's own performative authorization. Consequently, the presence of the law in literature can (and must) be felt even where its forms, processes, and practices are not the immediate object of representation at certain points in a specific literary text.

Yet, before we can turn to a more detailed discussion of the law-and-literature movement in the United States and its own struggle with the 'mystical authority' of the law, another intermediate step is necessary. This step concerns what I am tempted to call the rhetorical necessity of evidence. The problem sketched out by Derrida has its most obvious consequences where law and literature are regarded at once as rhetorical practices and as practices of proof or evidence. For, in yet another variation of the representational predicament which I have outlined so far, the question 'what is a just, what is a true fiction?' is inextricably bound to its antithetical version: 'what makes a fiction untrue or unjust?' Insofar as the latter question may immediately appear the easier one to answer, we can assume with some justification that the search for the truth and its conditions springs from the knowledge and the experience of its opposite. It is the fear of falsification and error which enforces the struggle for evidentiary practices, both in law and in literature. In other words, the cognitive and conceptual foundation of evidence may be described as an act of self-defense and resistance against the undeniable existence and power of false speech.

The concept of evidence as a representational relation enforces the self-reflection of language as a practice of power; truth outside language becomes the standard assumption to judge any claims brought forward with linguistic means. This is why the birth of rhetoric not only coincides with the need for forensic strategies of linguistic proof in trials but also with the conceptualization (and denigration) of fiction (poetry, drama, etc.) as potentially false speech. Legal evidence and literary evidence are from the beginning but two sides of one coin.

In the following part of my introduction I want to flesh out this observation a little more and trace the inherent link between the representational predicament and the problematic relation between rhetoric and evidence.

III

In a very basic sense, evidence may be understood as that quality of a thing or a statement which turns them into signs or expressions of true facts — or what we claim or believe to be true facts. In this sense, evidence is an important part or aspect of everyday cognitive practice, as Jeremy Bentham remarked in 1827:

> [Q]uestions of evidence are continually presenting themselves to every human being, every day, and almost every waking hour, of his life. … Whether the leg of mutton now on the spit be roasted enough, is a question of evidence … which the cook decides upon in the cook's way, as if by instinct; deciding upon evidence, as Monsieur Jourdan talked prose, without having ever heard of any such word, perhaps, in the whole course of her life.[40]

In contrast to the simple empirical certainty supported by the evidence of every-day practice and experience, the facts enlisted to support more ambitious claims to truth, whether in law, literature, religion, or science, are not as easily tested as a well-cooked roast and need more than the simple observation of an experienced chef de cuisine. Indeed, Bentham's own efforts to formulate a rational and scientific basis for legal evidence eventually led him to formulate a theory of fiction, based on the belief that fictions played a substantial role in establishing various grades of probability — in law as well as in literature.[41] Evidence is less something that stands as a sign for a fact but, rather, something that is assigned as a factual proof for a claim to significance:

> On their own, facts are notoriously inert — "angular," "stubborn," or even "nasty" in their resistance to interpretation and inference. … Only when enlisted in the service of a claim or a conjecture do they become evidence, or facts with significance. Evidence might be described as facts hammered into signposts, which point beyond themselves and their sheer, brute thingness to states of affairs to which they have no direct access.[42]

---

40 Qtd. in Twining, *Theories of Evidence*, 52.

41 See Stolzenberg, "Bentham's Theory;" Twining, *Theories of Evidence*; for a discussion of Bentham in the context of fictionality, see Iser, *Das Fiktive*.

42 Daston, "Marvelous Facts," 243.

This description already opens a perspective on the basic problem that regards the relation between evidence and rhetoric, especially where facts do not, and cannot, appear in their "sheer thingness." That is, where the factual can only be represented, it becomes a matter of linguistic constructions and their contestations of evidence, relying on their respective persuasiveness. It has become of course a trifle in contemporary debates on the very issue of facts and their representation to refer to the linguistic turn and, hence, to the fact that all 'facts' rely on linguistic constructions.[43] Yet even an observation like this will become evident — that is, convincing or even true — only for those who take it to be more than just rhetoric. In other words, evidence appears to be as much a matter of the presentation as of the construction of a claim (to truth, to significance) with the help of rhetoric.[44]

I will return to the rhetorical understanding again shortly; at this point there are two aspects of the public or cultural negotiation of evidence which are of special import for the discussion of literary representations of the law. Insofar as a claim is addressed to someone else, the evidence that is meant to support it must rely on (or result from) a rhetoric that is felt to be appropriate; that is, the linguistic presentation of evidence must appear to follow accepted, standardized, formalized, ritualized, etc., forms that are shared by both the speaker and the audience. Finally, where there are claims, there will be counter-claims; evidentiary practices that rely on public rhetoric are always contested and a source for adversarial conflict. Aristotle addresses these conditions, when he points to the common character of all rhetorical situations, insisting that a claim to truth can only be successfully presented if the speaker anticipates and reacts to the possible disposition of the audience:

> But since rhetoric is concerned with judgment (people judge what is said in deliberation, and judicial proceedings are also a judgment), it is necessary not only to look to the argument, that it may be demonstrative and persuasive but also [for the speaker] to construct a view of himself as a certain kind of person … for it makes much difference in regard to persuasion … that his hearers suppose him to be disposed toward them in a certain way and in addition if they, too, happen to be disposed in a certain way [favorably or unfavorably to him].[45]

This remark points to an understanding of situations of public judgment as a rhetorical struggle where claims are tested and contested. Since these claims

---

43 See Levine, *Realism and Representation.*

44 See esp. the contributions in Chandler, *Questions of Evidence*; also Dubrow, "The Status of Evidence" and Smith/Kroß, *Die ungewisse Evidenz.*

45 *On Rhetoric* 2.2. 1377b (Kennedy, 120).

are presented verbally, or in written form, that is, through linguistic representations, one could also describe the rhetorical address or appeal to judgment as a moment where linguistic representations are challenged and put under stress.

From an cultural-anthropological perspective this "forensic situation," as Joseph Kopperschmidt has argued, characterizes the basic structure of rhetorical practice and may thus be regarded as the originating situation of rhetoric itself — at least along the lines of conventional assumptions, according to which the first rhetorical treatises were scripted for parties in law suits in the 4th century B.C.[46] The courtroom trial can be taken as the model of the forensic situation, since it presents the fundamental conditions of rhetoric as a practice aimed at the solution of conflicting claims. Consequently, the trial model allows us to understand rhetoric from an anthropological perspective as an indispensable instrument of social survival.[47]

Kopperschmidt's description of the forensic situation suggests a profitable theoretical gaze on legal rhetoric that focuses on its function as a social and cultural practice. The model character of the forensic situation, moreover, may be used to explain why its literary and cultural representation could assume such omnipresence in the United States. However, Kopperschmidt's attempt to establish the anthropological dimension of the forensic situation also universalizes a specific description of this situation (his own), and must by necessity lose sight of the cultural differences between various legal practices and rhetorics, as well as the difference between the situation itself and its symbolic representation. The universalization becomes obvious when Kopperschmidt talks about the role of the judge as neutral arbitrator who is the addressee of the disputants' speeches. This may be so in the continental tradition of the inquisitional trial but much less so in the Anglo-American jury trial. And, despite the fact that most American trials are not jury trials, it is precisely the form of the jury trial which becomes the model for the cultural representation of the law. The trial situation may be taken as a model situation, yet one has to concede the different cultural manifestations of the model.

The representation of a trial in a literary fiction is not simply a fictional description of a forensic situation; it is in itself a forensic situation, since literature attempts to realize precisely what Koperschmidt calls *soziale Selbstbehauptung durch Reden*, social self-assertion through speech. The social and cultural self-assertion of literature in this way is always tied up with the necessities of

---

46 See Kennedy, *The Art of Persuasion.*
47 Kopperschmidt, "Anthropologie."

its historical and cultural situation — a fact that a rhetorical perspective has to take into account. In order to look at the law and literature relation from the perspective of rhetoric, it is necessary to understand both legal and literary discourse not just as different or comparable forms of rhetoric, but as different or comparable evidentiary practices: that is, as rhetorics of evidence. My preference for this specific combination of the rhetorical and the evidentiary dimension of the forensic situation is based on the thesis that this situation not only presents the foundational conditions for rhetoric as a practice, but also for the necessity of evidence as a central concept to guide and regulate and to test and contest conflicting rhetorical claims to truth.

Given these aspects, the courtroom trial may be said to represent a paradigmatic cultural situation where fundamental questions of truth, culpability, and justice appear to rely completely on both the versatility and the virtue of rhetorical practice aimed at the persuasive presentation and construction of evidence. As Austin Sarat notes, "Law is, generally, and trials are, more particularly, a stage for the display of verbal skill, linguistic virtuosity and persuasive argument in which words take on a seriousness virtually unparalleled in any other domain of human experience."[48] The evidence that is produced in these situations (construed, revealed, established, etc.) with the help of rhetoric is precisely what has to stand in for the facts, for the truth of the facts, and the belief in the truth of the facts. Evidence, as Lionel Gossman has stated, "is by definition a sign, and it signifies within a system of signs."[49] The term *evidence* is a reminder of the inherent representational dimension of the forensic situation.

I have said above that the literary portrayal of the law does not simply depict a forensic situation, say, a trial, but has to be understood as a forensic situation in itself as well. In face of the discussion of Derrida's "Before the Law," this double structure obviously regards the status and the success of literature's claims to truth. In the case of law in literature, the literary text, as it were, presents evidence concerning the law, i.e. its process, its practices, its motives, etc., by representing them in a certain way. Yet, this evidence is a sign within a system of signs and it can unfold its force (of signification and persuasion) only in relation to the system of which it is a part. As Derrida has suggested, this system must itself be regarded as a/the law, that is, a system of rules enforced under literary jurisdiction and the judicial authority of literature. The law as a literary representation therefore achieves the status of evidence only in compliance with the law of literature and the conditions it

48 Sarat, "Rhetoric and Remembrance," 367.

49 Lionel Gossman, "History and Literature," 32.

enforces or demands. Whatever 'truth' about the law Kafka's story may convey to its readers, it is based on literary evidence and thus it is most likely considered to be true as a literary statement only — and rather unlikely to be taken as evidence in a legal sense.

This observation obviously concerns an issue that has always been, and still is, of central importance in literary history and theory: the relationship between literature and reality. This is a thorny and complex issue, to be sure, which it is not my purpose here to discuss at any length or depth. However, since it touches on the question I stressed at the beginning: "What is a true fiction?" and its importance for the discussion of legal and literary evidence, I have a certain interest which cannot be denied or overlooked. Instead of discussing specific models of literary truth or evidence, however, my question will be what drives these models, what makes them necessary or possible, and how is this necessity or possibility related to what I have called rhetorics of evidence.

IV

In an essay on the possibilities of the novel and the concept of reality, Hans Blumenberg once wrote that the entire Western tradition in poetic or literary theory since antiquity could be understood as the struggle with the ancient dictum that the poets lie. The most interesting aspect of Blumenberg's remarks on this struggle, which is also most important for my own discussion, can be found in a footnote where he speculates about the origin of the debate and the motivation for the various theories about the truth of poetry or art in general. Before there is any systematic attempt to describe the relation between reality and art in antiquity, Blumenberg observes, one can only find admonitions emphasizing the duty of epic oratory to observe the truth: "The accusation of falsity becomes prominent only in relation to the principal condition of the epos that it ought to convey the truth."[50] That the poets lie turns into a more general allegation only with the increasing reflection about the technical conditions of representation and illusion on the dramatic stage; the difference between reality and art is seen from the perspective of dramatic practice itself and thus initiates a debate about poetic illusion.[51]

---

50 Blumenberg, "Wirklichkeitsbegriff," 9. [The original reads: "Der Vorwurf der Unwahrhaftigkeit hebt sich also vor dem Hintergrund der Voraussetzung ab, daß das Epos Wahrheit zu vermitteln habe." (English translation mine) PS.

51 Blumenberg, "Wirklichkeitsbegriff," 9, original emphasis.

The question of the truth conditions of poetical speech has thus only emerged through a process of theoretical reflection on the technical nature of the epos as a dramatic representation. However, the most consequential attempts at a more systematic description of the difference between true and false speech in general were developed in reference both to epic oratory and public oratory, that is, rhetoric. As Blumenberg explicates, the prejudice against the poets (and by implication against rhetoric as false speech) could only have developed from a point of view already informed by a concept of evident reality or truth, however unacknowledged and implicit it may be. On the other hand, this concept of evidence can only be developed further and become critically revised precisely because there exist techniques of illusion, dissimulation, and deception. In other words, what is accepted in the most general and implicit manner as real and true can become subject to critical negotiation and reflection only where acts and techniques of representation lay claim to truth and reality. In rejecting or correcting these claims, truth and reality become theoretically conceptualized:

> Any argument that questions the reference between a form of practice or a theoretical axiom and reality also reveals the very conditions that allow us to speak about reality in the first place. Thus the distrust of poetry which stands at the beginning of our tradition has also turned the theoretical reflection on literature [Theorie der Dichtung] into a methodical space where preexisting concepts of reality are forced to become explicit and can be confronted critically.[52]

Literary theory, Blumenberg seems to suggest, emerges as a reaction to a denial: the denial of the truth of (or in) art. At the same time, however, poetry and literature have become crucial instruments for the continuing critical investigation of concepts of truth and evidence.

Yet, the problematic question of truthful speech is not an exclusively literary or poetic concern. The denial of poetic, that is, mimetic, truth finds its parallel in the denial of rhetorical truth as mere probability, as brought forward both by Plato and Aristotle. Even though Blumenberg does not explicitly comment on this convergence, his prime examples (Gorgias, Plato, Aristotle) suggest a similar argument in regard to the emergence of rhetori-

---

[52] " … in dem Augenblick, in dem einem praktischen Verhalten, einem theoretischen Satz ihr Realitätsbezug abgesprochen wird, kommt zutage, unter welchen Bedingungen jeweils von Wirklichkeit gesprochen werden kann. Also gerade dadurch, daß dem poetischen Gebilde von allem Anfang unserer Tradition an seine Wahrheit bestritten worden ist, ist die Theorie der Dichtung zu einem systematischen Ort geworden, an dem der Wirklichkeitsbegriff kritisch hereinspielen und aus seiner präformierten Implikation heraustreten muß." Blumenberg, "Wirklichkeitsbegriff," 10 (English translation mine).

cal theory and criticism. In fact, the very term 'evidence,' which Blumenberg employs to explain the common foundation of Western concepts of artistic truth, must be seen as the contested ground claimed in similar ways by poetics and rhetoric.

That the term 'evidence' has a rhetorical history which in turn correlates in part with literary history has been generally acknowledged.[53] Cicero first used the term *evidentia* to translate the Greek term *enargeia*, which for him denoted on the one hand the sensible presence of objects perceived and, on the other, the aspect of vividness and effective representation in speech. Yet Cicero's translation actually presents already a combination of *enargeia*, meaning simply the detailed description of objects, with the Aristotelian principle of *energeia*, the vividness of dramatic speech achieved with the help of metaphors and similes.[54] To describe the effect of the latter rhetorical strategy, Aristotle employs a peculiar paraphrase that had some very fundamental theoretical consequences: vividness in speech, he says, is effected best by 'pro ommaton poiein,' that is, 'bringing-before-the-eyes' what is verbally represented. As Paul Ricœur has shown, the definition of metaphor and its underlying principle of *energeia* mark a crucial link between Aristotelian rhetoric and poetics.[55] The inherent linkage also suggests that the understanding of evidence as *evidentia*, as it attempts to establish a conceptual correlation of *energeia* and *enargeia*, will always be faced with the diverging options of rhetorical and poetical interpretations of the concept. This possibility is explicitly recognized by Ricœur when he talks about the "problems posed by the double insertion of metaphor in the Poetics and the Rhetoric."[56] The problem is twofold: on the one hand, 'bringing-before-eyes' is

---

53 See, for instance, Patey, *Probability*; Solbach, *Evidentia*; Campe, *Affekt*; Lausberg, *Handbook of Literary Rhetoric*.

54 Cf. *Historisches Wörterbuch der Rhetorik*, Vol. 3, 33; 39–42. For an extended presentation of the various elements and dimensions of *evidentia* in rhetorical theories since antiquity, see Lausberg, *Handbook,* 359–66. For my discussion, the definitions in Lausberg under § 810, § 811, § 812 are especially important. The difference between *energeia* and *enargeia* is described by Hagstrum: "*Enargeia* implies the achievement in verbal discourse of a pictorial quality that is highly natural. *Energeia* refers to the actualization of potency, the realization of capacity or capability, the achievement in art and rhetoric of the dynamic and purposive life of nature" (12). For Steiner, this contrasting definition makes the two concepts opposites (10), however, as Cicero's compound definition suggests, there is enough potential overlapping between both concepts for new syntheses — like Cicero's notion of *evidentia.*

55 Cf. Ricœur, *Rule of Metaphor,* 42–43.

56 Ricœur, *Rule of Metaphor,* 13.

a strategy that is neither exclusive to rhetorical oratory nor to poetical language. In itself, it therefore does not suffice to distinguish the rhetorical from the poetical. On the other hand, and even more unsettling for the defenders of poetic truth or literary evidence, the similarity of linguistic strategies would suggest that poetical speech was just another form of rhetoric, that is, a mode of persuasion. As Ricœur's explanation makes obvious, the Aristotelian definition of metaphor marks both a point of departure and of convergence since it establishes the functional difference between discursive practices and, at the same time, relates them through their structural correspondence:

> We said that rhetoric originally was oratorical technique; its aim and that of oratory are identical, to know how to persuade. Now this function, however far-reaching, does not cover all the uses of speech. Poetics — the art of composing poems … — as far as its function and its situation of speaking are concerned, does not depend on rhetoric, the art of defence, of deliberation, of blame and of praise. Poetry is not oratory. Persuasion is not its aim; rather, it purges the feelings of pity and fear. Thus poetry and oratory mark out two distinct universes of discourse. Metaphor, however, has a foot in each domain. With respect to structure, it can really consist in just one unique operation … but with respect to function, it follows the divergent destinies of oratory and tragedy. Metaphor will therefore have a unique structure but two functions: a rhetorical function and a poetic function.[57]

While Ricœur at this point merely appears to paraphrase the definitions and conceptual differentiations introduced by Aristotle, his description reveals a more general logic of correlation and distinction which, as we will see, is also prevalent in the theoretical positions of the law-and-literature movement. The main feature of this logic of correlation is that the specific function of poetical speech, or, more precisely, the distinct function of metaphor in poetical speech, rests on a denial of its potential rhetorical function as a means of persuasion. However, if we take the Aristotelian concept of metaphor as *energeia* — that is, in its latent dimension or function as evidence — then the denial of rhetoric in poetical speech (including prose literature) also appears as the necessary precondition for literary evidence. Ricœur's assessment that poetics does not depend on rhetoric should therefore be read with a grain of salt. As long as there is a common element, or, better, instrument, which poetical speech shares with rhetoric proper, literary evidence still retains a relation to rhetorical means of persuasion. Even if poetry does not aim at persuasion, its evidence can be persuasive. Metaphors may realize a rhetorical function even where they are meant to be poetical (and vice versa).

57 Ricœur, *Rule of Metaphor,* 12.

Rhetoric always remains the common foundation of all linguistic evidence that becomes functionally differentiated in different discursive practices.

Even though Aristotle does not relate *energeia* and *enargeia* in his three books on rhetoric, Cicero's combination of the two in his term '*evidentia*' only theoretically realizes a latent practical relation between them, facilitated in no small measure by the phonetic resonance of the original Greek terms. What is more important is the fact that the two concepts of *energeia* and *enargeia* formed shifting alliances in the course of Western art history and its continuous theoretical reflection. While neither is completely distinguishable, nor completely synonymous, they helped to develop and mutually revise opposing yet also complementary notions of evidence and proof in regard to the representation of truth (or of reality). No matter how elaborate and specific these notions appeared, they still referred back to the rhetorical tradition from which '*evidentia*' had originally sprung. *Energeia* and *enargeia* present the two poles that mark the extreme ends of an extended field of combinations and oppositions, and all their possible variants. Ricœur's reading of Aristotle clearly emphasizes the differences more than the similarities between rhetoric and poetics to the point where the latter is declared to be independent from the former. The only link that still exists is that 'enigmatic' concept of 'bringing-before-the-eyes.' Yet, this concept is not only at the heart of metaphor, it also describes in all its complexity and tormenting vagueness the evidentiary dimension of both oratory and poetry.[58] Thus, from a different perspective, one that is more interested in the evidentiary dimension of the concept and less in the various uses of metaphor, rhetoric and poetics must appear inherently related rather than functionally independent. As Kathy Eden has shown, for instance, Aristotle's discussion of dramatic mimesis and of *energeia*, which provides the linkage between his rhetoric and his poetics, draws on specific legal terms and repeatedly refers to legal practices and methods of proof known in his time. What holds the rhetorical and the poetical together, then, is their common character as linguistic methods of proof. And one central aspect of the two methods is the attempt to achieve the status of evidence with the help of visualization and vivification.

In a lucid discussion of the transformations and translations that helped *evidentia* in its sense as 'evidence' to emerge, Eden argues that both *energeia* and *enargeia* originally assumed their significance in rhetorical theory and practice in their forensic meaning, that is as methods of rhetorical proof. Even in Aristotle, as Eden demonstrates, the two meanings, though not di-

---

[58] It is important to insist on evidence as a 'dimension' rather than a 'function' of speech at this point.

rectly linked in the discussion of rhetoric, come together as complements when Aristotle tries to relate poetry to methods of legal proof. The Aristotelian relation of law and literature is based on certain essential characteristics which are shared by both. As Eden comments:

> the methods of dramatic poetry and forensic oratory, as conceived by Aristotle, overlap in many essential details — ranging from the most logical way to organize the presentation of events, to the psychological methods of arousing the appropriate feelings in the audience, to the even more practical details of acting … In tragedy as in legal oratory, the object presented is human action, usually as past action and often as hamartia, an error in judgment. … Insofar as the spectators at a theatrical performance or the jury at a legal trial witness, as if with their own eyes, an action that has been skillfully represented according to these requirements, they will — in Aristotle's view — learn from that representation not only what happened but why. And they will be moved in both cases to fear and pity and to reach the kinds of judgment that accompany those responses.[59]

The close affinities between the legal and the literary methods of forensic proof embrace the common rhetorical foundations of evidence in law and in literature. For Aristotle, as Eden's convincing discussion suggests, the rhetorical correlation between law and literature is not based in formal affinities, but in functional affinities. Legal oratory and dramatic poetry can be compared not because their rhetoric is similar, but because they share a similar purpose: to move an audience to judgment. In fact, it is the shared functional aspect of speaking purposefully in front of a judging audience that gives the rhetoric of poetic and legal oratory their similar form.

I will discuss the specific dimension of this relation with reference to Eden in a later chapter; here I am interested more in the perspective her argument opens on the law and literature relation and the rhetoricity of legal and literary evidence. The most obvious aspect in this respect lies in the fact that, even while Aristotle relates and compares the legal and the literary, his purpose is not to show that they are actually one. The correspondence between legal methods of proof and those of dramatic poetry serves as the basis for the conceptual framework which would then allow us to compare the functions of legal and literary rhetoric in order to distinguish them. In other words, to assume that their methods are alike, because forensic rhetoric and poetry share a central function, is a means to establish a critical relation between the two. The relation is critical in the sense that it allows both a distinction and a comparison and thus opens up the possibility of a whole range of differentiations whose critical force nevertheless remains controlled by the basic comparative thesis. It is, moreover, also critical in the

---

59 Eden, *Poetic and Legal Fiction*, 4–5.

sense that it furnishes the practices it compares and distinguishes with a common repertoire of critical and conceptual instruments that can be used to theoretically reflect on one practice from the position of the other. For the latter form of criticism, differences between law and literature might be more important than the comparative foundation they share.[60]

The theoretical reflection on truth and representation, which Blumenberg, Ricœur, and Eden describe in similar ways, though from different points of view, brings into being variable rhetorics of evidence as distinct ways of (re-)presenting the truth to the judgment of an audience. In regard to the relation between law and literature, the common rhetorical foundation of their respective evidence remained the source of dialogue and conflict. While insisting on their mutual independence, law and literature, as Martin Kayman has written, "appear perversely to need each other," because "[e]ach functions as a disavowal of the lack of autonomy that they denounce in each other."[61]

V

That one man's evidence may turn out to be another man's rhetoric and vice versa is a very common course of events in literary fictions concerned with the law and its evidentiary practices. For once, this feature can be traced back to the historical correspondence of the emergence of the novel and the increasing significance of eye-witness testimony in trials at law; a correspondence which found its obvious reflection in Anglo-American narrative literature and newly emerging concepts of fiction since the 18th century.[62] More important, however, is the fact that the literary representation of legal practices of truth finding, but especially in its most public and adversary manifestation, the courtroom trial, almost inevitably implies a comparative argument about different rhetorics of evidence. This observation not only

60 Thus Brook Thomas states: "it is precisely their differences that make it productive to place legal and literary documents in relation to one another, not to merge them, but interrogate and cross-examine them" ("Reflections," 532).

61 Kayman, "Lawful Writing," 765.

62 See in general Watt, *Rise of the Novel* and Davis, *Factual Fictions* and, more specifically, Schramm, *Testimony* and Welsh, *Strong Representations* for this argument, which will also be discussed in more length in my chapter on Charles Brockden Brown. As Bakhtin observed, this correspondence can be found as early as in Greek romances (Bakhtin, *Dialogic Imagination*, 123–24); a point also convincingly argued by Eden, *Poetic and Legal Fiction*.

concerns the representation and dramatization of contesting narratives or opposing points of view linked to individual characters in the fictional story.

The thesis I will argue throughout the chapters to come is that the literary representation of legal rhetoric and evidence always contains — and must eventually result in — a more or less conscious reflection on literary rhetoric and the potential 'evidence' of fiction. By looking at some more recent examples of critical readings in law and literature that raise questions similar to mine, I will carve out in more detail the significance of the rhetorical and self-reflective function of what I call the "legal moment" in literary texts. My central argument will be that these legal moments, which mostly take the shape of trial scenes, or other forms of legal procedure, on the one hand, present 'trials' in their own right: the literary examination of legal rhetoric and its claims to evidence and justice. On the other hand, however, these fictional trials also mark a moment of intense self-reflection about the potential and the limits of rhetorical evidence and, therefore, of the truth and justice of legal and literary fiction(s). My interpretations of the legal moments in several fictional texts thus aim to move closer to the intrinsic concern that binds law and literature together. This also entails the deliberate attention to other moments that compete with, contradict, or complement the representation of legal rhetoric and evidence in a literary text.

The mutual challenge of competing performative self-authorizations, which in the literary text is addressed by the specific correlation between the legal and the literary, cannot be acknowledged in full without also considering the extrinsic conditions that inform this correlation in the field of cultural and social practice in its specific historical situation. Here, the relation between law and literature must be considered as an effect of the formative histories of professionalization and institutionalization and the normative stabilization and revision that run parallel to these histories (the history of ideas, changing theories of evidence, etc.). In regard to the initial question about the intense mutual interest between the legal and the literary in American culture, there are several significant factors that have to be accounted for. On the one hand, there is a strong foundational affinity of law and letters in American culture that had considerable consequences during the early stages of functional differentiation from colonial times to the American Revolution.[63] On the other hand, the relation between American law and literature is marked by the emergence and increasing cultural dominance of a concept of adversarial evidence. This concept, which basically assumes that the antagonism between individual opinion in a pluralistic culture can only be

---

[63] See Miller, *The Life of the Mind*, esp. Vol. II; and Ferguson, *Law and Letters*.

solved through forms of regulated struggle, is of course not an exclusive trait of U.S.-American culture.[64] Yet, because of the particular conditions of the American public sphere, with its constitutional guarantees and the unrestrained force of strong commercial interests, there is a marked radicalization of the competitive aspects of cultural diversification and functional differentiation. These basic characteristics also form the (mostly unacknowledged) background for the various models of relation which inform the theoretical perspective on the law and literature nexus; that is, they have to be taken as competitive and functionally differentiated models where the relation between law and literature always implies a specific correlation of rhetoric and evidence. This observation, which for now must take the form of a leading hypothesis, will also inform the following attempt to form a heuristic synthesis from various theoretical perspectives of the law-and-literature movement that, finally, will serve as a link between the intrinsic challenge of legal and literary self-authorization and the extrinsic factors of cultural competition and functional diversification.

---

64 For the cultural function of dissent (and assent), see Bercovitch, *Rites of Assent*; for the USA as argument culture, see Tannen, *Argument Culture.* On adversarial legalism see Kagan, *Adversarial Legalism*; on litigiousness as a specific trait of American legal culture, see Lieberman, *The Litigious Society* and Marks, *The Suing of America.* I will address these issues in more detail in chapter six.

Chapter 2

Legitimate Fictions: Rhetoric and Evidence in the Law-and-Literature Movement

In my introductory chapter I sketched out a basic structural dilemma that concerns the critical representation of law in literature. In reference to Derrida's remarks on the 'mystical' foundation of legal authority, that is, the power of performative self-authorization and self-institution, I pointed out a fundamental affinity between law and literature in regard to the similar institutive force of their rhetoric. Both attempt to institute their rhetoric as evidentiary practices aimed at the representation and actualization of justice and truth. What I called the predicament of literary representations of the law results from the inherent ambivalence of this similarity of legal and literary rhetoric in respect to their institutive self-authorization. For while it allows literature to assume jurisdiction over the law in representing the law and thus to assert literary evidence over and against legal evidence, the close affinity between literary and legal self-authorization also threatens to expose, and therefore to challenge, literature's own 'mystical' foundation of authority. This challenge implies that the critical depiction of law in literature is inherently self-reflective, or self-critical, since it enforces a reaction to the conditions of representation within literary representation.

Moving from the general to the particular, I will reformulate my basic thesis in a more pragmatic and heuristically suitable form. This move will involve a closer look at the law-and-literature movement as it developed in the United States from the late seventies into the nineties. My goal is less to give a comprehensive survey of the entire field in its diversity, but rather to discuss at some length specific exemplary positions which then will serve as coordinates for a more succinct organization of the field. This organization is centered around the focus of my interest in the relation between rhetoric and evidence and the specific way in which this relation is expressed in each of the critical positions I will discuss.[1]

---

[1] The restriction to the period between the inception and the first culmination of the movement is intentional and meant to highlight the fundamental positions that informed (and still inform) most of the work done within the expanding interdisciplinary field of law and literature and law and culture, respectively. For some dissenting votes, see Mukherji, "Understood Relations" and Meyler, "The Myth of Law and Literature."

My focus is partly justified by the persistent attention given to rhetoric in the various strands of the movement itself. If one could "put the reasons for the law and literature revival in a nutshell," Brook Thomas has rightfully observed, "it is the increased acknowledgment in legal circles that the law has been and remains intricately tied up with rhetoric."[2] In his reflections on the different models of rhetoric presented by various approaches, Thomas has criticized the strong tendency in the law-and-literature movement to collapse the literary into the rhetorical and in contrast defended the status of literature as a particular mode of discursive criticism and critical reflection of the law, whose function differs fundamentally from other forms of public rhetoric. Thomas' cogent remarks are rather important for my own argument, not only because I agree with the central trajectory of his criticism of certain models of legal and literary rhetoric. More significant, at least in my view, is the fact that he has tried to advance his critical perspective by basing his argument on a concept of 'literary evidence.' This strategy at least suggests that, despite the fact that the term 'evidence' is rarely ever mentioned in discussions of legal and literary rhetoric, one could nevertheless use it as a conceptual and differential tool to resist certain essentialist claims about the rhetorical function of literature.

I think Thomas' suggestion is a valid one in this respect, and therefore I would like to assume a similar stance by looking, above all, at the debate about the rhetorical or literary character of the law, that is, the theoretical struggle over "law as literature." While this in part means that I will have to look at some of the same texts and approaches as Thomas has done, my main objective is radically different. In contrast to Thomas, I do not want to defend literary evidence against the law as literature approach; rather, I want to (re-)locate evidence within these approaches. More precisely, I intend to investigate into the particular correlation of evidence and rhetoric in some of the most influential texts and arguments of the law-and-literature movement. My hypothesis is that the particular correlation of evidence and rhetoric in turn defines the particular relation of law and literature which each of the discussed models proposes.

The first part of what follows is an attempt to isolate from the theoretical debate surrounding the law and literature relation four distinct, though in part overlapping, models of relation. These models are provisional categorizations of the much more complex configuration of the field and should be taken as the result of heuristic demands, that is, provisions made necessary by theoretical interest and investment. The first model, which one could dub

[2] Thomas, "Reflections," 523.

the conservative or classical correlation of law and literature, insists on the functional distinction of literary and legal discourse or rhetoric, though the latter is reserved strictly for literary discourse. The functional distinction, in turn, is based on a strict division between factual and fictional representation as a function of texts (or, more generally, of speech). The difference between literature and law is marked by the difference between fact and fiction.

The second position is characterized by its emphasis on rhetorical truth: the possibility of arriving at the truth in legal reasoning with the help of literary sensitivity and a reflection on the literariness of legal language. In this view, the right choice of words is the best way to make things evident. The conscious use of rhetorical means and of discursive strategies and linguistic composition, aimed at the union of substance and form, will eventually guarantee the realization of truth in legal language. As I will try to show, there are two more or less radical interpretations of this position to be found in the law-and-literature movement.

Finally, there is an even more radical rhetorical approach to law and literature based on a general notion of rhetoricity. In this view, rhetoric is not something that can simply be avoided, controlled, or optimized in order to guarantee truth in speech or writing. Such strategies are already part of a claim to truth that can only be advanced with the help of rhetoric. Rhetoricity is thus another name for the necessary rhetorical condition of linguistic claims to truth. In its most radical conception, rhetoric becomes the only way to think about evidence, to realize it and to stabilize it publicly. There are several prominent approaches in the law-and-literature movement that come to rest on the assumption of general rhetoricity.

Nevertheless, the various approaches that embrace the rhetoricity thesis also differ markedly in their reactions and their conceptual conclusions. One reaction is to favor literature over the law as the better, more humane, and inherently ethical form of communal rhetoric. Another reaction is to demand the institution of a critical counter-rhetoric within the law in order to reflect on and possibly correct legal constructions of evidence and justice. These claims are rejected by yet another perspective on the rhetoricity thesis, which insists that there is no way to use rhetoric to make rhetoric more true and that the different forms of legal and literary rhetoric are the inevitable result of their institutional practice.

The three basic positions I have sketched out can be said to more or less exhaust the possible correlations of law and literature in the 'law *as* literature' perspective. However, as I will argue in the second part of this chapter, there is another attitude towards this relation which tries to reinstall or reinforce the inherent difference between literary and legal rhetoric not just as a functional, but as a critical difference. I will therefore take a look at Thomas again, in order to establish a critical counter-definition of literary evidence. The position represented by Thomas insists on a supplementary relation of literature to law. It looks at both law and literature as distinct rhetorics of evidence with their own evidentiary practices. Starting out from this assessment, I will attempt to formulate a position that, in contrast to Thomas, has learned the lesson of rhetoricity yet still attempts to take into account the mimetic and creative particularities of literary fictions. Returning to an approach similar to that suggested by Thomas also means to return to history, specifically, cultural and literary history. Therefore the concluding part of this chapter will be concerned with the historical conditions of rhetorics of evidence, reminding us that the concept of evidence cannot be divorced from the specific historical and cultural conditions that ground it.

I

The contemporary interest in the relation between law and literature is not an unprecedented phenomenon. It must rather be considered as a "revival" that "attempts to reconnect disciplines" which already "have a history of connections."[3] Indeed, the "complicated politics"[4] of the actual movement can be traced back to specific conceptual residues of earlier historical configurations of law and letters in American culture. These residues also had some significant theoretical consequences, especially in regard to the assumed relation between the rhetorical and the evidentiary functions of legal and literary texts. Rhetoric and evidence are in fact always implicated in the critical examination of the "linguistic assumptions underlying the law" which Martin Kayman has identified as the central objective of the movement — an objective that has also made it an "important test case for the epistemological and political status of literary studies as a theory of reading and textuality.[5]

Given the variety of approaches that all lay claim to the law and literature master trope, then, the complicated politics of the movement are reflected by a theoretical complexity that cannot be described by the simple division between "law in literature" and "law as literature." The latter approach rather has to be read as a critical radicalization of the former — a radicalization which subsequently leads to the development of further specializations, as in

3 Thomas, "Reflections," 514.
4 Thomas, "Reflections," 512.
5 Kayman, "Questions of Jurisdiction," 8.

the hermeneutic, narrative, rhetorical, and cultural criticism of the law, that all rest on the original analogy of "law as literature": the claim that "law is like literature … and that the attributes law shares with literature are more essential, or more important, or more valuable … than those that distinguish it from literature."[6] In comparison, the 'law in literature' approach still appears to be a straight-forward affair, interested simply in the representation of law in literary fiction. However, it is precisely the nature and the limits of the law's literary representation which are at stake in the critical revision of the law and literature relation since the seventies.

The renewal of theoretical concern for the connection between law and letters during the last four decades gained considerable force in the United States as a critical reaction to another interdisciplinary connection, that of law and economics, which rose to conspicuous prominence during the Reagan years. This oppositional orientation is rather obvious in Owen Fiss' programmatic remarks in the opening issue of the *Yale Journal of Law and the Humanities* in 1988 where he explicitly asked to "alter the political direction of interdisciplinary work in the law" in order to "combat the instrumentalism and scientism of Law and Economics and to restore an appropriate place for value judgments in the study of law."[7]

Fiss' demand for a new alliance between legal studies and the humanities is based on a rather familiar opposition which contrasts the instrumentalism of the sciences with the moral responsibility of the humanities. The most interesting premise of this argument is that the nature of the law apparently depends on its extrinsic relation to some other discipline. By choosing the right 'partner,' as it were, the law may turn from a discipline with an "essential commitment to the market" to a discipline interested in moral values and a "deep and genuine commitment to pluralism."[8] While the interdisciplinary alliance between law and the humanities thus fills "urgent practical needs" and the turn to literature may "free contemporary law from its own barrenness," Fiss is clearly ambivalent about the disciplinary versatility of the law, supplementing his appeal for interdisciplinary work with a warning:

> looking outside of the law is risky — interdisciplinary work often blurs the distinctive qualities of the law, or widens the gap between the academy and the professional, rendering legal academic inquiries of limited relevance to the practicing lawyer.[9]

---

6 Binder, "The Law-as-Literature Trope," 63.
7 Fiss, "Challenge," x, xi.
8 Fiss, "Challenge," x.
9 Fiss, "Challenge," xi.

Fiss' warning reveals a certain anxiety of the law's interdisciplinary corruption and loss of disciplinary identity, an anxiety he ironically shares with Richard Posner, one of the most prominent representatives of the law and economics school.[10] Thomas has noted that both Fiss and Posner share a "reverence for literature"[11] as the repository of universal values, but for Posner, the dangers of interdisciplinarity result from a confusion of the legal and the literary, or, more precisely, from the "misunderstood relation" between law and literature, as the subtitle of his own contribution to the debate proclaims. In order to curb the risks of interdisciplinary corruption, Posner, in Thomas' words, works to "delimit connections" between law and literature.[12]

For Posner, there is a strict distinction between law as it appears in literature and the law as it appears outside literature. Law in literature is not law: it is not even a representation of the law, or a metaphor of the law as a practice. Literary law always represents 'something else' about the law, which is not representative of the 'real' law outside literature. Literature's intense interest in legal issues is for Posner exclusively aimed at the "broad features of the law," that is, the law as an "unchanging facet of human existence."[13]

Yet Posner's argument about the alleged intention and "social function"[14] of literary texts leaves no room for a concept of literary fiction as an interventional and critical historical practice, or indeed, as an immediate and specific reaction to legal practice and procedure at a certain point in time. Since literature represents only that about the law which transcends historical change, it can only be ahistorical in regard to the law, whose practice in turn is essentially defined by historical change. Interestingly, though, Posner attempts to support his definition of the representational function of literature by comparing it with other, non-literary texts — a comparison that, ironically, is only possible because the function of texts changes over time and from culture to culture. Thus Posner admits that even the literary representation of law may be taken as legitimate and authentic "in cultures where the only information about the law is found in what we call literature, though contemporaries thought about it as history." Yet this does not apply in our present cultural situation since, "in a culture that has non-literary records, those records generally provide more, and more *accurate, information* about the legal system than does literature."[15]

---

10 See Posner, *The Economics of Justice*, and Posner, *Economic Analysis of Law.*
11 Thomas, "Reflections," 512, 515.
12 Thomas "Reflections," 515.
13 Posner, "A Relation Reargued," 64.
14 Posner, *Law and Literature*, 17.
15 Posner, "A Relation Reargued," 64, my emphases.

If this comment seems almost like an afterthought, it nevertheless demonstrates that Posner's perspective on the law and literature relation is founded on a specific correlation between literary rhetoric and legal evidence. It also points at the paradox involved in Posner's claim about the social function of literature: while insisting that this function remains the same over time and is shared by different cultures — especially in regard to the representation of the unchanging features of the law — , Posner, at the same time, acknowledges that the function of texts may indeed change — from historical records into literary fictions, for instance. It seems obvious that Posner is performing an act of jurisdiction in the double sense characterized by Kayman. In prescribing the distinct functions of law and literature, Posner, on the one hand, attempts to define, in Kayman's words, "the area over which the court legitimately exercises its power (its field, as it were)," while on the other hand he is also "speaking or declaring (*dicere*) law (*jus*)" by "enunciating the legitimate principles and findings that operate in that field."[16] My focus here is on the central aspect of Posner's argument about the functional difference between law and literature (or between different genres in general), since his enforcement of jurisdiction rests on the supposed irrelevance of literary evidence for the law. The distinction between non-literary records, which can offer relevant information about the law, and literary fictions, which cannot submit such information, is reason enough for Posner to deny literature's admission into evidence. Relevancy is indeed the basis requirement for the admissibility of evidence, as defined, for instance, by the Federal Rules of Evidence:

> All relevant evidence is admissible, except as otherwise provided by the Constitution of the United States, by Act of Congress, by these Rules, or by other rules prescribed by the Supreme Court pursuant to statutory authority. Evidence which is not relevant is not admissible.[17]

This is not to say that Posner indeed follows this definition of admissibility by the Federal Rules of Evidence in any literal sense. Yet there is no doubt that the relevance of literature is defined in the legal sense of relevant evidence as "logically probative of a fact in issue."[18] The fact in issue in Posner's case is the determination of the nature of the law; and since its literary rep-

---

16 Kayman, "Questions of Jurisdiction," 6.

17 Fed. R. Evid., 401–03. The term 'relevancy' is used to denote the general concept, while 'relevance' mostly refers to a specific item or piece of evidence; see Reutlinger, *Evidence,* 22–25.

18 Reutlinger, *Evidence*, 22.

resentation has no logical, but only a "metaphorical"[19] relation to the law as a fact, the evidence of literature is irrelevant, and thus inadmissible. In a very literal sense, the law as a fact for Posner only includes legal practice, that is, "made" law (*facit*). Therefore, while literature is of high interest for the province of legal philosophy, it is much less so for legal practice; and, again, while jurisprudence may benefit from reading literary works, it is an "area of legal studies for which the ordinary professional training and experience of a lawyer provide scant preparation."[20] While this would suggest that there are indeed areas of the law which are closer to literature than others, these areas are as distant from legal practice as is literature.

Yet why, then, should lawyers turn to literature at all? Why, for that matter, does Posner turn to literary texts and literary criticism? To be sure, Posner's main interest is not in general values, like Fiss', nor does it lie in the new evidence provided by literary interpretations of legal texts. When he finally announces a "more promising direction for the law-and-literature movement to take," the respective chapter is significantly dedicated to the comparison of "masterpieces of rhetoric,"[21] ranging from Shakespeare's *Julius Caesar* to Oliver Wendell Holmes' dissent in the famous *Lochner* case.[22] Not only does Posner recommend literary works under the rubric of great rhetoric, but he also stresses the usefulness of literary criticism and its methods for the lawyer and the judge:

> the important thing is that lawyers and judges can learn from literary criticism of judicial opinions and perhaps of other legal writing — if nothing else, can learn how important rhetoric is to the law. More than rhetorical technique is involved. Also pertinent are the craft values … that inform great literature.[23]

This is not simply another, more positive, view of the possible contribution of literature and literary criticism to legal practice. In fact, this assessment only underscores and complements Posner's initial verdict about the irrelevance of literary evidence. It is no accident that a judicial opinion like Justice Holmes' should be comparable to great works of literature, while even the greatest literary works would never reach the status of being 'logically probative of a fact' under the particular jurisdiction of Posner's law of literature. This jurisdiction is enforced straight along the line between rhetoric and evidence: rhetoric being all literary (the best legal rhetoric is like a

---

19 Posner, *Law and Literature*, 16.
20 Posner, *Law and Literature*, 16.
21 Posner, *Law and Literature*, 17.
22 See *Lochner v. New York,* 198 U.S. 45 (1905).
23 Posner, *Law and Literature*, 18.

great literary work), while evidence is being exclusively defined in the legal sense.

More precisely, and more to the specific point which I will return to again and again in my own interpretations, Posner's correlation of law and literature according to an implicit distinction between the rhetorical and the evidentiary potential of texts denies the evidence of the law's presence in literature in order to allow the presence of the literary into the law as rhetoric. In an apparently paradoxical counter move, only this conversion of "law in literature" into "literature in law" in turn guarantees the transformation of literary rhetoric into legal evidence.

There is, of course, nothing new about Posner's particular understanding of the social and cultural function of literature. If my reading of his positions and his argument appear a little too close for their merits, it is due to my interest in the inherent reciprocity of the law and literature nexus in regard to the implied opposition between rhetoric and evidence. This opposition withstands even the invitation of rhetoric into the law (or the law's language), but only because Posner's initial move was to declare literature inadmissible as evidence. If we look at other correlations of law and literature that similarly emphasize the potential benefit of literary rhetoric for legal discourse, we will soon find that there are other ways to relate the legal and the literary to rhetoric and to evidence, respectively.

II

One early attempt to define the relationship between law and literature in reference to written expression and rhetorical style was presented in 1925 by Benjamin Cardozo, arguably one of the most influential voices in 20th-century American legal history. Under the programmatic (and rather predictable) title "Law and Literature," Cardozo made a strong case for the inherent literariness of judicial opinions, emphasizing the inevitable connection between the legal logic of its argument and the style of judicial writing and establishing himself as a reference point for the law-and-literature movement. Contrary to the common conception that "a judicial opinion has no business to be literature,"[24] Cardozo stresses the significance of literary means for legal writing. Literary rhetoric and style are a functional element or aspect of legal discourse for Cardozo; moreover, an appropriate understanding of the particular association of the legal and the literary is indispensable for the suc-

---

24 Cardozo, 699.

cess of judicial opinions. This understanding can only come from literature, or rather from its criticism, as Cardozo cites Henry James in defense of his conception of legal style: "there is no substance without [form]. Form alone *takes,* and holds and preserves substance, saves it from the welter of helpless verbiage that we swim in as in a sea of tasteless tepid pudding."[25] Cardozo comments:

> This is my own faith. … The strength that is born of form and the feebleness that is born of the lack of form are in truth qualities of the substance. They are tokens of the thing's identity. They make it what it is.[26]

With the help of James' emphatic understanding of the fusion of form and substance in literature, Cardozo is able to redefine the functionality of rhetoric as *style* in legal writing. Cardozo's peculiar translation of Jamesian substance into 'the thing's identity' gives his own union of substance and form an even more palpable materiality. It also already goes fairly beyond Posner's instrumentalist conception of rhetoric — a term that Cardozo significantly averts in his discussion. Moreover, Cardozo's peculiar fusion of legal substance and literary form could be read *in extremis* as the complete identification of evidence with rhetoric, as the closing phrase 'they make it what it is' indicates: (literary) rhetoric makes (legal) evidence what it is. Though Cardozo is not talking about the concept of legal evidence as it used in legal processes and trials, it will become clear that the emphasis on rhetorical strategies that characterizes Cardozo's perspective on judicial opinions (and the persuasiveness of the 'truth' they express) can be easily extended to include all those forms of evidence in the law whose persuasiveness likewise relies on rhetorical or literary strategies: successful argumentation, plausible narratives, and skilled cross-examination.

Certainly, such an interpretation of Cardozo's essay would run squarely against Posner's subsumption of the literary under the legal. Yet the point is precisely that once literary rhetoric is identified as an indispensable element of legal writing or discourse its function may be interpreted in very different ways. Cardozo's explicit emphasis on the literary and rhetorical quality of the law as text or speech has offered legal and literary scholars a vantage point for the assessment of the law's linguistic and aesthetic dimensions. While similarly oriented against Posner's conservative model of relation, the approaches of Richard Weisberg and Judith Koffler, respectively, present rather

---

25 Qtd. in Cardozo, 700. Cardozo is quoting from James' letter to Hugh Walpole, May 19, 1912 (James, *Letters of Henry James,* 236–37).
26 Cardozo, 699–700.

distinct variants of Cardozo's assumptions in regard to the affinities of literary and legal rhetoric.

As both a legal scholar and a scholar of French and comparative literature, Richard Weisberg has become one of the most outspoken proponents of the comparative study of law and literature in legal education. In this vein, he has offered his own approach as a constituting component within a general 'program' for the law-and-literature movement. The central aspect of what Weisberg has called "poethics," or "literary jurisprudence," is a "poetic method" for reading and writing law.[27] Like Fiss, Weisberg attempts to place his own understanding of the law and literature nexus in relation to conservative and radical positions in legal and literary theory, establishing an ethical model of legal rhetoric:

> Poethics … endeavours nothing less than to fill the ethical void in which legal thought and practice now exist. We find in this current environment the extremes of economic pseudoscientism and postmodern nihilism. … Literature provides a lively and accessible medium for learning about law in an ethical way. … [W]e return to the poetic method of the law, to the claim that form and substance, sound and sense, merge inevitably in the expression of a just legal system.[28]

As these phrases signal, Weisberg consciously turns to Cardozo's notions about legal and literary rhetoric in defining and defending his own approach. Weisberg's reading of Cardozo, however, has a peculiar edge to it, as it takes the latter's remarks about literary substance and form and transforms them into a fundamental statement about *legal* language and meaning. In declaring the conscious formal aesthetics of style as the most fundamental common feature of literary and legal rhetoric, Weisberg is in fact transforming Cardozo's aesthetic and rhetorical model of legal and literary writing into an ambitious program for a literary ethics of judicial opinion. Weisberg wants to align legal and literary rhetoric to the point where they become interchangeable — at least in their common feature as "carefully crafted utterances." In reference to Cardozo's statement that the lawyer, like the poet, must search for the "just word," Weisberg concludes that:

> Words create law, for Cardozo. They neither distort it nor stand in its way. Words do not translate the thought of justice, words *are* justice, and words can be the absence of justice.[29]

In light of Derrida's observations about the paradox involved in taking the law or literature as representations of justice, Weisberg's rhetoric should give

27 Weisberg, *Poethics,* 3–5.
28 Weisberg, *Poethics,* 4–5.
29 Weisberg, *Poethics,* 6.

pause. Even though it appears as if he is simply paraphrasing Cardozo, Weisberg is indeed extending the latter's perspective on the literary qualities of legal rhetoric in a radical way. Where Cardozo suggested that an awareness of literary style might help the judge to find the most persuasive form for legal thought, Weisberg makes style a matter of justice, and vice versa. This radical interpretation of aesthetic function is most obvious in Weisberg's emphatic assertion: "How an opinion means, how a negotiating session or an argument to a jury means, is more important that what it means."[30]

Weisberg's peculiar interpretation of Cardozo's credo concerning the unity of substance and form should not be taken simply as a manner of speaking, or as a defense of some sort of 'poetic justice.' It is, rather, a strong plea for the factuality of literature, for, in opposition to Posner, Weisberg strongly insists that the evidence of literature is relevant to the law. In a lively review of Posner's *Law and Literature,* Weisberg contrasts Cardozo's literary jurisprudence with Posner's "impersonal jurisprudence" that "appeals to literature only to denigrate its value for law."[31] What Weisberg criticizes most is Posner's inability or unwillingness to look at "the specificity and uniqueness of particular cases,"[32] because it is precisely the dimension of the particular and the specific where justice depends not on logic but on representation. Refuting Posner's emphasis on logical deduction and reasoning, Weisberg states that "[e]ven Posner's own opinions usually begin with the facts, the unique, individualizing elements that characterise our system's approach to the law." Consequently, there can be no abstract, universal representation of justice, neither in law nor in literature, without a factual foundation, "the statement of facts":

> Impersonal in its approach, Posner's thoroughgoing anti-inductiveness denies to the law what he even more inappropriately denies to literature: its origin in the specifics of the matter at hand. If something universal follows, whether in law or in literature, it is because of both the appropriateness of those facts to a universal claim and the craft of the narrator in structuring and describing the matter. … In legal and in literary culture … there can be no understanding and no universalizing apart from a base of specific, accurately observed data.[33]

Justice for Weisberg is impossible to conceive or understand, and, consequently, to realize, without the representation of the factual dimension of the case at hand: the unique, the individual, and the specific. This representation

---

30 Weisberg, *Poethics,* 7.
31 Weisberg, *Poethics,* 195.
32 Weisberg, *Poethics,* 195–96.
33 Weisberg, *Poethics,* 196.

can be achieved only by literature — by the literary 'crafts' of representation, of narration, and of description.

For Judith Koffler, Cardozo's description of the commonalities of legal and literary style indicate the interpretation of law *as* literature. As a law professor at Rutgers University, Koffler early on contributed to the important discussion of Melville's *Billy Budd* in the inaugurating number of the *Cardozo Studies in Law and Literature* (1989), and was one of the most prominent feminist voices in the early law-and-literature movement. From her critical viewpoint, the questions of legal justice and evidence cannot be divorced from issues of gender and the silence that surrounds the female presence in the representation of the law.

Similar to Cardozo, Koffler argues for the inherent affinity of legal and literary texts by reference to their shared linguistic disposition. Pointing to Plato's categorization (in the *Laws*) of both law and literature as "*constitutive* discourse," i.e. "fabrication in the root sense of the word," Koffler suggests that for Plato there is an intimate connection between a theory of law and a theory of literature.[34] Of course, Koffler is well aware that Plato's judgment of literature was rather critical, and thus hastens to assure her readers that her aim is not "to embrace the Platonic superiority of law to literature as forms of discourse."[35] Despite this disclaimer, however, the argument that follows comes to rest substantially on the implicit hierarchy proposed by Plato. In Koffler's interpretation, the common ground for legal and literary discourse can be found in Plato's understanding of a legal code as "the highest form of tragedy, a dramatization of a perfect and noble life."[36] This perfection of discourse can only be achieved, Koffler goes on to argue, when the constitutive discourse of law or literature assumes a diacritical form: "the intellectual ... discrimination [and] ... interweaving of the classes of ideas with one another" that engages "both the synthetic and analytic powers" of the mind.[37] In reference to Plato's high regard for *diacritics,* Koffler arrives at the somewhat un-Platonic (and rather Posnerian) conclusion that in order to learn and understand what a "diacrictical ... intelligent composition"[38] should be, one has to read "great literature": "To read a work of great litera-

---

34 Koffler, "Assimilation," 6. Although she does not give the exact location, Koffler obviously refers to Book 7 of the *Laws,* where Plato makes the comparison between the representation of the poets and those of the lawgivers.

35 Koffler, "Assimilation," 7.

36 Koffler, "Assimilation," 6.

37 Koffler, "Assimilation," 6.

38 Koffler, "Assimilation," 6.

ture involves the reader's active powers of judgment and imagination. … To read literature is to be *engaged* in an intense, diacritical activity."[39]

The important twist in Koffler's elaborate argument appears in her revision of the legal function of literary rhetoric with the help of a category that completely upsets the strict division between facts and their representation, that is, evidence and rhetoric, as Posner devised it; a category which also radicalizes Cardozo's and Weisberg's ideas about the 'identity' of substance and form. The concept of constitutive discourse which aligns law and literature, Koffler acknowledges, is not without problems; where fabrication is involved, there is always the danger of "forgery." The central term for Koffler, however, is 'fiction,' because it allows her to link the concept of constitutive legal discourse to a concept of imaginative literature. Moreover, 'fiction' comes to stand for a better, more suitable form of rhetoric, a form of diacritical persuasion, to which, in Koffler's view, law and literature should likewise aspire. To introduce fiction into the law is of course much riskier than the introduction of rhetoric, since fiction has a kind of unruly, unsettling quality:

> In law … the use of fiction has not always been legitimate. Good fictions are those which are imposed in order to effectuate some worthy results … Unworthy fictions, as for example the notorious Lochner-era fiction of the freedom of contract, have come to be considered … [as] legal cosmetic for oppressive economic theories. Yet Plato seems to be suggesting something different with regard to the law — namely, that all law partakes of the quality of fiction without regard to any criteria distinguishing good from bad. Unsettling as this position might be, it has a ring of truth insofar as the dispositive repudiation of a legal concept as fictitious often emerges only after a process of critical attack. Further, it reminds us that the use of fiction is to persuade, fiction in law serves as a tool for legitimizing judgment.[40]

Although, according to Koffler, Plato does not elucidate what would distinguish a good fiction from a bad one when he talks about law and literature, she points out such a distinction in Plato's *Phaedrus,* where the Greek philosopher had launched one of his famous attacks on rhetoric. There are two ways of speech which can be distinguished and should be valued according to their objective, as Koffler summarizes:

> One kind can help the soul to a happy state, a knowledge of reality. A second kind, properly called rhetoric, is of a different order, an inferior and dangerous sort. Its property is to stabilize our knowledge at its present inadequate level.[41]

---

39 Koffler, "Assimilation," 8.
40 Koffler, "Assimilation," 7.
41 Koffler, "Assimilation," 7.

Posner would certainly agree that a knowledge of reality will lead those who acquire it into a 'happy state.' Yet Koffler is far from subordinating rhetoric to the evidence of facts; what makes diacritical discourse superior to mere rhetoric are not its factual references, but rather its fictional properties. Words "are not communications of facts," and their "value lies not … in their containing some sort of positive truth." Ideally understood, that is, as 'good' fiction, diacritical discourse in law or in literature "presents a vision of a better life," it "creates an order of things possible … not so much by defining … objects as by enabling certain forms to appear."[42]

Koffler's assimilation of law and literature reaches beyond the mere functionality of literary rhetoric and style to make a case for the fictionality of legal writing. But still, even in her repudiation of rhetoric in favor of diacritical fiction she follows the logic of a distinction between a form of rhetoric that leads to 'falsehood,' and another form of superior discourse that gives us the truth, that is, evidence. This evidence, however, does not rely on or refer to facts. In the final analysis it is only the effect of a superior form of rhetoric.

Koffler's idea of the assimilation of law and literature through the category of fiction as a diacritical discourse presents a crucial revision of Cardozo's emphasis that legal writing "will need persuasive force" or "it may never win its way."[43] For Koffler, the persuasive force of legal and literary fiction is aimed at consent rather than victory. Therefore, the nature of literary persuasion "differs significantly" from other forms of rhetoric. In literature, Koffler writes, "the mode of persuasion is one of arousal; this is persuasion in a more diacritical sense, in that the persuasion arises through a *change in consciousness* and hence is more akin to self-persuasion."[44]

With all its utopian pathos and its indulgence in certain passages in deliberate allegorical flourish, Koffler's assimilation of law and literature could be dismissed all to easily as a rather too enthusiastic and hardly convincing theory of literary fiction. Yet it offers a rather instructive example of the critical trajectory of the revisions of the law and literature correlation which we have witnessed over the last decades. Setting aside the utopian and the pathetic dimension, the central focus of Koffler's criticism is clearly a legal and political issue: the "status-quo"[45] of *stare decisis.* This principle of Anglo-American law which demands adherence to precedents in judicial discretion is, in Koffler's

---

42 Koffler, "Assimilation," 8, 9.
43 Cardozo, "Law and Literature," 702.
44 Koffler, "Assimilation," 8, emphasis in the original.
45 Koffler, "Assimilation," 7.

eyes, an obstacle to social and political change. The study of literary texts, the "training in constitutive discourse,"[46] is thus a means to a more general end: countering and possibly even overturning the canonizing rhetoric of *stare decisis* which makes things 'stay the way they are.'

The fusion of the literary with the legal favored by Koffler has some very fundamental consequences, which become more obvious in comparison to the model propagated by Posner. The interpretation of facts, Posner seems to suggest, is a complex affair which must not be confused with the interpretation of fiction. Consequently, Posner's avowed purpose is "to protect statutes and the Constitution from … lawyers who have borrowed … techniques of literary interpretation."[47] This group definitely includes Koffler as well, who states that "the strategies" of interpretation in law and in literature "ought not to differ in kind, since the material does not differ." Not surprisingly, her conclusion is directly opposed to Posner's protective scheme:

> A training in law, in textual interpretation and analysis of statutes and court decisions, ought fundamentally to be a training in constitutive discourse, under which we may subsume literary texts.[48]

This remark is motivated by a considerable tendency to radicalize and universalize the function of literature in the law, a tendency which is characteristic for the law-and-literature movement and its attempt to revise the relation between the legal and the literary. Koffler's proposition to base legal education exclusively on the training in constitutive discourse is informed by an image of law as a fundamentally textual and interpretative exercise, that is, as an intrinsically *rhetorical* practice. This idea subsequently not only became one of the guiding tenets of the law-and-literature movement, but also a central point of conflict which inaugurated some important critical and self-critical reflections on some of the movement's basic assumptions about rhetoric and evidence.

The reason I have singled Koffler out was not to attack the apparent simplicity of her argument. But there are inevitable contradictions brought about by the radicalization and universalization of the legal and the literary as rhetoric. Universalization of legal and literary rhetoric places a severe restriction on the diacritical practice she wants to establish: subsuming both the legal and the literary under one category of constitutive discourse would eventually also mean to resolve the essential difference between law and lit-

---

46 Koffler, "Assimilation," 9.
47 Posner, *Law and Literature*, 17.
48 Koffler, "Assimilation," 9.

erature which allows their diacritical engagement as different rhetorics in the first place. What makes Koffler a special case is, on the one hand, the fact that her concept of assimilation so obviously displays the ambivalence of the rhetoricity thesis. Indeed, Koffler's explicit opposition of (bad) rhetoric and (good) fiction reveals that the correlation of the legal and the literary on the basis of their rhetorical, constitutive nature must always raise the central question I started out with: what is a legitimate fiction? Moreover, since Koffler links rhetoric to falsehood, from which only fiction may liberate its readers, the legitimacy of fiction appears always to be bound up with a claim to truth. Put in this way, the problem seems to be intrinsic to Koffler's particular argument; yet while her position maybe extreme, it is by no means a solitary one. In fact, the thesis about the law's inherent rhetoricity may be the most commonly shared and, at the same time, most ardently disputed issue within the law-and-literature movement. Koffler's fiction thus reminds us that the debate about the rhetoricity of the law is essentially a debate about the evidence of literature for and within the law.

There are at least two consequences which these observations suggest. One concerns the revision of the law-literature relation under the auspices of rhetorical criticism, specifically, the question how a revised understanding could contribute to a critical investigation of the correlation between the legal and the literary without assimilating or subsuming one to the other. The second consequence follows from the first, because it encourages the further inquiry into the revision as an attempt to renegotiate the evidentiary potential of the legal and the literary.

III

That the emergence of the contemporary law-and-literature movement is often associated with the rediscovery of the law as a rhetorical practice is certainly due to the writings of James Boyd White, whose book *The Legal Imagination* is said by many to have 'started' the movement in 1973.[49] One of purposes of the book was to suggest and legitimize the study of literature as a significant part of legal education — a claim that Posner could still find "audacious" in 1988.[50] Literary texts, especially classics like Plato's *Gorgias* or Sophocles' *Philoctetes*, become an important medium through which White approached the law, and in several articles from the 1980s, literature also

---

[49] See Gaakeer, *Hope Springs Eternal.*

[50] Posner, *Law and Literature*, 12.

presents the model for a more general rhetorical approach to the law. In "Law and Rhetoric: The Arts of Cultural and Communal Life" (1985), White suggests that the law should be considered as a branch of rhetoric; a perspective, he claims, that will "be more true to its actual nature as practiced and more valuable to us as critics."[51] Rhetoric in White's sense is neither the art of establishing probabilities where there is no scientific truth, nor is legal rhetoric simply an "ignoble art" of persuasion. The law is a rhetorical practice, a "rhetorical process" or a "rhetorical activity," simply because it offers and uses "a set of resources for thought and argument," because it involves a "creative process" that is "always argumentative;" and, finally, because the law is a "comprehensibly organized method of argument."[52] The most important aspect for White, however, is that legal rhetoric presents a form of "constitutive rhetoric":

> The domain of constitutive rhetoric as I think of it includes *all* language activity that goes into the constitution of actual human culture and communities. Even the kind of persuasion which Plato called dialectic, in which the speaker is himself willing, even eager, to be refuted is in this sense a form of rhetoric, for it is the establishment of community and culture in language.[53]

The law thus is a culture in itself: "a culture of argument, perpetually remade by its participants."[54] Even though it is hard to establish any direct connection between Koffler and White, they employ the term "constitutive rhetoric" in similar ways, both emphasizing the creative over the merely imitative (or rule following) function of the law, and, likewise, the beneficiary aspects of such rhetoric for the culture at large. White, however, does not use the term 'fiction' nor does he attempt to distinguish between good and bad (or true and false) rhetoric. Nevertheless, there is a close identification of the rhetorical with the literary in regard to the law's power to constitute what it speaks:

> The language the lawyer uses and remakes is a language of meaning in the fullest sense. It is a language in which our perceptions of the natural universe are constructed and related, in which our values and motives are defined, in which our methods of reasoning are elaborated and enacted; and it gives us our terms for constructing a social universe by defining roles and actors. … Law always operates through speakers located in particular times and places speaking to actual audiences about real people. Its language is continuous with ordinary language: it always operates by narrative, it is not conceptual in its structure; it is perpetually

---

51 White, *Heracles' Bow*, 31.
52 White, *Heracles' Bow*, 32, 33, 34.
53 White, *Heracles' Bow*, 39.
54 White, *Heracles' Bow*, 35.

> reaffirmed or rejected in a social process; and it contains a system of internal translation by which it can reach a range of hearers. All these things mark it as a literary and a rhetorical system.[55]

This is surely a remarkable image of the law, but it is even more remarkable as an image of literature. In contrast to Koffler, White's constitutive rhetoric, or better, the literature of law, does not fabricate diacritical fictions of possible things, but constitutes the very foundations of what we are used to presuming as facts. Legal rhetoric is about 'real' people and addressed to 'actual' audiences.

As often in White's argument, the line between the descriptive and the prescriptive becomes less and less distinct; yet, what is obvious nevertheless, is White's strong inclination, similar to Koffler's, to assimilate rather than to correlate law and literature. As Ian Ward aptly comments, White aims at the "integration," not the "identification" of the two practices,[56] but the term seems a little weak for his concluding prospect of a community where rhetoric becomes the only discipline and the only practice:

> Rhetoric in the highly expanded sense in which I speak of it might even become the central discipline for which we have been looking for so long — which "science" has proven not to be — by which the others can be defined and organized and judged. One reason rhetoric might be able to perform this role is its continuity with ordinary discourse and hence with real communities, real values, and real politics. It is at least contiguous to a ground common to us all.[57]

It is less the expansion of the meaning of rhetoric that must be considered critically here than the highly specialized way in which White defines it. The form of rhetoric which White desires to eventually organize the whole field of disciplinary inquiry, contest, and conflict — that is, the whole culture of argument — , is a rhetoric that does not constitute, but is itself constituted by, a community, its values, and its politics. How this can be done when the continuity necessary for this constitution of real rhetoric relies in turn on "ordinary discourse," that is, another form of rhetoric, remains as unclear as the question how an "ordinary" rhetoric could become a 'disciplined' way of speaking — in contrast to others which it then organizes and controls — , and yet stay in touch with some common ground of meaning, of value, and of identity. White's image of legal and literary rhetoric ultimately comes to rest on the hope that the pluralism of rhetorical communities will achieve a common ground precisely by consenting to the more general rhetoric of the

55 White, *Heracles' Bow,* 36–37.
56 Ward, *Law and Literature,* 20.
57 White, *Heracles' Bow,* 45–46.

law. Even though he never uses the term, evidence for White must be conceived of as the consensual meaning or effect of rhetorical strategies, the factual basis of a communally shared sense of justice.

In strong contrast to White, Peter Goodrich has argued that the rhetoric of the law is intrinsically adversarial and exclusory, that is, the law is an agonistic rather than a constitutive practice: "legal rhetoric complies with the adversarial form of all doctrinal discourse and is best understood as a form of antirrhetic or discourse of defense or denunciation."[58] Obviously, Goodrich's intention to introduce "the concept of a critical rhetoric"[59] into legal studies stands in stark contrast to White's ideal of rhetorical education as the foundation for a humanizing and ethical practice of legal reading and writing.

Both White and Goodrich carve their respective sketches of rhetorical practice from examples of classical rhetoric, yet while White seems to believe in the possible revitalization of republican virtues by a rhetoric rightfully understood and appropriately engaged, Goodrich appears to admit that his ideal rhetoric is a thing of the past. Republican rhetoric, Goodrich states, was both "radical and to a degree theoretically innocent;"[60] a state of bliss that is rather difficult to restore in today's highly professionalized and diversified theoretical debates.

What remains is to be even more radical, at least in the sense of imploring the specific rhetorical character of legal discourse. For Goodrich, the historical formation of legal discourse rests on the continuing repression and exclusion of its own rhetorical foundations. Legal discourse achieves its discursive autonomy and logical stability by denying its own rhetoricity. Goodrich's critical rhetoric aims, on the one hand, to investigate the specific, historically developed and instituted strategies of legal speech and writing, and the various processes of formalization, standardization, and ritualization of speech in legal situations, which are meant to assure the alleged objectivity and neutrality of the law's practice. On the other hand, rhetoric as legal criticism, or, as Goodrich calls it "rhetoric as jurisprudence,"[61] is an attempt to return the repressed to the law and confront it with its own unacknowledged literariness. Consequently, Goodrich has declared "[l]aw is a literature that denies its literary qualities,"[62] and extended his critical endeavors to use psychoanalytical concepts and theories for legal criticism.[63]

---

58 Goodrich, "Antirrhesis," 59.
59 Goodrich, *Legal Discourse,* 87.
60 Goodrich, *Legal Discourse*, 98.
61 Goodrich, *Legal Discourse*, 85.
62 Goodrich, *Law in the Courts of Love,* 112.
63 See Goodrich, *Languages of Law,* and Goodrich, *Oedipus Lex.*

The hypothesis about the law's repressed or strategically denied character as a fundamentally rhetorical practice has assumed common currency in the course of the law-and-literature movement. Gerald Wetlaufer's observation that "the particular rhetoric embraced by law operates through the systematic denial that it is rhetoric"[64] is as exemplary of the general sentiment as the following statement by Peter Brooks, which also demonstrates how the rhetoricity thesis can be extended easily to include other linguistic features commonly associated with literary fictions:

> Rhetoric, the art of persuasion, and, by extension, the organization of discourse, is a property of all statements. Narrative appears to be one of our large, all-pervasive ways of organizing and speaking the world — the way we make sense of meanings that unfold in and through time. The law, focused on putting facts in the world into coherent form and presenting them persuasively — to make a "case" — must always be intimately intertwined with rhetoric and narrative.[65]

This is a relatively straightforward description of the necessity of rhetorical practice in the law, and it is notable that Brooks still talks about this practice as "putting facts into coherent form" which strongly implies that while law may be like literature, its narratives are factual, not fictional. However, this implication is somewhat refuted by Brooks' subsequent warning to his colleagues from the legal profession:

> Lawyers and judges tend to assume that, as professionals, they work in reference to an objective standard or original intention that stands outside of the rhetorical system. But one may ask whether there is any outside of rhetoric — meaning the norms, the *topoi*, the commonplaces that govern legal thinking as a professional discourse.[66]

The contrast between the two paragraphs is not just one of degree — between various shades of linguistic skepticism, as it were. The difference is rather a principal one, particularly for the understanding of legal rhetoric and its relation to evidence. If we take only the first statement, the relation seems more or less unproblematic. The law's rhetorical practice does not run counter to its fundamental interest in the facts of the case. Indeed, one could still argue that legal rhetoric attempts to present the facts in such a manner as to give them a coherent and comprehensive form — a form that makes a judgment possible in the first place.

The problem indicated in Brooks' more skeptical question whether there is "any outside" of the law's rhetoric refers to the possibility that the rhetori-

64 Wetlaufer, "Denial," 1554.

65 Brooks/Gewirtz, *Law's Stories*, 14.

66 Brooks/Gewirtz, *Law's Stories,* 15.

cal character of the representation of evidence makes it impossible to decide whether it is deliberately made to conform to our assumptions rather than to any 'real' or 'true' correspondence between the object and its representation. Thus, evidence presented in a trial "will persuade a court of the truth or probability of the facts only if it is regarded as truthful, reliable and sufficiently cogent."[67] Moreover, the conformity of the representation of legal evidence in the Anglo-American legal tradition is itself heavily guarded and constricted by a complicated set of regulations, the rules of evidence. These rules present a rather central means of the suppression of legal rhetoricity by means of standardization, formalization, and exclusion. Brooks acknowledges this important feature of the rhetorical system of the law when he talks about rule-governed storytelling:

> Since the law at least implicitly recognizes the power of storytelling, it has been intent, over the centuries, to formalize the conditions of telling — to assure that narratives reach those charged with judging them in certain rule-governed forms. Against what may often appear as fragmented, contradictious, murky unfolding of narrative in the trial courtroom stand formulas by which the law attempts to impose form and rule on stories. … All the rules of evidence, including the much-debated exclusionary rule, touch on the issue of rule-governed storytelling.[68]

What we encounter, then, is the assimilation of two rather different ways of ensuring the legality of evidence and rhetoric: on the one hand, by their conformity to representational correspondence, and, on the other hand, by their conformity to the rules of evidence. As with Koffler's concept of assimilation, one never quite knows which way it will work: whether the enforcement of rules will encourage the representational correspondence to the alleged facts, or whether, on the contrary, they will simply produce a rhetorical conformity to the rules and to our assumptions.

One could argue that the radicalization of the rhetorical perspective on the law's evidentiary practices and the considerable attention in legal studies to the indeterminacy thesis merely mark the law's belated arrival on this side of the linguistic turn. For literary scholars, the debate between conservative intentionalists like Posner, liberal interpretivists like Fiss and Ronald Dworkin, and the more radical deconstructionists from the CLS movement must all bear traits of *déjà vu*, or, rather, *déjà lu*. Yet this impression not only demonstrates the identification of the legal with the literary — its theoretical assimilation — by the law-and-literature movement, it also may encourage the

---

67 Murphy, *A Practical Approach to Evidence*, 2.

68 Brooks/Gewirtz, *Law's Stories,* 19–20. See also Papke, *Narrative*; Bennett/Feldman, *Reconstructing*; Conley/O'Barr, *Just Words.*

question whether the debate about the rhetorical foundation of legal reason, logic, and evidence can be made heuristically useful for similar questions about the foundations of literary evidence.

IV

The 'belatedness' of the notion of the law's rhetoricity and the fundamental indeterminacy of legal 'evidence,' in contrast to similar claims about literature, is exemplified by an essay by Walter Benn Michaels from 1979, which predates much of the debate in the context of the law-and-literature movement. In his remarks on the alleged autonomy of the legal and the literary text, Michaels, whose theoretical assumptions were strongly influenced by Stanley Fish's neo-pragmatist approach to texts and interpretation, draws a parallel between the concept of textual intention held by the New Criticism and certain legal perspectives on intention in contract law. The proclaimed focus on textual meaning expressed by the New Critics, Michaels argues, was not meant "to deny the relevance of authorial intention but rather to limit what would be allowed to count as evidence of that intention" in regard to the text and its meaning.[69] This insistence on the autonomy of the text is in no way a position exclusive to literary criticism, as Michaels points out in reference to a 1911 opinion in a contract dispute, but it is also imminent to a legal understanding of textual evidence. Basically, the legal position holds that "if the written words are themselves plain and clear and unambigious," the text may stand as sufficient evidence for its own meaning.[70] However, if this is not the case, the judge may resort to extrinsic evidence in order to decide its original intention.

Referring to a more radical position, which holds that even a judgment which claims to be independent from extrinsic evidence cannot rest on intrinsic evidence alone, Michaels suggests that the basic distinction, assumed both in literary and legal interpretation, between intrinsic and extrinsic evidence, is completely dubious. The reason is that the decision about what would count as intrinsic and what as extrinsic evidence already presupposes an interpretation of intent and of meaning that comes to rest on extrinsic evidence — like the knowledge and conviction of the judge. In other words, there is no way to "refuse to admit extrinsic evidence in the grounds that it will tend to vary the meaning of the contract without having

69 Michaels, "Against Formalism," 24.
70 Qtd. in Michaels, "Against Formalism," 25.

already admitted extrinsic evidence in deciding what that meaning is."[71] Michaels' conclusion appears like a preemptive dismantling of the very assumptions of relevancy that serve as the basis for the admission of legal evidence:

> The implication is that while we must recognize the importance of extrinsic evidence … we must still insist in a principled way of distinguishing between relevant extrinsic evidence and … irrelevant extrinsic evidence. But … there can in principle be no such principle. Relevant evidence will be evidence that supports the interpretation we hold. Irrelevant evidence will be evidence that supports an interpretation with which we disagree.[72]

This brings us back to the initial observation about the basic nature of evidence as a reference to facts in the service of a specific claim. "Until evidence is articulated," Piyel Haldar states, "it is empty." In order to become evidence, a fact needs "articulated discourse in order to endow it with a meaning it would not otherwise have."[73] This meaning, Michaels insists, is always already a matter of interpretive choices that precede the enlistment of evidence for any specific claim to truth.

Again, this may sound like an all too familiar tune — yet my intention is not to state the obvious but rather to ask how an observation like this could contribute to a revised understanding of the relation between law and literature. At first sight, Michaels' correlation of legal and literary fallacies of intentionalism simply appears to acknowledge that when it comes to texts and evidence, both law and literature may fall prey to certain presumptions about the evidentiary potential of the objects of their respective judgment. It thus might be read in line with Goodrich's assertions about the artificial certainty offered by the law's rhetorical concealment of rhetoricity. Yet the most essential observations of Michaels' article run counter precisely to the fundamental assumptions of Goodrich's theses. Any critical observance of the rhetoricity of linguistic practice — be it that of law or of literature — could not avert the factual conditions under which these practices must operate. These conditions are the reason for the adversarial nature of meaning and evidence, not some inherent structure of language. Language may be ambiguous, yet, as Michaels asserts, it is not inherently so. In fact, we can scarcely assign with assurance any degree of inherent certainty or uncertainty to texts because "the properties we attribute to texts are functions … of the

---

71 Michaels, "Against Formalism," 27.
72 Michaels, "Against Formalism," 28.
73 Haldar, "The Evidencer's Eye," 184.

contexts in which texts are read."[74] To the possible objection that, after all, literary texts aim at and evoke quite different reactions from their readers than do legal texts and that the specific rhetorics of law and literature could thus not (and even ought not) be compared, Michaels concurs readily enough — but only to insist again that "while there are indeed differences between poems and contracts, they are institutional not formal differences."[75]

This appears to be nothing more than another version of White's and Goodrich's theses about the unacknowledged rhetoricity and literariness of the law. Legal language, Michaels seems to suggest in a similar vein, can assume its logical and unambiguous form only through the institutional repression of ambiguity. There is, however, an aspect in Michaels' reasoning which turns the radicalization of rhetoricity against White's and Goodrich's concept of a critical rhetoric that would help to restore the literary within the law and could thus be used to reform and ameliorate the practice of the law and its outcomes. For, in Michaels' account, literary evidence does not fare any better than legal evidence; consequently, a literary reading of a legal text must either run into the same indeterminacy trap as legal readings of legal texts do, or, if it wants to avoid this trap, a literary reading of the law must establish its own rules of evidence.

V

It must appear a bit surprising, if not ironic, that the most fundamental criticism of the notion of the law's rhetoricity at the center of both White's and Goodrich's arguments has been put forward by Stanley Fish. However, the most astonishing aspect of "The Law Wishes To Have a Formal Existence," in which Fish combines his criticism of the law with a critique of its critics, is that Fish finds White's and Goodrich's various concepts of integrating rhetorical criticism into legal practice not only thoroughly impractical, but even dangerous. At best, Fish argues against White, the "thesis of the law's rhetoricity will not … generate[] a new way of practicing law, it will merely … add[] one more resource to a practice that will be shaped, in large measure, by the goals the law will continue to have, the goals of winning an argument or crafting an opinion." White's ideal concept of an open, poetic, and pluralistic legal rhetoric can have no "place … in a process that demands single-

74 Michaels, "Against Formalism," 32.
75 Michaels, "Against Formalism," 32.

voiced judgments."[76] Likewise, even while Fish would agree to most of Goodrich's descriptions about the repressive formalism of legal rhetoric, he vehemently rejects the notion that the law would be better off if it would assume a more self-conscious and self-reflective rhetorical practice: "Were the law to deploy its categories and concepts in the company of an analysis of their roots in extra-legal discourses, it would not be exercising, but dismantling its authority, in short it would no longer be law."[77] In other words, both White and Goodrich are right to point out the law's inherent rhetoricity and literariness, but also quite wrong in assuming that this insight could be a part of good legal practice.

For Fish, the basic mistake is to read the law's formal rigidity, its artificial rules, and its self-centered logic exclusively as both the result and the instrument of ideology and power interests. This view overlooks the practical and "empirical conditions that give rise to the law and constrain its operation, conditions including the need for procedures to adjudicate disputes, and the pressure for prompt remedies and decisions."[78] The law's rhetoric and its claim to "a formal existence" are thus not simply a means to mask its ideological and political subservience, they also guarantee its practical, its pragmatic function. In his conclusion, Fish's anxious claim for the law's autonomy almost comes to resemble Posner's anxiety of interdisciplinary corruption:

> In a world without foundational essences … there are always institutions … that are assigned the task of providing the spaces … in which we negotiate the differences that would, if they were given full sway, prevent us from living together in what we are pleased to call civilization. And what, after all, are the alternatives? Either the impossible alternative of grounding the law in … immutable abstractions, or the unworkable alternative of intruding that impossibility into every phase of the law's operations … the effect [of which] would be so to attenuate those operations that they would finally disappear. That leaves us with the law as it is, something we believe in because it answers to … our desires.[79]

There is more than a need for anecdotal evidence which encourages me to dwell on Fish's peculiar version of the rhetoricity thesis for some time. My point is that the position which Fish advances in "The Law Wishes to Have a Formal Existence" is not a theoretical, but a practical position — in the sense that it marks the distance, or difference, between a theoretical and a practical claim to truth. This difference is the central assumption on which

---

76 Fish, "The Law Wishes," 174.
77 Fish, "The Law Wishes," 176.
78 Fish, "The Law Wishes," 177.
79 Fish, "The Law Wishes," 179.

Fish's arguments against White and Goodrich come to rest and which in the end also defines his own position as a practical rather than a theoretical one. The processes and procedures that guarantee the law's function as a practice are based on certain evidentiary presumptions and rules which are an essential part of its rhetorical practice. In this observation, Fish readily agrees with White and Goodrich. Arguing as they do, however, that the law's rhetorical practice could be (or even should be) replaced with this observation, or more precisely, with the self-reflective critical rhetoric that allows for the insight into the rhetoricity of the law, runs not only counter to their own theoretical premises, as Fish points out, but would also turn the law from a practice into a theoretical and critical enterprise.

It may be argued that this conclusion will not prevent a more radical legal rhetoricist from asserting that such a change would be beneficial to the law or would even make it more just. But this assertion fails to understand the real thrust of Fish's polemics. Replacing the rhetorical practice of the law with a critical theoretical rhetoric will not help it to better fulfill its desired function — the solution of conflicts in a regulated, non-violent manner with results that are felt to be both justified and just — simply because it is precisely this function that requires the law's rhetorical practice as it is. Thus, even if one could replace the law 'as it is' with something else in order to better serve the function as described, this something else would become subjected to the same practical demands and constraints which make the law's rhetorical practice what it is in the first place. Consequently, even a critical or communal rhetoric, when attempting to meet these functional demands and constraints, would eventually be transformed into a rhetorical practice, which will look, in Fish's eyes at least, very similar to the practice of the law they want to replace.

Hence it will not do to replace the rhetoric of the law with the rhetoric of theory and criticism as it is practiced in seminars and academies in order to break "down "the closure of legal discourse," as Goodrich hopes. Yet to believe in such a theoretical claim all the time is practicable only in theory, i.e. only under the conditions of the practice that advanced this claim to validity; from the perspective of a different practice the claim must remain purely theoretical, or rather, rhetorical.[80] As Fish retorts tartly, Goodrich's project would be a purely "academic project determined in its shape by norms of academic inquiry (themselves forms of closure): once the seminar is over …

---

[80] Adam Thurschwell offers a very thorough reading of Fish's argument. My own discussion of the practice-theory opposition at the center of Fish's claim is based in part on Thurschwell's observations ("Reading the Law").

the law will resume the task of simultaneously declaring and fashioning the formal autonomy that constitutes its precarious, powerful being."[81]

It is not my aim to demonstrate the theoretical and practical merits or shortcomings Fish's arguments in "The Law Wishes" might have in regard to the study or the improvement of the law's rhetorical practice. Although this is obviously the essay's major concern, it nevertheless also implies a perspective on the relation between rhetoric and evidence that appears to be rather useful for the discussion of this relation in the context of the law-literature nexus in American culture. As I have pointed out, there is an operative distinction at work in "The Law Wishes" between the theoretical assumptions about the law's rhetoric and the practical function of legal rhetoric. That is, Fish looks at the rhetoricity of the law from two perspectives at once: from a theoretical point of view, the rhetorical dimension of legal rhetoric can be critically or self-critically reflected and deconstructed; yet from a practical point of view — from the perspective of legal rhetoric itself — this cannot be done, and the law's rhetoricity must appear to itself as an evidentiary practice. The mistake of the rhetoricity thesis, Fish holds against Goodrich, White, and Critical Legal Studies, is to assimilate the practical to the theoretical point of view and to argue that legal rhetoric would improve if it acknowledged its rhetoricity, became self-reflective, and disavowed its evidentiary claims. This assimilation is itself based on denial: not only the denial of the validity of the law's practical perspective on its rhetoric, but also the denial of the evidentiary dimension of critical rhetoric as a way of practicing theory. This observation allows some fundamental suggestions in regard to the rhetorical approach to evidence implied in the 'law as literature' perspective.

First, what is regarded as evidence from the point of view of one practice may appear as purely rhetorical from the point of view of another practice. This also means that the critical reflection of the rhetoricity of specific evidentiary procedures and protocols must remain blind to the very rhetoric of evidence which helps to advance its own claims to truth. Evidence is an indispensable requirement of *practical* rhetoric, even where it critically (i.e. theoretically) may claim that there is no evidence at all, only rhetoric. In other words, since evidence without rhetoric is empty and rhetoric inevitably produces evidence, the difference between various competing rhetorics of evidence becomes manifest only in the specific correlation they (must or can) realize between the evidentiary dimension and the (self-)critical potential of their rhetoric under the specific conditions that define their practice. This

[81] Fish, "The Law Wishes," 177.

correlative balance between evidence and rhetoric again has both a theoretical and a practical dimension, which allows precisely for the criticism of other correlations, as well as for the self-critical revision and practical adjustment of the original correlation.

The relation between law and literature proposed by the 'law *as* literature' trope precisely illustrates this dialectic of evidence and rhetoric even in its resistance to acknowledging it. The attempt to 'assimilate' legal and literary discourses according to the assumptions of the conceptual essentialism and literary exceptionalism implied by the rhetoricity thesis is driven by the idea that the incorporation of the literary into the legal would restore, or implant, a self-critical or self-reflective dimension within the law's rhetorical practice, making it a more suitable practice for the achievement of justice. However, the alleged self-reflective potential of literary rhetoric is, as Michaels maintains, not a formal, but an institutional, or, in Fish's definition, a practical disposition of literary discourse. By failing to recognize that the critical function of the literary in respect to the legal rests on their practical incompatibility — their "lack of relationship" as distinct practices — , the assimilation of law and literature threatens to remove an essential pre-condition for both the evidentiary and critical function of literary rhetoric: its very distinction and independence from the functions of legal rhetoric.

VI

One dimension of the evidentiary function of literary rhetoric is its propensity to stage, enforce, or otherwise foreground its rhetorical quality, a privilege that would become useless if literary rhetoric were subsumed under the requirements of legal practice. Nevertheless, the rhetoricity thesis may help to understand more clearly the relationship of literature to law, especially in those cases that interest me most: the literary representation of legal processes. For once, such representations appear to realize what White and Goodrich propagate, even if only in reverse: law has become, in these texts, an integral part of literature's rhetorical practice. Hence the rhetorical perspective on the law, emphasized and radicalized by the concept of rhetoricity, is always implied in the literary representation of legal discourse. As I suggested in the preceding chapter, the possibility for the criticism of legal practice and procedure in or through literature rests to a great extent on literature's own rhetorical practice and its knowledge of the rhetorical foundations of legal authority. One central strategy in the critical representation of law in literary fictions must therefore be a more or less pronounced revelation of the law's inherent rhetoricity, its performative and interpretive violence, the linguistic fabrication of its evidence, and the fictionality of its 'truths.'

This strategy might result in good literature based on bad representations of the law, as Tony Sharpe has argued, but that does not invalidate the critical function of these fictions.[82] In fact, one insistent argument that informs my interpretations is that literary representations of the law must be interpreted as the performance of legal rhetoric in literature. Law as it appears in literature is not 'the law,' it is first of all literature, that is, part of a specific rhetorical practice with specific evidentiary assumptions and specific claims to truth, a practice that is called, or calls itself, literature. This perspective is necessary in order to observe in full the critical potential of law in literature: as an examination of different correlations of evidence and rhetoric that claim to be at once just and true. The criticism of the law is but one part of this examination, and it is the part that is most visibly acknowledged and pronounced. The other part, though less visible and hardly acknowledged, is equally indispensable for the critical examination of law in literature. The radicalization of the rhetoricity thesis tends to obscure the specific correlations, i.e. the possible correspondence, interdependence, or supplementarity which governs the relation between the legal and the literary and thus correlates the evidentiary function of legal and literary rhetoric as cultural practices within specific historical situations. A rhetorical perspective on the law-literature correlation is always challenged by the fact that rhetoric has both a theoretical and a practical history, and, moreover, that these histories are related in various ways that cannot be described exclusively by reference to a 'trial situation' of forensic conflict. Nor is rhetoric best understood, as Goodrich demands, by "imag[ining] a history prior to, or other than, that of the division of labour, be it in an economic, legal and political or theoretic and semantic form."[83] One cannot escape one's own historical perspective by imagining another. As Fish counters Goodrich, "one who has learned the lesson of rhetoricity does not thereby escape the conditions it names."[84]

This is also a central point in Brook Thomas' critique of the insufficient concepts of literary fiction that are implied (or even applied) by some positions in the law and literature debate. The fictional reflection of the law, Thomas insists, can help to better understand certain aspects of legal history by

---

82 See Sharpe, "(Per)Versions."

83 Goodrich, *Legal Discourse*, 98.

84 Fish, *Doing What Comes Naturally*, 552.

bringing to light the repressed or denied dimension of that history. Since Thomas' central concerns are very close to mine, his understanding of literary evidence offers a valuable counter perspective to the rhetoricity thesis.

Thomas clearly opts for staying within the Aristotelian paradigm, and he defends his own concept of literary evidence in reference to Eden's discussion.[85] Noting the correspondence of the central significance of ocular proof in legal and in poetic discourse stressed by Aristotle, Thomas asserts that the importance of vivid display and description in both law and literature is due to their common interest in affecting the responses of an audience. The most effective tool to achieve this common aim are those rhetorical strategies that produce evidence — in the combined sense of *energeia* and *enargeia*. Thomas then goes on to make an important distinction in regard to the conditions of evidence in law and literature — a distinction that clearly resonates with the one made by Ricœur already discussed in the first chapter:

> But if for Aristotle rhetoric was a technique to present evidence, its effectiveness was governed by different criteria in the court and on the stage. The truth of rhetoric in court depended on an accurate retelling of what actually happened. Its effectiveness was measured by its ability to persuade. In contrast, the truth of poetic language is not measured by what actually happened, nor does it aim at persuasion. Instead, its aim is mimetic. Not an act of persuasion, *mimesis,* when successful, brings into existence a plot whose truth about human action is self-evident.[86]

This distinction, Thomas claims, is already inscribed in Aristotle's conceptual framework and the various distinctions it could establish in reference to the foundational functional correspondence between legal and poetic discourse. On the other hand, Thomas' form of the distinction cannot be found in Aristotle, and not just because the term "self-evidence," that most evidently American form of evidence, was unknown to Aristotle. This is not to quibble with an approach I find persuasive enough to use as evidence in my own argument. My problem with this passage — which is crucial because it refers to the difference between legal and literary evidence — is that it links one distinction to another.

The first dividing line between the evidence of legal and poetic rhetoric is that the former produces a story which presumably has happened, while the latter can freely dispense with this presumption. The second distinction runs along the familiar line of truth versus persuasion — with a sophisticated twist. Legal evidence for Thomas must always rely on persuasion, no matter

---

[85] See the discussion in Eden, *Poetic and Legal Fiction,* 36–38.

[86] Thomas, "Reflections," 532.

whether a story told in court is true or not in accordance with the presumption noted above. Literary evidence, in contrast, is not established in reference to a real event, but rather as the result of a mimetic process which does not retell a true event but actualizes another through the plot it presents. The main point, however, is not that mimetic evidence is different from legal evidence, nor that they both might be considered true in their own right. Poetical truth is only possible, Thomas claims, because poetic language — its evidentiary practice — is not aimed at persuasion. Nevertheless, Thomas also suggests that rhetoric, as "a technique to present evidence," was used both in the court and on stage. Somewhat paradoxically then, poetic *mimesis* turns out as a non-persuasive rhetoric — something that Aristotle would presumably take as a contradiction in terms — more than the simple presentation of evidence with rhetorical means, but rather the realization of self-evidence.

Despite the obvious similarity of their insistence on poetic language as non-persuasive, Thomas' description of literary evidence is more problematic than Ricœur's definition of the living metaphor. It is the very concept of evidence which resists the denial or repression of rhetoric and its potential persuasiveness.

It seems to me that Thomas is comparing two different notions of evidence: a weak notion, in which evidence is linked to persuasion, and an emphatic notion, in which evidence appears to be free from rhetoric and thus can come into its own, as it were. This also separates legal *enargeia*, the accurate description of things and events, from poetic *energeia*, the actualization of truth as event and experience. What gives this distinction its own persuasive evidence is the denial of the double structure of *mimesis,* namely actualization through imitation. This particular notion of literary evidence is needed to distinguish literature not only from the law but from other forms of public rhetoric as well. In maintaining its critical distance to the law, literature also functions as a corrective of the *doxa* of public opinion. Since literature is mimetic, it is not aimed at persuasion, and thus differs essentially in function from the practical rhetoric used in public and political debates. For Thomas, literature is no part of *phronesis,* for the truth which it may offer can have no value in debates surrounding practical concerns.[87]

Unlike the doxic truths of public opinion, the truth of literature is not the result of persuasion, and therefore it can not be believed in the same way as

---

[87] *Phronesis,* or 'practical wisdom,' is an Aristotelian category which is to be distinguished from pure wisdom, *sophia,* and the more abstract and universal knowledge of *episteme.* See *Eudemian Ethics*, 1141b9–14.

the rhetorical truth of *doxa*. In this sense, Thomas maintains, the self-evident truth of literature is paradoxical: "[f]or those experiencing it, its truth is self-evident; for those who don't, no amount of persuasion will work." Yet this character of literary evidence makes it especially well-fitted for fulfilling a critical function in regard to the law and legal evidence. The paradoxical evidence of literature, Thomas writes, has to be related to the

> contradictions produced by the conflicting deployments of rhetoric within particular societies, contradictions that often surface in the conflicts faced by a society's legal system. If the function of the law is to resolve those conflicts, literature's paradoxes result from a failure to do so. This failure continues to give literature a supplementary relation to the law, because it draws attention to inequities committed by the law's exclusions.[88]

In his attempt to wrestle literature both from Posner's normative instrumentalism and the paralyzing grip of radical rhetoricity, Thomas wants to prove that literature is neither simply imitative or metaphorical, nor just another form of rhetoric. Literature is a non-persuasive rhetoric, which turns its relation to rhetoric proper into a critical one: "literature … is a rhetorical means of marking the limits of human-made rhetoric."[89]

Insofar as all rhetoric is still made by humans, this definition seems puzzling. Does it mean that literature is limited, or a limited form of rhetoric? How do you mark the limit of rhetoric with the help of rhetoric? Where, for that matter, is the limit of rhetoric? Thomas offers two explanations in his essay. What he wants to argue is that literature can work as a rhetorical check on another rhetoric, that of the law. But that could be said of the law as well, after all, since the law is indeed a rhetorical means that sets limits to other forms of rhetoric. Thus it may mark the limits of literary rhetoric by acts of copyright, by laws against libel, against pornography, etc.

If I understand Thomas' argument correctly, he is not talking about the limits of rhetoric, but the limits of evidence, the line where rhetoric denies itself and attempts to stand in for evidence. Literature, he appears to suggest, can expose the limits of the law's rhetoric of evidence by showing where its evidence is just rhetorical. But in his second, more pronounced explanation, Thomas declares this critical function of literature to depend on a limitation. Literary rhetoric may be able to expose the inequities of the law and thus confront legal justice with literary equity, but this ability results from its own failure as *mimesis*. Thomas acknowledges the difference between what he first had described as the Aristotelian notion of mimetic truth or evidence and

88 Thomas, "Reflections," 536.
89 Thomas, "Reflections," 531.

his own revised notion of mimesis as paradoxical and inherently lacking. The revision, he argues, is necessary because in its emphatic understanding, mimetic truth presents an ideal rather than an actual description of what literary evidence can be. But even the rhetorical versatility and mimetic power of literary fiction will never achieve a full representation of what Thomas calls the untold story of the law:

> the untold story that I have in mind remains untold. It is a story that could equitably resolve the contradictions produced by a society's conflicting stories about justice. This story remains untold because it can never be fully represented within a text. Literary paradoxes that point to, but never speak, this untold story have the potential to stimulate an audience to generate new ways of constructing evidence, evidence that does not easily fit into accepted public opinion, evidence that is not deemed admissible in existing courts of law. If accepted, such evidence can alter a society's sense of justice.[90]

There are several observations about Thomas' argument which are important for my own interpretation of the critical function of literary representations of the law. Most essentially, the emphasis on literary evidence as paradoxical and inherently lacking connects Thomas' notion of the "untold story of the law" with Derrida's description of the mystical foundation and the force of law and the predicament of representation I have discussed in the first chapter. Both Derrida and Thomas point out certain impasses concerning the adequate or comprehensive representation of the law and of justice. There are of course significant differences between the two arguments, depending on the scope and the focus of their respective interests and concepts. However, there is an interesting, and I think very profitable, affinity to be noticed that relates to the idea of a legitimate or just fiction. To understand this affinity, we have to look less at what such a fiction would represent, but rather at what such a fiction would *do* — if it were ever possible.

The story of the law can never be told in full, Thomas notes, because such a story would *equitably resolve* the conflicts between all other partial representations of justice, including, I would add, the law itself. In other words, this story would not only represent but moreover realize justice — it would bring about justice by offering itself as justice. The full representation of law in literature thus becomes the full realization of justice, which also means that this story of the law would immediately achieve the form of emphatic literary evidence that Thomas described at the beginning: *self-evidence.* If we take another look at this unlikely scenario, this time from the perspective of Derri-

---

90 Thomas, "Reflections," 538.

da's moment of performative self-authorization, the literary representation of the untold story of the law *as a fiction of justice* could be said to effectively institute literature as both law and justice. In other words, the untold story of the law stands for the 'mystical source' of literary authority, the foundation of its legality.

Given the affinity in notions of the predicament of representation, I would agree with Thomas that literary evidence has a certain paradoxical character, as I would also admit that a full textual representation of equity is impossible. Yet I do not assume that the exposure of the law's inequities is the only, or most dominant motivation, for literary and cultural representations of the law. That might be the dominant motivation of the specific texts that Thomas has in mind, but it could hardly serve as a category to decide which of all the various representations would count as literature, because their evidence about the law is paradoxical in contrast to other narrative fictions whose evidence is merely 'doxic.'

Finally, it may be stated that persuasion is neither 'un-literary,' nor does literature abstain from attempting to persuade its readers. In fact, one of the basic presumptions that informs my interpretation of several literary texts from different periods of American literary history is that there is a persistence in the public function of literary rhetoric, an eagerness to prove its power in the realm of *phronesis*. That does not mean that literature must perceive itself as rhetoric or even as doxic to understand itself as a form of intervention in regard to public opinion. Indeed, when literature self-consciously tries to realize the "potential to stimulate an audience to generate new ways of constructing evidence," that stimulation must be regarded as a form of persuasion.[91]

The lesson I draw from the Aristotelian correlation of law and literature is a different one. My central focus is not aimed at extracting a definition of literature from Aristotle, rather, my interest is in the specific way in which the model attempts to define the literary in reference to, and distinction from, the legal. This also means to acknowledge the double thrust of a rhetoric that wants to be mimetic to unfold its "stimulating" power. For literary evidence to be effective under the conditions of public rhetoric, more is at stake than the success of *mimesis*. As I suggested in my discussion of Derrida's notion of institutive self-authorization, part of the interest of literature in the law is an interest in power and linguistic authority that has an ambivalent character. The attempt to expose the inequities of the law, to mark the limits of human-

91 Thomas does not entirely rule out this motivation. See Thomas, "Reflections," 538.

made rhetoric in the law, also threatens to expose the limits of literary rhetoric in regard to evidence. Thus literature, like the law, is forced to comply to the constraints which its practice places on its evidentiary rhetoric. It is my interest to show how in specific literary texts the representation of certain evidentiary predicaments of the law reflects on, and in fact, reinforces the representational predicaments of literature. The representation of law in literature always implies a representation of the law *as* literature, for in this way literature can best expose the rhetorical pretensions of legal evidence. However, this is not without risk since the same could be done to the rhetorical construction of literary evidence.

Moreover, the similarity of some of the evidentiary practices of law and literature enforces a certain competitive dynamic every time literature strives to represent legal rhetoric as a form of critique. As I will show, the critical representation does not operate simply along a line that divides the realm of the law from that of literature, with the intent to comment from one position on the other. Even where this simple contrast appears to be the main operational strategy, one will always be forced to admit that the law in a literary fiction must assume some literary aspects in the process, while it cannot be denied that literature must take on a legal character, if only in acquiring, in specific moments, a legal voice. This also belongs to the mimetic dimension of literary evidence, this time in the sense of imitation. One focus of my discussion will be the complex negotiation between the legal and the literary that is a constitutive element of literary representations of the law.

My last point of departure from Thomas' argument about legal and literary evidence is related to my observations about the intent or motivation of literature to enter the realm of public discourse. In doing so, literature has to face the competition of other forms of rhetoric and other forms of evidence. The Aristotelian model which Thomas wants to maintain has to take into account that the realm of *phronesis*, the public sphere, is not immune to cultural and historical change. A society's sense of justice is intimately related to the images of the law which circulate in the public sphere. Literature offers its own, as do other arts and media. If the representation of legal processes and practices is a constant in American culture, it is also true that the forms and interests of this ongoing representation may change over time. Thus, the critical relation between law and literature must be realized at different moments under different conditions — conditions which concern the general assumptions about legal and literary evidence, as well as specific evidentiary practices and their rhetorical strategies. The founding configuration of American law and letters, which Perry Miller and Robert Ferguson have described so impressively in its rise, its glory, and its decline, was a very decisive, but not the only period in American history in which both the critical exchange and the common interests of law and literature expressed themselves. In this respect, the law-and-literature movement only reinforces a negotiation that is a constant in the American culture of argument.

VII

The following chapters present interpretations of several works of fiction from various periods of American literary history. Even though the sequence of the chapters follows a chronological order, they should not be read to suggest a historical development, nor do they attempt, as a whole, to rehearse an argument for such a development. In fact, they present separate case studies which combine extended contextual investigations with close textual readings of one, or more than one, fictional representation of legal processes and procedures. While the argument is in each case meant to be autonomous from the others, all share an intense interest in the problematic relation between evidence and rhetoric and between the truth of the law and the truth of literature.

The choice of the specific texts and contexts is not accidental. They represent, each in their own way, certain key aspects and legal questions, which are of central importance for American legal culture. The problems addressed by and negotiated in the literary texts are thus inherently felt and represented as problems both fundamental and specific to American law and culture. This does not mean that more universal questions, such as legal justice and truth or the fairness and justification of legal processes, are absent from the literary representation of law in the United States. On the contrary, these questions clearly form the indispensable background for the close investigation of more immanent characteristics of American law and justice.

The first of my textual investigations in chapter three is concerned with the central question of literary and legal evidence, and the gradual emergence of the modern understanding of the term during the 17th and 18th centuries. This emergence was connected to a readjustment of rhetorical theories to certain epistemological assumptions about human perception and language propagated by Enlightenment philosophies. The emancipation of individual reason created political subjects who could claim their autonomy from traditional authority and religious doctrine with the help of truth claims based on the laws of nature. In the American Declaration of Independence, this claim most famously and successfully became founded on the notion of 'self-evident truths': truths that needed no accepted authority to sanction them and that were immediately accessible and understandable for everyone endowed with natural reason and perception.

Especially after the American Revolution, however, the latent conflict between the ideal of perceptive reason and the threat of its potential deception through (political or religious) rhetoric became a central problem both in the politics and the poetics of the young republic. I look at a specific moment in this ongoing conflict which was characterized by the attempt to realign the empirical grounding of truth claims with a concept of testimony based on probability. The consequences of this process were far-reaching and have been reflected in various ways in literary fiction, as Jan Melissa Schramm and Alexander Welsh, among others, have shown. Taking their discussions as a background, my interpretation will focus on Charles Brockden Brown's first novel, *Wieland* (1798), an early attempt to establish a concept of national fiction, an "American Tale," as Brown subtitled his work. *Wieland* offers an engaging negotiation of the new concepts of empirical evidence during the 18th century. In contrast to the dominant readings of the novel as an anti-empiricist critique and an early expression of linguistic skepticism, I try to relate it to the debate on evidence in legal treatises and philosophy on the one hand, and to the rhetorical theories of the so-called New Rhetoric of George Campbell and Hugh Blair on the other. As I will argue, the law plays a central part for Brown in his attempt to find a form of fiction whose evidence is not addressed to private sentiment but to public judgment. The legal moment at the center of the novel, the testimony of the tragic murderer Theodore Wieland, serves Brown to confront his audience with a reader who falls prey to his own illusions, based on wrong assumptions about literary evidence and the power of rhetoric. Neither American law nor American literature, Brown seems to suggest, can trust the self-evidence of its fictions.

The fourth chapter returns to my initial question, "what is a legitimate fiction?," by looking at two novels by James Fenimore Cooper, which at first sight appear rather different. The relation between *The Pioneers* (1823) and Cooper's last novel, *The Ways of the Hour* (1850), which my interpretation attempts to investigate, concerns Cooper's specific notions about literature as a form of public discourse on the underlying principles of American democracy. As has been demonstrated by a host of readings, *The Pioneers* is both an argument for and against the law and tries to outbalance the inherent tension between the necessity of the law for social order and its misuse and corruption through the hands of individuals. While *The Pioneers* offers a powerful national fiction of the inevitable progress of American democracy from wilderness to civilization, the successful negotiation of the tension between nature and culture was also employed by Cooper to present the Americanization of the English Common Law as the perfection of natural law through common sense. The legal order which *The Pioneers* attempts to justify is thus both cultural *and* natural; like many influential American jurists of his day, Cooper believed that American law was the inescapable result of the ongoing adaptation of common law principles to the conditions and the experience of democracy. American legal history in Cooper turns out be an integral part of a cultural fiction of progress, safeguarded and defended by an exclusive class of legal and literary authors and interpreters.

Consequently, Cooper's common law of literature, as I call it, also institutes a fiction of the law to delineate the jurisdiction of literature and to establish the authority of historical fiction over other forms of public discourse. This literary legality is based on the latent complicity between legal and literary fiction and expressed in the similar form they assume. Yet, since to the law this form is and must remain invisible, it can only be properly acknowledged and represented by literature. Cooper's law of literature thus gives the law its proper public representation and thereby assures its own legitimacy as lawful writing or rhetoric. In contrast to the celebrated *Pioneers*, the complicity of law and literature is completely undermined in *The Ways of the Hour,* where the law appears only in one form: as an instrumentalized medium for the manipulation of public opinion. What Cooper decries above all is that the law has turned from literature to journalism to find its proper public form. As journalism, however, the law falls prey to public opinion and completely loses its evidentiary integrity. The most dramatic effect of this situation is that literature, Cooper's literature, to be precise, has lost its function, and all that remains is either to join the struggle for public opinion or to disavow its claims for literary legality.

The critical perspective on the variable conditions and effects of the negotiation of the legal and the literary within the sphere of culture must also include an awareness that the rhetorical struggle between law and literature does not take place in an isolated arena. While for Brown and Cooper this struggle was certainly dominated by concepts of reading, writing, and speech, that is, by verbal rhetoric in its various forms and modes, the nature of the arena, as well as the nature of the various modes of rhetoric have changed considerably from the 19th to the 20th century. Consequently, there will be a noticeable shift of emphasis in the last two chapters as their critical viewpoint will give special attention to the complex interdependence and interaction between representations of the law in literary fictions and in other media, especially visual media like film (chapter 5) and television, as well as popular culture in general (chapter 6).

This attention is due to the claim that literary evidence emerges and develops in contrast to other cultural rhetorics of evidence. The 'truth' of literature is effective or persuasive only in relation to and distinction from the evidentiary discourses it wants to (or has to) compete with as a public rhetoric. Therefore, another aspect whose significance must be addressed is the relation to the public sphere in which literature sees or projects itself. In a very direct sense, for example, the distinction of literary evidence can become a matter of legal protection and regulation, as the definition of literary property makes very obvious. Copyright law treats literature not as a private, but as an essentially public property, which it will protect only for a certain time. At the same time, to insist on literature as an autonomous mode of writing does not prevent the law from restricting that autonomy, precisely when its public effects are seen to be detrimental to legal order. Moreover, while the predicament of representation must by necessity concern all media, it is obvious that the double-faced nature of modern evidence, oscillating between *energeia* and *enargeia,* will be realized quite differently in different media, which in turn will affect the concept of evidence and its rhetorical understanding.

Chapter five therefore is concerned with both a literary text and the cultural effects it continues to unfold, which appears to present a unique example of the paradoxical evidence of fictions of the law. Harper Lee's *To Kill a Mockingbird* (1960), arguably the most successful legal novel of this century, both nationally and internationally, is generally praised by lawyers and shunned by literary critics. There is no denying the persistent cultural presence of the novel, which has become a center piece in many educational projects concerned with law and racial injustice. On the other hand, the novel's celebrated appeal for legal equality in the face of racial difference and conflict reveals the troubling paradoxes inherent in the notion of legal 'color blindness,' still thought to be the ideal of legal objectivity and justice.

One institutive element of legal rhetoric which is held to be especially distinctive for American law is the claim of the universality and objectivity of justice in face of individual difference. Equal justice under the law is one of the founding principles of American legal order — and one of its most troubling fictions. From the beginning, the claim of equal justice could hardly be reconciled with the reality of racism and racial injustice in American law and society. One of the most enduring concepts which American law had conceived in order to justify and maintain the claim of legal equality over and against racial bias and injustice was the notion of the law's 'color blindness' in matters of racial difference. While the Civil War brought the abolition of slavery in the U.S., it did not bring equal justice under the law for

African American citizens. On the contrary, the Supreme Court's infamous decision in *Plessy v. Ferguson* (1896) introduced the so-called "separate but equal" doctrine which effectively offered a legal foundation for the system of institutionalized racial segregation and repression in the American South.

Racial segregation, however, was not only a Southern phenomenon. In fact, the underlying logic of racial identification generally supported the social and cultural superiority and dominance of white Americans and the legal equality of white subjects. In the 1950s and 1960s, the legal ideology of color blindness and the cultural ideology of racial segregation were increasingly challenged. On the one hand, institutionalized segregation in the South was declared unconstitutional by the Supreme Court in 1954. On the other, the decades during and after the Civil Rights movement also witnessed a heightened awareness and increasing visibility of conflicting images of race and racial identity. The prominent cultural visuality of race and racial difference in the United States has become a persistent challenge to the claims of color blindness in American law and justice.

That American law cannot escape the problem of race is even more obvious when we look at the evidentiary complexity involved in the acknowledgment of racial identity. The phenomenon of cross-racial (mis-)identification by crime witnesses, for instance, demonstrates how the epistemological assumptions of legal evidence are subverted and rendered useless by the persuasive force of racialized perceptual judgments. As I will argue, it is no accident that the concern with racial inequality and injustice that obviously motivates *To Kill a Mockingbird* is most significantly expressed by the problem of racial identification and misidentification. I will analyze the specific connections and linkages between two different rhetorics of evidence, one that is based on words, and another, based on images. Never completely autonomous, these two rhetorics work together to allow both a rhetorical identification of and a psychological identification with the black body. As I will show, the novel's rhetoric of identification can unfold its force only by denying the existence of a contemporary public sphere and the highly charged images of conflicting racial identifications which it presents. Suppressing the representation of these conflicting images, the novel assumes that racial identity and identification should remain the exclusive responsibility of law and literature. As will become clear, the appeal to legal equality which has made *To Kill a Mockingbird* so successful is based on the difference between the legal and the literary evidence of race and racial identification.

As recent developments have made obvious, the representation of the legal process in literature and in other media is increasingly challenged by the competition of the law's self-representation in the cultural arena. As the presentation of real trials or tribunals on television and on the internet make obvious, the sensational aspect of legal conflict in the United States has created its own public rhetoric, and turned the entire public sphere into one gigantic courtroom. As Richard Sherwin has observed, in the contemporary age of "tabloid justice" and "media frenzy,"[92] the line between law and popular culture is rapidly eroding.[93] The search for justice has become a public spectacle, which has installed the "popular trial" as a "new genre of public discourse."[94] My concluding chapter will discuss two very different literary reactions to the contemporary spectacles of justice: William Gaddis' *A Frolic of His Own* (1994) and Alan Dershowitz's *The Advocate's Devil* (1994).

Pairing a lawyer and law professor (Dershowitz) with a high media profile, together with a postmodern author (Gaddis), whose novels are admired by critics for their intricacies and complexities but ignored by a larger audience (for the same reasons, one suspects), must at first sight appear rather odd. However, it allows an unfolding of the complex double structure of the contemporary law and literature relation in American culture that cannot be reduced simply to a matter of representation and aesthetics, but always involves questions of self-representation and professional identity. In this respect, as I will demonstrate, both books are transgressive since the lawyer becomes the writer, and the writer assumes the role of a lawyer. At the center of both works stands the problematic status of literary and legal evidence overwhelmed by the rhetorics of spectacle and performance, which not only includes the conflict of representation versus self-representation, but also the question of imitation, copying, and parody.

The conflicting forces in an increasingly adversarial legal culture are reflected in the American culture of litigation, in which, as both authors acknowledge, the most imminent danger to both law and literature stems from a universal penchant for dramatized evidence. In a culture where most people tend to confuse drama and visual effects with facts and evidence, the respective evidentiary functions of verbal rhetoric in law and literature are more and more threatened with irrelevance. This is a rather problematic situation for the status and the professional autonomy of legal and literary discourse and their engagement in the negotiation of cultural 'evidence.'

The persistent interest in the changing nature of the competition of cultural rhetorics of evidence also means that a historical perspective is indispensable for the interpretation of each of my 'case studies.' Another reason

---

92 Fox/van Sickel, *Tabloid Justice,* 2.
93 See Sherwin, *When Law Goes Pop,* 15–39 and 171–203.
94 Hariman, *Popular Trials,* 18.

why the critical reflection of law in literary fiction is always tied to specific historical circumstances is because literary mimesis unfolds its evidentiary force where historical and sociological details are recognized and represented in their specific contexts.

The following case studies therefore attempt to avoid the pitfalls of still current universalist interpretations of law and literature and their relation. As the preceding discussion of the law-and-literature movement has shown, a monolithic understanding of the terms would run counter to any detailed investigation of the case at hand. The critical function of literature in regard to the law implies a self-critical dimension, which unfolds through the specific correlation of the legal and the literary. The domains of legal and the literary are specific, cultural, and historical, and they are constantly changing. What the law is, what it possibly could or should be, literature can only present and project when it reflects the conditions of the legal and the literary that inform its own practice.

Chapter 3

Wieland's Testimony: Charles Brockden Brown and the Rhetoric of Evidence

The following chapter is concerned with the relation between law and literature in Charles Brockden Brown's novel *Wieland* (1798). Although the prominence of legal concepts and forensic procedures in Brown's fiction in general, and in his first novel in particular, has long been acknowledged, closer readings of the specific nature of the connection between the legal and the literary in Brown are still rare, even in face of the influence of the law-and-literature movement in American literary criticism. Using two of those readings of *Wieland,* by Christopher Looby and Laura Korobkin, respectively, as my starting points, I want to challenge their historical assumptions about the law and literature nexus in Brown's time. My focus will be particularly on the concept of evidence and its problematic relation to rhetoric.

To single out Looby's and Korobkin's discussion of Brown's novel is not meant to bypass or ignore the important work that has been done in the study of Brown's novels and essays by other scholars — including the elucidating discussions of legal aspects in Brown's work by Chad Luck, Marcia Nichols, and Frank Shuffleton, for instance.[1] The latter are brilliant illustrations of the increasing sophistication and historical sensitivity invested in the study of Brown's work in recent years. In regard to the question about the relation between legal and literary rhetoric and evidence, Luck's and Shuffleton's interpretations share the strong interest of the following discussion in the status and impact of literature as a public rhetoric in the early American Republic, while Nichols in similar ways is interested in Brown's concern for the rhetoric of the law. They also emphasize Brown's awareness of and interest in legal issues and concepts of his time. Whereas Luck convincingly demonstrates how Brown uses literary fiction as a tool for philosophically investigating questions and concepts of property and native American dispossession, Shuffleton's discussion contrasts Brown's engagement of his reader's judgments in questions of law and rights to the revisionary force of judicial review and its impact on the public debate of legal issues in the context of the famous *Marbury v. Madison* decision. In their respective interests

---

1 See Luck, "Re-Walking"; Shuffleton, "Juries of the Common Reader"; Nichols "Rhetorical Strategies."

and perspectives, Luck, Nichols, and Shuffleton must be read as significant contributions to our understanding of literary fiction as a public rhetoric of intervention and debate in Republican America. Without being able to refer to their arguments in detail, in the course of my own argument I will return to some of their central issues and concerns, e.g. Shuffleton's discussion of the acts of judgment that novel reading "simultaneously necessitates and problematizes," as well as Nichols' comments on the status of sensory evidence in relation to rhetoric within the legal system.[2]

For now, my main points of departure will be Korobkin's and Looby's interpretations of *Wieland*, since they are both explicitly concerned with the relation between evidentiary procedures and concepts on the one hand, and their linguistic regulation and standardization (and literary transgression), on the other. Thus, it is the particular interest they share in the relation between rhetoric and evidence which makes their discussions especially significant for the focus of this chapter.

During the 18th century the status of evidence both as a central epistemological and as a legal concept became increasingly complicated and ambiguous. Especially in the realm of public discourse, concepts such as evidence, fact, and truth were being instrumentalized as rhetorical claims. The ambiguity of evidence became the common focus of legal and literary debates on the probability and credibility — and consequently the authority — of conflicting narratives of events. Both the emergence of the novel as the dominant literary genre and as a mode of public discourse, as well as the parallel development of a system of rules of evidence in Anglo-American legal proceedings must be seen as resulting from the general debate over the ideological uses of rhetorics of evidence. Like those of his English predecessors and contemporaries, Brown's literary notions are deeply indebted to these discussions. Yet as I will show in the second part of my discussion, his attempts to establish a distinct national form of fiction — the American romance — were based on a unique revision of both legal and rhetorical concepts of evidence. This is most obvious in one of the central passages of *Wieland*, the courtroom testimony of Theodore Wieland. Brown's use of the trial scene combines the rhetoric of confession and witnessing in order to reflect on the rhetorical force of narrative literature, especially in contrast to the spectacular narratives of Gothic romances and magazine journalism. Wieland's madness and illusions are shown as the result of his misguided belief in original evidence and unmediated truth and his insufficient understanding of textual

---

2 Shuffleton, "Juries of the Common Reader," 91; Nichols, "Rhetorical Strategies," 471–73.

authority and authenticity. Neither a simple refutation of Enlightenment epistemology nor a relentless deconstruction of the ever-present rhetorical nature of truth, *Wieland* attempts to make a case for literary evidence as a necessary contradiction of ideological truth and a challenge to the universal foundation of moral judgment.

I

The relation between law and literature in the work of Charles Brockden Brown remains as elusive as it appears to be obvious. The general agreement among literary critics about the significance of the legal aspects of Brown's writings contrasts sharply with the lack of scholarly attention given to these aspects — a discrepancy noted as early as 1984 by Robert Ferguson in his influential study, *Law and Letters in American Culture.* Ferguson observed that "nowhere is the bond between vocation and literature more important, or more consistently ignored, than in the writings of America's first major novelist."[3] Ferguson's book certainly did a lot to increase the critical awareness of the significant dialogue between American legal and literary culture. Yet even the highly productive law-and-literature movement during the last decades has been surprisingly reluctant to deal with Brown's complex negotiations of the legal and literary. Thus in her essay on Brown's first novel *Wieland* (1798), Laura Korobkin could state that "detailed explorations of the novel's legal aspects have been virtually absent from critical discussions," even though *Wieland,* in Korobkin's words, is clearly "obsessed with law."[4] While there are obvious signs of an increasing scholarly interest Brown's obsession with matters of law — *vide* Luck, Nichols, and Shuffleton — the particular correlation of the legal and the literary in his novels and essays still deserves closer scrutiny. One reason to call for a deeper investigation of the way that Brown conceived of the relation between law and literature is the conspicuous ambivalence the author himself displayed at various times toward either component of the relationship.

Despite their similar assessments of the lack of critical attention, Ferguson and Korobkin approach the law and literature relationship in Brown's work (and more specifically in *Wieland*) from different perspectives. For Ferguson, this relationship is beset with "vocational anxieties,"[5] resulting from

---

3 Ferguson, *Law and Letters,* 129.
4 Korobkin, "Murder by Madman," 723.
5 Ferguson, *Law and Letters,* 134.

Brown's "uncertain place" as a novelist in early Republican culture where "fiction lacked respectability as a literary genre … while law represented a major topic of general interest within the realms of letters."[6] Law and literature represented "opposing worlds" for Brown, and the novelist's "need to trivialize the law," Ferguson explains, is both an attempt to cope with feelings of occupational inferiority and an expression of deliberate self-empowerment. As Ferguson writes, Brown "defensively insists on the law's inapplicability to real problems or its shallowness as a solution to those problems."[7] The negative image of the legal system in Brown's texts, especially its "inability … to control or even define human behavior,"[8] stands in stark contrast to the imaginary realm of fiction, which served Brown as "a fantasy world for projecting" and thereby negotiating "occupational difficulties."[9]

This perspective is criticized by Korobkin, who insists that Brown's obsession with the law in *Wieland* must be regarded as a conscious authorial strategy to enforce a specific reading of the novel's characters and events. As Korobkin points out, the novel is not only "saturated with the vocabulary of evidence, testimony, proof, inference, corroboration, and judgment."[10] Moreover, the text itself is structured like a trial, as it attempts to recover past events and resolve "conflicting narratives of such events by making factual determinations."[11] By turning his readers into jurors, Korobkin argues, Brown asks his audience to approach the narrative as if it presented the testimonies of various witnesses. The "reader-jurors" thus have to sift and weigh evidence, decide its contradictory or corroborative nature, and finally reach a verdict. Korobkin's interpretation of the novel therefore suggests that the relation between law and literature in *Wieland* is not simply antagonistic, as Ferguson maintains, but offers a more complex dialogue:

---

6 Ferguson, *Law and Letters,* 131.
7 Ferguson, *Law and Letters,* 138.
8 Ferguson, *Law and Letters,* 139.
9 Ferguson, *Law and Letters,* 129.
10 Korobkin, "Murder by Madman," 723. See Seed, "The Mind Set Free," 109. Even without reacting to the legal terminology, critics have always assumed the role of jurors, with very different verdicts concerning accountability and liability. For Shuffleton, in contrast to Korobkin, but also in difference to Davidson and Warner, the engagement of his reader's potential competence to discern and judge was central to Brown's strategies as a writer of fictions — his novels thus become 'democratic lessons' less based on their moral content but rather on reflected acts of reading and interpretation.
11 Korobkin, "Murder by Madman," 723.

> Though Brown used the novel to mock the law's ineffectiveness, he also carefully designed a plot that demonstrates how key principles of law and evidence can supply the conceptual links that restore accountability in a fragmented world. As in a courtroom, the law helps reader-jurors complete their job because it provides rules for determining responsibility.[12]

In her reading, Korobkin refers to various legal texts from the 18th century, especially to Sir William Blackstone's *Commentaries on the Laws of England* (1765–67) and Sir Geoffrey Gilbert's *Law of Evidence* (1754), to emphasize how the novel both addresses and complicates notions of legal evidence, legal insanity, and accountability, which were all prevalent during Brown's time. In Korobkin's view, the particular achievement of Brown's novel as a literary, rather than a legal, text is that *Wieland* translates "theoretical examples" from legal commentaries and treatises into "fully realized situations."[13] The translation of legal templates into the fictional analogy of a trial moreover aims at the criticism or subversion of certain categories of the law by literature. While Brown relied on Blackstone and Gilbert, Korobkin writes, the novelist also used "the resources of fiction to pull the rug out from under their complacent analyses."[14] In contrast to Ferguson, Korobkin thus describes the relation between law and literature in Brown's work in terms of a critical engagement, which is less determined by specific vocational tensions or cultural constraints than by a more general conflict between literary and legal notions of truth, evidence, and accountability.

The suggestion that Brown uses legal concepts to criticize basic epistemological presumptions of the law has also been emphasized by Christopher Looby. Like Ferguson, Looby stresses the central political and cultural power of the law in the early American Republic. Yet, beyond the particularities of Brown's vocational difficulties and subjective anxieties, Looby maintains that the author's engagement with legal discourse and ritual in *Wieland* also "reflects Brown's serious, incisive, and destructive analysis of the early republic's faith in legal order" and an attack on the "validity of the procedures of legal reasoning."[15] Similar to Korobkin, Looby calls attention to the significance of the court trial as a "scene" where "otherwise abstract questions of epistemology and individual psychology" are turned into the "very mundane questions of how facts are known, how words can be trusted, and how judgments can be reliably entered."[16] Looby, however, does not read *Wieland* simply as a

---

12 Korobkin, "Murder by Madman," 725.
13 Korobkin, "Murder by Madman," 724.
14 Korobkin, "Murder by Madman," 724–25.
15 Looby, *Voicing America,* 186.
16 Looby, *Voicing America,* 149.

literary analogy of a trial but, more fundamentally, as a "social and political allegory" whose critical force is directed against the "epistemological edifice" at the heart of the legal ideology of the early Republic.[17]

Korobkin and Looby both take Ferguson's observations as a starting point for their highly original readings of *Wieland* and arrive at distinct assessments of the law and literature relationship in Brown's work. In obvious ways, they both attempt to move beyond Ferguson in claiming that the antagonism that governs the relationship reflects not so much a tension between vocation and inclination as it presents a more fundamental conflict between legal and literary notions of evidence and truth. They both insist, moreover, that the presence of the law in *Wieland* serves a critical and strategic function. The law enters Brown's text not simply as a motif or as a target of criticism; its rhetoric and terminology are also employed by Brown to give structure and form to his novel in order to entice a specific response or create a particular effect. As Korobkin shows, the conflict between various narratives at the center of *Wieland* follows the adversarial logic of a legal trial: a structural device meant to "implicate" Brown's readers in the "project of assessing evidence and reaching a verdict."[18] In a similar vein, Looby observes that Brown's "conspicuous" use of legal terminology must be regarded as "a calculated effect" which establishes a "subliminal sense that the action of the novel is permeated by a legalistic aura."[19] Even though they do not argue the point explicitly, both Looby and Korobkin thus suggest that it is the entanglement of the legal with the literary which finally makes *Wieland* into a "deeply political text"[20] with a "message … for the newly formed Republic" that "Americans should assess policies by their actual impact in the world … rather than by a politician's character, ideas, or articulated intentions."[21]

These legal interpretations of Brown's novel add a new dimension to Ferguson's perspective in pointing out the intrinsic and reflective character of the law and literature relationship in *Wieland*. Rather than refuting Korobkin's and Looby's readings in the following discussion, I would like to challenge some of their underlying assumptions concerning the historical background in legal philosophy and the practices of the law which informed Brown's literary works and ideas. Moreover, I want to use this investigation

---

17 Looby, *Voicing America,* 192.
18 Korobkin, "Murder by Madman," 724.
19 Looby, *Voicing America,* 186.
20 Looby, *Voicing America,* 193.
21 Korobkin, "Murder by Madman," 725.

to reframe the law and literature relationship in Brown's work with regard to the problematic status of literary fictions in the public discourse of the early Republic. Brown was obviously torn between his vision of literary achievement and the threat of cultural inferiority associated with narrative fiction, since his remarks concerning the literature of his day range from enthusiastic approval at the outset of his writing efforts to taunting criticism and ridicule in his later years after he had dropped literature altogether.[22] As many critics have noted, Brown's intense struggle to formulate convincing criteria for the political and moral function of literary fictions in a Republican culture represents an important contribution to the formation and configuration of literary authorship and culture in the United States.[23] As I will argue in more detail later, Brown's literary notions owe much to certain legal concepts of his time. The transfer from the legal to the literary must be seen as a conscious transformation: the law becomes for Brown an indispensable element in a new, yet-to-be-realized American literature.

While Looby and Korobkin make a strong case for Brown's strategic use of the law in *Wieland*, they do not consider or remark upon how this choice relates to the status of the novel as a form of public discourse. While the use of legal terminology certainly represented an almost inevitable option for Brown, given his personal training and the general cultural climate emphasized by Ferguson, I argue that the particular function of legal rhetoric in *Wieland* was motivated and encouraged by Brown's notions about literature in general, but especially about narrative fiction. If we look at the deep distrust with which these forms were regarded during the early Republic, the decision to use a work of fiction to negotiate, or even debate and criticize fundamental notions of the law and its political power, does not appear obvious at all. Indeed, if Brown's determination to "write a gothic romance in the land of Enlightenment was already a reactionary move,"[24] as Looby states, this move in itself asks for closer inspection.[25] Brown's activities as a

---

22 For Brown's literary criticism, see Clark, *Brown;* Cahill, "Lawless Fancy." See also the collection of Brown's essays edited by Weber, *Literary Essays and Reviews.*

23 The sentiment is already well captured in Clark's seminal work on Brown as the "pioneer voice" in American literature. However, the critical acknowledgment was somewhat ambivalent about the relation. See, for instance, Clark, *Brown*; Hesford, "'Do You Know the Author?'"; Bell, "'The Double-Tongued Deceiver'"; Fliegelman, "Introduction"; and Jordan, "On Rereading *Wieland*."

24 Looby, *Voicing America,* 194.

25 Brown is of course not the only 'reactionary' in this sense. For the relation of Brown's gothic tales to other literary productions of his time, see Davidson, *Revolution and the Word,* esp. 238–54 and Kafer, *Birth of American Gothic.*

fiction writer and as a publisher of magazines were clearly driven by the attempt to increase the recognition and the reception of imaginative literature among his contemporaries.[26] During a time when the novel had not yet reached the status of a cultural institution and fictions were seen by most people as detrimental to sound education and rational thinking, Brown became an early advocate for a national American literature. Although his literary ideas were very much influenced by English authors and styles, he nevertheless supported the development of indigenous genres of narrative fiction, most obviously in the famous note "To the Public" in *Edgar Huntly*, where Brown stated "that the field of investigation, opened by our own country, should differ essentially from those which exist in Europe, may be readily conceived."[27] Both Brown's first attempt at a novel, the later abandoned "Sky Walk," and *Wieland* were announced in their subtitles as "American tales," clearly pointing to their author's aspirations for a distinctive national form of fiction.[28]

The following discussion, therefore, addresses the law and literature relationship in Brown's work, and especially in *Wieland*, from the perspective of literature and the historical development of narrative fiction in the cultural context of the early Republic. This is meant as a necessary complement to the readings of Korobkin and Looby. Like them, I want to stress the significance of notions, such as evidence, testimony, and witnessing, for Brown's intense engagement with the law in *Wieland*, yet since my perspective is different, I will also explicitly acknowledge and address the literary employment and reconceptualization of these notions.

The close association of legal and literary debates around evidence and testimony in the eighteenth and nineteenth centuries has been most recently emphasized by Alexander Welsh and Jan-Melissa Schramm, respectively. In his investigation on narrative and circumstantial evidence in English law and literature, Welsh states that after the Enlightenment, new narrative strategies for the presentation of facts emerged. What characterized these strategies was their rhetorical effort (and their success) to present the truth by weaving an unbroken chain of circumstantial evidence into one coherent narrative. Both in the courtroom and in the novel, facts could not simply stand on their own; they had to be arranged and presented in a convincing way to their

---

26 See Clark, *Charles Brockden Brown,* 126–54; for Brown's role as editor during the emergence of American magazine publication, see Cody, *Cultural Journalism*; Chielens, "Periodicals."

27 Brown, *Edgar Huntly,* 3.

28 The ambivalence that haunted Brown's hopes in this respect also informed his literary criticism. See Cahill, "Lawless Fancy."

respective audiences. Both lawyers and novelists thus came to favor what Welsh calls "strong representations," i.e. "carefully managed [narratives] of circumstantial evidence."[29] Characteristically, Welsh explains, "strong representations … openly distrust direct testimony, insist on submitting witnesses to the test of corroborating circumstances, and claim to know many things without anyone's having seen them at all."[30] For Welsh, the two most distinct features of strong representations, the emphasis on inferential reasoning from circumstantial evidence by way of narrative synthesis and the rejection of direct testimony in favor of discrete auctorial control over a narrative of facts, present the "evidentiary basis of … realism"[31] in English literature since the eighteenth century.

The central status of inferential reasoning and narrative conclusiveness has been stressed as well by Schramm in her book on testimony and advocacy in Victorian law, literature, and theology. In contrast to Welsh, however, Schramm points to the much more complex relation between factual narratives and testimonial positions in both law and literature. Calling attention to the fact that all evidence must be presented to the court by way of testimony,[32] Schramm concludes that the simple binary opposition of testimony versus circumstantial evidence has to be revised. Instead, she writes, "it is perhaps more accurate to argue that testimony was co-opted to serve in the proof of facts which were increasingly seen as multi-faceted and open to professional manipulation."[33] In other words, the strength of narrative representations of evidence in law and literature also depended on the way in which such narratives could account and compensate for the vicissitudes of testimonial presentation. Consequently, lawyers and novelists alike were forced to reflect on, as Schramm puts it, "the ways in which testimonial declarations are appropriated to serve in the proof of facts."[34]

While both Welsh's and Schramm's observations are of considerable importance for the following discussion, their results cannot be transferred to the American situation without qualifications. Schramm's claim that in the late eighteenth and early nineteenth centuries "law and prose narrative … saw themselves as competing for the right to provide an authoritative account of the 'facts' of an event" might also be true for Brown's attitude towards the law. However, the author of *Wieland* may have found different

29 Welsh, *Strong Representations*, 17.
30 Welsh, *Strong Representations,* 8.
31 Welsh, *Strong Representations,* 49.
32 Schramm, *Testimony*, 19.
33 Schramm, *Testimony*, 21.
34 Schramm, *Testimony*, 22.

answers to the question of what fiction could bring "to the task that the law could not,"[35] if only for the fact that both law and literature in the early American Republic were trying to redefine their respective function according to the political realities in which they found themselves.

The undeniable presence of the law in all of Brown's work must be seen to reflect more than their author's troubled position between the law as an unwanted profession and literature as the vocation of choice. As Brown's numerous remarks on the function of literature in the context of a democratic society make evident, the lawyer-turned-novelist was deeply concerned with what I would like to term the 'evidentiary value' of fiction: the way in which imaginative literature could be acknowledged as a reliable and even necessary form of 'testimony.' Indeed, it is the concept of testimony that is central both to the novel and to the legal and literary discussions that surrounded it. Brown's keen interest in advanced rhetorical theories of his day, which were of great import for both legal epistemology and the emerging theory of the novel, greatly influenced his ideas about the power of literary fiction in the public life of a democracy. These ideas include the questions of the persuasive power and the credibility of fictions and the responsibility and competence demanded of both authors and readers in order to account for the effect of fictional events on individual conviction and collective beliefs.

My main thesis thus is that Brown's "American tale," as *Wieland* is conspicuously subtitled, struggles with the translation of legal and philosophical concepts of evidence and probability into an effective, but also highly problematic, rhetoric of literary evidence and testimony.

At first I want to look at two major strands of criticism of the novel, which are in agreement that the central concern of the text is the truth or untruth of alleged facts. On the one hand, there are readings of *Wieland* as a critique of Enlightenment principles and empiricist notions of factual knowledge. These readings invariably stress the uncertainty and unreliability of sense perception as the major source of error and illusion. On the other hand, there are important interpretations which focus on the linguistic skepticism expressed in *Wieland*, arguing that facts in the novel are constructed and manipulated deliberately in the narratives of the different characters to serve their conflicting interests.[36] Both sides agree that the major conflict in *Wie-*

---

35 Schramm, *Testimony*, 13.

36 Following the history of the novel's criticism, one may notice an observable shift of focus from problems of perception and experience to problems of language, such as reference, performance, or ambiguity. See also Russo; Voloshin, "Wieland"; Hesford, "'Do You Know the Author?'"; and Kreyling, "Construing Brown's *Wieland*." For an interesting combination, see O'Shaughnessy, "'An Im-

land is the struggle between evidence and rhetoric — with the latter winning out. Despite their differences, these approaches suggest that the novel rigorously deconstructs any notion of epistemological certainty beyond mere subjective belief. From this perspective, *Wieland* appears as a radical anti-empiricist novel, whose major target is the philosophy of John Locke. The assumption, however, that the skepticism of *Wieland* lacks a distinct notion of evidence simply because it so obviously attacks a Lockean concept of sensual evidence fails to take into account the actual debate about the concept in legal and rhetorical theories during Brown's time.

Unfortunately, this is also where most of the 'legal' readings of Brown's novel like those by Looby and Korobkin miss some important points. Thus it will be necessary to reconstruct the particular concept of evidence which not only informs Brown's novel but also his theoretical notions about literary narratives as fictions in general. These notions are clearly indebted to new theories of rhetoric which were developed during the 18th century and which also served as a common ground for literary and legal definitions of evidence. A closer look at one of the first American contributions to the philosophy of evidence in the law will point out the close affinities between law and literature concerning the central role of testimonial evidence and the concept of moral certainty, or probability.

The concluding part of my discussion will turn once more to the novel itself. The significance of the rhetoric of testimony, of evidence, and of witnessing is highlighted throughout *Wieland*, but especially in the courtroom testimony of Theodore Wieland. From the law and literature perspective, the trial scene presents a particular challenge. It introduces within the novel a difference between two distinct realizations or manifestations of the law. If the text as a whole assumes the form of a trial, the fictional representation of a 'legal moment' at the center of its narrative must be seen as a doubling of its own logic. This doubling is emphasized by the fact that what is presented in the courtroom is indeed a fiction: the gothic romance of supernatural powers and mysterious phenomena, which lead to a horrible murder, all told by the assassin himself. Paradoxically, then, Wieland's testimony marks an effective and conscious staging of literary performance in the novel, using a form that belongs to the law's repertoire of rituals to ascertain guilt, but also

---

perfect Tale,'" who uses Locke's theory of language to analyze Brown's linguistic skepticism. The contrast between epistemological and linguistic skepticism also informs the third wave of Brown studies over the last two decades, even though its efforts at contextualization are oriented much more towards the political and social than to the philosophical or cultural. See Barnard/Kamrath/Shapiro, *Revising Charles Brockden Brown.*

to reveal the truth. The performance of the law in literature thus turns into an intense moment of literary self-reflection, a demonstration of the power of rhetorical evidence, but also the culmination of the self-destructive force of a rhetoric that confuses its effects with pure evidence.

II

If the struggle for independence was not only a "war of words fought between Britain and the Colonies" but, moreover, a "war about words,"[37] the excessive force of political rhetoric culminated in the 1790s during the bitter debates over the future of the American Republic. Especially in response to the French Revolution, American political rhetoric turned from the ideal of rational and enlightened argument, aimed at the conviction of assemblies, to an emotionally charged exchange of vile vituperation obviously meant to discredit one's political opponents in the eye of the public. The age of reason thus turned into an "age of passion,"[38] as Marshall Smelser aptly described the heated atmosphere of the controversies between Federalists and Republicans: "the political activity of the Federalist period was strongly influenced by passions of hate, anger, and fear … a good deal of the writing was much less concerned with informing the intellect than it was with whipping up [the] passions."

In the 1790s, then, both the ideals of the American Revolution, put forward in the Declaration of Independence, and their legal foundation and framing in the American Constitution were shattered and almost destroyed by the reality of political abuse of eloquence and the "harshness of partisanship."[39] The dream of a Republic based on the freedom of speech had turned into a nightmare.[40] What many Americans realized was that certain truths, especially those which had been declared as 'self-evident' during the Ameri-

---

37 Gustafson, *Representative Words*, 207.

38 Smelser, "The Federalist Period," 391–419.

39 Smelser, "The Federalist Period," 396.

40 See also Warner, *Letters*; Fliegelman, *Culture of Performance*; Gustafson, *Representative Words;* and Looby, *Voicing America*, for the debates about public rhetoric from the revolution to the framing of the constitution, which were perpetuated and radicalized in the political struggles during the late 1790s. For the shifting concepts of public speech in the early Republic, see Potkay, "Theorizing Civic Eloquence." For later developments, see Warren, *Culture of Eloquence*. Wilf has argued that the increase of public debate also reverberated with the legal profession ("The First Republican Revival").

can Revolution, were more elusive than evident. Truth no longer served as a unifying principle with universal viability; instead it turned into an instrument of particularism and partisanship, especially in the "war of words" fought in the magazines and newspapers of the day. Truth — and its antithesis, falsehood — thus gradually transformed into ideological categories and rhetorical claims in the highly adversarial process of winning public opinion in the favor of the respective faction or party. Commenting on the development of the novel as a public discourse in Britain, Lennard Davis remarked how an intensified political debate changed conventional assumptions about the truth or authenticity of printed texts and records. Especially in regard to printed news, the word "false" began to

> be used to signify ideological position. False news is the news printed by the opposition party. In this sense, news may be factually true, yet for political purposes the opposition must see it as false. … Now truth would lie much closer to the surface; true-speaking had much more to do with language and politics …[41]

During the last decades of the 18th century the American Republic was dominated by similar political fractures and public debates, and even though the arguments were fought mainly in newspapers and magazine articles, these debates doubtlessly reverberated in the discussions about the 'truth' of literary fictions.

In light of the disturbances in the social and political atmosphere of the Republic, it seems only natural that Brown's first novel, *Wieland*, published in 1798, has been read mainly as a literary reaction to and commentary on the Federalist age of passion and its adversarial rhetoric. Since the events are placed in the years between the "conclusion of the French and the beginning of the revolutionary war," as Brown announces in his "Advertisment"[42] to the novel, the story apparently achieves its relation to the historical reality of the time of its publication by means of allegory rather than by direct allusion or reference. Despite the historical distance of the fictitious events, however, critics have interpreted the novel as a rather explicit description of the fears and passions which moved Brown and his contemporaries and as an open critique of both excessive libertarianism and religious fanaticism.[43] Beyond these immediate references, *Wieland* has been interpreted as a rejection of the belief in "the Enlightenment's supreme fiction of an autonomous rational individual making free and thus accountable choices and its attendant cel-

---

41 Davis, *Factual Fictions*, 79, 82–83.

42 Brown, *Wieland*, 3. (In the following *W* with page number).

43 Cf. Samuels, "Wieland: Alien and Infidel"; and Kindermann, *Man Unknown to Himself*.

ebration of voluntarism over coercion, liberty as self-sufficiency, and Newtonian narratives of simple cause and effect."[44]

What is undisputed then is Brown's denial of authorial explanation and closure. In a final letter, "written three years after the foregoing" (*W,* 234), as Brown adds in an editorial note, Clara Wieland, the central narrative voice, is still unable to give a satisfying explanation of the disturbing events she has been witness to. Thus she leaves her readers with the even more disturbing conclusion that even the victims of delusions must be held responsible for the catastrophic events:

> I leave you to moralize on this tale. That virtue should become the victim of treachery is, no doubt, a mournful consideration; but it will not escape your notice, that the evils of which Carwin … [was] the author, owed their existence to the errors of the sufferers. … If Wieland had framed juster notions of moral duty, and of divine attributes, or if I had been gifted with ordinary equanimity or foresight, the double-tongued deceiver would have been baffled and repelled. (*W,* 244)

There is then neither consolation nor relief at the end of Brown's American tale. It ultimately suggests that the experiment of a democratic and liberal society must utterly fail in the United States since the "moral constitution of men" (*W,* 4) is too weak a defense against one's own delusions and the treachery of others. Declaring the individual unfit for building a society on the principles of reason and severely questioning the Enlightenment's empirical trust in the reliability of factual perception and its hope for the rational control of the passions and the imagination, *Wieland* apparently presents a devastating critique, if not a demolition, of the very ideals that informed the foundation of the American Republic.

But what precisely are the reasons for this failure? Is it a matter of cunning deception or fatal disposition? What does Brown mean when he leaves his readers to 'moralize' on his narrative? In order to solve these questions, critical interpretations of *Wieland* have mostly focused on two major issues which could be classified, roughly, as the epistemological problem, on the one hand, and the linguistic problem, on the other. To use a terminology closer to the law, the epistemological problem in the novel may be said to concern the quality of witnessing as an act of perception and observation, while the linguistic problem centers on the reliability of verbal — both written and oral — testimony. While the former addresses the question of direct sensual evidence, the latter is more interested in the rhetorical aspects of witnessing.

---

44 Fliegelman, "Introduction," xv.

Readings that focus on direct evidence stress the novel's highly critical view of the naive trust in the senses, as in Winfried Fluck's statement that *Wieland* "is a novel about the terrifying instability of sense perception. Its catastrophic events are inaugurated by phantasmatic perceptions whose sources are unknown, and which therefore seem questionable and unreliable."[45] Because the characters are unable to discern between real and projected phenomena — especially those affected by the central villain, the ventriloquist Carwin — , their accounts constantly contradict each other until any sense of what was (or is) objectively real and what is (or was) subjectively projected gets lost. In other words, their testimony as witnesses is compromised by their faulty sense perception.

The important point is that the disturbance on the epistemological register serves to highlight the potential status of the various testimonies offered by the protagonists to each other and to the readers as merely rhetorical statements, invented stories or simply lies. Cynthia S. Jordan has stressed how the characters in *Wieland* become story-tellers and authors of fictions in their own right. But if, as she concludes, in Brown's world "*all* mental processes are shown to be fiction-making,"[46] there is no way to tell the record of the competent and honest witness from that of the disturbed or deliberately falsifying one. The novel thus becomes an arena of contesting fictions, all based on and legitimized by a similar rhetoric of witnessing and evidence. This contest is made obvious by numerous pleas and claims such as this one: "Listen … to my narrative. If there be anything in his story inconsistent with mine, his story is false" (*W,* 109). Moreover, even Wieland, while confessing to his horrible deeds, insists on his status as a true witness to the real existence of the divinity. And finally, since the entire text is presented by the principal protagonist and narrator, Clara Wieland, as her "testimony" (*W,* 5), the latent unreliability of all witnesses reaches beyond the action of the novel to include its author, and possibly its readers, as they are witnesses as well — a point that I will return to at the end.

More recent interpretations of *Wieland* have even more radically denied that there is any direct evidence, free from any linguistic intervention, which the protagonists (let alone the readers) can access. The narrative of the novel, Christopher Looby states, is "produced by nothing but speech acts, a sequence of utterances," which means rhetoric does more than to precede ac-

---

45 Fluck, *Das kulturelle Imaginäre*, 73, my translation. See also Hagenbüchle, "American Literature"; Voloshin, "Wieland"; and Limon, *The Place of Fiction.*

46 Jordan, "On Rereading Wieland," 170.

tions and events. It is the condition *sine qua non* of what can be perceived *as* evidence. In *Wieland*, it is indeed the "saying [that] makes it so,"[47] as Mark Seltzer explains:

> On every level of the narrative, one finds a confusion, a transformation, of ways of saying into modes of being. Words and acts appear as equivalents … [l]anguage displaces events … in this novel saying becomes a form (the only form) of doing.[48]

According to such interpretations, any direct evidence in *Wieland* must be regarded as an illusion brought forth by rhetorical manipulation. Even Clara turns out to be a rather incompetent witness, as she readily concedes at one point: "[m]y narrative may be invaded by inaccuracy and confusion. … What but ambiguities … can be expected from the historian who is, at the same time, the sufferer of these disasters?" (*W,* 147) The readers of Clara's letters are thus faced with an unreliable narrator, whose claims for the truth and accuracy of her account are severely complicated by the fact that she had been an active party in the events she relates. Of course, from there it is only a small step to announcing that Brown himself, like Carwin, is an "authorial ventriloquist"[49] who cannot be trusted, and the intent of the novel is to point out not only the ambiguity of narrative fiction, but also the principal instability of linguistic constructions of the real, of evidence, and of truth, in general. No wonder that readers of *Wieland* are left with a sense of "epistemological despair," as Roland Hagenbüchle noted, since the "lack of a stabilizing frame or context" renders all "texts … utterly ambivalent" and tends to "undermine stability on all levels."[50]

III

In the face of the fundamental uncertainty and unreliability concerning evidence based on human perception and testimony, there is something daunting about Laura Korobkin's challenge to the reader to approach the novel as an attentive jury member "at whose 'bar' evidence is presented for judgment."[51] For Korobkin the task only appears futile because, as she optimistically asserts, even though the evidence is "confusing" it "is nevertheless

---

47 Looby, *Voicing America,* 81.
48 Seltzer, "Saying Makes It So," 84–85.
49 Looby, *Voicing America,* 171.
50 Hagenbüchle, "American Literature," 131.
51 Korobkin, "Murder by Madman," 723.

possible to sort most of it out."[52] Korobkin's efforts in sorting out the evidence are impressive, but what remains confusing is precisely the concept of evidence Korobkin employs. On the one hand, Korobkin concurs with readings of the novel as a severe criticism of empiricist and sensualist models of knowledge. She agrees, for instance, that Brown wanted "to demonstrate weaknesses in the philosophical theories of Locke and others who argued that all knowledge derives from the senses."[53] On the other hand, Korobkin reduces the complexity of 18th-century notions of evidence and the debates surrounding them to subsume different categories of legal proof under a single form of what she calls "direct sensory evidence." Korobkin's insertion of the adjective 'sensory' is obviously meant to emphasize the aspect of immediate perception, which is indeed a central feature of the law's understanding of 'direct' evidence in contrast to 'indirect' or 'circumstantial' evidence.[54] Yet the presumption that courtrooms in Brown's time "evinced a strong preference for direct sensory evidence"[55] is misleading because it suggests a hierarchy of proofs that was not yet established. What is more, even the specific eighteenth-century legal model, which Korobkin refers to, does not rank 'sensory evidence' at the top of the hierarchy of evidence it proposes.

Brown's skepticism in regard to factual knowledge based on sense perception, Korobkin claims, may be extended to include legal theories as well: "[b]y showing how easily the senses can be misled, Brown also challenges related legal principles that privilege sensory evidence."[56] But the conclusion is hardly convincing. Nothing that happens to the characters in the novel would make them ineligible as witnesses as far as their senses are concerned. With the exception of Theodore, whose state of mind might be problematic, no one would be incompetent as a witness to testify what they heard and saw. What is 'misled' is their judgment, not their senses.

As the main target of the legal principles that Brown presumably attacks, Korobkin identifies the concept of legal evidence laid down by Sir Geoffrey Gilbert in his influential treatise *The Law of Evidence.* Written before Gilbert's

---

52 Korobkin, "Murder by Madman," 744.

53 Korobkin, "Murder by Madman," 735.

54 According to textbook definitions of legal evidence, the term 'direct' evidence can refer to a type of evidence or to the use of evidence. In the first instance it points to the manner of perception as the relation of the witness to the fact in question. 'Direct' evidence also designates testimonial evidence of the type above in its use and relevance in distinction to circumstantial evidence, which can either be testimonial or physical. See Reutlinger, *Evidence,* 5.

55 Korobkin, "Murder by Madman," 735.

56 Korobkin, "Murder by Madman," 735.

death in 1726 but first published only in 1754, the treatise was widely read by Anglo-American lawyers and law students well into the 19th century and highly praised as the first systematic and accessible essay on the subject.[57] There is certainly much evidence to support the assumption that Brown, like most of his teachers and fellow students, knew Gilbert's work well and most likely learned to apply the elaborate system of rules that Gilbert had devised. The Lord Chief Baron's system of the basic categories of evidence and the rules which should be applied to evidence in legal trials is clearly based on Locke's principles, as Barbara Shapiro and others have convincingly demonstrated. Locke's influence is acknowledged explicitly in a short introduction, where Gilbert defines the various degrees of evidence. Knowledge about facts, Gilbert states, may differ in degree of certainty, which ranges from "perfect Certainty and Demonstration, quite down to Improbability and Unlikeness, even to the Confines of Impossibility."[58] These "degrees of evidence" correspond to another hierarchy of mental states, which Gilbert calls, after Locke, "degrees of Assent" ranging from "full Assurance and Confidence, quite down to Gonjecture, Doubt, Distrust, and Disbelief."[59] The highest form of assent possible and therefore the ideal mode of epistemological confidence is again defined by Gilbert in Lockean terms:

> All Certainty is a clear and distinct Perception, and all clear and distinct Perception depend on a man's proper Senses, for this in the first Place is certain, and that which we cannot doubt if we would, that one Perception is not another … and when Perceptions are thus distinguish'd on the first view, it is called Self-Evidence or Intuitive Knowledge.[60]

This definition seems to support Korobkin's claim about the "preference for direct sensory evidence." It is important, however, not to confuse the system of legal evidence developed by Gilbert with the evidentiary preferences of his epistemological framework. First of all, Gilbert rules out perfect certainty when it comes to legal trials. In a courtroom, there is no certainty based on "clear and distinct perception" and "intuitive knowledge," because these perceptions and the knowledge they would yield must first be "re-

---

57 See the similar assessments in Twining, *Theories of Evidence*; Shapiro, *Probability*; Landsman, "From Gilbert to Bentham;" Langbein, "Historical Foundations."

58 Gilbert, *The Law of Evidence.* 1. Here and in the subsequent quotes, Gilbert is paraphrasing (sometimes quoting verbatim from) Locke, *An Essay Concerning Human Understanding*, Book 4, Ch. 15: 2.

59 Gilbert, *The Law of Evidence,* 1–2.

60 Gilbert, *The Law of Evidence,* 2. Gilbert's argument already contains a legal interpretation of Locke's empiricist model, see 2, 30–31.

trieved by Memory and Recollection"[61] during the witnesses' testimony. Gilbert then distinguishes between the highest form of knowledge based on demonstration and a lower grade of knowledge, which can be obtained by the presentation of evidence in a trial. Thus there are two realms of certainty: on the one hand, knowledge based on demonstration and sense perception, on the other hand, knowledge based on testimony and rational inference. The latter pair, which today is usually called 'direct' versus 'circumstantial' evidence, is subsumed by Gilbert under one single category. After his definition of the degrees of evidence and their corresponding "Acts of the Mind," Gilbert declares that "what must be done in all Trials of Rights, is to range all Matters in the Scale of Probability."[62] Gilbert's conclusion, that the "the rights of Men must be determined by probability"[63] shows that for him the highest grade of assent and therefore the ultimate degree of certainty in a legal trial clearly remained within the realm of mere probability. The certainty of knowledge about facts which was to be achieved by evidence in a trial therefore could never reach beyond the probable. For this degree of probability there was already an established category in the legal proceedings of the time, which usually aimed at "moral certainty" as the basis for a verdict.

As Shapiro has pointed out, the category of moral certainty can be found in scientific, historical, and religious as well as legal treatises from the 17th century onwards.[64] There is reason to believe that the association of probability and moral certainty was made possible before Gilbert's treatise by reference to existing legal rules and practices, especially those concerned with the evaluation of witnesses and their testimony in criminal trials. Scientists and historians thus found courtroom investigations a useful model for their own inquiries and often referred to legal proceedings in their writings. Robert Boyle, the eminent 17th-century chemist, for instance, explicitly pointed to "the practice of our courts"[65] when discussing the reliability of scientific reports. Faced with similar problems, historians, scientists and lawyers in the 17th century felt the common need for a theoretical foundation and terminology that would allow for a more systematic approach and evaluation of

---

61 Gilbert, *The Law of Evidence,* 3.

62 Gilbert, *The Law of Evidence,* 2.

63 Gilbert, *The Law of Evidence,* 3.

64 The emergence of a modern concept of probability in the sciences, theology, philosophy, and literature has been treated in a number of important texts; besides Shapiro, *Probability,* and Patey, *Probability,* see also Hacking, *The Emergence of Probability,* and Daston, *Classical Probability.*

65 Qtd. in Shapiro, *Probability,* 179.

credibility and probability. One of the first attempts even before Locke to apply a theory of certainty to legal thinking appeared in Sir Matthew Hale's *The Primitive Origination of Mankind* (1677), which suggested a new categorization of proven knowledge. Concerning matters of fact which were precluded from direct observation and experience, for instance, events which happened "before our time, and out of the immediate reach of our Sense," Hale insisted that in these cases "only 'moral and not demonstrative' evidence was available."[66] By the mid-18th century, the mutual identification of moral judgment, belief, and probability was generally accepted. Thus Bishop Butler, in his influential *The Analogy of Religion* (1736), could state that probability should be the "very guide of life."[67]

The interesting twist in Gilbert's revision of these well-established notions appears in his treatment of moral, or probable evidence as if it were a demonstration of a second order. Gilbert's definition of legal evidence first follows Hale in stating that in order to make judgments of things which we did not experience ourselves, "we must see and hear by the Reports from others; which is one Step farther from Demonstration … founded upon the View of our own senses." However, even though there can be no immediate demonstration of the facts, their representation by the reports of others can achieve the same *effect* as demonstrative evidence, due to the "Faith and Credit to be given to the Honesty and Integrity of credible and disinterested Witnesses." Evidence in this sense completely relies on the trust in others, which can be so strong, Gilbert writes,

> that the Mind equally acquiesces therein *as on Knowledge by Demonstration*, for it cannot have more Reason to be doubted than we ourselves had heard and seen it; and this is the original of all Trials and all Manner of Evidence.

The crucial term in this definition is 'demonstration,' an expression Gilbert (following Locke) had initially used for the highest form of certainty, based on clear and distinct perceptions. Since facts in a trial cannot be presented directly to perception, they have to be demonstrated — in modern critical usage: represented — by using the strongest evidence for the fact in question: "the Design of Law is to come to rigid Demonstration in matters of Right, and there can be no Demonstration of a Fact without the best evi-

---

66 Shapiro, *Probability,* 180.

67 Qtd. in Rescher/Joynt, "Evidence," 563. As early as 1705, the British novelist Mary de la Rivière Manley wrote that the author of fictions should aim at "the probability of truth, which consists in saying nothing but what is morally to be believed" (Qtd. in Davis, *Factual Fictions,* 111).

dence that the Nature of the Thing is capable of."[68] Gilbert's notion about the origin of legal evidence — the inevitable necessity to base one's judgment in what others have seen and heard — would suggest that the account of credible eye-witnesses must be ranked as the most valuable, and therefore best, evidence. However, in Gilbert's understanding of the Lockean "scale of probability," not oral, but written evidence "has the first Place in the Discourses of Probability."[69] The reason is explained in a curious reference to Cicero — a reference that will surely ring a bell with attentive readers of *Wieland* — when Gilbert rejects the rhetorician's argument in favor of unwritten evidence and "the Freedom of the Poet," arguing that in cases where oral reports and written documents oppose each other, the "Balance of Probability" should always be on the side of written evidence,

> for the Testimony of an honest Man, however fortified with the Solemnities of an Oath, is yet liable to the Imperfections of Memory, and as the Remembrance of Things fail and go off, Men are apt to entertain Opinions in their stead, and therefore the Argument turns the other Way …

In contrast to the flawed recollection of witnesses, written documents "are more advantageously secured from all Corruption," precisely "by the Forms and Solemnities of the Law." Gilbert's assertion that "Contracts reduced to Writing are the most sedate and deliberate Acts of the Mind"[70] shows the strong civil law orientation of his treatise, but it also generalizes his legal textualism by connecting it to his epistemological and psychological framework. The reason that texts are better evidence than oral reports is not simply because documents per se are more credible than people, since Gilbert was certainly aware of the fact that documents could be forged or tampered with. The more immediate motivation is, rather, that a document made for better demonstration since it offered a material object which could be scrutinized and inspected in court — as a 'fact' in itself, it allowed for clear and distinct perception of the fact for which it stood. Thus written documents presented textual objects — objectified acts of the past — in which epistemological and legal demonstration could converge to produce a persuasive psychological effect: the acquiescence of the mind by the satisfaction of belief. Moreover, this effect relied on the 'forms and solemnities' of the law which precisely prescribed the function and the value of the written text in a legal demonstration. Before cross-examination assumed its crucial status in the trial process, the testimony of witnesses in court was also deemed less re-

---

68 Gilbert, *The Law of Evidence,* 4 (my emphases).
69 Gilbert, *The Law of Evidence,* 5, 6.
70 Gilbert, *The Law of Evidence,* 6.

liable because it was less manageable by the law. Since there was no way to control what a witness would say and how it would be said, oral testimony assumed a dangerous ambivalence as an effective demonstration (of a text) in its own right.[71] While a written document offered a 'fixed' and therefore stable text, oral reports, given in 'real time,' as it were, appeared to be texts 'in the making,' which had yet to be molded into a form that would have made them acceptable as legal evidence. Gilbert's association of oral testimony with poetic license betrays an obvious uneasiness with the rhetorical and creative potential of orality, and his objections are informed by the well-established convention that unchecked rhetoric will inevitably favor opinion over truth in language. This sentiment goes back to Locke's famous diatribe against rhetoric in his *Essay*, where he calls rhetoric a "powerful instrument of Error and Deceit." Locke's solution for the antagonism of truth and rhetoric was the abandonment of all rhetorical devices from rational discourse:

> if we would speak of things as they are, we must allow, that all the Art of Rhetorick ... are for nothing else but to insinuate wrong Ideas, move the passions, and thereby mislead the Judgement; and so indeed are perfect cheat. And therefore ... they are certainly, in all Discourses that pretend to inform or instruct, wholly to be avoided, and where Truth and Knowledge are concerned, cannot be thought a great fault, either of the Language or the Person that makes use of them.[72]

Locke's legacy in Gilbert's system of legal evidence is twofold. On the one hand, Locke's degrees of probability are adapted to the trial situation, where no direct demonstration of the facts is possible and where all knowledge must rest on the testimony of others, i.e. on probabilities. On the other hand, the law of evidence that Gilbert codifies tries to give probable evidence the certainty of demonstrative evidence by turning it into a factual element within another demonstration: the courtroom trial. Gilbert does favor direct sensory evidence, however, the evidence he champions does not refer to the report of eye-witnesses, but rather to the indisputable sensory factuality of written documents. The hierarchy of evidence proposed in Gilbert's treatise is less based on Locke's empiricism than on the distrust of rhetoric which underlies Locke's empiricism. Oral reports by witnesses are less reliable than legal evidence because compared to written texts, their form is less defined by the law and therefore less controllable. In contrast to the evidentiary po-

---

71 Langbein and Landsman discuss the development of the rules of evidence and their practical implementation in Anglo-American judicial practice at the close of the eighteenth century and beyond as a result of various interconnected trends. Even Gilbert's treatise was less a philosophical text than a systematization of rules already in practice. See also Twining, *Theories*, 34–41.

72 Locke, *Essay*, 34.

tential of writing — especially in legally acceptable form — oral testimony is tainted by rhetorical ambivalence and excess and tends to express opinion rather than truth.

IV

Gilbert's references to Locke's theory of knowledge were meant to allow for a systematic treatment and quasi-scientific categorization of legal evidence, of which the testimony of eye-witnesses was only one category. The main objective of Gilbert's treatise is to treat the process of fact-finding in the legal trial as a process of cognition and to approach probabilities as distinct degrees of certain knowledge rather than as inferior and merely conjectural forms of opinion.[73] When it came to witnesses, first hand knowledge of facts based on direct observation was highly valued by Gilbert and his contemporaries; nonetheless, oral testimonies were but one element within a much larger configuration of factual evidence derived from other sources.

The focus of Gilbert's treatise is consequently not on the plausibility or credibility of verbal records but, rather, on the authenticity of documents. Most of the volume deals with written evidence, documents, titles, deeds, and the like, while only a very small rest deals with unwritten evidence, including testimony. As Stephan Landsman observes: "Gilbert conceived of the judicial process as, and foremost, a search for the determinate piece of written evidence."[74] Gilbert's system thus presents a certain paradox: while it propagates a more scientific approach to legal evidence based on empiricist and sensualist theories of knowledge, it does not favor "direct sensory evidence," and its major concern is obviously not with the credibility of witnesses and the probability of their accounts. Credibility is less of concern for Gilbert than competence, one reason being that one can hardly find legal 'rules' for credibility that could be enforced before the witness testifies. The test of credibility after Gilbert is marked by the rise of cross-examination. Gilbert's notion of the 'best evidence rule' became a central part in Anglo-American legal thinking of the time. It was not until around 1800, with the rise of counselling and cross-examination, that judges and juries began to regard oral testimony as the most important form of evidence. The shift in

---

[73] See Shapiro *Probability,* 189. The change of the use of the term 'probable' during the 17th century from 'approved (by) opinion' to its modern meaning is discussed at some length in Patey, *Probability,* 1–35.

[74] Stephan Landsman, "From Gilbert to Bentham," 1154.

focus from Gilbert's system to modern rules of evidence, which occurred in the late 18th and early 19th centuries, has been aptly summarized by legal historian John Langbein:

> [T]he pre-modern law, the law found in Gilbert and the lesser eighteenth-century treatises … was preoccupied with the authenticity of writings and the competency of witnesses. The modern law of evidence, centered on the oral testimony of witnesses at trial, supplanted the older law at the end of the eighteenth century and across the nineteenth century. The modern law abandoned the effort to treat the document-preferring best evidence rule as the organizing principle of the law of evidence. Cross-examination replaced oath as the fundamental safeguard for the receipt of oral evidence, defeating the competency regime that had disqualified the parties for interest, and allowing the hearsay rule to assume its ultimate character.[75]

This rather detailed discussion of Gilbert's treatise is not designed to question Korobkin's claim that Brown was attacking a Lockean "preference for direct sensory evidence" expressed in Gilbert's treatise and also, at least in Korobkin's opinion, dominant in the practice of American courts during the 18h century. As I said before, these assumptions tend to limit the Lockean aspects in Gilbert's treatise, and consequently in Brown's novel, to the question of sensory evidence and oral testimony. It is certainly fair to suggest that Brown's anti-empiricism also covers the Lockean framework of Gilbert's treatise. Given the peculiar nature of Gilbert's system, however, I want to shift the perspective on the connection between Gilbert and Brown by calling attention to some central features of Gilbert's system which are obviously addressed in Brown's novel. If we look at Gilbert and Brown in light of the remarks by Langbein, Landsman, and others about the changes in trial procedure and the handling of evidence during the late 18th century, there are several observations to be made.

Most importantly, there is the question of the competing authenticity of the various reports in *Wieland*, a competition that engages both oral testimonies and written documents. The novel is conspicuously filled with printed and written matter of all sorts, ranging from scribbled notes, letters, collected correspondence, newspaper and magazine articles, collections of works from classical authors to religious tracts, broadsides, and legal papers. The public realm described by the novel is completely dominated by printed and written communication. While the protagonists live in splendid isolation from their neighbours, they nevertheless communicate with correspondents near and far, even in Europe, and regularly receive fresh information about

75 Langbein, "Historical Foundations," 1194.

political, social, and artistic developments. The novel itself presents a string of letters by Clara Wieland; even though Brown does not follow the conventional form of the epistolary novel, the reader is repeatedly reminded that Clara is recounting her past calamities in writing; she is indeed acting as a 'historian' who is also a 'sufferer.'

From the perspective of a system like Gilbert's, the readers may ask how the evidentiary value of the various verbal and written records is to be assessed. If the characters display a fatal naiveté in regard to sensual impressions, their trust in written communication seems likewise untouched by a healthy suspicion. Of course, what apparently triggers the tragic events are mistaken voices, but Carwin's sinister manipulations are by no means limited to his vocal performances. At crucial points of the action, the cunning ventriloquist chooses to rely on his writing skills rather than his elocutionary powers. In one revealing instance, Carwin sends a letter to Clara, asking her to meet him in secrecy in order to deliver some obscure information which, as he promises, will affect her greatly. The letter comes after their rather dramatic confrontation in Clara's house late at night, in which Carwin allegedly tried to take her life but was stopped by some mysterious *Doppelgänger* who antagonized him, thus saving Clara. In the meantime, Clara had also been confronted by Pleyel, who told her about an intimate conversation between herself and Carwin, which he allegedly overheard and which he takes with great resentment as proof of Clara's faithlessness. For Clara, and of course for the reader, Carwin's letter appears to be alluding to both incidents:

> To Clara Wieland,
> What shall I say to extenuate the misconduct of last night? … I have no means of removing any fears that you may entertain of my designs, but my simple and solemn declarations. These, after what has passed between us, you may deem unworthy of confidence. … If you chuse [sic] to admit me to a conference, provided that conference has no witnesses, I will disclose to you particulars, the knowledge of which is of the utmost importance to your happiness.
> Carwin
> (*W*, 137)

What is important is the way in which a written text is employed to restore confidence and regain credibility in cancelling out the effect both of direct sensual impressions, i.e., Clara's encounter with Carwin, and of the corroborating report by an eye-witness, i.e., Pleyel's account of the secret meeting between Clara and Carwin, which Clara knows did not happen and which consequently points to Carwin's subversion of Pleyel's trust in her. At this point it is far from clear how these two events relate, but this is one of many instances in the novel where a written document is inserted — in this case even quoted in full — to acknowledge a serious breakdown of credibility and at the same time to ask for a renewal of trust. In fact, it is exactly with such a statement that Clara had begun her epistolary narrative: "If my testimony were without corroborations, you would reject it as incredible. … Listen to my narrative, and then say … if, indeed, every faculty be not suspended in wonder that I am still alive, and able to tell it" (*W*, 6). In this respect, even Brown's introductory advertisement must be read along the same lines as an appeal to his readers to suspend their incredulity, since "the incidents related are extraordinary and rare" and even "approach … to the nature of miracles" (*W*, 3). Again, the veracity of the events, or better, their probability, is assured by reference to "historical evidence" to be found in the reports from others, whose texts Brown resorts to in footnotes whenever he feels that his readers would have reason to doubt the truth of a particularly improbable phenomenon.

The attempt to bolster the probability of oral testimony by written communication, or by reference to some external written document, suggests a hierarchy of proofs similar to the one described by Gilbert's law of evidence. Thus Jordan states that in *Wieland* "written narratives are privileged over oral ones,"[76] implying that textual fictions provide a better basis for acting and judgment than oral confabulations. Jordan argues that the various vocal and written reports are used by Brown as metaphors for the different modes of experience associated with them — listening versus reading — contrasting the ambivalence or even danger of unmediated sensual impressions with reading as a more reflected, distanced, and therefore less harmful mediation of experience. She concludes that *Wieland* is a "defense" of fictions as "necessary mediations."[77] Jordan's observation that the novel is concerned with the "proper … uses of fiction" is central for my discussion, but her conclusions about the saving graces of literature are somewhat inconclusive.[78]

Yet Jordan also emphasizes that "the veracity of … second-hand narratives" in *Wieland* must be regarded with suspicion: fictions like Wieland help their readers "to learn to distrust happy endings" and to "turn their attention … to a careful scrutiny of the psychological complexities, especially disguised self-interest, leading to action."[79] She draws attention to the fact

---

[76] Jordan, "On Rereading Wieland," 171.

[77] Jordan, "On Rereading Wieland," 169, 171.

[78] Brown was well aware of both the power and the ambivalence of emotional address in fictional narratives. The ambivalence in regard to its own function and potential is a trademark of early American fiction, as both Davidson and Fluck have emphasized.

[79] Jordan, "On Rereading Wieland," 171.

that the novel must by necessity try to establish its own veracity not only in contrast to oral narratives, but also by its difference from other forms of textual reports. The question in what sense the novel as fiction may be regarded as superior to other narrative texts is closely related to its evidentiary value in terms of what Gilbert called the original situation of all trials and evidence, that is, the obligation to judge without immediate access to events or actions. Using Jordan's phrase then, the problem for Brown is how to save narrative fiction from being regarded as a suspicious "second-hand narrative," or, according to a legal category already used by Gilbert, as mere hearsay.[80]

The problem with second-hand narratives and hearsay is that they only present reports of others' reports, or testimonies about testimonies, thus being one step farther removed from the events or actions which they pretend to communicate than the reports of eye-witnesses. In terms of Locke's and Gilbert's scales of assent, such narratives therefore must be regarded as mere opinions and should be disregarded as evidence. This concept of testimonial evidence defines the relation between an event and a report about the event according to a logic of cause and effect, with the event as the real cause and the report or testimony as the discursive effect. As Christopher Looby observes, this is precisely the logic which is rather effectively subverted in *Wieland*. In contrast to Jordan, Looby maintains that the novel effectively undermines any attempt to discriminate between facts and fictions. Not only does everything in *Wieland* happen "on account of voice,"[81] but even the facts of the past are merely "a linguistic construct,"[82] open to revision. As Looby states, "facts" in *Wieland*

> are, in truth, functions of discursive *accounts* of those putative facts; they are, quite without exception, the products of reconstructive "inference" from those discursive representations.[83]

The difference between fact and fiction is thus no longer secured by material causality, but rather subject to disruption and destabilization by discursive interventions and inferential interpretation. If facts are merely products of linguistic operations, the search for truthful accounts of facts must appear a rather futile endeavor, and indeed, Looby claims, all the novel offers are

---

80 For Gilbert's treatment of hearsay, see Langbein, "Historical Foundations," 1174–76; and Landsman, "From Gilbert to Bentham," 1156–57. Both note that for Gilbert hearsay was inadmissible not because cross-examination was impossible, but rather because the original statement was not made under oath.

81 Looby, *Voicing America,* 165.

82 Looby, *Voicing America,* 153.

83 Looby, *Voicing America,* 154, emphasis in the original.

"vocal and verbal substitutions" of facts. The narrative consists of a "series of interlocked recourses"[84] to various written and oral reports that render the search for the true meaning of past and present events rather frustrating. Conflicts about the truth of alleged facts can therefore never be resolved, simply because there are only reports which are endlessly disputed, reinterpreted, and revised, only to become disputed again. The question of fact versus fiction thus appears to be a moot one in *Wieland*, considering the universalism of discursive production in the novel; for Looby at least, *Wieland* thus testifies to "Brown's discovery that truth … is an effect … of utterance"[85] — that Looby makes no difference between vocal and written utterance is less problematic than the notion of linguistic universalism which he believes to be presented in Brown's fiction.

Obviously, this state of affairs would completely upset any ordering of evidence according to the principles of Locke or Gilbert. To evaluate the 'reports from others' in reference to Gilbert's neatly ranked hierarchy of probable evidence would be rather accidental, or even illusory, since the natural order which Gilbert's system presupposes is turned upside down ever so often during the course of events. Take, for instance, the fact of the sudden death of Pleyel's German sweetheart, Theresa de Stolberg. The tragic incident is first communicated to Pleyel in miraculous ways by the voice of his absent sister — apparently another of Carwin's secret performances. The report is then confirmed a little later by the passenger of a Saxon ship, who vividly describes "the particulars" of Theresa's "death and funeral" (*W*, 48). In Gilbert's scheme, the first report would hardly count as testimonial evidence, while the second report would be valued as highly probable, considering that the passenger was an eye-witness to the tragic event (To be sure, the best evidence for Gilbert would be an official death certificate). Since the latter report supports the former, it in fact enhances the credibility of the improbable, convincing even the ever skeptical Pleyel to accept it: "[h]ere were proofs of a sensible and intelligent existence, which could not be denied. Here was information obtained and imparted by means unquestionably super-human" (*W*, 45). Much to the reader's surprise, however, it turns out a good deal later that even the super-human intelligence had been duped: "Theresa de Stolberg was alive. She had conceived the resolution of seeking her lover in America. To conceal her flight, she had caused the report of her death to be propagated" (*W*, 183). This revelation clearly shows how apparent facts are brought into existence by con-

84 Looby, *Voicing America,* 165.
85 Looby, *Voicing America,* 166.

vincing accounts, especially when these reports assume their high likelihood by reference to the testimony of an eye-witness. Moreover, such false accounts are obviously circulated rather deliberately precisely in order to hide one's own actions from being witnessed by others. Under such conditions, Gilbert's hierarchy of evidence must appear too simplistic, if not naive, since neither the report of (so-called or self-designated) eye-witnesses nor simply the fixed form of a written document can be taken as assurances for the truth of the facts thus reported.

However, if this is a "discovery," as Looby has it, neither Clara nor Pleyel show any surprise about it, and neither does anyone comment, critically or otherwise, on the disturbing ease with which the Baroness de Stolberg fabricated her own death. This lack of surprise suggests that Brown found the deliberate construction of facts less disturbing than symptomatic of his own cultural situation. Moreover, it reveals the possibility that the novelist aimed at contrasting Theresa's 'fiction' with that of Carwin, less to demonstrate the unreliability of all fabricated facts, but rather to make possible a comparison of their different goals and motivations. In other words, just because truth is merely an "effect" of linguistic operations — the result of rhetorical acts — it does not follow that the difference between fact and fiction, between true and false testimony becomes indeterminable, and therefore, irrelevant. Of course, the combined effect of the novel's open epistemological and linguistic skepticism would strongly suggest such a conclusion, yet there is a danger in radicalizing Brown's skeptical attitude in both areas to the point where his own motivations and goals might be misconstrued or even obscured. In my mind, this is what happens when Looby tries to subsume the issue of perceptual knowledge in the novel to its critical investigation of language and testimony. Throughout the novel, Brown makes repeated use of phrases like "testimony of my senses," or "testimony of my eyes," which almost read like verbatim quotations from Locke's *Essay on Human Understanding.* For Looby, this usage is yet another sign of Brown's epistemological skepticism, because the author "insinuates a terrible doubt of the reliability of sense-impressions into the phrase." As Looby explains:

> in this familiar but complex figure of speech the supposed immediacy of sense-impressions is already compromised by the term "testimony," which implies a verbal redaction — a linguistic mediation — of the supposedly simple sense experience.[86]

---

[86] Looby, *Voicing America,* 191.

This conclusion seems to me a radical interpretation of the reputed incompatibility between sensual perceptions and verbal accounts of perceptual experience because it suggests that for Brown, and for his readers, the term 'testimony' might have been incompatible with perceptual experience. Looby appears to believe that in the late 18th century people would find testimonies of sense-impressions unreliable (or even their own impressions) simply because they involved some sort of 'linguistic mediation.' To be sure, during Brown's time Americans had many reasons to distrust allegedly true reports of events, especially since there were so many in circulation. But they would hardly have found the term 'testimony' to be 'compromising' in the way suggested by Looby. Like Korobkin, Looby overstates the presence of Locke as a target of criticism in *Wieland*, and by seeing Brown's concerns with perception as simply an example of linguistic skepticism, he fails to recognize that in *Wieland* both the reliability of the senses and of the various testimonies become a question of probability and moral judgment. Indeed, as the rest of my discussion will show, Brown's emphasis on perception as 'testimony' rests on the assumption that perceptual knowledge, like any other form of testimony about actions and events, yields only probable evidence asking for moral judgment. It is this assumption that links Brown's novel and his ideas about narrative fiction to the philosophy of evidence in eighteenth-century American law.

V

At the time that Brown was receiving his legal education, Locke's indictment of rhetoric and his critical attitude toward testimony had already been criticized and revised by proponents of the Scottish Common Sense school. There is "much greater similitude than is commonly imagined," Thomas Reid wrote in 1764, "between the testimony … given by our senses, and the testimony of men given by language," the reason being that in both 'testimonies' "things are signified to us by signs."[87] Twenty years later, Reid again stressed the "analogy between the evidence of sense and the evidence of testimony," which for him was acknowledged "in all languages" by "the analogical expressions of the *testimony of the senses* … and the like." The "real difference," Reid maintained, was that "[i]n believing upon testimony we rely

---

87 Thomas Reid, *An Inquiry into the Human Mind,* 170, 190. See also Limon, *The Place of Fiction*, who likewise proposes that Reid's epistemology is a more likely source for Brown than Locke's.

upon the authority of a person who testifies; but we have no such authority for believing our senses."[88]

In light of these remarks, the function of the analogy between testimony and perception, as well as the decisive difference between testimonial and direct sensual evidence, as both are inscribed in Brown's text, appear to be less aimed at the opposition between simple sense experiences and their 'verbal redaction.' It rather seems to me that Brown wants to emphasize what Reid had described, namely, that the testimonial nature of sense experience always implies the interpretation of signs, only that this interpretation and the testimony it provides completely relies on our own authority. Both Reid and Brown, then, already know that the Lockean insistence on truth conveyed by the senses has hardly any currency in social affairs and the knowledge which guides them, since they are almost completely reliant on human testimony, i.e., on the words of others. Reid's conception of testimony as a distinctively "social operation of the mind"[89] marks an important revision of the individualistic conception of knowledge in Locke and others; as C. A. J. Coady claims, Reid was "one of the very few important philosophers of the European tradition to have recognized the epistemological significance" of our reliance upon the testimony of others, which therefore "should be regarded as fundamental to the justification of belief in the same sort of way as perception, memory, and inference are."[90]

An interpretation of Brown's concerns in *Wieland* that considers testimony the most basic foundation of human knowledge is also supported by the fact that James Wilson, arguably one of the most important lawyers and legal theoreticians in the early Republic and most likely an influence on Brown's legal training,[91] put the same emphasis on testimony as Reid when he wrote: "[t]he greatest and most important part of our knowledge, we receive by the information of others."[92] What is even more important, and a point which deserves special attention in regard to Brown's notion of literary testimony and evidence, is that both Reid and Wilson stress that most of our knowledge, even in its highest degree as moral certainty, relies on what we have *learned* from others, even though we are commonly unaware of the fact when we apply this knowledge. As a result, such knowledge consists of mere probable truths. Given this probability, even the testimony of our senses can

---

88 Thomas Reid, *Essays*, 181, emphasis in the original.
89 Reid, *Essays*, 48.
90 Coady, *Testimony*, 120, 23.
91 For Wilson's role in the Revolution and in the early Republic, see Schwartz 43–53.
92 Wilson, *Works,* 1: 384.

be measured only in the scales of probability; an observation which runs counter to both Gilbert's and Blackstone's conception of evidence, as Wilson carefully points out in his lecture on evidence:

> Demonstrative evidence has for its subject abstract and necessary truths … Moral evidence has for its subject the real but contingent truths and connections, which take place among things actually existing. … If these observations are just … we may see the impropriety of my Lord Chief Baron Gilbert's remark, when he says, that "all demonstration is founded on the view of a man's proper senses." From hence we may see likewise the inaccuracy of Sir William Blackstone's description of evidence, when he mentions it as demonstrating the very fact in issue. *The objects of our senses are objects of moral, not demonstrative evidence.*[93]

I quote the passage at length for two reasons. First, it suggests that Brown used the term 'testimony' in conjunction both with direct sense experience and with the verbal records of others' sense experience not to highlight the distinction between perception and testimony in terms of unmediated versus redacted 'truth,' but rather to stress their similarity in terms of probable (i.e., moral) evidence. If the testimony of the senses in *Wieland* is misleading, this is not due to the failures of sensual perception nor to the incompatibility of sense impressions with language. What Brown describes is a lack of moral perception, the failure to perceive the probable nature of all evidence and to judge it accordingly. The second conspicuous feature of the passage is its definition of moral evidence, which at first glance looks like an elaborate paraphrase of Reid's "the field of probable reasoning is contingent truth."[94] But it is in fact a verbatim quote from another source, George Campbell's *Philosophy of Rhetoric*, which was published in Scotland in 1776, and became one of the most successful books on rhetoric in the United States well into the 19th century. Together with Hugh Blair, Thomas Sheridan, John Ward, Richard Whately, and others, Campbell belonged to a number of philosophers and writers on rhetoric who tried to revise the theory and practice of eloquence and persuasion and thus helped to develop the so-called "new Rhetoric" of the 18th and early 19th centuries.[95] Campbell, Blair, and Sheridan all are in one way or another present in *Wieland*, and the novel's obvious obsession with rhetoric has been noted by a number of critics.[96] One could even argue that Brown's novel is indeed a thorough comparative study of the

---

93 Wilson, *Works*, 1: 395, my emphases.

94 Reid, *Essays*, 432.

95 See Johnson, *Rhetoric*; Moran, *Rhetorics and Rhetoricians*; and Wallace, *Speech Education*. For Campbell, see especially Stieglitz, *George Campbells Philosophie*.

96 The novel's obvious connection to Blair, for instance, has been discussed by Nichols, "Rhetorical Strategies," 460–61.

various models which the new rhetoric developed. Apart from the obvious interest in the epistemological and cognitive function of rhetorical modes, which are central both in Campbell and in Blair, Brown's descriptions of Wieland's attempts to bring classical texts to life by performing them clearly alludes to Sheridan's elocutionary theories about natural language and the force of modulation and stress, among other things. Of course, the elocutionary model is more present in the figure of Carwin, which aligns these two figures even more.

That Brown read Gilbert and Locke can be surmised with sufficient certainty; that he read Hugh Blair with approval has been recorded[97] and would suggest that he shared at least some of the theoretical ideas of the new rhetoric. Moreover, Campbell's influence both in legal and literary circles would have made his *Philosophy* an obvious point of convergence where Brown's legal training met with his literary ideas. It is indeed a convergence because the notable passage already quoted from Justice James Wilson, which could have been taken from Campbell, resurfaces in yet another version in Brown's theoretical notes on the evidence of literature. Let us take another look at the division of evidence as explained by Campbell. As the "most eminent" difference between moral and demonstrative (scientific) evidence, Campbell lists the following:

> [t]he first difference … is in their subjects. The subject of [demonstrative evidence] is … abstract … truth, or the … necessary relations of ideas; that of [moral evidence], the real … and contingent connexions that subsist among things actually existing.

This passage is clearly indebted to Reid; but note the similar emphasis on contingency and the actual existence of things in both Campbell and Wilson. Nonetheless, whereas Wilson found the realm of moral evidence a suitable and legitimate foundation for legal reasoning about matters of fact ("real truths"), Campbell insisted that moral evidence was the "proper providence of rhetoric."[98] This latter claim is indeed a radical revision of the distinction between evidence and rhetoric implied by Locke.

In this respect, Brown's own thoughts on probability mark an even more radical revision, or rather, a deliberate terminological shift from Locke's original opposition between evidence and rhetoric. In an essay about "The Difference between History and Romance" (1800), Brown draws upon the now familiar difference between demonstrative and probable evidence to elucidate the distinction between fictions and historiography. The most in-

---

[97] See Clark, *Charles Brockden Brown,* 45.
[98] Campbell, *Philosophy*, 43.

novative deviation from traditional doctrine happens when Brown calls up the famous scales of probability of Locke and Gilbert, only to turn the hierarchy they implied upside down. At the outset, Brown states that, in common understanding, history deals with "the probable and certain" whereas fiction is "a tissue of untruths." This distinction is subsequently corrected when Brown maintains that while the historian deals with "certainties," the romancer deals with "probabilities."[99] In an interesting twist, Brown projects the legal and philosophical distinction between demonstration and probable evidence onto the difference between history and romance. Historiography thus becomes a matter of demonstrative evidence in the sense of Reid, Wilson, and Campbell, while romance gains the status of probable evidence, and therefore, of testimony and moral certainty. In doing this, Brown is able to revise the claims of both history and fiction as reliable and essential sources of true knowledge. Curiously enough, it is precisely the close relation to the truth as demonstrative evidence which limits history, while fiction — like moral evidence and testimony in the sense of Campbell and Reid — gains almost unlimited authority:

> If history relate what is true, its relations must be limited to what is known by the *testimony of our senses.* Its sphere, therefore, is extremely narrow. The facts to which we are immediate witness, are, indeed, numerous, but time and place merely connect them. *Useful narratives* must comprise facts linked together by some other circumstance. They must, commonly, consist of events, for a knowledge of which the narrator is indebted to the *evidence of others.* This evidence, though accompanied with different *degrees of probability,* can never give birth to certainty. How wide, then, if romance be the narrative of mere probabilities, is the empire of romance? This empire is absolute and undivided over the motives and tendencies of human action. Over actions themselves, its dominion, though not unlimited, is yet very extensive.

Fiction is for Brown what for Campbell was rhetoric and what for Reid and Wilson was testimony as probable evidence: both a principal source of human knowledge and a way to describe and probe into the contingent and changeable relations between actual things and events. As Brown insists, history can merely describe these events and the actions of human agents, "but the connection between them, that quality which constitutes one the effect of the other, is mere matter of conjecture, and comes within the province, not of history, but romance."[100]

In a nutshell this passage presents the various tenets of the philosophy of evidence from Locke and Gilbert on the one hand and Reid, Campbell, and

---

[99] Brown, "History and Romance," 83.
[100] Brown, "History and Romance," 85.

Wilson, on the other. It is also rather obvious how these concepts are negotiated in *Wieland*, where Brown emphatically presents a useful narrative consisting of the testimony of others, which indeed never gives birth to certainty. However, Brown's insistence on the universal claims of literary fiction also implies that what appears as uncertainty and mere probability on the epistemological level — as merely factual knowledge — may be the source for a different form of knowledge and certainty. Since, in contrast to Brown's protagonists, who are either historians bound to the facts or bound to suffer by their senses, the readers of *Wieland* can assume a different position and read the evidence differently to gain insight into the motives and tendencies underlying the action. The knowledge they have gained this way can again be only probable, yet it may in the end amount to 'moral certainty.'

To be sure, achieving this moral certainty is no easy task, and it demands a high competence on the side of the reader to distinguish between various modes of rhetoric and their different value as evidence. Here the law offers Brown yet another means to make his case for literary evidence. The testimony of Theodore Wieland marks a 'legal moment' within the novel, where the claims of competing rhetorics of evidence converge in one single demonstration, allowing Brown not only to highlight their conflict but moreover to demonstrate how rhetoric may turn into evidence and become the basis for moral judgment.

VI

That evidence should be both visible (or sensible) and an effect of utterance would hardly have been surprising to Brown. A devoted student of classical authors and fervently interested in the rhetorical theory of his day, he was most likely aware of the fact that apart from its derivation from the Latin *videre*, to see, evidence had its more immediate root in the traditional philosophical category of *evidentia*. As Douglas Patey notes, Locke

> consistently uses *evidence* in a sense descended from the Greek εναϱγεια … What we mean by evidence, Locke calls 'grounds'; his 'evidence' is a shining forth to the mind whose … direct ancestor is scholastic *evidentia*, a term which never lost its etymological connection with seeing … and hence with light.[101]

Yet Locke's concept of evidence is also close to an explicit rhetorical understanding of *evidentia*, which above all acknowledged the power of speech in

---

[101] Patey, *Probability*, 31.

bringing forth vivid images to the mind of the listener.[102] *Evidentia* in this sense meant the description of scenes as if they were present to the senses; rhetorical evidence thus addresses the audience as spectators or listeners, that is, as *witnesses*. According to Carlo Ginzburg, the aspect of effective persuasion by the description of scenes and characters *in absentia* was especially important for classical legal rhetoric, since "the lawyer … was expected to make a convincing argument by communicating the illusion of reality, not by exhibiting proofs collected either by himself or by others."[103]

The emergence of probability during the 17th century is closely connected to the attempt to wrestle evidence from the authority of opinion and rhetoric and to ground it on sound empirical observation and direct experience of reality. As Ian Hacking remarked, the Lockean system of probability tried to replace evidence provided by people with the evidence provided by things.[104] But evidence and probability still remained within the scope of rhetoric and *evidentia*, especially where things by necessity had to be represented by people, and thus by speech. As the example of Gilbert's system of legal evidence has shown, questions of representation and rhetoric are always implicated where human judgment has to rely on the report from others. From this perspective, *Wieland* oscillates between evidence and *evidentia* on all levels, trying to navigate and negotiate the antagonistic claims of both concepts without fully subscribing to either.

The protagonists in Brown's novel are clearly aware of the ambivalent status of narratives of "mere probabilities" between evidence and *evidentia*, as an early reaction of Clara and her friends to Carwin shows. Asked to speculate about the mysterious vocal phenomena which so upset Wieland, Carwin (whose part in the mystery is yet unknown) offers some very persuasive explanations of his own:

> His narratives were constructed with so much skill, and rehearsed with so much energy, that all the effects of a dramatic exhibition were frequently produced by them. Those that were the most coherent and most minute, and, of consequence, least entitled to credit, were yet rendered probable by the exquisite art of this rhetorician. (*W*, 74)

Skill, energy, dramatic exhibition, combined with coherence and attention to detail: Carwin is a natural 'new rhetorician' who can 'produce' probability ac-

---

102 For the discussion of these principles underlying *evidentia* in ancient and classical rhetorical models, see Eden, *Poetic and Legal Fiction*, esp. 71–75; 85–96; and Solbach, *Evidentia.*

103 Ginzburg, "Checking the Evidence," 291.

104 Hacking, *The Emergence of Probability*, 32.

cording to the theories of Blair, Campbell, and Sheridan. Yet his listeners are not convinced because they, too, know the difference between real evidence and rhetorical evidence and are able to see how probabilities are being constructed. But that is not the only reason for their incredulity. Carwin's explanations, which actually come very close to the truth, fail to match the distinct concept of evidence which each of the characters unwittingly presumes. While neither Clara nor Pleyel believe in the supernatural source of the voices, they find Carwin's narratives lacking evidence in certain respects. Pleyel bases his belief on the same ground of factual knowledge as Brown's historian: "he scrupled not to deny faith in any testimony but that of his senses." Like the historian, Pleyel is bound to a definition of factual knowledge and demonstration, and his range of belief is rather narrow. If testimonies contradict one another, he starts "not to mould his belief, but merely to give birth to doubt" (*W,* 75). In contrast, Clara is clearly fascinated by Carwin's probabilities, yet she does not put faith in them because all his skillful explanations still do not elucidate essential aspects: a plausible connection between the single events and, more important for Clara, a motive. If Clara is more willing than Pleyel to give credit to mere probabilities as long as they are supported by consistency and motivation, there is something ambivalent about her fascination with the mystery and the promise of revelation which Carwin appears to offer. As it turns out, the most dangerous concept of evidence as a basis for judgment is propagated by Wieland, since he not only "maintained the probability of celestial interference" (*W,* 75) as an explanation for the voices, but he also eagerly asks for direct sensual evidence to support this probability, to transform the existence of God from a moral certainty into a demonstration of self-evidence. Even after he committed his atrocious deeds, he still defends his concept of evidence in his testimony:

> God is the object of my supreme passion. … I have thirsted for the knowledge of his will. … My days have been spent in searching for the revelation of that will, but … my search failed. I have not been wholly uninformed; but my *knowledge has always stopped short of certainty.*
>
> O! that I might be admitted to thy presence; that mine were the supreme delight of knowing thy will, and performing it! The blissful privilege of *direct communication* with thee, and of *listening* to the *audible enunciation* of thy pleasure! … Would that a momentary emanation from thy glowy would visit me! that some unambiguous token of thy presence would *salute my senses*! (*W,* 165, 166–67; my emphasis)

In Wieland's appeals to the divine will, we can observe a regressive mixture of empiricist groundings of truth in sense impression and pre-Lockean notions of the revelation of truth as "emanation," which never lost its religious meanings. Certainty about the truth in this sense is absolute and mystical in its longing for direct communication with the divine. Yet at the same time, Wieland insists on direct sensual address; he demands to *see* and *hear* in order to know the will of God. This demand is different from a mystical understanding of revelation, and it appears to be a strange combination of external empirical evidence and *evidentia* as, in Patey's words, the 'shining forth' of truth. Wieland's account of his encounter with the Supreme Being demonstrates the powerful effect of this peculiar alloyment of evidence:

> How shall I describe the lustre, which … burst upon my vision.
>
> I was dazzled. My organs were bereaved of their activity. … A nameless fear chilled my veins, and I stood motionless. …
>
> I opened my eyes and found all about me luminous and glowing. It was the element of heaven that flowed around. Nothing but a fiery stream was at first visible; but, anon, a shrill voice from behind called upon me to attend.
>
> … It is forbidden to describe what I saw: Words, indeed, would be wanting to the task. The lineaments of the that being … no hues of pencil or of language can pourtray. (*W*, 167–68)

This description clearly matches the categories of the gothic sublime, yet if we read it as a moment of evidence and revealed truth, Wieland's testimony presents an account of a miracle: an event which is overwhelmingly sensual and defies all efforts of representation. This is of course what Wieland had been waiting for all along: the revelation of truth as pure demonstration to the senses.

The way in which Brown describes Wieland's ideal of evidence bears a remarkable resemblance to the concept of 'pure evidence' which flourished shortly in late 17th-century debates on miracles. This concept developed out of a certain embarrassment, since even with the rise of scientific models of explanation, based on empirical observation and experiment, the potential veracity of supernatural phenomena like miracles could not be ruled out so easily because such events had always been interpreted as proof of the existence of God. In the attempt to distinguish authentic miracles from mere fabrication and hallucinations, the nature of supernatural or divine evidence was defined in such a way as to limit "the function of miracles to that of providing irrefragable evidence for the truth of Christian revelation."[105] According to one authority, a necessary condition was that the "supernatural Effect" must be "evident and wonderful to Sense" at the same time.[106] But the sense of wonder was only one precondition for pure evidence, as Lorraine Daston has pointed out:

---

105 Daston, "Marvelous Facts," 265.

106 Qtd. in Daston, "Marvelous Facts," 265.

> Ideally, [the evidence of miracles] was pure evidence, unequivocal in its interpretation, and irresistible in its persuasive power. The evidence of miracles straddled the distinction between the 'internal' evidence of things, and the 'external' evidence of testimony … In both cases, the evidence of miracles was saturated with intention, God's intention to suspend the natural order to certify his messenger, and God's intention to establish certain doctrines. Because miracles accompanied doctrine, their meaning was clear; because God was the author of miracles, they proved beyond a shadow of a doubt.[107]

The most impressive feature of such a concept — one that seemed particularly attractive to Wieland — is that it presents a closed system of belief, interpretation, and evidence. Meaning and event become one, and by its sensual force the event evidences — authorizes — its meaning beyond any doubt. Miracles as pure evidence were thus not only proof for the existence of God, their exegesis also turned out doctrine — miracles revealed the divine will in the form of irresistible orders. Theodore Wieland thus appears as the enlightened subject in desperate search of divine doctrine, revealed directly to his senses and authorized by the 'author of his being.'

In light of Brown's remarks about probability and the empire of romance, Wieland's choice of words in his testimony suggests yet another interpretation of his yearning for the sensual revelation of truth. In his essay on history and romance, Brown argued that "the evidence of others" might yield only probable knowledge and that it "can never give birth to certainty."[108] This situation, however, is unbearable for Wieland when he realizes that his knowledge always falls short of being certain. In fact, his desire to go beyond this insufficient knowledge and partake in the 'supreme pleasure' of knowing God shows that Wieland is not satisfied with "mere probabilities" and that he will not settle for knowledge which only relies on human testimony. But as Wieland's own testimony makes glaringly obvious, to transcend the realm of human testimony and mere probability only affords an illusory certainty of moral judgment that is deeply inhumane and anti-social. Indeed his direct communication with God puts him out of touch with his family and with himself, as his wife exclaims with horror: "it is too plain: thou art undone — lost to me and to thyself" (*W,* 171).

According to Reid and other contemporary authorities, Wieland could never be a competent judge in moral decisions about right or wrong, and even according to the legal standards of the time, he would have been con-

---

107 Daston, "Marvelous Facts," 266.
108 Brown, "History and Romance," 85.

sidered mad and therefore unaccountable.[109] Yet something more is at stake than the defendant's individual accountability in regard to his actions. How can the jury — be it a real one or one comprised of readers — base its own moral judgment on the evidence provided by someone who is mad? What seems the most reasonable and responsible reaction from our historical point of view may not intuit the urgency and the full complexity of the problem that Brown is addressing. The uncomfortable question that is implied in all the various presentations of proof is whether one must need the idea of God to ground and to judge the morality of one's conduct and that of others. In this respect, Wieland's testimony can also be read as a straightforward comment on and criticism of the concept of individual duty and accountability formulated by Wilson in his lectures on natural law. For Wilson, the assurance of moral legitimacy and the goodness of individual action relies on the correspondence of one's conduct with the will of God:

> If I am asked — why do you obey the will of God? I answer — because it is my duty so to do. If I am asked again — how do you know this to be your duty? I answer again — because I am told so by my moral sense or conscience. If I am asked a third time — how do you know that you ought to do that, of which your conscience enjoins the performance? I can only say, I *feel* that such is my duty. Here investigation must stop; reasoning can go no farther.[110]

If one could imagine Wilson rising to Wieland's defense, the judge's moral self-assurance would turn into outright travesty — indeed, one could very easily imagine Wieland himself quoting the exact passage as a justification, thus adding further evidence of his disturbed state of mind. But what, precisely, is the difference between the moral assurance of Wieland and that of Wilson? Whether Brown was aware of the passage or not is hard to establish. But it seems more than obvious that he is severely complicating the kind of moral justification of individual action which Wilson suggested. What makes Wieland a madman and Wilson a competent judge is the different concept of evidence they employ to ground their respective beliefs and moral convictions. Whereas Wieland desires to communicate with God in order to get moral direction for his actions, Wilson communicates with his 'moral sense' or conscience. The evidence needed for Wilson is all internal, while for Wieland it must, by necessity, be external. In contrast to Wilson, however, Brown radicalizes the inherent similarities between the two concepts to the point of

---

109 Korobkin refers to Blackstone's *Commentaries* to make this point. The reasoning can also be found in Reid's *Inquiry,* 429.

110 Wilson, *Works of James Wilson*, 1: 332–33, emphasis in the original.

moral confusion. Both modes of communication are solipsistic; whether one listens to the voice of one's conscience or the voice of God, the evidence of moral justification thus afforded is purely individualistic and subjective. There is no way to investigate this evidence or to put its witness on the stand, as it were, since there is no common concept of moral evidence. The notion of moral duty that Wilson presents could not have prevented the disaster described in *Wieland*.

But Brown's novel is also a challenge to Wilson's final verdict that the 'investigation' of moral evidence 'must stop' because 'reasoning' could 'go no farther.' It is precisely such an investigation of moral evidence that *Wieland* offers to its readers, and if the readers are free to moralize, as Brown insists, they are also asked to reason before they judge. In order to do so, however, the readers must avoid the confusion of evidence with *evidentia*: they must read the novel as a rhetoric of evidence on its own terms. As Cathy Davidson has remarked, Brown, like any other novelist in the early Republic, chose "to write fiction precisely for what the form allows and for what it disallows." In contrast to Davidson, however, I would argue that Brown did not write *Wieland* to be read mimetically and that the novel challenges the attitude of early Republican readers to take fiction as a "paramount reality of its own."[111] For, to mistake fictions for reality would impair their usefulness as "narratives of mere probability" designed to be read as probable evidence for moral reasoning. Literary fictions, Brown implies, should not be internalized as evidence for some subjective reality, but rather be used to externalize individual moral reasoning (with all its confusions) to establish a common discourse on moral certainty.

That Brown leaves his readers to moralize, refusing to offer a moral of his own, may be an indication of his idea of the novel as a demonstration of probable — moral — evidence, not as an agency of moral instruction and judgment. If one compares the representation of the historical evidence in magazines with Brown's literary treatment of the original case, the appeal to moral reasoning becomes even clearer. Commenting on the murders committed by John Yates in 1781, the *New York Weekly Magazine* speculated in 1796 that the "cause for his wonderfully cruel proceedings is beyond the conception of human beings." The unnamed reporter then offered both insanity or "a strong delusion of Satan" as possible explanations for the killing, only to conclude with a note of epistemological despair:

> But what avail our conjectures, perhaps it is best that some things are concealed from us, and the only use we can now make of our knowledge of this affair, is to

---

[111] Davidson, *Revolution and the Word*, 262.

> be humble under a scene of human frailty to renew our petition, "Lead us not into temptation."[112]

Such humbleness in face of the inexplicable was far from Brown, who designed his narrative of probability in a way precisely to encourage conjectures, to ask for inference, and to challenge his reader's capacity for moral judgment. In an ironic twist, the final conclusion of the news article, that the appeal to divine direction and support would help in times of moral confusion, becomes the very source of delusion and immoral demeanor in *Wieland.* Moral justification, Brown seems to suggest, needs the best evidence the facts are capable of, and this evidence can only be literary.

VII

It seems that all the evidence presented through Wieland's testimony and all the conclusions drawn from it still follow the law of analogy. After all, we have heard the witness, we have seen his appearance before the jury, just like in a real trial, and we can deliver our opinion with conviction. However, this sense of unmediated access to the evidence provided by Wieland's testimony is as carefully staged as the testimony itself. This staging is not history — a description of actions and events — but literature — a narrative of mere probability. In his essay, Brown makes the distinction clear:

> That which is done beneath my own inspection, it is possible for me to know and exactly to record; but that which is *performed at a distance*, either in time or place, is the theme of *foreign testimony.* If it be related by me, I relate not what I have witnessed, but what I derived from other witnesses. The subject of my senses is merely the existence of the record, and not the deed itself which is recorded. The truth of the action can be weighed in no scales but those of probability.[113]

Once again, Brown translates the legal standard of probability into an argument about the nature of fiction. The paragraph even reads like an accurate description of Brown's own role as the author of *Wieland.* He is only relating 'foreign testimony,' derived from other witnesses. But it also contains an appropriate description of the role of the reader, whose only direct evidence is the mere existence of the record of events (Clara's letters, Brown's novel), whose probability nevertheless must be weighed. Finally, and most importantly, one of the characteristics of such testimonies is that they are "per-

---

112 "An Account," 28. For an interesting discussion of the historical context of this and other similar cases, see Hughes.

113 Brown, "History and Romance," 85 (my emphases).

formed at a distance," which means that the actions and events — the evidence allegedly seen and heard — cannot be inspected closely but only be watched like a dramatic spectacle. The author is a witness that cannot be cross-examined, and his fictional document can only be read. What is at stake in *Wieland* is how such documents should be read — a question that ultimately rests on an evaluation of Wieland's testimony as evidence.

Brown's 'scales of probability' are taken straight from Locke and Gilbert, yet his acknowledgment of the performative quality of witnessing and testimony adds a distinct rhetorical dimension to the concept of probable evidence — which was one of the major revisions prepared by the new rhetoric of Campbell and Blair. It is this rhetorical, performative dimension of evidence which Brown highlights again and again in *Wieland.* Thus, if readers are confronted with things "performed at a distance," they are also challenged by the uncanny ability of the various performances to affect direct sensual impressions, i.e., to turn into evidence. This capacity becomes obvious through Carwin's ventriloquism: the projected voices — performed at a distance — are taken by the listeners for evident signs of the presence of others. But this fatal transformation of rhetoric into evidence is not simply a matter of deliberate manipulation. The delusions of the protagonists are also triggered by their loss of distance to the subject of their senses — which is, in most cases, a written text, or a verbal record. Once the distance is lost, they start to confuse the performance, with its effects, i.e., the testimony with the illusion of direct sensual evidence.[114]

In the tragic figure of Wieland, Brown presents a reader who falls prey to such a confusion. Wieland is not only a fervent admirer of the famous rhetorician Cicero, in whose divinity he believes and whose bust decorates the temple built by Wieland's father. Wieland also attempts to regain the original significance of Cicero's speeches by performing them with his friends, "embellishing his rhetoric with all the proprieties of gesticulation and utterance," thereby "settling and restoring the purity of the text" (*W,* 24). These performances clearly reveal a desire for re-translating rhetoric — the textual documents — into direct, sensual evidence. And because he wants his rhetoric to become self-evident, Wieland is obsessed with the perfection of its performance. Thus he can identify with its effects: he can "feel" its evidence.

In the carefully staged courtroom appearance, Brown directly confronts his readers with Wieland's fatal notion of rhetorical self-evidence. His testimony is the only instance in the novel where the events are not mediated by Clara — where Wieland himself acquires a voice and becomes the "narrator

---

[114] Jordan makes a similar point, but her emphasis is on time and action.

of his own tale" (*W*, 162). If Clara's tale follows the logic of witnessing and testimony, her brother's confession now turns her into the reader of another tale, and as a reader she is overwhelmed by her impressions. The disturbing result of this entanglement of legal procedure and fictional performance in Wieland's testimony is indeed a transformation, because it presents the law in the story *as* a story, and we enter the courtroom only through an act of reading:

> "One of the hearer's faithfully recorded [Wieland's] speech. There it is ... you may read it at your leisure." With these words my uncle left me alone. My curiosity refused me a moment's delay. I opened the papers, and read as follows. (*W*, 163)

Even this moment of unmediated and direct communication is thus just another instance of a performance whose distance has been overcome by rhetorical means. Wieland's testimony has been "faithfully" recorded by another unnamed witness of the trial; hence it is what Brown called "evidence of others." But since this witness does not comment on the evidence he presents, we cannot become witness to his witnessing — we are merely readers, directly exposed to the effects of Wieland's rhetoric.[115]

Which is, of course, Brown's own. Thus, in the 'advertisement' which precedes the novel, Brown announces the text as "the first of a series of performances" (*W*, 3). Whatever evidence we may be able to 'sort out' as readers of *Wieland*, it always demands to be witnessed as evidence brought about by a rhetorical performance. Indeed, the evidence that Brown presents to us must be read or even witnessed for what it is, not in the legal or moral but in the literary sense. The novel attempts to transform and translate a legal ideal of evidence as independent of rhetoric into a literary notion of evidence as emphatically rhetorical and performative. This 'literary evidence' then demands to be witnessed as a rhetorical effect. Paradoxically, *Wieland* confronts the reader with conflicting rhetorics of evidence and witnessing in order to force us into witnessing its own rhetoric as evidence.

---

115 See Baym's comments on the particular presentation of Wieland's speech in the novel ("Minority Reading").

Chapter 4

The Judge and the Code: James Fenimore Cooper and the Common Law of Literature

I

Given the foundational affinities that link American literary and legal culture, the epistemological despair that so obviously pervades Brown's *Wieland* may be more than just an expression of subjective disturbances in the face of extreme social and cognitive challenges. It also points to a more general ambivalence and collective insecurity that surrounded the various 'fictions' of law and literature in republican America. Some of these fictions were clearly built on the claim of the distinctiveness of American culture and experience; at any rate, as we have seen in the examples of Brown's novels and James Wilson's legal philosophy, there was a comparable tendency in both fields to emphasize, in contrast to European traditions, the differences which conditioned the relation between rhetoric and evidence in a democratic society, based on 'self-evident' truths and the principles of 'natural' law. In 1798, when *Wieland* was published, neither American law nor American literature existed as fully established institutions — a situation which Brown and Wilson tried to change both in their own respective ways. During the first half of the nineteenth century, American law and literature intensified their struggles to find a distinct national form and identity. Legal historians have long acknowledged the fundamental significance of this period in American legal history, calling it the "golden age" or the "formative era" of American law, which not only brought about the "Americanization" of the common law, but also the gradual formation of a specific American understanding of the law and of legislation as tools for economic expansion and progress.[1] Between 1790 and 1830 American politics and culture became severely legalistic in the sense that emerging concepts of social organization, order, and progress used the law and especially the ideal image of judicial integrity and power as a frame of reference. As Perry Miller wrote, "[t]he formation of American law in this era … embrace[d] a mental adventure of heroic propor-

[1] See Pound, *Formative Era;* Horwitz, *Transformation;* Nelson, *Americanization*; and Mann, *Neighbors and Strangers.* For the sectional and regional foundation of this 'Americanization' of the law, see Newmyer, "Origins."

tions"[2] — and more often than not the self-declared heroes in this adventure were the judges. The "harmony and … the stability of the union, depends in a very material degree, upon the just and discreet exercise of judicial power," Justice James Kent stated in 1824 and he added that "[i]t may be said of [the Supreme Court], and certainly with as much propriety, as it has been said in reference to the *Roman sages,* that justice has there unveiled her mysteries and erected her temple."[3]

Arguably, one of the most memorable representations of the pioneering spirit of these judges and lawyers that helped to shape American law after the revolution was a fictional character: Marmaduke Temple, the determined judge of the little frontier settlement Templeton in James Fenimore Cooper's novel *The Pioneers* (1823). Cooper's portrait of Judge Temple and the legal conflict at the center of *The Pioneers* are meant to serve as a complex fiction. While it in some respects echoes the sentiments of Kent, Cooper's portrait of Judge Temple in *The Pioneers* is that of a pathfinder preparing the way for an American legal tradition, even though Temple does not have the learning and the social standing of Kent or figures like Joseph Story.

As I will argue in the first part of this chapter, *The Pioneers* presents the Americanization of the Common Law as a process that appears to be both inevitable and beset with inherent contradictions and oppositions. The most obvious of these has always been interpreted as the conflict between nature and culture, or more precisely, between the law of nature and civil law. In my view, however, the complexities of Cooper's fiction of American law result from the confrontation between two rather different notions of 'natural' law which Cooper translates into the irreconcilable conflict between an individualized law — of the state of nature — and a common law — of the state of civilization —, thus demanding an option for one or the other. In fact, in the end the conflicting models of a 'natural' legal order turn out to be compatible, even complementary, yet only if the pragmatic superiority of Temple's judge-made law is accepted, while Leatherstocking's 'nateral' (in his words) law is relegated to the confines of an imaginary nature that can be claimed as 'property' only by aesthetic appreciation.

The relation between the two conceptions of laws and rights that are in conflict with each other in *The Pioneers* may be taken as a fundamental one, especially if discussed in regard to the similarly conflicting claims of law and literature. The fiction of the free individual, owning a natural right to prop-

---

2 Miller, *The Life of the Mind*, 109.

3 Qtd. in Miller, *The Legal Mind*, 104. For the close affinity of Kent's and Cooper's notions about law and legal order, see Thomas, *Cross-Examinations*.

erty, for instance, is central to American law and American literature alike. Cooper's fictions of the law react to the radical revision of these concepts in the field of law during his time. As I will try to show, the basic constellations and contrasts that Cooper employs, especially in his trial scenes, emphasize the complementary nature, the interdependence even, of emerging legal and literary fictions. The imaginary figure which allows this reconciliation of law and literature results from a model of historical development and teleological progress restrained and guided by unchangeable principles. For Cooper, as for many of his contemporaries in the legal profession, the American Constitution, in combination with the principles of an American Common Law, would serve as a guarantee for a legal order which could both allow and withstand the constant changes within a democracy.[4] The question, however, which common law principles would be suitable for the American situation or could be reconciled with the principles written down in the Constitution was of course highly debated during the nineteenth century.

The decisive changes in the various fields of American law did not occur without intense public debates and rhetorical struggles; like the federalist controversies, the political and legal conflicts of the Jacksonian era were fuelled by passion on all sides. As Miller notes, "even after the violent passions of 1800 were diminished, other passions — sometimes political, but often purely conceptual — continued to inspire assaults on the Common Law."[5] One of the most embattled questions was what kind of law would be better suited for the further progress of American democracy. On the one hand, there were the uncodified, time-honored principles of the British Common Law, with its reliance on precedent and its unique practice of pleading, which had been initially accepted widely in the colonies, but had increasingly become the target of "bitter antagonism" and even "primitive hatred"[6] like all things deemed British or feudal since the Revolution.[7] However, even radical critics of the Common Law like William Sampson acknowledged its inherent character as "the law of a free people" which "has freedom for its end"[8] and which had served as a formidable instrument in the hands of the American lawyers drafting the Declaration of Independence. On the other hand, there was the newly written law created and auth-

---

4 For this shared belief see the discussion in Adams, *The Guardian of the Law,* and Thomas, *Cross-Examinations.*

5 Miller, *The Life of the Mind*, 107.

6 Miller, *The Life of the Mind*, 108, 109.

7 "The common law, as something English, was under a cloud after our revolution" (Pound, *The Formative Era,* 40).

8 Sampson, *An Anniversary Discourse*, 36.

ored by American judges and legislators as they responded to the rising challenges of urbanization, industrialization, and territorial expansion. Faced with the growing mass and complexity of legal decisions and commentary and the lack of a federal frame for the diverse legislation and court decisions of the various states, many nineteenth-century American lawyers and politicians felt a growing need for the simplification and standardization of American laws.

One possible remedy suggested by a number of lawyers and politicians alike was the translation of the Common Law into some form of a written code, or digest, which would be both concise and comprehensive enough to make the law more accessible to the layman and more practicable for the professional lawyer. Yet, even though it was not completely foreign to the Common Law tradition, the concept of legal codification had never been very dear to English or American lawyers, and earlier attempts to codify American laws had been met with skepticism rather than with approval.[9] After the introduction of the Napoleonic Code in continental Europe, however, the idea of a comprehensive yet transparent set of codified rules and laws also began to appeal to Americans. Codification accordingly became one of the most debated concepts in American legal culture in the first half of the nineteenth century, and the codification movement which emerged from these debates turned into "one of the set pieces of American legal history."[10] Even though the success of the various attempts at legal codification during the time must be considered rather minor since eventually the resistance of the Common Law supporters proved to be too strong — the Louisiana codes and the New York Field codes being the prime exceptions to the general situation[11] — the passionate discussions clearly left their mark and severely challenged some of the most fundamental assumptions about the Common Law, especially with regard to the source and extent of its authority.

At the center of the conflict between the Common Law supporters and the codifiers was the conflict between the law as authorized *interpretation* versus the law as an authored *text*, which was highlighted in the antagonism between an unwritten legal tradition and the new creation of law through writ-

---

9 See Herman, "Fate and Future"; Weiss, "The Enchantment of Codification"; and esp. Cook, *Codification Movement*, 3–22.

10 Friedman, *History of American Law*, 402; see also 187–88, 391–93. Additional in-depth discussion of the various arguments and debates can be found in Cook, *Codification Movement*. While I cannot discuss them at length, these earlier debates will form the background of my discussion of Cooper's positions both in *The Pioneers* and in *The Ways of the Hour*.

11 See Herman, "The Fate and Future," and Kadish, *David Dudley Field*.

ing. Did the latter simply realize and reflect, or rather revise — and thus possibly subvert — the former? How could a written code, as a presumably fixed set of laws, account for all the unforeseeable changes in cultural and social experience and the emergence of new fields of legal conflict? The codification debate of the nineteenth century gradually revealed that the idea of the Common Law as a fixed moral law, endowed with some pre-ordained, stable 'meaning,' which existed before its verbalization and remained unchanged by it, was irreconcilable with the increasing dominance of textual production and interpretation in every field of legal practice and, more generally, in the public sphere. Far more significant, however, was the revision of the Common Law concept of property, especially in its radicalized understanding as a natural and absolute right. New forms of social and mercantile interaction radically changed old and opened new fields of legal conflict for which the Common Law had no ready concepts or precedents. Especially in areas like contract and tort law, new concepts of property emerged and more and more undermined the traditional understanding of property as absolute dominion over material things.[12]

Thus, the dephysicalization and relativization of property during the nineteenth century posed a severe problem because it challenged traditional notions of property rights and the laws which were meant to protect those rights. More fundamentally even, the creation (or condemnation) of property through acts of legislation or judicial discretion questioned the republican ideal of individual liberty based on an inviolable right to personal property. In short, nineteenth-century Americans learned, if somewhat reluctantly, that life, liberty, and property (the original Lockean term for the Jeffersonian 'pursuit of happiness') as basic individual rights in a democracy were not of the same nature; indeed, that property rights could no longer be called *natural* rights at all. Both the anxieties of conservative property holders — mostly land holding gentry — and the legal revisions effected by progressive judges and politicians in the name of economic development also resurfaced in the debate about the Common Law between the traditionalists and the codifiers.

---

12 See Horwitz, *The Transformation,* 31–62; Nedelsky, *Property,* esp. ch. 2 and 6; and Vandevelde, "The New Property," 325–57.

II

The struggle over different concepts of property and the distinction between unwritten (i.e. common) versus written (i.e. codified) law debated in 19th-century American culture are closely related. The debate, however, is not unprecedented in the history of Anglo-American Common Law. In fact, its basic dilemma that informs the debate, that is, the defense of static and unlimited rights to property in the face of an increasing fluidity, fluctuation, and abstraction of property interests can be traced back to the legal definition of the literary work as a new kind of property by 17th-century English common lawyers. As Martin Kayman has shown in his discussion of the important early copyright case *Donaldson v. Becket* (1774), the modernization of the Common Law, especially in regard to the revision of traditional concepts of property to include the immaterial sources of the literary — i.e. the imagination — *within* the law, was made possible by a revision of legal authorship and the redefinition of the source of its authority.[13] Curiously enough, both the proponents of the new 'literary property' and their adversaries based their arguments in rather similar ways on the crucial difference between literary writing and authorship and its legal counterparts — a difference that became instrumental in establishing the modern dialectic of legal and literary rhetoric. It did so by pointing at the different sources of the legal and the literary: one the product of communal custom and experience, the other merely the result of individual fancy. The traditionalists could thus sustain the authority both of the authorless Common Law and of legal writing (as in a statute) by defining the latter "in terms of a collective authorship expressive of the *public* interest, as opposed to the … *personal* authorship and interest"[14] of literary writing. The same dialectic can be seen at work in the defense of the modernizers. For when they claimed that the literary work was emphatically the most personal of private properties, the argument implicitly rested on the distinct character of the Common Law and the interpretive texts based on it as inherently public and impersonal. After this "crucial moment in the historical relation between law and literature," Kayman states, the legal and the literary — as distinct forms of writing, languages, or texts — can only be constituted in reference to each other. While this inevitable

---

13 See Kayman, "Lawful Writing." On the copyright debate and the emerging definition of modern literary authorship, see also Rose, "Author as Proprietor"; Woodmansee, "Genius and Copyright"; Ross, "Invention of Tradition"; Saunders, *Authorship and Copyright*.

14 Kayman, "Lawful Writing," 773.

reference more often than not took the form of mutual disavowal, negation, or denial, the question of the relationship between law and literature became imminent to their own self-definition and -understanding.

Not surprisingly, the conflict between the American supporters of the Common Law and the reformist movement for legal codification also touched upon certain presuppositions regarding the nature and function of literary fiction in nineteenth-century American culture. Again, in this respect, the work of James Fenimore Cooper is clearly exemplary, since his novels are almost invariably concerned with questions of ownership, linguistic authority, and the nature of property, both in the legal and the literary sense. Using Kayman's observations as my background, I will return to the properties of literature in my discussion of Cooper's last novel, *The Ways of the Hour* (1850), which has been characterized as the author's "final word on the judicial system"[15] but which was also almost generally dismissed as a rather "poor performance"[16] and as artistically flawed. However, the faults of Cooper's *Ways* are of considerable interest for the discussion of the function of the law in his fictions. More than anything else, they betray an intense "aesthetic and moral anxiety,"[17] which obviously forced Cooper to experiment and present the law from a perspective rather different from that of his other novels, especially his historical fictions.

However, the main difference, as I will suggest, must be seen in Cooper's radicalization of an internal conflict within the law, which is already inherent in *The Pioneers.* In certain respects, *The Ways of the Hour* breaks with a system of balanced opposites that had given Cooper's historical romances their convincing and suggestive power as national fictions. The aging author's diatribe against what he felt to be the newest perversions of legal practice and the flagrant manipulation of the laws by judges, juries, the public, and the press not only signifies the collapse of an ideal legal order, which Cooper had championed in his earlier narratives and in his political essays. *The Ways of the Hour* moreover demonstrates to what extent the author's ideas about American literature as a democratic rhetoric and the creation of common fictions of the past in turn relied on a certain fiction of the law — what I have ventured to call the common law of fiction.

In order to better understand the complexities behind Cooper's polemical realism in his last novel, I will first take a closer look at *The Pioneers* (1823), the center piece of his political and legal fictions, and also at some of

15 Bardes/Gossett, "Cooper," 499.

16 Dekker, *James Fenimore Cooper*, 246.

17 Ickstadt, "American Democrat," 22.

the more convincing interpretations of the legal aspects in Cooper's work. My focus will be on the contrast that Cooper inscribes into the novel between the law as principle, that is, in its unwritten, invisible, or 'natural' form, on the one hand, and the law as a force, as a written, visible, and cultural phenomenon, on the other. The basic distinction between written and unwritten law, which I will subsequently discuss in regard to the American codification debate, must be regarded as a central functional relation within Cooper's fictions. More precisely, Cooper's idea of fiction depends on an inherent, naturalized 'Common Law' that governs the relation between the unwritten and the written 'codes' of democratic experience and reality.

III

Cooper's notions about the great potential and interest of American literature in 1828 display a degree of authorial self-assurance that is a far cry from Brown's agonizing bouts of self-criticism and self-doubt. "The literature of the United States," Cooper asserted in his *Notions of the Americans* (1828), "is a subject of the highest interest to the civilized world," whose power as a form of public rhetoric

> will be felt with a force, a directness, and a common sense in its application, that has never yet been known. If there were no other points of difference between this country and other nations, those of its political and religious freedom, alone, would give a colour of the highest importance to the writings of a people so thoroughly imbued with their distinctive principles, and so keenly alive to their advantage.[18]

American literature in Cooper's view was distinguished most of all by political institutions and principles and the collective experience they informed. Yet the function of "polite literature," as Cooper stated six years later in his *Letter to His Countrymen* (1834), was more than simply to "illustrate" the "peculiar principles of his country." Rather, literature was an "agency" to "enforce" these principles.[19] Cooper's choice of the term 'enforce' is peculiar yet revealing, particularly in the context of his attempted public defense against politically motivated criticisms. It clearly demonstrates the author's understanding of his fictions as deliberate and corrective interventions in political and public affairs — an understanding, however, which his contemporary readers did not entirely agree with. Cooper's unique attempt to defend him-

---

18 Cooper, *Notions of the Americans*, 359.
19 Cooper, *A Letter*, 98.

self publicly against the unfair and clearly politically motivated criticism of his so-called 'European' novels (*The Bravo, The Heidenmauer*) enraged the American public and press even more. Clearly, the author's understanding of a critical audience differed markedly from that audience's understanding of the function of 'polite' literature. In addition, the legalistic connotations of Cooper's terminology point to a close identification of literary and legal institutions and their democratic functions. And finally, any enforcement of principles, especially when it has to rely on rhetorical means, is a matter of potential power and sanctioned authority. Here Cooper's word choice is obviously meant to suggest the compatibility or even complementarity between law and literature. Both enforce the peculiar principles of American democracy. Yet, in the sense that these principles can only be transformed into social and political realities by enforcing the laws, the deeper implications of the particular term also suggest that the implementation of democratic principles can only be successful if literature, like law, can be enforced.

The strong presence of the law in Cooper's novels has scarcely escaped his readers. Critics have readily acknowledged the legal aspect as one central component which reconciles Cooper, the romantic historian, with Cooper, the social and political critic of his times and mores.[20] Indeed, The trial must be regarded almost as a basic structural element in Cooper's narratives, given the fact that there are trial scenes, according to McWilliams, "in twelve of [Cooper's] novels and impending trial alters the outcome of many more."[21] The representation of the law in its various manifestations in Cooper's narratives serves, on the one hand, as an essential element of dramatic composition, that is, as an important literary device. On the other hand, the law also marks the point where the literary converges with the political and the actual dimension of Cooper's national fictions. Cooper's legal fictions are always meant as political arguments and interventions. As John McWilliams has observed, "Cooper saw himself as a defender of American political values," and consequently "the search for political justice became the dominant concern of his fiction."[22] Building on "concepts of the law in their broadest sense," most of Cooper's narratives "rely upon legal conflicts."[23] Underlying these conflicts, critics like McWilliams, Charles Adams, and Robert Ferguson, among others, have observed a basic opposition between the laws of nature

---

20 See, for example, Thomas, *Cross-Examinations*; Dimock, *Residues of Justice;* and Smith, *Law and American Literature.*

21 McWilliams, *Political Justice*, 15.

22 McWilliams, *Political Justice*, 5.

23 McWilliams, *Political Justice*, 15.

and those of men that informs Cooper's literary perspective on American law and society. A short discussion of this common assumption will demonstrate that the categorization has its problems if we want to understand the function of Cooper's law in (and for) his literature.

As McWilliams states, the "primary function of Cooper's appeal to natural law … is to emphasize that natural law is the mirror of divine or moral law."[24] Consequently, "[w]henever Cooper theorizes about ideal political systems, natural, moral, and divine law become nearly interchangeable terms." This potential affinity between divine, moral, and natural law, McWilliams concludes, serves as the fundamental contrast which allows Cooper to judge human, i.e. civil law, in terms of political justice: "the measure of political justice [for Cooper] is the proximity of the civil to the divine law."[25] In contrast to this principal identity of natural and moral law with divine law, civil law appears to be merely the necessary result of an inevitable lack — or even impossibility — of identity. As McWilliams writes, the "necessity of having civil law, Cooper insists, arises from man's failure to live within the moral or divine law."[26] Paradoxically, then, Cooper's "view of government" is based on the recognition that although "natural justice must always be [the] standard, natural justice will always be perverted."[27]

What is most significant in this context is that the perversion of natural justice through the application — the enforcement — of civil laws can be, and must be, read as a problem of representation, or 'mirroring.' In other words, the chain of reflexive imitation that leads from divine to moral and finally to natural law is broken once civil law comes into play. Civil law in Cooper is simply another term for a legal order characteristic of human affairs and culture. This means that any cultural reproduction of natural law must fall short of the original, since human law will always lack the 'identical principles' which ground the affinity of divine and moral laws. As we will see, this difference is negotiated in Cooper's narratives mainly through the inevitable conflict (and the subsequent reconciliation) between the unwritten — as the natural — and the written — as the cultural code of law. The major problem of Cooper's law is thus characterized by a conflict of representation: how can cultural (i.e. man-made) law legitimately represent (or stand in place of) natural law, and how can it be made to preserve rather than to pervert the principles of the latter.

---

24 McWilliams, *Political Justice*, 18.
25 McWilliams, *Political Justice*, 19.
26 McWilliams, *Political Justice*, 21.
27 McWilliams, *Political Justice*, 18.

What I wish to emphasize as one of the main threads of my discussion of Cooper's laws, however, is that, in contrast to more familiar readings of his novels, I do not understand the problem of representation as arising from the conflict between natural and civil law. In fact, I would like to argue the reverse, namely, that the legal conflict in Cooper is indeed another way of staging and solving the vicissitudes of cultural representation. The conflict of different legal orders in Cooper's fictions is also, and most emphatically, a conflict of different literary or, more precisely, rhetorical orders and their principles of authorization.

The law in Cooper's novels thus describes a space of cultural contest where various conflicting claims have to be tested and negotiated — they are quite literally put on trial. But this central conflict is legal in more than one sense. On the one hand, as has been said, it often involves, or is engendered by, the violation of rights or laws. On the other hand, however, it is legal in the sense that it always addresses an implicit inconsistency within the law, presenting a potentially dangerous contradiction between different notions of justice, rights, and legal authority, which is made explicit in Cooper's novels precisely by the struggle between warring factions and interests, both individual and collective. For Cooper, legal conflicts thus become the mark of American identity. In fact, the very possibility of American identity, understood both in its individual and collective sense, relies on the proper use and function of the law.[28] The inherent problem in Cooper's novels sketched out by Adams in this passage is characterized in a fashion similar to McWilliams' conflict of laws. Like McWilliams, Adams stresses the problem of representation at the core of Cooper's interest in the law. The legitimacy of the law can only be judged according to an "abiding standard": the coherence and comprehensiveness of the "picture of man" represented by the law. Also like McWilliams, Adams distinguishes between the natural and the unnatural as the fundamental difference which Cooper draws in his novels between legitimate and illegitimate forms of legal representation:

---

[28] Adams puts a similar thesis in more universalist terms, when he writes: "Central to Cooper's investigations of the legitimacy of law is his conviction that the law is always essentially an interpretation of human nature, and that the abiding standard for judging its interpretation at a given historical moment is the extent to which it provides a coherent picture of man, and functions as a means of promoting cohesiveness in society" (*Guardian of the Law*, 19). My point is that for Cooper the law is the central institution and practice for the definition of an American identity — American democracy is defined by its legal system.

> When the law divides man unnaturally into warring legal and nonlegal selves, or when it facilitates the disruption of social bonds by individuals willing to manipulate legal forms and rhetoric for personal ends, the law loses its legitimacy.[29]

The major problem with such a strict distinction, as I understand it, must be seen in the use of terms like 'natural law' or 'law of nature' as if these were clearly defined by Cooper. This somewhat skews the perspective on Cooper's fictions of the law, especially when these fictions are read as legal histories. Robert Ferguson, for instance, describes Cooper's crucial theme as "the unfolding nature of the republic of laws in American culture."[30]

In his comparison of three of Cooper's novels, *The Pioneers* (1823), *Home as Found* (1838), and *The Ways of the Hour* (1850), Ferguson states that even though each of the works in question presents a different stage in the social and cultural development of American civilization, the dramatization of the legal process in all of them is motivated by the same concern: "The problem, as Cooper makes clear, is that the law has been displaced from its *natural* function."[31] On closer inspection, this phrase obviously does imply more than just one thing. On the one hand, if 'function' designates the purpose, performance, or office of the law, the term 'natural' may be assigned either to the character, or, indeed, 'nature' of the law's office: its unhampered performance free from any regulative or artificial intervention. On the other, 'natural' may point to the effect or result of the law's performance. The two meanings may be easily reconciled by arguing, for instance, that the natural performance of the law will lead to equally natural effects. But the two aspects will always diverge exactly when the 'natural function' of the law is in question; that is, once the law appears to be 'displaced' from its natural function, we are forced to ask what precisely decides the natural function of the law — its performance or its results? This is also the dilemma at the heart of the codification debate, with the codifiers arguing for more regulation and the traditionalists fighting against the law's further displacement from its natural form and function. Ferguson can, of course, hardly be criticized for lack of discussion of the very problem he detects as central in Cooper's novels.

---

29 Adams, *Guardian of the Law*, 19.

30 Ferguson, *Law and Letters*, 298.

31 Ferguson, *Law and Letters*, 299. His interest in Cooper, however, is focused on the latter's exemplary expression of the general decline of legal optimism in American culture between 1800 and 1850. From this perspective, the novelist's work may appear even more subject to a common development from 'vision' to 'despair' in American legal culture.

But if we agree with Ferguson, Adams, and McWilliams that Cooper's central critical concern was the perversion of natural law by civil law, or the displacement of the law from its natural function, the law represented in his fictions must appear 'displaced' twice over. Cooper's law is not presented in its 'natural,' but in a fictional form, and moreover, the law in Cooper's fictions has lost its natural function and thus its natural lawfulness. As Ferguson remarks, none of Cooper's novels depict the law in its "natural" function, since all "take place in Cooper's middle period or least inviting stage of civilization,"[32] where the law has been turned into an instrument in the struggle for wealth and power. Ferguson is referring to Cooper's model of progress and civilization which the latter described in *Home as Found* (1838): "using human development as a metaphor, Cooper … describe[s] the three stages in the growth of the new country from childhood through adolescence to adulthood."[33] The Templeton community in *The Pioneers* is somewhere between an early state, characterized by the "careless association" between the members, and the evolving state of a more competitive and agonistic social formation, characterized by "struggles for place … and the jealousy of competing families." The final, ideal state is described by Cooper's opening panoramic view of the New York country side in *The Pioneers*, which shows the most mature state of social organization where "man and things come within the control of more general and regular laws."[34]

The question is how Cooper nevertheless manages to establish the very idea or concept of the 'naturalness' of the law. Thus, at the core of Cooper's representation of the law there appears to be a paradox. On the one hand, the law cannot be represented in its natural function because as a social and cultural phenomenon, it always appears displaced. On the other hand, only through the representation of its absence, or more precisely, its representative (i.e. symbolic) negation, can the natural function of the law assume the status of a principle that should be enforced. This would suggest that, in regard to the law's natural function, legal enforcement and literary representation cannot be separated; in fact, literature may become the only way to both represent and enforce this function.

There is, of course, much evidence to be found to support interpretations which highlight the oppositional structure of Cooper's notion of social pro-

32 Ferguson, *Law and Letters*, 299.
33 Ferguson, *Law and Letters*, 298.
34 Significantly, the 'big picture' at the beginning of the novel leaves out what Cooper states as a necessity in *Home as Found,* the "division into castes that are all more or less rigidly maintained" (qtd. in Ferguson, *Law and Letters,* 299).

gress, and the advance of American civilization, as it is represented not only in the Leatherstocking tales, but also in his other fictions. However, the persuasive power of binaries like nature versus culture, freedom versus law, individual versus community, etc., only comes at a certain price. Especially where the role of the law in Cooper is concerned, these convincing categorizations may in turn enforce a much too categorical reading of the 'kinds of law' which are at stake in Cooper. What is worse, they may suggest that *the* law in Cooper could be defined and localized, as it were, precisely on either side of the dividing line between nature and culture.

The identification of nature with 'natural laws' and culture with 'civil laws,' respectively, has also become widely accepted in interpretations that focus on the legal dimension in Cooper's work. Since *The Pioneers* holds such a domineering status in relation to Cooper's other fictions, this identification is used as a yard stick even where Cooper is definitely not discussing 'nature' or 'natural law' at all. Yet, the distinction between 'natural' and 'civil' law in this way is unfortunate and misleading: not only does it reduce Cooper's range of legal representations to its most obvious extremes, but it also, and more importantly, misunderstands Cooper's notions about the nature of a civil legal order and its literary 'enforcement.' A close look at the legal conflict at the heart of Cooper's *The Pioneers* will help to clarify this issue.

IV

In his thorough discussion of *The Pioneers,* McWilliams states that Cooper uses a "trivial and local event," i.e. Leatherstocking's killing a deer out of season, and the resulting trial in order to express in length his ideas "concerning the nature of political justice and the necessity of law on the American frontier."[35] Smith's earlier assessment of Cooper's "conflict of allegiances" and of the novel's "genuine ambivalence"[36] in regard to a 'natural' versus a 'cultural' order is rejected by McWilliams. Instead, he describes the legal conflict and its solution as steps within the stadial logic of cultural evolution:

> If we apply the *Second Treatise on Civil Government* to *The Pioneers*, we find that Cooper's characterization of Natty Bumppo exactly corresponds to Locke's definition of the just man in a State of Nature. Judge Temple, however, exactly corre-

---

[35] McWilliams, *Political Justice*, 101.
[36] Smith, *Virgin Land*, 61, 62.

> sponds to Cooper's definition of the just man in a State of Civilization. *The Pioneers* records the evolution from one state into the other. … As the life of the hunter yields to the life of the farmer, so must natural justice yield to civil justice.[37]

While McWilliams insists that the conflict between Natty and the Judge may not be read as Cooper's internal struggle and that the two representatives of different stages of settlement should not be compared by the same standards, his initial distinction between natural and civil justice becomes the very foundation of his comparative interpretation of the legal concepts which each of the characters apparently represents. Leatherstocking is "governed by natural laws," and consequently, "he does not recognize the validity of the civil law at all." Indeed, as McWilliams argues, Cooper seems to indicate that the civil law does not have "any jurisdiction over a hero such as Natty, who has prior natural rights, belongs to an earlier state of civilization, and is governed by a superior moral law."[38] Judge Temple, on the other hand, personifies the notion of the law as a necessary means to maintain social order and the survival of the frontier community: "[F]or Judge Temple, as for Fenimore Cooper, the civil law is the only guarantee of liberty," and his "legalistic attitudes … stem from his recognition that a frontier community has special need for the strict discipline of law."[39] Leatherstocking's adversary thus "exemplifies Cooper's definition of a just judge."[40]

In his attempt to do justice to both Natty's position and that of the Judge, however, McWilliams finally defines Leatherstocking as an anachronistic figure just like his Indian companion, Chingachgook, alias John Mohegan. Their heroic antics may be admirable, yet they can no longer be accepted in the more advanced civilized society which Judge Temple is trying to establish and maintain through his laws. For McWilliams, Cooper's conflict of alliances is thus resolved by reference to the inevitable logic of genealogical succession and cultural development. More precisely, Natty's fate stands for the complete revision and replacement of an older, pre-revolutionary order and the notions of natural law and justice it was built on by a new, instutionalized legal order and its cultural manifestations. He concludes that

> Natty's resentment against civilization, his reliance on moral rather than civil law, are heroic, compelling and true within the context of the … wilderness. *The Pioneers,* however, describes a frontier that is rapidly being settled and institutional-

---

37 McWilliams, *Political Justice*, 102.
38 McWilliams, *Political Justice*, 112, 113.
39 McWilliams, *Political Justice*, 119, 117.
40 McWilliams, *Political Justice*, 117.

> ized … Surrounded by the institutions of a village, Natty and Mohegan may still be heroic and compelling, but their views cannot be true in any meaningful sense. Within a settled society, they are magnificent anachronisms.[41]

Yet Cooper's play of interrelated opposites can be read both ways and does not necessarily present an inherent, or inevitable, contradiction at the heart of American democratic individualism. The problem with McWilliams' categorizations is that his descriptive terminology undermines his initial claim that Natty's and Judge Temple's notions of justice and law must be incompatible because they belong to different stages of social settlement and progress. Even if this was the case, their comparison would appear perfectly justifiable, given the fact that Cooper continuously encourages his readers to assume a simultaneous perspective on both characters and thus on the legal concepts they stand for and try to defend.

Instead, Cooper's "fiction[s] of self-sufficient individualism," as Brook Thomas has argued, have played an important, but rarely recognized role for the cultural understanding of the alleged function of law and legal order in the United States. Commenting on Cooper's treatment of the law in *The Pioneers*, Thomas remarks that many Americans look at the law both as a necessity and as a potential threat to their individual freedom. Yet most cultural notions about the law and its role as a civilizing force are taken from literary works and popular culture and are much less the result of accurate historical knowledge. While *The Pioneers,* as Thomas states, can hardly be said to truthfully "reflect a historical reality," Cooper obviously found a most "persuasive way to narrate the conflict between the individual and the law that so many Americans have felt."[42] Cooper's novel thus stages the legal conflict in *The Pioneers* as a confrontation between individual freedom and collective order. As a consequence, most readers feel that there really is no other choice than to sacrifice one man's freedom for the good of the greater part. This feeling of the unbending force of necessity, however, does not reflect the development of American law in the nineteenth century, as Thomas concludes:

> Natty's sacrifice, though lamentable, [appears] inevitable, because Judge Temple's laws are necessary for the orderly civilizing of America. We get a very different sense of the conflict when we juxtapose Cooper's fictional narrative with an interpretation of antebellum law relying on the evidence of actual court cases and statutes. Judge Temple's legal order may not have been the only possible order available.[43]

---

41 McWilliams, *Political Justice*, 102–03.

42 Thomas, *Cross-Examinations*, 21.

43 Thomas, *Cross-Examinations*, 21–22.

The ideal of the individual's natural freedom and rights in Cooper's fictions serves as the mythical foundation of legal justice and order as legitimate restraints on the individual's social freedom and rights. Like Robinson Crusoe, Thomas states, Leatherstocking Natty Bumppo is thus the "necessary fictional product[]" of an "individualistic ideology" central to Jacksonian democracy and its agrarian ideal of independent yeomen, which celebrated natural freedom while "advancing market capitalism."[44]

Thomas' interpretation of *The Pioneers* offers an important revision of the dominant readings of Cooper's fiction in terms of the parallel evolution of American legal order and the progress of a democratic civilization. I would like to extend this revision in reformulating its main premise in a more dialectical fashion. What interests me here is the necessary function of the law for the kind of literature Cooper defined as an agency for the enforcement of democratic principles. For it seems to me that Cooper's Judge Temple is as much a necessary fiction as his counterpart, Natty Bumppo. If we agree with Thomas that one should not read Cooper's characters as representing mutually exclusive legal orders, we may go one step further and read them as presenting mutually dependent and complementary fictions. The struggle between 'natural' and 'civil' law could thus be recast as an argument between two distinct, yet closely related models of 'lawful fictions.'

Judge Temple's law aims as much at civilizing the wilderness as it attempts to regulate and keep in check the excesses of civilization — including those of the law. In fact, this is where the real conflict of the novel must be situated: an internal conflict within the law, or rather, an inherent contradiction between the abstract legal principles on which the Judge's authority and power rest and the concrete practice of the law, i.e. the way this power is used on others. Natty's confrontation with the law is exactly the result of a manipulative scheme by Hiram Doolittle, the magistrate, and the 'real legal villain' in *The Pioneers.* Only through Doolittle's misuse of the power of his office does the central legal confrontation in the trial of Leatherstocking become possible. As Adams comments: "the entire series of Natty's misfortunes with the law results from Hiram's ability to use his legal power — specifically his power to obtain a search warrant — to satisfy his curiousity and greed regarding the silver ore that he thinks Leatherstocking and his friends are mining on the far side of Mt. Vision."[45] The way, however, in which the fatal search warrant is obtained deserves a closer look because here Cooper exam-

---

[44] Thomas, *Cross-Examinations*, 42.
[45] Adams, *'Guardian of the Law,'* 65.

ines how the transfer of legal power and authority from the abstract, or symbolic, to the concrete, or practical, runs counter to the intentions of the law itself. When the complaint is presented to the Judge, the latter has just learned that Leatherstocking saved the life of his daughter and her friend, Louisa Grant, when they had been attacked by a panther in the woods. The Judge's personal feelings are therefore rather favorable towards Natty, which only highlights the inherently contradictory nature of the legal process that is triggered by the search warrant. After the magistrate has assured Temple that "we will have a pretty dull court," he carefully leads the Judge through the prospective cases. His remarks about "some folks" who "talk of a deer or two being killed out of season" are answered by the Judge with a strong commitment to the enforcement of his laws: "'Let a complaint be made, by all means,' cried the Judge; 'I am determined to see the law executed, to the letter, on all such depredators.'" Only then does the magistrate come forward with his own complaint, and the Judge realizes "how completely he had been caught by the other's cunning."[46]

Part of the success of Doolittle's strategy relies on the fact that the Judge cannot overlook a violation of the law once it is formally placed before him. The magistrate thus forces the Judge into issuing formal commitments to the law which he then cannot revoke without impairing his authority. As both the judge and his magistrate know quite well, a great deal of Temple's power rests on his reputation, i.e. his authority is legitimate because it is accepted by most parts of the Templeton community.[47] This symbolic understanding is made even more obvious by the fact that Doolittle asks for a search warrant which he could have easily and quite legally issued himself. His answer to Judge Temple's angry question, "thou art a magistrate … why bother me with the matter?," also demonstrates why Doolittle needs to secure the highest authority possible in this matter:

> "Why, seeing it's the first complaint under the law, and knowing the Judge set his heart on the thing, I thought it best that the authority to sarch [sic!] should come from himself. Besides, as I'm much in the woods, among the timber, I don't altogether like making an enemy of the Leather-stocking. Now the Judge has a weight in the county that puts him above fear. … But if the Judge don't conclude to issoo [sic!] the warrant, I must go home and make it out myself."

---

46 Cooper, *The Pioneers*, 328, 329, (in the following *P* with page number).

47 Adams severely misunderstands this aspect — see Adams, *'Guardian of the Law,'* 64. "Pride," as Adams has it, is much too weak a term for the Judge's need to preserve his symbolic power, a need that is described by Bourdieu, *Language and Symbolic Power,* 129.

> "I have not refused your application, sir," said Marmaduke, perceiving, at once, that his reputation for impartiality was at stake; "go into my office, Mr. Doolittle, where I will join you, and sign the warrant." (*P*, 329)

Even though Doolittle's office already comes with the authority to issue search warrants, provided that the formal conditions of a complaint — an oath by at least two witnesses — are met, he nevertheless insists on the Judge's signature. One reason is the nature of the law that is to be enforced. The game laws have just been introduced by the Judge and are an important part of his ideal of civilization and progress as orderly and regulated, that is, lawful processes.[48] Yet these laws still exist only as an abstract principle; they have not yet been enacted. To become a reality and, more importantly, to become enforceable as a rule, there must be a precedent. Since the law in question has not yet been added to the accepted corpus of legal rules (the game laws are statutes, not part of the Common Law), its legitimacy rests on the authority of its author. Thus, what the magistrate insists upon is the signature of the Judge as the creator and author of the law, since this alone will allow him to assume the authority of the law in turn. Moreover, the cunning officer also hopes that the signature will protect him in case his warrant is met with resistance. The act of transferral of the symbolic power of the law thus works as a magical transformation of persons and things: by signing the warrant, the Judge transfers his power to a piece of paper and in this form hands it to the magistrate. This in turn allows the magistrate to assume the authority of the Judge; any resistance against the warrant and the magistrate thus turns into an attack on the Judge and the law itself.

The initial signature of the warrant then starts a chain of transfers, ending with the crucial encounter between Leatherstocking and the law that will lead to his indictment and trial. Cooper carefully describes this chain as a deliberate manipulation of legitimate entrustment in which letters, writings, and books are the prime means and medium of transfer. In a very literal way, Judge Temple's emphatic demand to execute the law "to the letter" can only be fulfilled by enforcing the law *through* letters. Enforcement here becomes completely a matter of authority based on and transferred by written or printed documents.

Thus, Magistrate Doolittle's first step is to swear in Billy Kirby, the woodchopper who, as Cooper notes, "prided himself on the powers of the physical man, like all who have nothing better to boast of" (*P*, 333). Kirby's

---

48 As the Judge later explains to his daughter: "Society cannot exist without wholesome restraints … the laws alone remove us from the condition of the savages" (*P*, 383).

qualities are indeed exactly what Doolittle will need in order to enforce the law by translating its abstract principle into very concrete effects. Like most of his fellow settlers, Kirby is primarily interested in the pecuniary aspects of his prospective legal office, but Cooper also keeps an eye on the details of the process:

> "What's the fees?" said Kirby, laying his large hand on the leaves of a statute-book, that Hiram had opened in order to give dignity to his office, which he turned over, in his rough manner, as if he were reflecting on a subject, about which he had, in truth, already decided; "will they pay a man for his broken head?"
>
> "They'll be something handsome," said Hiram.
>
> "Damn the fees," said Billy, again laughing … and, stretching out his broad hand, with the palm downward, he said, keeping his eyes fastened on his own bones and sinews —
>
> "Come, give us a touch of the book. I'll swear, and you'll see that I'm a man to keep my oath." (*P,* 332–33)

It is hardly imaginable that the book on which Kirby swears would be the very same statute-book he had already touched before. However, in this way Cooper underlines again that the authority and the binding force of the oath relies on statutes, that is, written law. Ironically, the abstract principles of the written law can only unfold their power over people and their actions when they are brought into physical contact with its material medium, the statute-book, or, in Natty's case, the search-warrant as a written document. Therefore, before Leatherstocking can be brought to the letter of the law, the letter of the law has to be delivered to him, as Cooper comically, but truthfully has the wood-chopper explain to Natty: "the good people of the state have been writing you a small letter, and they've hired me to ride post. … If you can read it it's all well, and if you can't, here's Squire Doolittle at hand to let you know what it means" (*P,* 334–35). Not surprisingly, the old trapper, who had prided himself earlier that he "never so much as looked into a book, or larnt [sic!] a letter of scholarship" (*P,* 134) and therefore has lived outside the reach of the written law, does not respond to Kirby's offer, who is quite willing to leave the matter at that. Yet to enforce the statute, the letter has to reach its destination, as the magistrate well knows:

> But Hiram, emboldened by the advance of the deputed constable, now ventured to approach also, and took up the discourse with the air of authority that became his commission. His first measure was to read the warrant aloud, taking care to give emphasis to the most material parts, and concluding with the name of the Judge in very audible and distinct tones. (*P,* 335)

Cooper describes Leatherstocking's reaction to this performance of the law as a subtle reminder of the real foundations of the magistrate's legal power:

"Did Marmaduke Temple put his name to that bit of paper!" (*P*, 336). The tone of this exclamation vacillates between irritation and resignation, yet the message is clear: in Natty's eyes, the power remains with the name and the person of the Judge; the warrant, however, is just a piece of paper. For the old hunter, there is no transfer of legal authority from the Judge to the paper and thus to the magistrate — and much less so in the transfer from the magistrate to his sworn deputy, Billy Kirby. Legal authority, for Leatherstocking, always stays with the person. More precisely, the power of the law can only rest in, and emanate from, an immediate presence; enforcement thus can only mean force. This understanding is also obvious in Leatherstocking's repeated references to physical harm during the attempted search of his hut. Violation of the law thus can only mean, quite literally, violence against things or persons.

For Natty, the law — as an enforceable rule — does not exist in the abstract, only in the concrete, physical form; Natty does not understand the law as a purely formal procedure. When Doolittle tries to assure him that the search would be "nothing but form" and suggests to "go in and talk the thing over in reason" (*P*, 336), the old man immediately interprets the gesture as an infringement of his rights and as a direct attack on his person and property. This literal, physical interpretation of the attempted entry of magistrate Doolittle and his constable is fatal since it helps to turn the violation of a statute, i.e. civil law, into a crime under the Common Law. In other words, Natty's defense of his hut against magistrate Doolittle and constable Kirby not only prevents the enforcement of the new game law, but his physical resistance also questions the principle of legal enforcement itself; Natty has indeed, as the Sheriff puts it, "set an example of rebellion to the laws" (*P*, 355). The tragic irony of Natty's incapability to understand and properly react to the symbolic power of the law becomes very clear in his subsequent trial.

In the central trial, Cooper highlights the internal conflict within the law by confronting its principles with its practice and by revealing that enforcement without principle must lead to obvious injustices. Yet Cooper's method is not a simplistic denunciation of injustice and the perversion of legal principles. His perspective on the legal proceedings is rather characterized by mild irony and a keen eye for the absurdities and the incomprehensibilities of the process, which are especially obvious in the laywers' penchant for a language which is "ancient," "vague," and apt to "utterly confuse the faculties" of their audience (*P*, 361, 365, 368). For Adams, Cooper's ironic emphasis on formulaic legal terminology and the misunderstandings resulting from it point at "the law's linguistic rigidity" and reveal the "extreme dependence" of legal procedure on language.[49] He concludes that Cooper's intention in the trial is to show the "extent to which the culture which threatens Natty is a verbal one":

> In this sense the misunderstandings in the trial sharpen our perception of the central conflict in *The Pioneers* as one between two value systems, one spontaneous and the other formulaic. The intention of the legal system described here is to translate into professional tropes the existence of an individual the basis of whose life is intuitive. The effect is to devalue Natty's individuality by linguistically turning his acts into a mere reflection of the law's social and intellectual basis. The law's purpose, in essence, is to rearticulate the world, and thus force life to wear the mask constructed by its conventions.[50]

There is a lot to be said for such a reading, and especially for the focus on the linguistic violence which is so obviously displayed in Cooper's description of the trial proceedings and which will help us to understand why the trial and its language are so important for Cooper's idea of literary enforcement.[51] I find it appropriate, though, to first point out again that the sharp contrast stressed by Adams, between the formulaic rigidity of the law and Natty's intuitive and spontaneous individuality, must be read in both ways. That is, through Cooper's emphasis of the law's formal rigidity, legal language not only appears completely and utterly inadequate for the description and translation of the existence of an individual. It also ironically turns Natty into an exemplary individual in the first place. The paradoxical nature of the process is essential: what makes Natty Bumppo a tragic hero is exactly his open victimization by the enforcement of the law for the law's sake. Even Adams has to acknowledge that Cooper does not condemn the system as a whole. For the tragedy of legal enforcement also concerns the Judge, who is very well aware that he, too, has become subjected to the force of the law — the force which springs from its unsolved internal conflicts. Yet, in contrast to Adams' statement about Judge Temple's tragic predicament of being "often forced to wear a public mask that violates his private convictions," I believe that Cooper's foremost interest was to show how much the Judge is moved by Natty's verbal plea. More importantly, there is a decisive difference between the legal rhetoric of the lawyers on both sides and the way the law is spoken by the Judge. This difference is most obvious in his instructions to the jury, so often quoted by the critics, where Temple also surprisingly links his demand for the necessary protection of civil legal order with an expla-

49 Adams, *'Guardian of the Law,'* 62.

50 Adams, *'Guardian of the Law,'* 62.

51 On the violence in Cooper's verbal exchanges, see also the brilliant essay by Cheyfitz, "Frontier of Translation."

nation of the old man's motives that opens a potential alternative for the jury's verdict:

> It was now the duty of the Judge to deliver his charge. It consisted of a short, *comprehensive* summary of the testimony, laying bare the *artifice* of the prisoner's counsel, and placing the *facts* in so *obvious* a light that they could not well be misunderstood. "Living as we do, Gentlemen," he concluded, "on the skirts of society, it becomes doubly necessary to protect the ministers of the law. If you believe the witnesses, in their construction of the acts of the prisoner, it is your duty to convict him; but if you believe that the old man, who this day appears before you, meant not to harm the constable, but was acting more under the influence of habit than by the instigations of malice, it will be your duty to judge him, but to do it with lenity. (*P*, 368–69; my emphases)

Asking the jury for leniency is, of course, a rather inconsequential attempt to counter the clear language of the facts of the case. Mercy in legal matters is something which lies outside the jury's office, which concerns matters of fact, not law (a distinction that serves as an essential element of Common-Law adjudication). Nevertheless, the judge here offers an important insight into his own explanation of the motives behind Natty's resistance. The latter's "rebellion to the law," Temple's charge makes clear, may have been completely unintended, a result of an habitual attitude towards any infringement of what he thinks are his 'natural' rights. But the jury can only convict or acquit the defendant, and with so little room to move the double necessity to protect the law is interpreted by the jury members as including more than just deliberate acts of rebellion. Natty's disapproval of the 'new' law, which he has made clear throughout, may be acceptable as an opinion, yet his radical understanding and physical defense of what he presumes are his natural property rights has no place in the new legal order.

It is significant that Cooper has the jury, and not the judge, decide about the limitations of those rights which Natty tried to defend with his trusty rifle. While Leatherstocking is soon acquitted of the first (and minor) charge of assaulting magistrate Doolittle, who after all had no legal right to enter the trapper's cabin, the jury wastes little time in pronouncing Natty guilty of threatening constable Billy Kirby, that is, an officer of the law, with a deadly weapon — of threatening the law itself, as it were. The way Cooper comments on this second, decisive verdict, however, is most peculiar. "There was but little surprise manifested in the court-room at this verdict," he states, almost a little disappointed, only to offer an explanation that surely is more surprising than the verdict: "the testimony, the greater part of which we have omitted, was too clear and direct to be passed over" (*P*, 369). The sudden appearance of the pronoun "we" reveals an invisible agency presiding over the courtroom proceedings, one that immediately draws a line between the trial as the space of legal enforcement and the literary representation of the trial as the imaginary enforcement of the law. The line, however, becomes obvious only through the transgression, or rather, the *presumption* of judicial practice: Cooper's literary authority asserts itself not by representation, but by omission.

The entire trial scene is thus marked by the continuous redaction of language on all levels; linguistic rigidity is indeed the mark of legal discipline, a mode of self-restraint which Judge Temple is at pains to enforce: "This is an improper place for such dialogues" (*P*, 367), he admonishes Billy Kirby when the witness strikes up a conversation with the defendant. In other words, in his apparently unobtrusive comment, Cooper reveals that, beyond the sphere of legal redaction and regulation in the courtroom, there is another even more powerful linguistic authority at work, which may deliberately omit precisely what the law cannot pass over.

Yet this revelation only emphasizes the significance of what is not omitted, that is, those parts of the trial which Cooper choses to describe in detail: the dialogues, indeed, that are not 'improper' but 'proper' in the confines of literary jurisdiction. This would explain why Cooper concentrates on certain aspects that may seem irrelevant, while he exempts other parts of the proceedings — especially the facts which are "too clear and direct" — from the literary record. On the one hand, this is to stress that while Leatherstocking's case may be clear to the law, it must appear far less so to literature. On the other hand, however, Cooper's strategy also signals the literariness — the potential literary function — of those aspects of the law that from a legal perspective may appear contradictory, highly conflictual, and even mutually exclusive, yet from the perspective of literature assume a different, and much more complementary character.

Here I have to return again to the question of 'verbal culture' versus 'nature' on the one hand, and the culture of writing, exemplified by the 'letter' of the law, on the other. What Cooper presents in the trial scene is clearly a struggle, yet not between two, but three different models of legal — or, better, lawful — rhetoric. The language of the law, Cooper suggests, may assume different rhetorical attitudes which in turn are shaped both by their respective sources and by the medium which dominates their arguments. Similar to the search warrant episode, the confrontation in the courtroom trial displays the gap between the letter of the law and the experience of the law as it is expressed in Leatherstocking's reactions and testimony. As a consequence, the reader is faced on one level with mutually exclusive models of verbal expression: the ancient and vague language of Common Law pleading is clearly incompatible with Leatherstocking's plain and simple speeches. On the other hand, however, Cooper also emphasizes the fact that, in contrast to lawyer Lippet (the defense counsel) and his colleague Dirk Van der School (the prosecutor), Judge Temple speaks the language of the law in such plain and simple fashion that the illiterate yeomen who compose the jury are all able to comprehend the facts of the case. In the preceding episode, Temple's legal authority and his capacities to enforce the law were clearly linked to written documents and to the transfer of legal power by writing and signature, thus revealing how much the mechanics of legal enforcement relied on the successful combination of form and symbolic power. In the trial, however, the Judge's power is much more direct, a matter of immediate address and utterance. In short, the Judge is able to negotiate between the two basic modes of lawful rhetoric that Cooper brings into confrontation in the trial.

While Temple knows the letter of the law and is well versed in the intricacies of Common Law pleading and procedure, he is not bound to formulaic legal rhetoric. In fact, he is the only one in the novel who is able to translate the letter of the law into comprehensive speech — and thus also the only one powerful enough to translate the letter of law into direct experience. Cooper takes great care to record both of Judge Temple's instructions to the jury, thus also calling attention to the fact that there are two charges which have to be decided separately. In both cases the jury obviously bases its verdict on Temple's remarks, which indicates how much the latter's ability to translate the incomprehensive legal rhetoric of the respective representatives of the defense and the prosecution into a clear basis for judgment. If, as Pierre Bourdieu remarks, even the "most rigorously rationalized law is never anything more that an act of social magic which works,"[52] Cooper's trial demonstrates how much translation must go into the effort to make the magic of the law succeed.

It appears obvious that Cooper, by calling attention to the different linguistic 'self'-representations of the law in this scene, wants his readers to critically judge opposing modes of lawful rhetoric. One that does indeed address and reach the people — and in this respect, at least, Leatherstocking and Judge Temple are two of a kind — and another that is incomprehensible to common sense, either because it is excessively formal ("delivered to the letter" [*P*, 362]), or because it is deliberately constructed as an "artifice" (*P*, 369). Since the law itself has been offended, these distinctions are important, and the question that Cooper wants his readers to ask is whose pleading is the most convincing. In other words, Cooper wants the law to speak for itself, to define and defend its jurisdiction by a mode of speech that is legit-

---

52 Bourdieu, *Language and Symbolic Power*, 42.

imate because it is comprehensive and convincingly eloquent. From this perspective, Natty and the Judge emerge from the trial scene as equally strong spokesmen for the respective conceptions of the law they represent. To describe Leatherstocking's conflict with the law as a conflict with the "verbal culture" of civilization, however, overlooks the latter's peculiar rhetorical abilities. In a very interesting earlier episode, Bumppo tells young Oliver Edwards, the secret claimant to Temple's property, about his favorite places in the wilderness. His vivid descriptions of spectacular sights from the mountains, but most of all the image he recalls of a waterfall hidden in the woods, are so impressive that the highly cultured Edwards praises the woodsman with amazement: "'You are eloquent, Leather-stocking!' exclaimed the youth" (*P*, 294). What impresses Edwards is the unexpected display of 'natural' eloquence that produces aesthetic effects by composing, as it were, images of nature after the conventions of landscape painting.[53] Even more impressive and moving is the old hunter's own appeal in his confrontation with the Judge which concludes his trial.

While Natty remained mostly silent during the legal proceedings which ended with the jury's verdict, his emotional charge to the Judge, after the latter has pronounced his judgment and the sentence, builds up into what is clearly meant by Cooper as another *literary* mode of pleading. Most critics have quite rightly taken the eloquent pathos of Leatherstocking as a signal for the central significance the image of natural law and justice sketched out by the old hunter has for Cooper himself. In the following, often quoted, passage, the roles between Leatherstocking and Temple are reversed, and the defendant assumes the rhetoric of prosecution and judgment. The most obvious sign of this reversal is Natty's censoring of Temple's attempts to speak:

> "Talk not to me of law, Marmaduke Temple," interrupted the hunter. "Did the beast of the forest mind your laws, when it was thirsty and hungering for the blood of your own child! She was kneeling to her God for a greater favor than I ask, and he heard her; and if you now say no to my prayers, do you think he will be deaf?
>
> "My private feelings must not enter into" —
>
> "Hear me, Marmaduke Temple," interrupted the old man, with melancholy earnestness, "and hear reason. I've travelled these mountains when you was no judge, but an infant in your mother's arms; and I feel as if I had a right and a privilege to travel them ag'in afore I die. Have you forgot the time that you come to the lake-shore, when there wasn't even a gaol to lodge in; and didn't I give you my own bear-skin to sleep on and the fat of a noble buck to satisfy the cravings of your

---

53 See my discussion of Cooper's ekphrastic rhetoric ("Pictorial Desires and Textual Anxieties").

> hunger? Yes, yes — you thought it no sin then to kill a deer! And this I did, though I had no reason to love you, for you had never done any thing but harm to them that loved and sheltered me. And now will you shut me up in your dungeons to pay me for my kindness? A hundred dollars! where should I get the money? No, no — there's them that say hard things of you, Marmaduke Temple, but you an't so bad as to wish to see an old man die in a prison, because he stood up for the right. (*P*, 370–71)

For most readers, the meaning of Leatherstocking's impassioned plea must appear clear enough. In a series of rhetorical questions, Natty exposes "the wickedness" (*P*, 370) of the law Judge Temple wants to enforce, and by reminding the latter of their common hunting days, the defendant even exposes the arbitrariness of the game laws. The main image of the argument, however, is a somewhat revised description of the state of nature as a rather precarious mode of existence. Man in the state of nature is endangered, both by wild animals that no human laws can tame and by their fundamental helplessness as individuals which makes them dependent on the help of others. This revision of the Lockean concept suggests a fundamental opposition between the laws of nature and the laws of man — but in a sense quite different from the conflict of legal orders expounded by McWilliams.

The central topoi in Natty's speech about the state of nature are not natural justice or the laws of nature — such terms are completely absent here — but human survival and the means of mere subsistence. Given these conditions, it is indeed hard to imagine any form of order, let alone a legal order, which could emerge from a state of natural existence so completely driven by necessity. The picture that Natty 'paints' may be eloquent and moving, yet on closer inspection it appears rather counterintuitive, since it in fact proves the Judge right in his efforts to "tame[] the wilderness" (*P*, 344). Cooper even, and not without irony, has Leatherstocking answer his own question, "why can't the law leave me to myself?" (*P*, 336), in a rather unexpected twist. Without the intervention of the law, the state of nature would persist — a point that, again ironically, both the Judge and Natty make the center of their respective arguments. Both may even agree that this state does not offer a stable or comfortable form of existence; in order to survive in nature, one has to become a part of it, like Leatherstocking. The main point of contention, however, is the character of economic and social relations which are implied by Natty's natural mode of existence. In this state, social intercourse and cohesion emerge from dependency alone and completely rest on the willingness of individuals to share what rudimentary possessions they call their own.

That Natty in the end again insists that he was merely standing up for his rights must appear surprising, if not contradictory. On first sight, his glimpse of the early settlement history apparently refers to the Lockean state of nature and to the natural property rights which for Locke already existed in this 'original' state.[54] Yet Cooper uses Leatherstocking's tale to mark the difference between the state of nature as a necessary — and desirable — *fiction* versus the state of nature as an undesirable and unjust reality. As McWilliams observes, for Locke there are "three deficiencies to justice in the State of Nature: the lack of established law, the lack of a single judge to decide the law, and the lack of a magistracy to execute the law."[55]

Natty's insistence on remaining within nature and without the law thus makes him a fictional character indeed; however desirable such an existence may appear for the individual imagination, it cannot serve as a foundation for collective survival. For Cooper, the danger lies in confusing the rights which the imagination of unlimited, unrestrained individualism presupposes with the real rights that are guaranteed and can be protected by real laws. The last point is essential, since the protection of rights, even imaginary rights, is always a matter of enforcement, which ultimately means the employment of force. Leatherstocking's rights are individualistic to the degree that their protection becomes a matter of direct physical resistance and violence between individuals. In *The Pioneers,* such an extreme individualistic understanding of laws and rights exists not only in Natty's natural state, but it also works as the basic motivation for most of the settlers and is a real threat to Judge Temple's ideal of a civilized society. The obvious similarities between the Lockean state of nature and Natty's way of life in the wilderness notwithstanding, it does not follow that Natty's rights to his hut and the land it stands on (let alone the deer on the estate) are more 'natural' than the Judge's property claims. In fact, Locke's famous dictum, "in the beginning all the world was America," only states what served as the legal foundation for English charters granted to the early settlers. America was indeed a *res nullius,* another legal fiction which the state of nature theory was meant to support. The judge's claims to the Otsego estates are thus secured both in terms of natural and Common Law property: first taken into possession by the Crown as a thing belonging to nobody, then granted to Temple and Major Effingham, the latter's part held in trust by the Judge after his death by drowning. In these transactions Natty had no part, and there is no way he could legally lay claim to something that is already secured by legal title. The "*kind* of natu-

54 McCoubrey stresses some points on Locke and the construction of property that are essential for my interpretation of 'nature' and 'natural rights' in Cooper (*Naturalist Legal Theory,* 69–70).

55 McWilliams, *Political Justice*, 117.

ral right" which the Judge concedes Natty may possess is indeed a privilege based on custom and granted by the real owner of the land. Of course, these 'English' legalities are supplemented by Cooper with American features; the Americanization of the Common Law in this respect includes the history of Indian grants or 'gifts' to white settlers, a 'fact' resting on the fiction of compatible concepts of property shared by Indians and white settlers. As it turns out, Edwards' challenge to Temple's property claims rests on his ignorance of the legal consequences of Locke's theory, which he only understands, as does Natty, in its emphasis on the individualistic foundations of property.

The legal order of Judge Temple is thus challenged on both sides by highly individualistic conceptions of law and rights; and the threat to Temple's authority as a restraining agency becomes especially clear near the end of the novel. When, in the midst of the devastating fire on Mount Vision, the Sheriff's posse launches its attack on the escaped Leatherstocking, the Judge tries to intervene in the name of peace and order: "Silence and peace! why do I see murder and bloodshed attempted! is not the law sufficient to protect itself, that armed bands must be gathered as in rebellion and in war, to see justice performed! … I command the peace!" (*P,* 435)

The question — "is not the law sufficient to protect itself?" — may sound merely rhetorical, given the impression that the Judge's power and authority can indeed put an end to the threat of social anarchy and the blatant misuse of the law.[56] Yet the question also points to the central problem of enforcement which the law must face in the frontier situation. Characteristically, though, Cooper does not reveal how effective Temple's effort to 'command' the peace actually is; on the contrary, the Judge's order is effectually supplanted by another, more powerful appeal, issued from a higher station: "'Hold! shed no blood!' cried a voice from the top of the Vision — 'Hold! for the sake of Heaven, fire no more! all shall be yielded! you shall enter the cave!'" The language strongly reminds one of Carwin's performances in *Wieland,* and Cooper leaves no doubt that its effects result from the successful combination of surprise and suspense: "Amazement produced the *desired effect.* Natty, who had reloaded his piece, quietly seated himself on the logs … while the 'Light infantry' ceased their military movements, and waited the issue in suspense" (*P,* 435, my emphasis). It also appears obvious that the latter appeal is the stronger one because it promises the satisfaction of the interests of all parties: "all shall be yielded!"

While the Judge can only demand submission to the abstract authority of the law which he personifies, the abstract voice from the mountain offers

---

[56] At least that is McWilliams' impression. See *Political Justice,* 115.

something in return: a visit to the mysterious cave, which presumably holds unknown riches and eventually presents the unexpected solution to the conflict of ownership between Oliver Edwards and Judge Temple. Even while Cooper does not comment on the almost comical contrast between the two appeals to law and order, it reveals for a short moment the weakness of the law and the power of literature. In exploiting a standard strategy of the sentimental novel and the gothic romance, i.e. the unravelling of a secret, Cooper contrasts, but at the same time also complements, the authoritative rhetoric of the law — "I command the peace!" with the literary promise of denouement — "You shall enter the cave!"

The promise is meant to prepare Cooper's readers for the final revelation of Edwards' identity, the clarification of Temple's disputed property claims and the restoration of legitimate legal authority. As Adams has noted, the novel's conclusion "describes a trial scene"[57] in which Judge Temple once again transfers his legal power, this time directly, to Oliver Edwards: "Thou shalt be thyself the judge" (*P,* 439). The formal congruence with the preceding trial signals a similar function of this last challenge to the authority and legitimacy of Judge Temple's legal power. And as before, Cooper contrasts the formalities of legal rhetoric with the persuasive power of a lawful rhetoric that bears all the marks of literature. At first the Judge tries to calm the enraged temper of the rightful heir to the estate by explaining to Edwards how, through a combination of unfortunate events, his efforts to preserve the rights of Edwards' father to the land and to further secure them after his death for his heirs had all failed, so that finally the land had fallen to him. This testimony is emphatically supported by the old German Major Fritz Hartmann, who has witnessed all of Temple's efforts: "He's true as ter steel! … [d]ere is not a hair as of ter rogue in ter het of ter Tschooge" (*P,* 438–39).

The most convincing evidence in the concluding trial, however, is a legal document, Marmaduke Temple's will, which he had felt his "sacred duty" to draft immediately after he received the first news of Edwards' father's death at sea (*P,* 275–78). The way Temple presents his testament to his youthful 'judge' demonstrates how much he trusts that the written document will finally exonerate him in the eyes of Edwards:

> "Read this paper, Oliver," said Marmaduke … "and thou wilt find that, so far from intending thy family wrong during life, it has been my care to see that justice should be done at even a later day." (*P,* 442)

---

57 Adams, *'Guardian of the Law,'* 69.

It is certainly significant that Cooper chooses to present a written legal document as crucial evidence and as an "undeniable testimony of the good faith of Marmaduke" (*P*, 443) in order to restore and legitimize the latter's authority. It is even more significant if we consider that this act of restoration is also meant to finally decide what lawful fiction must be — in the sense that its function is in turn sanctioned by the law. This is precisely why the Judge symbolically transfers his office to his prosecutor in the first place, because in this way Edwards can become a reading judge and a judging reader at the same time. And, quite appropriately, the Judge can assume the role of an author while still remaining a judge bound to legal procedure.

One should note first that the Judge's employment of his will is, legally speaking, improper. Even though it serves as a 'testimony' and is recognized as such, the disclosure of the will happens prematurely, before the Judge's death. Moreover, it is presented by the author of the will himself, which is quite unimaginable under normal conditions of lawful disclosure. Removed from its proper context, the legal document thus not only testifies to past events but also already announces the future. Adams describes this effect of the will accurately: "the written document makes the Judge's effort to do justice part of an intellectual structure with a unique ability to operate across generations to bind past, present, and future in a firm covenant of trust." The will thus restores to the law the "virtue of historical depth," as Adams concludes. Yet on closer inspection it appears obvious that this virtue is not due to the will's legal, but rather to its *literary* character. True enough, as Cooper notes, the will starts out "with the usual forms, spun out by the ingenuity of Mr. Van der School" (*P*, 442). But the description of the content which follows makes Adams' statement that "the will is full of legal phrases"[58] sound a little too sweeping. After the legal formalities are "fairly exhausted," Cooper writes,

> the pen of Marmaduke became plainly visible. In a clear, distinct, manly, and even eloquent language, he recounted his obligations to Colonel Effingham, the nature of their connexion and the circumstances in which they separated. He then proceeded to relate the motives of his long silence, mentioning, however, large sums that he had forwarded to his friend, which had been returned, with letters unopened. After this, he spoke of his search for the grandfather, who had unaccountably disappeared, and his fears that the direct heir of the trust was buried in the ocean with his father. (*P*, 443)

Temple's ability to break through the formal rigidity of the law and become visible as an author is due to the quality and style of his writing. Eloquent,

---

58 Adams, *'Guardian of the Law,'* 71.

clear, distinct, manly, these are the established virtues of classical rhetoric, both in law and in literature. These are also the qualities that Cooper claims for his own literary record, as the sentence that concludes the first part of the will suggests. Marmaduke's account appears only in paraphrase; this author's pen, at least, does not become visible to Cooper's readers. Like in the trial scene, Cooper acts as a censoring agency, restraining the full force of Temple's testimony to leave only those parts exposed which are of literary interest. After all, Cooper summarizes the Judge's tale, the latter only "recounting, in a clear narrative, the events which our readers must now be able to connect" (*P*, 443). *Our* readers: the pronoun clearly admits Cooper's possessive claims to his authorship. Since the Judge is only recounting the tale which Cooper has already unravelled for his readers, the Judge's document turns literary into legal rhetoric. Like Judge Temple, Cooper wants to clarify and assure property rights, and both also act as legators promising to hand on their rightful possessions to their "heirs at law" (*P*, 443).

The powerful fusion of legal and literary rhetoric into a lawful fiction has the desired effect, since Oliver Edwards, the reader and designated judge, is visibly moved when he receives the document:

> The youth took the paper, which his first glance told him was the will of the Judge. Hurried and agitated as he was, he discovered that the date corresponded with the time of the unusual depression of Marmaduke. As he proceeded, his eyes began to moisten, and the hand which held the instrument shook violently … The tears fell from the eyes of the young man, as he read this undeniable testimony of the good faith of Marmaduke … (*P*, 442–43)

Edwards here is described as a sentimental reader, who reacts to the psychological force of the document rather than to its legal form. This is only fitting, since the promise of future possession and authority, expressed in the rhetoric of legal succession and inheritance, can only become true if Edwards willingly accepts those parts of the document which relate the historical fiction on which both the Judge's claim and his own are based. Since Adams does not pay any attention to the function of the will in regard to Cooper's own interests and claims, he argues that the judge "puts his faith into formulaic prose, and merges his personal agency with the law's."[59] However, as I tried to show, the will presents at least a hybrid between a legal and a literary document. If the more legalistic second part of the will (where Temple details the conditions of the trust and the succession of his legacy) appears 'numbing,' the question is: for whom? Certainly not for the reader who is addressed in the first place, because Edwards seems pretty agitated

---

59 Adams, *'Guardian of the Law,'* 72.

and excited. While I do not doubt that the will as a legal document tries to project an image of the historical continuity of legal authority, it appears obvious to me that Cooper insists that this continuity and the legitimacy of legal power and property claims can only be enforced with the help of literary rhetoric.

The truth of the legal claims thus depends on the accepted truth of the "clear narrative" of events put into writing and signed by its author — a letter of the law, yet also a *belle lettre.* This placement of the reader, on the other hand, also positions the author. In other words, if the law in this way depends on the literary rhetoric of historical fictions, these fictions are acceptable only when their author, even though assigning his office symbolically to his readers, remains the real judge and the real authority in matters both legal and literary. Cooper thus assumes a stance similar to that of Lord Mansfield in the latter's opinion in the copyright cases; presumably acting as a Judge who merely interprets the legal principles inherent in the precedent, while, in fact, creating the foundational myths to authorize his lawful fictions.

The continuing challenge and the final restoration of legal authority is indeed a sequence of conflicts between various linguistic appearances of the law: the search warrant, the trial, the will. These appearances Cooper asks his readers to compare in regard to their justification and their potential enforcement. Thus, for instance, the search warrant is marked as unlawful even though it is perfectly legal. The letter of the law which the duplicitous magistrate employs to claim access to Natty's hut abuses the signature of its original author and thus the law itself, which Doolittle pretends to represent. In contrast to such unlawful representations that nevertheless have to be enforced to uphold the law, Judge Temple's will stands as the most perfect and persuasive example of lawful writing, whose enforcement, however, is due to its literary features and the force of the fiction it contains. It is moreover important to note that the Judge's testament offers a history of the settlement's early foundations which sharply contrasts with Leatherstocking's fiction of the state of nature. Both accounts are lawful in the sense that they presume an order based on concepts of laws and rights, which they want to preserve. Yet while Natty eloquently evokes a past before the existence of a collective or Common Law, the Judge describes, in all the details of legal language, a legal past that is always already ruled by Common Law contracts and titles, grants, patents, and entrustments. Consequently, the two fictions of the foundational history of American law follow different trajectories. While Leatherstocking projects the past onto the present and the future and celebrates the pathos of true origin and eternal order, his counterpart, the jurist, projects the future onto the past, celebrating in turn the pathos of progress based on principle. There is indeed a rather different ideal of history in Leatherstocking's and Judge Temple's fictions. For the former, history is an ongoing attempt at the imitation of the state of nature, an attempt which never fully succeeds, only, Cooper seems to suggest, in art. For the Judge, history is all creation, vitalized by progress and regulated by the law.

Drawing a distinction along these lines also allows us to overcome the allegedly irrevocable opposition between natural and civil law. While imitation in the strictest sense would exclude creation, creation in turn does not necessarily exclude imitation. The Judge's fiction thus has the advantage over Natty's since it may preserve the principles of natural law through the perfection of lawful creation. This, indeed, represents one of the founding ideas of American legal history and its attempts to naturalize the English Common Law.[60]

Cooper's particular fusion of law and literature in *The Pioneers* needs the fiction of Leatherstocking. Yet the reason, as the final chapter makes clear, again relates to the translation or transfer of authority from unwritten principles into writing. When the old hunter takes his final parting to vanish into his proper realm — the imaginary wilderness of the fictional state of nature — Cooper makes sure that Leatherstocking will stay, nevertheless. In the place where Natty's hut had been, there now stands a monument, a grave shared by the white and the Indian founding fathers of Cooper's Common Law, Major Effingham and John Mohegan. The monument's headstone is decorated with images of Indian life and warfare and bears an epitaph, which binds the living Leatherstocking to the two deceased friends. Of course, only the hunter understands the images: "There's something that I suppose is reading; but I can't make any thing of it; though the pipe, and the tomahawk, and the moccasins, be pretty well …" (*P*, 450). When Edwards reads the inscription aloud, Leatherstocking is startled "at the sound of his own name" and asks: "[s]how me the name, boy … let me see my own name placed in such honour: 'Tis a gin'rous gift to a man who leaves none of his name and family behind" (*P*, 452). Thus the transfer of Natty's name from the register of spoken language to that of a written text offers a symbolic remedy for the lack of genealogical continuity — on which, after all, both legal authority and property rights depend in *The Pioneers*. It also fixes his memory forever in the state of a "faithful servant" to the founders of the law and their descendants (*P*, 451). Before the real Natty must go so that his fiction may live forever, Cooper reminds the lawful heirs to Judge Temple's land and authority —

60 Indeed, as a state 'naturalizes' a foreign subject.

and his readers — once again of the invaluable service of the servant to his master, the law. When Edwards reads the epitaph of Natty's old Indian companion, John Mohegan, the illiterate hunter offers the cultured young Tory a lesson in linguistic correctness:

> "But what have ye put over the redskin?"
> "You shall hear: —
> "'This stone is raised to the memory of an Indian chief, of the Delaware tribe, who was known by the several names of John Mohegan; Mohican' —"
> "Mo-hee-can, lad, they call theirselves! 'he-can."
> "Mohican; 'and Chingagook' —"
> "'Gach, boy; 'gach-gook; Chingachgook, which, intarpreted, means Big Serpent. The name should be set down right, for an Indian's name has always some meaning in it." (*P*, 452)

The transfer of names and authority from experienced history to its written record is a delicate business, and there is always the danger that the true or original meaning of words becomes impaired or even lost in the process. But where, precisely, does that truth come from? The passage is clearly meant by Cooper to give priority to the spoken meaning saved by Leatherstocking's intervention. Yet, the complex play of parentheses, dashes, and other means of typography, which order the confusing switches between reading, quoting, correcting, and repeating, reveal the extent to which the meaning of speech is subject to the laws of writing and grammar. Moreover, we are tempted to wonder how the outspoken foe of books and letters can know that Edwards' pronunciations are the result of the misspelling of a name. How would he ever know when a name is "set down right" so its meaning can be preserved? In light of these questions, Edwards' assuring answer to Natty's admonition acquires a rather ambivalent sense: "I will see it altered" (*P*, 453). The promise of preservation turns into the announcement of inevitable change: "some meaning" will always be altered. And one of the first meanings to change is that which denotes the implied office of the faithful servant of original meanings in regard to Cooper's common law of literature. For Natty, interpretation means translation, the natural transfer of meaning and linguistic authority from one language to another, in fact, the faithful imitation of nature through language. Yet, as Eric Cheyfitz has convincingly argued, Cooper's novel stages this ideal of translation as natural imitation in order to mask "the rhetorical alienation of a language from itself."[61] This alienation is most obvious in the trial scene where the very terms 'law' and

---

[61] Cheyfitz, "Frontier of Translation," 58. For the distinction between oral culture and writing in *The Pioneers,* see also Dudensing, *Die Symbolik von Mündlichkeit und Schriftlichkeit.*

'right' continuously shift between the literal and metaphorical register of speech:

> While throughout *The Pioneers* Natty Bumppo and Judge Temple stand upon the same ground and ground their opposing arguments in the same term, *legal,* the alienation of the term from itself — its state of being in translation between what we usually term the literal and the metaphoric — calls into question the absolute literalness of all ground, the literalness of the literal, by suggesting the alienation of any term from itself, in asmuch as a term can never settle completely in a single context, but necessarily inhabiting a number of contexts simultaneously, comes to unsettle itself with its own foreigness when these contexts conflict …[62]

Leatherstocking's tragic fate thus allegorizes the vanishing ideal of legal principles untouched by adversary rhetoric and hence by interpretation; his fiction, however, is meant by Cooper to establish a 'law of writing,' based on the unwritten, imaginary laws of history. The term 'law of writing' is Adams',[63] a rather fortunate phrase for my purposes, although I do not subscribe to the strict definition attached to it. It is meant less to block the assaults of 'verbal culture' against the meaning and properties of law and literature. The law of writing, as I understand it, rather aims at the regulation of writing according to an ideal of unwritten, original principles of linguistic order — a founding speech as the foundation of speech. This is what the monument stands for: the depth and tribute which writing owes to speech even as it drives the latter from the common ground of meaning. Like natural laws, natural eloquence can only survive in fiction, yet this survival is the very legitimation of writing as a substitute for speech. Bumppo's tragic alienation thus may be said to be Cooper's as well, since his written narrative of events, too, becomes displaced, like the law, from the natural function of spoken language.

The delicate balance between the conflicting roles of author and judge and correspondingly between those of readers and interpreters, as Cooper was to find out, cannot be upheld for long without effort, especially when readers are no longer as trusting and as easily moved as Oliver Edwards. For Cooper, the increasing criticism of his work after his return from Europe felt like a revolt against the common law of literature and its enforcement, a revolt he linked in his writing to the mounting forces of legal reform and the codification of the American Common Law. This will be the focus of the conclusion of this chapter.

---

62 Cheyfitz, "Frontier of Translation," 81.
63 Adams, *'Guardian of the Law,'* 78.

V

Cooper's ideal of a commonwealth "under the dominion of mild laws" (*P,* 15) rests, as we have seen, on the delicate balance between natural liberty and rights on the one hand and cultural restraints and laws on the other. The stability of this balance in turn presupposes a specific interdependence between the realm of unwritten and written meaning — both in law and literature. In fact, the presence of the unwritten *in* the written and therefore the enforcement of natural principles in the practice of a democracy depends on the power of a lawful literary rhetoric: the authoritative expression of judicial opinion inspired by, yet also transcending, its historical precedents. Cooper's ideal of literary fiction thus follows and incorporates the ideals and the ideology of interpretation inherited by the tradition of the Common Law. Even though these traditions were revised and redefined for the American context and its specific conditions by leading nineteenth-century American jurists like Kent, Story, Hoffman, and DuPonceau, the basic understanding of the legitimate source of legal authority remained the same.[64] This authority was ultimately presented by the judges, who interpreted the written opinions of their predecessors according to unwritten principles, embodied both in the Common Law and the Constitution. Just as the records of precedents were seen as the translation of principles into legal decision and action, judicial discretion was described as an interpretation which merely translated, in reference to the inevitable changes of condition and circumstance, the unchanged meaning of the underlying legal principle into writing. The triple role of the judge as author, interpreter, and translator clearly fitted Cooper's understanding of his own office as the author of historical fictions. Like Chief Justice James Kent, whom he revered, Cooper wrote commentaries on the American Constitution, based on and authorized by the traditions of the Common Law.

The strong didactic impulse in all his novels is an indication of Cooper's functional concept of literary rhetoric as the enforcement of principle. Yet this function cannot be conceived of without the existence of an audience, and although it is completely missing from the early settlement community in *The Pioneers,* the concept of a public sphere — or, in Cooper's terminology, public opinion — is at least already implied: "Long before Billy reached the village … the news of his danger, and of Natty's disrespect of the law, and of Hiram's discomfiture, were in circulation" (*P,* 338). There are, of course, no

---

64 For an introduction of the relation between these jurists and their common ideals, see Miller, *The Legal Mind.*

newspapers, broadsheets or other forms of printed matter as part of a wider system of public debate, yet Cooper's terms ('news'; 'circulation') nevertheless hint at the role of the (absent) press in a democracy. Nevertheless, the field of cultural conflict in the novel is exclusively defined by the rhetoric of law and literature, and the solution consequently rests on a specific reconciliation of legal and literary jurisdictions. Cooper's historical fictions could be said to include a fiction of the public sphere in early American culture, where the adversary impulses inherent in the individualistic pursuit of happiness are regulated and 'tamed,' as it were, by lawful writing.

Cooper's most extensive description of the literary institutions in the new republic appeared in his *Notions of the Americans* (1828), which must be regarded, in many respects, as the companion piece to *The Pioneers*. This series of letters relates the peculiarities of American nature, society, and culture to a number of European correspondents and presents a portrait of America in which the vision of the prosperous commonwealth at the start of *The Pioneers* has become a reality. In the twenty-third letter Cooper attempts to "write freely"[65] about the state of American literature. The letter in fact offers two perspectives on the subject: one that is concerned with the aesthetic merits and the specific genres of American literature, and another more interested in the political function of American letters in general. Hence, before he enters into the discussion of the conditions of American literature proper, the author finds it necessary to remark on the law and the press, and their "effects" as "[l]iterary institutions of the United States."[66] Given the close identification of the legal with the literary it comes as no surprise that Cooper should include the profession of the law. More interestingly, however, is what he has to say about public journals and newspapers, which he even ranks as the "first and most important … branch [of American literature]."[67] What holds these passages together — and, by extension, may define a common link between law, literature, and the press as literary institutions — is not at all obvious on first sight. Yet there is a common concern that is signalled by terms like 'opinion,' 'principle,' and 'truth' which appear at central points of the argument Cooper is trying to project.

In the comments on the profession of the law we easily recognize the familiar argument for an indigenous American Common Law, revised by experience and adapted to American circumstances. "Instead of existing in a state of dreaming retrospection, lost in a maze of theories," the American

65 Cooper, *Notions of the Americans*, 337.
66 Cooper, *Notions of the Americans*, 339.
67 Cooper, *Notions of the Americans*, 342.

lawyer "seizes the natural truth for his sheet anchor," and in this way "usages and opinions which … are … inapplicable to the present state of the world" like all "feudal absurdities, come to receive their death warrants." American legal practice, Cooper argues, grows out of "sheer experience" and the "collision of intellect" and will lead eventually to the "framing of laws, that are not to harmonize with … an elaborate theory, but which are intended to make men comfortable and happy."[68]

Cooper's emphatic preference of 'natural truth' against 'inapplicable usages and opinions' obviously resonates with the idea of the Americanization of the Common Law according to the principles of natural law. On the other hand, this process of the naturalization of the Common Law should not rely on any theory, but on experience alone. Only then will legislation — the writing of the law — follow intended principles rather than just precedents and opinions. The latter term, as it turns out in the following, must be read in more than its legal sense.

Between the discussion of the law and that of the press, Cooper inserts a few observations about the emergence of a "National literature." While English and American literature in Cooper's view "must be fashioned after the same model," he holds that the "only peculiarity that can, or ought to be, expected in their Literature, is that which is connected with the promulgation of their distinctive political opinions."[69] Whatever else it could be and eventually will be, American literature for Cooper is, first of all, a medium for political opinion. In this respect, however, literature, almost by necessity must compete with public journals and newspapers. After all, as Cooper writes, "[p]ublic Opinion … is … completely the offspring of a free press."[70]

Yet the essential office of the press, as Cooper insists, is less to express public opinion and more to "keep it alive" by "imparting facts" about the "public acts of public men."[71] Cooper readily admits that the "great freedom of the press," although guaranteed by the law, also contains "a constant temptation to abuse" this freedom. This, however, rarely ever happens, because public opinion "which is not only in consonance with the law, but which, in this Country, makes law" has "imperiously prescribed … that certain limits shall not be passed."[72] The enforcement of Cooper's "law of public opinion" is a rather precarious one, since it appears to rely mostly on

---

68 Cooper, *Notions of the Americans*, 340.
69 Cooper, *Notions of the Americans*, 342.
70 Cooper, *Notions of the Americans*, 346.
71 Cooper, *Notions of the Americans*, 343, 345.
72 Cooper, *Notions of the Americans*, 346.

the self-restraint of both public opinion and its medium, the press.[73] While Cooper's trust in this self-regulating system is still considerable in *Notions of the Americans,* the one example that he uses to illustrate the severe violation of his 'law of writing' already foreshadows the legal conflicts which inform his later works. Despite the fact that the American press is "more decent" than its English and "less decorous" than its French counterparts, there is a disturbing "habit" in which American journals seem fatally willing to follow the Europeans: "the practice of repeating the proceedings of the Courts of Justice, in order to cater to a vicious appetite for amusement in the public."[74] In the paragraphs that follow, Cooper shows how the representation of legal procedures in the reports of journals and magazines amounts to a perversion of the principles which should inform any legal trial. In these cases, publication does not — and cannot — impart facts, but, rather, only creates an unjust public opinion. In light of the central function of Leatherstocking's trial in *The Pioneers* and the implied argument about the competing, yet also related, function of law, literature and the press in *Notions,* Cooper's passionate tirade is most revealing and deserves a full quotation:

> It is pretended that as a court of Justice is open to the world there can be no harm in giving the utmost publicity to its proceedings. It is strange that the courts should … permit the gross injustice that is daily done by means of this practice. One would think that if a court of Justice is so open to the world, it should be the business of the people of the world to enter it, in order that they might be certain, that the information they crave should be without coloring or exaggeration. It is idle to say that the reports are accurate, and that he who reads is enabled to do justice to the accused by comparing the facts that are laid out before him. A reporter may give the expression of the tongue, but can he convey that of the eye, of the countenance or of the form, without regarding all of which no man is perfectly master of the degree of credibility that is due to any witness of whose character he is necessarily ignorant. …
>
> It is an unavoidable evil of the law, that it necessarily works some wrong in order to do much good, but it is cruel that even the acquittal of a man should be unnecessarily circulated in a manner to make all men remember that he had been accused. … There are undoubtedly cases of that magnitude which require some sacrifice of private feelings in order that the community should reap the advantage, but the regular books are sufficient for authorities, the decisions of the courts are sufficient for justice, and the utmost possible oblivion should prove as nearly sufficient as may be to serve the ends of a prudent and righteous humanity.[75]

---

73 See Grossman, "Cooper and the Responsibility of the Press," for a detailed discussion of Cooper's notions about the press. See also Outland, *Effingham Libels;* Waples, *Whig Myth;* and McWilliams, *Political Justice.*

74 Cooper, *Notions of the Americans*, 344.

75 Cooper, *Notions of the Americans,* 344–45.

This passage must appear especially prophetic in light of the protracted libel suits which Cooper fought against several American journals and their editors, beginning in the late 1830s. These suits, in which the author tried to defend his reputation against disparaging accusations of anti-Americanism, are in themselves interesting examples of the difficulties Cooper was to face in enforcing the law of writing he had envisioned in *Notions*. The Effingham libels, as they have come to be called after the name of the family at the center of his critical novels *Homeward Bound* and *Home as Found* (both 1838), are also linked by the name Effingham to Cooper's undisputed American myth in *The Pioneers*. Even today, Cooper's critique of biased journalism and the sensationalist tendencies of courtroom reporting must strike a familiar chord — which only proves that the problem is not a recent one but rather one which has always been inherent in American legal culture.

More precisely, and more important to the discussion of Cooper's own work, the practices of courtroom reporting he decries concern the delicate balance and mutual interdependence between unwritten legal principles and their cultural enforcement with the help of writing — lawful writing, that is. By the intrusion of the press into the space of the law this balance is disturbed to the point where the transfer of law from its practice to written record completely subverts the intentions and principles of legal practice. The law's proceedings, Cooper suggests, do not suffer their translation from public experience to exaggerated publicity without losing some of their dignity and purpose. The loss is due to the character of the press as an insufficient medium of representation. On the one hand, the reports 'color' or 'exaggerate' the information they present to the reader, and on the other hand, the information presented in this way lacks some crucial aspects of the experience which a member of the jury or of the audience would have had. In other words, these reports do not represent the full presence of the law *in its procedure*, since as written texts they remain both artificial and incomplete.

In the discussion of *The Pioneers* we have seen how closely Cooper looks at the law's practices and procedures. Only by carefully attending to these practices (as a writer and as a reader) is it possible to see — and judge — the enforcement of principles in any given case. This is the service and the duty of lawful writing to the enforcement of the law: "that he who reads is enabled to do justice."[76] In Cooper's eyes, a press report of a courtroom trial is thus another example of a failed linguistic representation of the law; it cannot be lawful writing, or lawful fiction, precisely, because it is lacking in the law.

---

[76] Cooper, *Notions of the Americans*, 344.

From another perspective, however, it should also become rather clear how Cooper attempts to defend his own literary fictions of the law in the quoted passage. Like Judge Temple, Cooper decides what is proper and improper speech in his courtroom. And Cooper's efforts to regulate and control the cultural representation of the law are even more prominent than in his own representation of Natty's trial in *The Pioneers*. In the latter, he had omitted those parts of the evidence and the testimony that undoubtedly declared Leatherstocking guilty in the eyes of the law. Instead, he had focused on the law's literary presence, as it were, in describing not only "the expression of the tongue," but also that "of the eye, the countenance" and "the form." In this way, he tried to make his readers aware of dimensions of experience inherent in the legal process that, although they must remain unspoken (and thus unwritten) for the law, are yet indispensable for judging the credibility of the law. In one of his rare literary reviews, Cooper once remarked that any author of literature, in order to become a "true historian" and "a describer of society as it exists, and of men as they are," should transcend the function of a mere "recorder[] of statutes" in giving a fuller, more comprehensive picture of reality.[77] Fiction, Cooper asserts, may "correct our false opinions" because it presents a truth that is indeed lawful:

> We love an interesting fiction, because, however paradoxical the assertion may appear, it addresses our love of truth — not the mere love of facts expressed by true names and dates, but the love of that higher truth, the truth of nature and of principles, which is a primitive law of the human mind, and only to be effaced by the most deplorable perversion.[78]

These earlier observations, written even before the publication of *The Pioneers* in 1822, are perfectly compatible with Cooper's conclusion in the passage quoted from *Notions of the Americans.* Only literature may join the "regular books" and the "decisions of the court" as a legitimate form of lawful writing in order to aid them with the cultural enforcement of the law.

Cooper's law of writing thus depends as much on the unwritten, the natural laws of language, as on the cultural 'unwriting' of the law. The "utmost possible oblivion" Cooper asks for is a command for silence, similar to the one uttered by Judge Temple, or, to paraphrase one of Leatherstocking's desperate exclamations, it is an appeal to the press to 'leave to law to itself.'

---

77 The term 'true historian' is taken from Fielding, who is quoted by Cooper: "Those dignified authors who produce what are called true histories, are indeed writers of fictions, while I am a true historian, a describer of society as it exists, and of men as they are" (Cooper, *Early Critical Essays,* 98).

78 Cooper, *Early Critical Essays*, 99.

Cooper's final novel, *The Ways of the Hour,* shows how utterly the press disregarded his appeal, with disastrous consequences for the law — and for Cooper's literature.

VI

When Cooper attempted to defend himself in the late 1830s against what he felt to be libellous criticisms of his novels by journal reviews, he went to the law, assuming that it would protect him against public accusation and the damages he was suffering by the falsehoods of the press. He soon learned, however, that the "law in action was quite different from the law on the books."[79] The libel suits presented only one episode of an ongoing legal quarrel in which Cooper was engaged during that time, a quarrel whose essential point was, ironically, the precarious legal protection of literary property and the properties of literature. For Cooper, these legal battles were less about money and much more about reputation. However, the decisions on punitive damages which were decided in the course of the legal proceedings did not exactly encourage Cooper's trust in the law. Literary property and its protection meant nothing to the juries:

> The law, as represented by judges, was on Cooper's side, but the law, as represented by juries, was less favorable to him. Judges instructed juries to bring in verdicts for Cooper and sometimes suggested that the damage should be substantial; but the juries' verdicts were on the whole only for relatively small amounts.[80]

This state of affairs is clearly reflected in Cooper's preface to *The Ways of the Hour,* where he writes that "in a state of society like our own, … juries get to be much too independent of the opinion of the court." Only when the judge guides the jury, and its members attune their power of discretion to the "proceedings of the court," the "greatest benefit [will be] found to accrue from this institution."[81] Yet Cooper's motivation did not entirely rest on personal experience; *The Ways of the Hour* also reacted to a capital criminal case which had aroused public interest and emotion during the 1840s. Beginning in 1844, Mary Housman Bodine, known as 'Polly,' was put on trial three times for the murders of Emeline Housman, her sister-in-law, and her child during the Christmas season of 1843. When the first local Staten Island jury was hung, Polly was tried again in Manhattan — which by then had become a

---

[79] Grossman, "Responsibility," 147.
[80] Grossman, "Responsibility," 146.
[81] Cooper, *The Ways of the Hour*, vi (in the following *Ways* with page number).

veritable circus. P.T. Barnum, the famous entrepreneur in human sensations, had installed a wax figure of the accused as the "Witch of Staten Island," which showed the young defendant hacking her victims to death. The trial was a disaster, with witnesses changing their stories and revoking their earlier identification of the defendant, but nevertheless the jury returned a guilty verdict. This verdict, however, was overruled by the New York State Supreme Court in 1845, calling for a retrial. For the next trial, 6,000 jurors were called in the county, yet only ten were found to be unbiased. After the case was moved to another county in 1846, the jury finally acquitted Polly Bodine and she was finally set free, the case remaining unsolved until this day.[82]

Cooper uses some characteristic details of the Bodine case in his tale about a young woman who is put on trial for murder and arson in the little town of Biberry, not far from Manhattan. It is clear, however, that the author's interest was less in the legal particularities connected to the case but much more in the character of the Bodine trial as a popular spectacle. The Bodine affair provided Cooper with the perfect example of a "most deplorable perversion" of the inherent principle of the law, the "love for truth." Instead, what the novel shows with almost gleeful detail, is how the adversarial forces, so essential to American legal culture, go almost completely out of control. The result is utter chaos and the gross perversion of principle. *The Ways of the Hour* certainly is Cooper's most intense confrontation with the specific procedures and practices of the American legal system; in fact, the novel may be said to be one of the first examples of the courtroom thriller, combining a criminal mystery plot with detailed descriptions of lawyer-client consultations, courtroom proceedings, the complex public warfare of opinionated journalism, and the intrigues and counter intrigues of the respective parties. At the center of the turmoil stands the accused, Mary Monson, a young stranger, who had recently moved in as a lodger with the Goodwins, an elderly couple, whose mutilated bodies were found in the remnants of the fire that destroyed their house. When the townspeople discover that Mrs. Goodwin's hoarded gold is missing, Mary, who barely escaped the fire, is soon suspected of having robbed the couple and of attempting to conceal the deed by burning down the house. Public feeling is very strongly against her, especially since it is obvious that she is highly cultured and wealthy. When she is indicted, a well-known Manhattan counselor, Thomas Dunscomb, offers his services and, with the assistance of Squire Timms, a slick, ambitious country lawyer, prepares to defend Mary Monson.

---

82 See *The Early Life and Complete Trial of Mary, alias Polly Bodine.*

This, however, proves to be no easy task, because the defendant refuses to disclose essential information about her person, her background, and her motive for staying alone in Biberry. Moreover, Dunscomb soon learns that his client also has some thoughts of her own about the law and the handling of her defense strategy. The mysterious stranger, whose beauty, cultured habits, and excellent education do not fail to impress the counselor and his peers, tries to influence public opinion in her favor by spreading rumors and attempting to win over jurors with the help of her considerable financial means. Yet the secret machinations and chicaneries all fail. On the contrary, the public mind is thoroughly stirred up against what the common people deem to be Mary Monson's unacceptable aristocratic, anti-democratic, and foreign manners. Foreseeing that the trial will be disastrous for their client, Dunscomb and Timms plead with her to accept a deal with the nephew and heir of the Goodwin's and to return a sum of 5,000 for the gold allegedly stolen. But Mary Monson vigorously insists on her right to trial: "It is indispensable that I should be *acquitted*" (*Ways,* 210). For counselor Dunscomb, this almost fanatical determination to see justice done in a case that has so obviously turned against her lends some support to his growing suspicions about Mary's instable state of mind — the "secret principle of her peculiar temperament," as Cooper describes it (*Ways,* 198).

Despite the combined efforts of Dunscomb and Timms to establish reasonable doubt in a trial completely resting on circumstantial evidence, the jury is quick to find Mary guilty of all charges. Yet the spirit of the defendant remains unbroken when Mary Monson takes the stand herself and, in a lengthy exchange with the judge, proves with clear reasoning that the verdict was based on rumors and opinions rather than sound facts and evidence. While many in the audience and, indeed, the jury members themselves are beginning to have second thoughts about the trial, the law has been satisfied and the judge announces the sentence: death by hanging. At that very moment, one of the presumed victims staggers up to the bar: "twenty voices cried aloud the name of '*Peter Goodwin*!' Every word that Mary Monson had stated, was true!" (*Ways,* 299).

This of course changes things more than a little, and the court immediately empanels another jury to try Mary again. Curiously enough, the defendant asks for and is granted permission to question the principal witness for the prosecution, Sarah Burton, herself. In an impressive display of examination skills, Mary is able to extract the truth from the witness — who turns out to be the real villain. Mrs. Burton had stolen Dorothy Goodwin's stocking with the hoarded gold coins and then slipped one of them into Mary's purse. The presumed arson was indeed an accident, caused by the flaring of a faulty flue, and the two poor victims — Mrs. Goodwin and her faithful German servant Jette — had been killed by a plough falling from its storage place above their heads. When the testimony of Sarah Burton is corroborated by other witnesses, the charges are withdrawn and Mary Monson is finally acquitted.

This astonishing denouement, however, is not enough for Cooper. As it turns out, Mary Monson is indeed Mildred Millington, the granddaughter of Mary Millington, the only woman the notorious bachelor Dunscomb ever courted in his youth. His courting was unsuccessful, since Mary Millington married a richer man and moved to France. Her granddaughter inherited not only a considerable fortune but also a streak of mild insanity. Unhappily married to a French aristocrat, Mildred took her money, changed her name, and went to America, where a new law had given married women the right to their inherited property. The novel ends with Dunscomb retiring from his practice, all young couples happily married, and Mary Monson, whose insanity is gradually diminishing, remaining under the guardianship of her former lawyer.

The rather topsy-turvy solution of Cooper's plot has disturbed critics as much as they have been appalled by his outright misogynistic statements scattered throughout *The Ways of the Hour.* Yet what is truly amazing about this "most damaging of Cooper's attacks on American society," is the energy which the author devoted to the task of describing the utter disintegration of the "whole social organization … into a kind of chaotic madness."[83] Indeed, Mary Monson's insanity stands for the more general state of affairs in American politics, culture, social life, and, last but not least, the law.

On the face of it, there seems to be no common denominator for all the various evils which Cooper chooses to attack, and yet the despicable "ways of the hour" are all encouraged by one single motivation, "to court change for its own sake," as Cooper states in his foreword, a tendency that is "erroneously termed a love of reform" (*Ways,* vii). The reforms which Cooper detested most were those that affected the extension of voting rights, the reform of the New York land holding system, and the revision of women's property rights in the wake of the codification movement. The latter point, as Barbara Ann Bardes and Suzanne Gosset have convincingly suggested, provides the focus for Cooper's attack on contemporary legal reform:

> In *The Ways of the Hour,* the town of Biberry … represents American life, and the trial that takes place there exhibits all that has gone wrong with the political system. Even though Cooper does not discuss the debate over codification, he ex-

---

83 Ringe, *James Fenimore Cooper,* 117.

> presses his outrage at the reforms which have been adopted in New York. *The Ways of the Hour* is unified by its depiction of the legal changes in the 1840s, of which women's increasing independence, since it affects the very fabric of society, is the worst.[84]

Women's increasing independence is signaled by the conceptual revision of both property and authority; indeed, what is at stake in *The Ways of the Hour* is the idea of 'proper' authority and its foundation in, and dependence on, property in the most general sense. As Cooper implies in his foreword, the spirit of false reform is fuelled by the public sentiment against "the enjoyment of the ordinary rights of property" (*Ways*, vii). The most disturbing point of the argument, at least in our contemporary eyes, is that for Cooper women do not possess the same 'ordinary rights of property' as men. The so-called "cup-and-saucer law," which, under the New York Civil Code of 1846, granted married women the right to their own property, is deeply resented by Cooper's spokesman in the novel, counselor Dunscomb:

> unless the courts interpose their prudence to rectify the blunders of the legislator … the labourer's wife may have her action against the husband for the earthen bowl he has broken; and the man may be sued by the wife for rent! … This very law will produce twenty-fold more unhappiness in families … by setting up distinct, and often conflicting interests, among those who ought to live as "bone of their bone, and flesh of their flesh." (*Ways,* 199)

The democratization of property, Cooper suggests, encourages some dangerous tendencies of the adversarial potential intrinsic to American culture. In fact, it introduces the damaging controversy between conflicting property interests into the very heart of the family, thus destroying the stability of the 'natural' association between husband and wife. Interestingly enough, Cooper describes the internal struggle in terms of legal conflict, i.e. as actions and suits, thus emphasizing that the law serves as the structural model for societal and even familial argument. This point becomes even more prominent when we compare Cooper's final fiction of the law with the one on which his reputation had been founded.

In *The Pioneers,* as I have tried to show in detail, the courtroom trial marks the crucial scene in the novel where different linguistic representations of the law — what I have called lawful fictions — are contrasted. The intricacies and antics of the 'lawyering' notwithstanding, Cooper leaves no doubt that judge and jury agree about the fundamental principles of the law. Nobody in the audience is really surprised at the second guilty verdict — only

---

[84] Bardes/Gosset, "New Reading," 507–08.

Cooper's readers may feel that there is a certain injustice in the law's formal power. This is precisely what Cooper needs to ground the necessity of another form of representation, unbound by the formal rigidity of the law, yet still lawful because it is bound to legal principles.

The synthesis of legal and literary rhetoric aimed at in *The Pioneers* is exemplified by the judge's will, which in turn comes to represent, on the legal side, the power of literary enforcement that Cooper claims for his own fiction of the law. The self-authorization by virtue of the rhetorical signatures of authorship ('the visible pen,' the 'manly style') serves the same end in both texts. Temple's will and Cooper's novel are claims to property whose lawfulness rests completely on the rhetorical power — the force — of their fictions. Moreover, both claims depend on similar conditions which bind the changing modes of legal and literary representation to the principles enshrined in authorless traditions and customs. Because they are unwritten, these customs become the 'natural' source of legitimacy for the principled writings of American Common Law — and literature. The linguistic stability which saves even the new statutes from the vicissitudes of interpretation is linked by Cooper to the genealogical and historical continuity of property rights; a continuity that may overcome the rupture caused by the revolution and the gap between the unwritten laws of nature and the written rights of men. In the end, the figure of Leatherstocking has been inscribed into the new fiction of legal and cultural progress as a reminder of the original meaning of principle and the proper meaning of words and names.

The complex interplay of and the interdependence between the legal fictions of property and the properties of lawful fiction, which Cooper so successfully negotiated in *The Pioneers*, are completely disrupted and subverted in *The Ways of the Hour*. The main reason, as Cooper stresses very early in the novel, is the existence of the press as a system of writing whose fictions are not meant to guard and shield old property but, rather explicitly, are geared towards the creation of new property. In a discussion that centers on the different functions of the law and the press in a democracy, Dunscomb tells his friend, Dr. McBrain, that the American press threatens to "overshadow justice" because it misuses its influence on public opinion to interfere with the administration of the law. Despite the fact that the press is thus "guilty, at common law, … of libel on the courts of justice," Dunscomb observes bitterly, "in a country … where the virtue and intelligence of the people are said to be the *primum mobile* in everything, there is no one to enforce the ordinances that the wisdom of our ancestors has bequeathed to us" (*Ways,* 49). The system of the press, whose original function was to "extract facts, and to do justice to their warranty," has succumbed to the sheer "mania ... of putting everything into print" and to the invention of "ten thousand schemes to make money" (*Ways*, 49). Facts have become news, and news, especially that which is taken from courtroom proceedings, sells. In Dunscomb's sweeping proposition for censoring measures that recall Cooper's appeal for the "utmost possible oblivion" in *Notions of the Americans,* the close identification of news and money reveals an underlying anxiety over new instable forms of property, explicitly associated with the circulating, floating, and imaginary values of bonds and shares:

> I would ... forbid the publication of any statement whatever, touching parties in the courts, whether in civil or in criminal cases, pending the actions, that the public mind might not be tainted by design. Give the right to publish, and it will, and is abused, and most flagrantly, to meet the wishes of corruption. I tell you, Ned, as soon as you make a trade of news you create a stock market that will have its rise and fall, under the impulses of fear, falsehood, and favour, just like your money transactions. It is a perversion of the nature of things to make of news more than a simple statement of what has actually occurred. (*Ways,* 53)

Facts are thus not only turned into news by the press, by this very transformation they also become a form of printed money — and a form of printed fiction. Dunscomb's concluding remark moreover implies that it is not only the nature of things that is perverted by this transformation, but also the nature of fiction. In its natural form, Cooper seems to suggest, news is merely a lesser category of historiography — and in this sense comparable to Cooper's own "clear narrative of events" in *The Pioneers.* In its emphatic sense as a commodity, however, news is not only a dangerously manipulative form of fact, it also appears to be, in Cooper's eyes, a degraded form of fiction. When Dr. McBrain objects that "it is surely natural to lie!" Cooper's common lawyer draws a familiar line between the natural and the unnatural. While the lie "issued from the mouth of man" can only rely on the "natural member," the press has at its command "a thousand tongues which speak by means of type." The news of the press is thus "ten thousand times a lie" (*Ways,* 53). A later remark from Mary Monson's trial refers to this multiplication of lies and emphasizes their unlawfulness which upsets the clear distinction between fact and fiction:

> it is not an easy thing for either judge, counsel, or jurors ... to keep distinctly in their minds that which has been obtained under legal evidence, from that which floats about the community on the thousand tongues of rumour — fact from fiction. (*Ways,* 183)

The stories in the news are dangerously unlawful fictions because they bypass the formal rules — the rules of form — of legal evidence and procedure. Due to this confusion of journalistic fiction with legal evidence, "popular opinion has replaced the law" as Ferguson summarizes Cooper's message in *The Ways of the Hour.*[85] But what, one is tempted to ask, does that mean for literature?

Cooper's last novel would be negligible indeed if one were to simply read it as one of the countless conservative ramblings about the decay of law and order in America. It certainly implies in its bitter criticism the inevitable end of the original "configuration" (Ferguson) of law and letters in American culture. However, the most interesting aspect of Cooper's final word, in my view at least, is his representation of the displacement of literary fiction from its natural and lawful function: the "love of truth." This displacement is marked both by the creation of law without literature, the "infernal code" (*Ways,* 86), and the creation of literature without law, the reports of the press. For Dunscomb, and presumably for Cooper, the very foundations of 'natural' order are shattered in the process:

> Heaven knows what the country is coming to! There is Webster, to begin with, cramming a Yankee dialect down our throats for good English; then comes all the cant of the day, flourishing finical phrases, and *new signification* for good old homely words, and changing the very *nature* of mankind by means of terms. Last of all, there is this infernal code, in which the ideas are as bad as possible, and the terms still worse. (*Ways,* 86, my emphases)

Obviously, Dunscomb is no friend of flourishing rhetoric, and in his admiration for the Common Law of Coke and Blackstone, he appears even more traditional than his predecessor, Judge Temple, in *The Pioneers.* The balance between legal and natural (or literary) eloquence and authorship which informed the latter is nowhere to be felt in *The Ways of the Hour.* In fact, Cooper's revision of the innocent defendant, who reveals the law's inherent conflicts from the figure of Leatherstocking to that of Mary Monson, reveals a deep seated ambivalence towards the force of literary rhetoric that at times borders at anxiety. When Dunscomb first encounters Mary, she literally presents an *image* of innocence that naturally follows aesthetic rules and does not fail to impress the spectator:

> Although nothing could be more simple or unpretending than the attire of Mary Monson, is was clearly that of a lady. … Our lawyer … could see the hands, feet, figure, hair, and general air of the female … but he could not see her face. The last was again covered with a cambric handkerchief, the hand which held it being ungloved. It was a pretty little American hand, white, well-proportioned, and delicate. … The foot corresponded with the hand, and it was decidedly the smallest,

---

[85] Ferguson, *Law and Letters,* 302.

> best-formed, and best-decorated foot in Biberry. John Wilmeter [Dunscomb's nephew] thought it was the prettiest he had ever seen. It was not studiously exhibited, however, but rested naturally and gracefully in its proper place. The figure generally, so far as a capacious shawl would allow of its being seen, was pleasing, graceful, and a little remarkable for accuracy of proportions, as well as attire. (*Ways,* 31)

The proper female figure that appears so agreeable to the eyes of the male is characterized, nevertheless, as much by its visible form as by her invisible face. This detail already hints at a potential force within the figure that may disturb or exceed precisely the formal rules it is bound to follow in order to remain agreeable. When Mary's face is finally revealed, the full image exposes a somewhat paradoxical character:

> it was when answering some questions …, that Dunscomb first got a glimpse of his intended client's face. The handkerchief was partly removed, and remained so long enough to enable him to make a few brief observations. It was then that he felt the *perfect justice* of [Dr. McBrain's] *description.* It was an *indescribable* countenance, in all things but its *effect* … (*Ways,* 31, my emphases)

I would not hesitate to point out this little passage as an accidental definition of both the ideal and the inherent paradox of Cooper's notion of lawful fiction. The ideal is a description that does 'perfect justice' to what it attempts to describe, yet only at the price of conceding its own futility and the collapse of its descriptive function. Moreover, the paradoxical nature of such a description even affects the logic of representation, which it nevertheless struggles to uphold. Mary's countenance is indescribable — but in what sense? The final clause seems to suggest that there is, after all, an exception to this total denial of description: the only thing that is not indescribable is the effect of Mary's face. This effect — its felt force — is somehow both within and beyond description. On the other hand, it appears obvious that the effect that is felt by Dunscomb in the first place is that of a perfectly just description. Thus every attempt to describe the effect would lead back to a description that does justice precisely by defying any regular form of describing. Perfect justice is an effect beyond the law, a force that cannot be enforced, a description that does not describe and in turn cannot be described; in short, a representational paradox whose apparent logic is purely rhetorical.

The growing suspicion on Dunscomb's part that the effect which at first "was quite … marked" on him was less the result of perfect justice, but rather the "proof" of rhetorical "management" (*Ways,* 31) is signaled by Cooper by the repeated description of Mary's countenance as "cunning." Mary's innocence thus gradually turns out to be less 'natural' than artificial, a cultured, civilized innocence which is the result of a rather artful mode of self-representation. The defendant not only speaks several languages in a "wonderful soft and musical voice," and her words are "correct and well-pronounced" (*Ways,* 67); this "singular being" (*Ways,* 198) also plays the harp and the guitar in her prison cell which she has transformed with the help of a servant into a veritable parlour filled with flowers and artwork (*Ways,* 260). When she feels like it, she even leaves the gaol for an evening stroll among the locals to find out how public opinion stands on her case.

Again, it is obvious how Mary's 'effects' not only transgress the formal restraints the law wishes to enforce upon her, but utterly disable the symbolic power of the law's form by aesthetic means. Like Leatherstocking, Mary Monson is in "rebellion to the laws," yet hers is not the resistance of nature against the law. Rather, the "handsome prisoner" (*Ways,* 196) in *The Ways of the Hour* sets a disturbing example of the insubordination of art against the law and its forms. Cooper's leading lady, which was "always [the] symbol of civilization,"[86] here follows a "treacherous nature" when she declares her own independence from the laws and from men: "I can feel my own longings … they are all for independence. Men have not dealt fairly by women. Possessing all the power, they have made all the laws, fashioned all the opinions of the world, in their own favour" (*Ways,* 198). All this, of course, is no longer agreeable to Dunscomb, and soon it "flashed on his mind that Mary Monson might be a lunatic" (*Ways,* 196).

The most significant threat of this madness, however, and the one where the anxiety of Dunscomb's Common Law merges with Cooper's literary anxiety, results from Mary's dangerous claims for authority and authorship. The prisoner's attempts to manage public opinion in order to ensure her triumphant courtroom victory over the law (*Ways,* 263) consist of spreading numerous fantastic rumours about herself. In contrast to the press, however, Mary's rumours are less distortions of facts by biased news reporting; they are rather deliberate inventions of facts, that is, they are fictions. At least, this is what Mary thinks they are, and consequently, she turns into an author who is quite proud of her stories. Yet the reasons for her pride are completely opposite to Cooper's idea of fiction as a servant to the love of truth. Mary thinks of literary fiction as falsifications and illusions aimed at deluding its audience into false beliefs. In an exchange with Squire Timms, whose knack for legal trickery sits well with Mary's own literary tricks, the defendant draws some astounding parallels, yet also reveals the unlawfulness of her 'fictions':

---

[86] Ferguson, *Law and Letters,* 303.

"It is now time, Mr Timms, to set the other story in motion," [Mary] said quickly. "Let one account follow the other; that will distract people's belief. We must be active in this matter."

"There is less necessity for our moving in this affair, as [the other party] has got a clue to it … and … will spread it far and near, long before the cause goes to the jury."

"That is fortunate," exclaimed the prisoner, actually clapping her gloved hands together in delight." … I regard that tale as the cleverest of all our schemes … And [the other party] believes it true!"

"It is not surprising; there are so many small and probable facts accompanying it."

"I suppose you know what Shakespeare calls such an invention, Mr Timms?" said Mary Monson, smiling.

"I am not particularly acquainted with that author …" …

"Shakespeare is a writer very generally esteemed … I believe he is commonly placed at the head of our English literature, if not at the head of that of all times and nations — Homer, perhaps, excepted."

"What! higher, do you think Miss Mary, than Blackstone and Kent?"

"Those are authors of whom I know nothing, Mr Timms." (*Ways,* 264)

Comparing her fantastic stories with the inventions of Shakespeare must appear more than just a little presumptuous. What is even worse, Mary's own fantastic delusions of authorship are based on a complete ignorance of two eminent legal authorities whom she dismisses offhand as if they were merely lesser writers of fiction. That Cooper mentions the most venerable representatives of the English Common Law tradition and its American continuation, William Blackstone and James Kent (who was called the American Blackstone), is not without significance. For, in contrast to those unknown writers of the infernal code and the new property laws, Blackstone and Kent are legitimate authors, who indeed rank with Shakespeare and Homer at the head of all times and nations. That Timms knows the jurists but does not know their literary counterparts is just as bad for Cooper. Neither Squire Timms nor Mary Monson can create lawful fictions, since one is as ignorant of legal authority as the other is of literary authority.

Nowhere in *The Ways of the Hour* is the breakdown of what Ferguson has described as the original "configuration" of American law and letters more striking than in this confession of mutual ignorance. The Common Law of legal and literary authorship, which depended, in Cooper's understanding as well as in the understanding of jurists like Kent or Joseph Story, on the force of forms through which change and progress could be molded into tradition and history, was swept away by the new professionalism in law and literature and the populism of politicians and legislators. "How can a Republic … continue," asked Justice Story in 1845, "when the People … refuse to listen to the counsels of Wisdom and Experience?" As Ferguson comments: "The lawyer as a man of letters had lost his audience and knew it. No one was listening."[87]

In a similar way, the audience of Cooper's lawful fictions was dwindling from the 1840s on, while, at the same time, his law of writing was literally written out of circulation by the self-ordained authorities of public justice. While Story appeared to resign, however, Cooper invested considerable energy to argue with *The Ways of the Hour.* In a final ironic twist, yet one not without logic, Cooper in this way also abandoned his ideal of the literary enforcement of principle by disavowing the role of an impartial judge. In his final novel he stepped down from the bench and became another party to the never-ending lawsuit of American culture with itself.

87 Ferguson, *Law and Letters*, 279.

Chapter 5

Evidence and Identification: The Case(s) of *To Kill a Mockingbird*

Many critical perspectives on the relation between law and literature tend to emphasize the rhetorical and textual dimensions of the courtroom trial as one of the most obvious common characteristics shared by legal and literary practices. Thus the 'scripts,' which form the basis of the conflicting rhetorical strategies of the parties at trial, are often identified as 'narratives' or 'stories.' David Ray Papke, for instance, calls the legal trial "a battle of narratives," in which "[e]ach side uses pieces of evidence, witnesses, testimony and striking revelations to construct a narrative, and each side also tries to poke holes in the other side's narrative."[1]

Similarly, Laura Korobkin has argued that in the U.S.-American legal system trials are "run as a storytelling contest in which each narrative must battle for acceptance against challenges and counter narratives." Without these narratives, there can be no trial, Korobkin states, because "it is simply not possible *not* to tell stories in court. Even the dullest civil negligence suits necessarily generate stories whose persuasive power derives more from 'literary logic' than from 'hard data.'"[2] Especially in the context of Critical Legal Studies (CLS), Critical Race Theory (CRT), and the so-called law and storytelling movement, it became major currency in theoretical exchanges about the trial to look at it predominantly as a constructed text and to approach the rhetorical struggle in the courtroom as, in Kim Scheppele's words, an all-comprehensive "textualization of social life at trial."[3] While there are "obvious differences between texts and events," Scheppele explains

> these differences are minimized in trials … At a trial, actions and harms are converted into accounts and claims. Events are made into texts. And these are texts that, like legal texts, are open to interpretation.[4]

---

1 Papke, "Law in American Culture," 9.

2 Korobkin, "Narrative Battles in the Court Room," 226–27.

3 See Brooks/Gewirtz, *Law's Stories,* for a collection of essays on narrative and rhetoric in law and literature; on CLS, see Kelman, *Critical Legal Studies;* Unger, *Critical Legal Studies Movements;* and Hutchinson, *Critical Legal Studies*; for key texts on CRT, see Delgado, *Critical Race Theory*; and Crenshaw, *Critical Race Theory.*

4 Scheppele, "Facing Facts," 44.

That linguistic practices and strategies are as central to the law as they are to literature can hardly be disputed. However, there is something reductive to the textualization thesis. On the one hand, it undercuts the sense for the theatricality of courtroom proceedings: the presentation of evidence, the cross-examination of witnesses in front of judge and jury, and the real time confrontation between the defense and the prosecution. As Jeremy Bentham already observed in the early 19th century, the courtroom is the "main theatre of justice,"[5] and the presence of things and persons, as well as their dramatic *mise en scène*, are of considerable significance for the outcome of any trial. On the other hand, the emphasis on language, text, and narrative suggests that both in law and in literature rhetorical strategies could simply be reduced to discursive operations. This also limits the awareness of the interaction, but also the potential conflict between discursive and non-discursive elements of the trial scene. The "textualization of life" at trial does not mean, as Scheppele has it, that in a courtroom "we don't have events before us," but only "verbal accounts" of events.[6] It rather means that the trial inevitably involves a dramatization of texts, which in turn characterizes it as an event in its own terms. Hence any trial, as Patricia Williams has rightfully observed, is a "rhetorical *event*,"[7] i.e. the dramatic synthesis of speech *and* gesture, discourse *and* action.

One of the central concerns of the following discussion thus will be with the "tactical aspects of legal aesthetics,"[8] which is the specific way in which the law enforces its theatrical appearance — its spatial setting and procedural rhythm, its dramatic presentation of persons and things — in order to control the *perception* of its audience and sustain an image of itself inside and outside the court. My main interest will be in the way in which this identity and this image of the law rely on and, at the same time, express themselves through specific acts of identification. By these acts of identification I mean the explicit procedures and the implicit concepts they rely on, through which the law identifies the status, the importance, or even the very nature of persons and things in reference to itself. Such procedures and concepts, for instance, characterize the very foundation of the definition and admission of legal evidence, including the privileges and constraints that mark the conditions and acceptability of testimony or the presentation of pieces of evidence. Legal identification in this sense always involves a certain perception,

---

5 Qtd. in Papke, "Law in American Culture," 9.

6 Scheppele, "Facing Facts," 44.

7 Williams, *Alchemy*, 11.

8 Goodrich, *Languages of the Law*, 11. See also Goodrich, "Specula Laws"; and Vismann, "Tele-Tribunals."

and nowhere is this perception and the identification it allows more problematic in American legal culture than in regard to the legal identification of race. As a first step in the following discussion, I will describe the inherent perceptual assumptions of the legal identification of racial difference in American law. Identifying race or racial differences presents a particular problem for the presumed universalism and evidentiary objectivity of the law and its processes; at the same time, racial difference has always served as an implicit basis for the definition of white personhood and property rights in America. This intricate interdependence of racial identification and white identity has also been inscribed into American literature, especially at times when habitual schemata of the cultural and social identification of race lost their paradigmatic force and had to be revised or redefined.

I

One of the most fundamental claims on which American law has grounded its authority and which has from the beginning often been characterized and emphasized as its most specific trait is the concept of equality before the law. Arguably, this concept is already implied in the famous statement about the 'self-evident truth' in the American Declaration of Independence that 'all men are created equal.' Yet even more evident than this truth was the fact that the universalism of the original founding claim of American law and justice did not embrace certain subjects but rather excluded them from the enjoyment of their 'inalienable rights' — if not so much of life, then certainly of 'liberty and the pursuit of happiness.' The paradoxical logic of exclusion that informs the universalism of the rights to freedom and property was on the one hand poignantly documented by the professed author of those memorable lines, Thomas Jefferson, celebrated champion of individual liberty but also a slave owner. On the other hand, the logic inaugurated by these claims relied precisely on the inextricable dialectical relation between property and liberty. In other words, as the concept of free individuality became implicitly defined by the rights of ownership and possession, it excluded precisely those who were seen as personal property rather than as free individuals.

As Cheryl Harris has noted, the conflation of property and personhood on which the American understanding of individual liberty and rights came to rest was implicitly racialized from the start.[9] It was above all the standard

---

[9] See also Hall/Wiecek/Finkelman, *American Legal History*, 245; and Haney López, *White by Law*, esp. 37–77. The term 'race' appeared first in connection to citizen-

of the "white person" which served as the foundation of the legal identification of race. This standard was first introduced in 1790, when Congress made it the prerequisite for naturalization and acquiring American citizenship. The "white person" standard remained effectively in place as a condition until 1952. Thus the most valuable kind of property was an unacknowledged form of racial identity that could be owned only by those who were not owned by others:

> Slavery as a system of property facilitated the merger of white identity and property. Because the system of slavery was contingent on and conflated with racial identity, it became crucial to be 'white,' to be identified as white, to have the property of being white. Whiteness was the characteristic, the attribute, the property of free human beings.[10]

Consequently, the legal identification of whiteness as property from the beginning implicitly relied on the identification of race and racial difference.

As Harris shows, one can trace the development of this logic with the help of crucial legal decisions in which the Supreme Court subsequently attempted to define the scope and the limits of the universalism of American justice. After the Civil War and the adoption of the Fourteenth Amendment which guaranteed equal rights of citizenship to African Americans, the explicit relation between racial identification and property rights could no longer be maintained. Nevertheless, whiteness as cultural and social property still continued to be defined in its implicit relation to racial otherness and especially in opposition to blackness as the most devalued form of racial identity. This is fairly obvious in the Supreme Court's decision in *Plessy v. Ferguson* (1896), which effectively established the so-called "separate-but-equal" doctrine that became the bedrock of the Jim Crow system, the specific Southern system of racial segregation lasting from the late 1890s to 1954, when another Supreme Court decision, *Brown v. Board of Education of Topeka, Kansas,* prohibited institutionalized segregation. The reasoning of the majority of the court in *Plessy* claimed that segregation based on a legal distinction between black and white had no impact on the equality of the races, since a mere separation could not be interpreted as a statement about racial inferiority or superiority. This was clearly an attempt to justify racial segregation by denying its discriminatory character. The language of the *Plessy* decision is revealing since it suggests a dual mode in the legal percep-

---

ship in the Civil Rights Act of 1866. See Banton, *Racial Theories*, 1. For a history of racism and the constitution, see Berry, *White Law.*

10 Harris, "Whiteness as Property," 1721; see also 1721 n45.

tion and identification of race which from then on would continue to haunt American law:

> A statute which merely implies a legal distinction between white and colored races — a distinction which is founded in the color of the two races, and which must always exist so long as white men are distinguished from the other race by color — has no tendency to destroy the legal equality of the two races. … Laws permitting, or even requiring, their separation … do not necessarily imply the inferiority of either race to the other …[11]

In the court's opinion, a legal distinction on the basis of color simply expresses and translates a natural division between the visible appearance of black and white persons — and it is important to notice that the *Plessy* court insists on the inevitability and invariability of *perceptible* racial differences. Moreover, this naturalized legal distinction was then used by the court to insinuate that racial inferiority was something that African Americans feel because they fail to understand the naturalness of racial division. The "underlying fallacy" of Plessy's argument, the court unabashedly stated, consisted in

> the assumption that the enforced separation of two races stamps the colored race with a badge of inferiority. If this be so, it is not by reason of anything found in the act, but solely because the colored race chooses to put that construction upon it.[12]

While the conclusion of the majority must surely appear cynical, the guiding assumption that racial identification was basically a matter of perception, and of physical differences, which could not be undone merely by the discursive assertion of equality, was even carried over into the remarkable dissenting opinion of Justice John M. Harlan that clearly exposed the faulty logic of the majority opinion. For, in order to support his assertion that "[i]n respect of civil rights, all citizens are equal before the law," Harlan, like the majority, had to assume a certain mode of the legal perception of racial difference. "[I]n view of the Constitution, in the eye of the law, there is in this country no superior, dominant, ruling class of citizens. … Our Constitution is color-blind … [t]he law regards man as man, and takes no account of his … color when his civil rights … are involved."[13] The notion of 'color-blindness' has

---

[11] 163 U.S. 537, 550 (1896).

[12] 163 U.S., 551. For the notion of inferiority as a leading presumption of racial law and injustice, see Higginbottom, *Shades of Freedom,* esp. his discussion of *Plessy* 108–26. As Harris demonstrates, the *Plessy* case is also clearly informed by the notion of whiteness as property, as, for instance, the remarks in the brief by Albion Tourgée, one of Plessy's attorneys, make obvious. See Harris, "Whiteness as Property," 1746–50. A concise and comprehensive presentation of the case and its context can be found in Thomas, *A Brief History.*

[13] 163 U.S. 559 (1896).

survived until today, and the tragic paradox of its survival points at the sad fact that Harlan's cherished concept only makes sense as long as one has to assume that the perception of color alone could lead to the discriminatory identification of racial differences — as in fact it still does today.[14]

The use of perceptual metaphors in both the majority and the dissenting opinion therefore is no accident. In fact, these metaphors present the dialectical opposites of the perception and identification of race and racial discrimination in American law and culture until today. One could in fact argue that only after the Civil War and the Fourteenth Amendment and after the introduction of Black Codes and the institution of the system of racial segregation in the South did the "black/white paradigm," as Adrienne Davis calls it, gradually assume the status of a central dichotomy from which racial difference in all its variations could be implicitly derived. The perceptual paradigm of racial discrimination has survived even the later-day revision of *Plessy* in *Brown.* Even though race has come to be recognized as "a concept that we continually invent and construct," Davis writes, "most Americans, of all races, do not view race as indeterminate, but rather as physically cognizable, stable, and culturally significant. Moreover, as a culture, we locate race primarily in black and white."[15] As Davis emphasizes, the rule of determining race according to ancestry or bloodline, which so strongly dominated 19th-century scientific and legal definitions of race, finds its more modern equivalent — already clearly obvious in *Plessy* — in the 'scopic rule,' that is, a determination of race which "relies on the inspecting and scrutinizing gaze of a (white) individual in order to discern and assign racial identity."[16]

Davis' scopic rule refers to Neil Gotanda's "rule of recognition," which "holds that any person whose black African-American ancestry is visible is black." The complementary concept is the "rule of descent," which "holds that any person with a known trace of African ancestry is black, notwithstanding that person's visual appearance, or, stated differently, that the offspring of a black and a white is black."[17] Together, these two rules characterize a specific American system of racial classification, which is also system of "social reproduction." Gotanda uses a term by anthropologist Marvin Harris, "hypodescent," for this specific American system of racial classification. For Gotanda, the combination of hypodescent and the concept of color-

---

14 See also Sarat, *Race, Law, and Culture;* Crenshaw, *Critical Race Theory;* Delgado, *Critical Race Theory.*

15 Davis, "Identity Notes," 695.

16 Davis, "Identity Notes," 705.

17 Gotanda, "A Critique," 258.

blindness "conveys a complex and powerful ideology that supports racial subordination […] through its implied validation of white racial impurity."[18] In other words, the racial purity of American whiteness relies on a definition of race founded on blackness.

Racial identification and discrimination are grounded in perceptual assessments implicitly informed by the identification and discrimination of value, and even in present multicultural America, passing as white still presents a strategy of economic and social survival. Whiteness then continues to be the basis for an unacknowledged economy of the evaluation and devaluation of persons in the eyes of others — a situation that presents a perplexing paradox in (and to) the eye of law. For, if it wants to aspire to the ideal of equal justice before the law, the law must both be color blind and acutely perceptive to racial discrimination: the law must be able to discriminate without being discriminatory. If based on color-blindness, racial equality before the law may turn out to be mere rhetoric in the face of the overwhelming evidence to the contrary. The precarious passage that has to be negotiated in the eye of the law in this way is that between the rhetoric of equality and the evidence of race and racial discrimination. This, however, as we will see, is not simply a problem of definition or description, i.e. of texts, but fundamentally a problem of perception and identification, i.e. of images — both imaginary and real.

While acknowledging the intense interest of the law-and-literature movement in the legal complexities of racial identification, my focus in what follows will not be on a real but on a fictional case: the trial at the center of the most successful American legal novel of the 20th century, Harper Lee's *To Kill a Mockingbird* (1960).[19] There are several reasons for this. For one, the question I have tried to pose consistently in the preceding chapters was how literature responds to and negotiates the evidentiary claims of legal rhetoric and the changing concepts of evidence inscribed into the process of the law. In doing so, I have argued that literary fiction has to reflect on its own evidentiary assumptions and on both the potential and the limits of a literary rhetoric of evidence. This includes the problematic authority and the dilemma of enforcement of literary legality in relation to the law, but also in relation to other cultural representations of law and justice.

---

18 Gotanda, "A Critique," 259.

19 The first and only novel of the Alabama writer has sold a staggering 20 million copies world-wide, and has never been out of print since its first publication. See Johnson, *Threatening Boundaries*, for more numbers and details from the book's publication history and Weisberg, "Procedural Novel," 226, on its status as a legal novel.

Like the law, American literature has from the start negotiated the black/white paradigm and constructed its own powerful versions of whiteness with the help of imagined and imaginary racial opposites, as Toni Morrison has argued convincingly in *Playing in the Dark*. What Morrison calls the "Africanist presence" in American literature and culture is not simply a response to the reality of "the four-hundred-year-old presence of, first, Africans and then African-Americans in the United States." In fact, for Morrison, the "dark, abiding, signing Africanist presence" has shaped the very character of American literature in its response to it:

> It has occurred to me that the very manner by which American literature distinguishes itself as a coherent entity exists because of this unsettled and unsettling population. Just as the formation of the nation necessitated coded language and purposeful restriction to deal with the racial disingenuousness and moral frailty at its heart, so too did the literature, whose founding characteristics extend into the twentieth century, reproduce the necessity for codes and restriction. Through significant and underscored omissions, startling contradictions, heavily nuanced conflicts, through the way writers peopled their work with the signs and the bodies of this presence — one can see that a real or fabricated Africanist presence was crucial to their sense of Americanness.[20]

My interest in *To Kill a Mockingbird,* a popular novel from the 1960s and written by a white female writer from the American South, is informed both by Morrison's observations about the Africanist presence in (white) American literature and by the debate within the law-and-literature movement concerning the legal identification of race and racial difference. As the novel clearly attempts to respond to the *Brown* decision and its hostile reception in the South, *To Kill a Mockingbird* tries to negotiate a more general crisis of the dominant paradigms of racial identification and discrimination in the South, but also in American culture at large. *To Kill a Mockingbird* in this way answers to *Brown's* legal challenge and revision of the cultural perception of race.

My question is how the Africanist presence, or more precisely the representation of the racial body as legal versus literary evidence, is employed by the novel to review the black/white paradigm and to find a revised image of Southern whiteness. As I will show, the trial at the center of the novel is a crucial element within this strategy because it serves as the regulated space of the public representation and identification of race and racial difference. However, this chapter does differ from the preceding two in that my discussion will have to pay even more attention to the contexts of the produc-

---

20 Morrison, *Playing in the Dark,* 5–6.

tion and reception of the literary text. Although the novel will be the focus of the argument, the various ways in which its public effects have unfolded and still unfold today, cannot be neglected.

In fact, I will spend some time sketching out these effects in order to characterize and, accordingly, to interpret *To Kill a Mockingbird* as a cultural event. This event cannot be reduced to the novel or its filmic adaptation; it has grown into something larger, nationally as well as internationally. It is certainly no exaggeration to claim that *To Kill a Mockingbird*, certainly much more than *Wieland* or *The Pioneers,* has helped to project a certain iconic image of American law and the American legal process.

More than fourty years after its first publication, Harper Lee's *To Kill a Mockingbird* is still praised by many readers for being one of the most powerful representations of racial injustice and the law in American literature.

The high cultural esteem of both the book and its filmic adaptation has transformed *To Kill a Mockingbird* from a literary fiction into a highly recommended moral primer for aspiring lawyers, a principal text for high school classes on the issues of racial justice and civil rights, and, last but not least, into an exemplary representation of two principal ideals of the American legal system: due process and equal protection under law.[21] The novel was awarded the Pulitzer Prize in 1961; the movie, starring Gregory Peck in the leading role as lawyer Atticus Finch became a four-time Academy Award Winner in 1962. The reverence is not unanimous, though. Literary critics have more than often dismissed the book as merely children's literature, hopelessly naive and severely flawed by its regressive regional nostalgia.[22] Moreover, both the novel and the film have been severely criticized as the last stand of white Southern liberalism, as a contemporary version of *Uncle Tom's Cabin*, or, even worse, as being more or less racist.[23]

Obviously, there must be something in the novel (and, by extension, in the movie) which touches on some central and still unresolved questions regard-

---

[21] For the use of the novel in legal and ethical education, see Shaffer, "Growing up Good," and Shaffer, *American Legal Ethics;* Hall, *American Legal History;* Johnson "Without Tradition," and Asimov, "When Lawyers Were Heroes."

[22] Famously, Flannery O'Connor delegated the book to the juvenile genre — whether critically or appraisingly, is not altogether sure (see Johnson, *Threatening Boundaries*). For the novel's nostalgia, see Bloom, *Modern Critical Interpretations;* and Sundquist, "Blues for Atticus Finch;" for its regionalism, see Woodward, "Listening to the Mockingbird."

[23] See Freedman, "Atticus Finch Esq. R.I.P."; Freedman, "Atticus Finch — Right and Wrong"; Osborn, "Atticus Finch"; and Sundquist, "Blues for Atticus Finch," for the implied racism of the novel. Nicolson's remarks in "Hollywood and Race" about the same issue focus on the filmic version.

ing the reality of racial difference and the ideal of legal equality in American culture. More precisely, *To Kill a Mockingbird* demonstrates how prejudice and racial discrimination enter into the legal process and how as a result the very concept of legal evidence becomes tainted and even untenable. Yet, in their response to these critical observations, both novel and film reveal some important differences in their treatment of the image of racial evidence and in the rhetorical strategies they employ to make their case. My discussion will center on the conflict and the complicity of what I call verbal and visual rhetorics of evidence; i.e. discursive strategies of proof that aim at the containment or the empowerment of images. One central argument here is that both the novel and the movie react to a deeper conflict between words and images which became crucial for the formation and the radicalization of the civil rights movement during the late 50s and early 60s.

Locating *Mockingbird* within its cultural and historical contexts shows the discrepancies which it tries to negotiate between the image of justice the law at the time aimed to project through its discursive power — most prominently by the Supreme Court in *Brown v. Board of Education* — and the images produced by the perversities of 'southern justice,' both inside and outside the courts, which were exposed daily and with great resonance by the media. The law's own image becomes severely threatened by the powerful specularity of injustice presented by images of the media. At the center of the threat is a crisis of the legitimate identification of evidence, more precisely, the conflict between the cultural and the legal recognition of racial injustice and the visibility of its evidence. Thus, the cases of the *Mockingbird* touch upon an unsolved problem which is still being argued passionately today in the debates between liberal and radical perspectives on legal action against racial injustice and discrimination. While *Mockingbird's* enormous success as a novel may be explained in part by its regression into legal nostalgia and its profound (if naive) trust in the power of evidence and procedure to overcome the blind routines of racist stereotyping, I would like to call attention to its inconsistencies and ambivalences as a potential for debate; a potential that more than often tends to be glossed over and lost in the readings which the filmic adaptation imposes on the reception of the novel.

One of the ironies of the reception of *To Kill a Mockingbird* lies in the fact that while the cultural recognition of the image of the law it projects relies so heavily on the novel's unconscious identification with the movie, and vice versa, it is precisely this kind of unconscious identification of the visual with the verbal which the novel asks its readers to reflect upon and to revise. As a central concept in legal procedures, identification presents a complex interaction of recognition and ascription, a linking of visual perception and discursive 'naming.' This link is clearly obvious in the deictic moments of identification in any trial when witnesses are asked to point out persons or things, and, at the same time, are asked to give a verbal verification of their status within the respective narratives of evidence. The complexity of such moments of identification lies in the fact that the connection between the two registers — the visual and the verbal; image and text — is far from being obvious or fixed in advance. For there is always more than just one sense in which a person or an object can become identified (or mis-identified) — especially if they are to be identified as evidence in a legal trial. The link between object or person and any verbal ascription in fact always implies an active 'linking' by the agent of identification, which in turn always implies a selection and an interpretation.

Within the adversarial logic that informs the American courtroom trial, the identification of evidence presents a focal point in the 'battle' between the conflicting narratives; hence in a trial, identification is always contested and attacked. Yet, it is important to notice that this contest always already rests on a prior act of identification, which made the evidence admissible in the first place. Thus the federal rules of evidence state as the "general provision" for "authentication or identification" that the

> requirement of authentication or identification as a condition *precedent* to admissibility is *satisfied by evidence* sufficient to support a finding that the matter in question is what its proponent claims. (Rule 901.a; my emphases)

In other words, in order to become admitted as evidence in a trial, the identity of objects, persons, documents, etc. has first to be decided upon. This founding act of identification in turn rests on evidence sufficient enough to support a certain 'claim' of identity. If the trial is a contest between stories, then this contest is also, and in a very fundamental way, about the specific claims of identity that allowed the admission of evidence on which these stories are built. Consequently, the dramatization of evidence always includes an implicit or even explicit dramatization of identity — or, to put it differently, the courtroom trial always involves a drama of identification.

In this respect, the complexities of legal identification cannot be explained by reference to processes of textualization or perception alone. Rather, as I will argue in more detail below, these moments of identification rely on the precarious passage and transfer between visualization and verbalization, between image and text. They thus belong to the repertoire of rhetorical means shared by law and literature; an affinity which has been recognized and discussed very early in ancient rhetorical theory. I will at first explore these connections with the help of certain concepts like *eikôn,* or image, and *anagnôrisis*, or dramatic recognition, which figure prominently in Aristotle's *Poetics.* As Kathy Eden has shown, Aristotle's ideas about the poetic-rhetorical image and dramatic recognition have to be understood in relation to the concepts and the terminology of legal procedure, which also influenced his *Rhetoric.* The fundamental role of the image both in legal demonstrations of proof and in scenes of recognition or dramatic discovery in literary texts shows how the verbal and the visual register participate in rhetorical and poetic strategies of persuasion and dramatization. These observations will also serve as a basis for the comparative analysis and interpretation of what I call visual and verbal rhetorics of evidence in the novel and the movie.

To Kill a Mockingbird is full of moments of dramatized and contested identification, the most prominent being the identification of the black defendant in the trial. The crucial scene in the process allows us to understand not only the logic which underlies such moments in the novel (and in the movie), but also *Mockingbird's* perspective on the more general, i.e. the cultural identification of racism and its evidence. Advocating a poetical rather than a political rhetoric of identification, the novel successfully projects an imaginary public space in which the struggle over racial injustice and equality is directed and confined by the rhetoric of due process and the images of literature. The conclusion of the chapter will reveal and discuss the complementary relation between legal and literary modes of racial identification and their respective evidence. In the end, the mutual exclusivity of the legal and the literary allows the novel to identify an image of Southern whiteness that is grounded in consensual misidentification.

II

According to Aristotle, "rhetoric [may] be defined as an ability, in each [particular] case, to see the available means of persuasion."[24] As the first attempt to formulate a systematic approach to the art and the various elements of oratory, Aristotle's treatise focused almost exclusively on 'means of persuasion' that are linguistic, or verbal. In fact, the complex architecture which Aristotle develops in the course of his three books on rhetoric starts out with a crucial basic distinction. In a language that implicitly refers to the conventions and the terminology used in the legal proceedings of Athe-

---

24 Aristotle, *On Rhetoric,* 1.2.1. All translations are from Kennedy (1991), unless otherwise noted.

nian courts, Aristotle very early draws a line between two different kinds of proof or *pisteis,* which he terms 'inartificial proofs' or *atechnoi pisteis* — everything that may be introduced and presented in a trial, but which is external to the speeches of the litigants and the lawyers in the sense that it is not provided by their invention or argumentation — and 'artificial proofs,' *entechnoi pisteis* — the strategies and arguments chosen by the speakers to make or defend their respective cases.[25] This initial division proved to be rather consequential for the understanding of rhetoric as an art exclusively concerned with words.

On first sight, however, Aristotle's strict separation might appear to be somewhat counter-intuitive in the face of the initial definition of rhetoric because inartificial proofs were always regarded as 'available means of persuasion' in a trial, as Kathy Eden has shown.[26] In his discussion of the powers of emotional appeal in the second book of the *Rhetoric,* Aristotle in fact "takes account of the enormous psychagogic power of objects (*semeia*), such as the clothing of a victim, exhibited directly before the eyes of the jury (*pro ommaton, en ophthalmois*)."[27] Yet while Aristotle was clearly aware of the effectiveness of such demonstrative or real evidence, Eden goes on to argue, the basic division between non-rhetorical and rhetorical proofs and Aristotle's concentration on the latter must be seen as an attempt to give "priority to rational argument over physical proof."[28] This in turn suggests that for Aristotle physical proof could play little or no part in rational argument. More precisely: for Aristotle, persuasion can be logical or rational *only* in the sense that it is based not on physical but on linguistic proofs. Even if this conclusion may overstate the overall objective of Aristotle's system, there can be no doubt that his *Rhetoric* attempted to conceptualize rhetorical persuasion as a strategic effect of utterance controlled by a theory of language.[29] From

---

25 Aristotle, *On Rhetoric* 1.2.2–11. and 3.16.1. See also Eden, *Poetic and Legal Fiction,* 13; and Kennedy's note in Aristotle, *On Rhetoric,* 37.

26 See Eden, *Poetic and Legal Fiction,* 15–16.

27 Eden, *Poetic and Legal Fiction*, 16.

28 Eden, *Poetic and Legal Fiction*, 18. Although Eden does not explicitly comment on this, Aristotle's preference for the "logic of probability" (Eden, *Poetic and Legal Fiction*, 18) over inartistic proofs was shared by juries (and by handbooks on rhetoric) in Athenian trials: "Greek juries distrusted direct evidence such as witnesses and documents because they thought these might be bribed or faked" (Kennedy, trans. in Aristotle, *On Rhetoric,* "Introduction," 9).

29 Quite literally, this theoretical dimension of *Rhetoric* is contained in Aristotle's definition which emphasizes not use but insight: to "see" the available means of persuasion "translates *theorôsai* 'to be an observer and to grasp the meaning or utility of'" (Kennedy, trans. in Aristotle, *On Rhetoric,* 37).

this perspective, inartistic means of persuasion may have undisputable psychagogic power — like the bloody cloak of a victim — but since they are not verbal or linguistic, they are not rhetorical. This is exactly what the term *atechnos* points at: proofs are inartificial when the source of their persuasive power is not language and therefore outside the reach of rhetoric as a *technê*.

Focusing exclusively on the *Rhetoric* and its argument, however, means to overlook the prominent role Aristotle assigned to non-linguistic or pre-discursive modes of cognition and judgment in his other writings, like the *Poetics* and *De Anima*. Especially where rational argument and dramatic presentation come to work together, the psychagogic power of inartificial proofs has to be accounted for — an aspect that will also be at the center of my interpretation of *To Kill a Mockingbird*. I will try to make a case for a rhetorical understanding of inartificial proofs, especially when the latter are employed as visual means of persuasion, that is, when they become part of a dramatized argument or an *exhibition* of proof. Such an understanding is obvious, for example, in the following remark by a contemporary trial lawyer:

> I'm a big believer in demonstrative evidence. … Recreations, photographs, bringing a part of an aircraft, bringing in part of a railroad crossing signal. It all creates drama which makes it interesting for the jury vs. dry … testimony.[30]

The inclination to dramatize, however, hardly presents a contemporary trend in forensic rhetoric, because it had been one of its basic ingredients ever since the introduction of public trials in ancient Greece. Moreover, as David Summers has remarked, the *attempt* to turn words into images to make them more persuasive became one of the "most basic principles of rhetoric itself." It meant that "the first appeal of speech was to the inner eye of the beholder, and conviction was achieved … when the matter being argued stood as if real before the inner eye of the listener."[31] Rhetorical evidence in its most convincing form was conceived of as a visible and vivid image, and this, of course, is what the term evidence as *evidentia* was meant to connote in the first place: the vivid description of actions, figures, and events, as if they were visible and alive.[32]

Naturally, there is a crucial difference between the images that address the inner eye of the listener and images or objects that are presented to the perceiving eye of a spectator or beholder. From the perspective of Aristotle's *Rhetoric*, only the first would be considered 'artistic,' that is, within the

---

30 O'Leary, "Masters of the Legal Universe," 39.
31 Summers, *The Judgment of Sense*, 39–40.
32 See the discussion of evidence and *evidentia* in chapter 1.

reach of the art (*technê*) of rhetoric. The latter, by contrast, would fall under the category of demonstrative evidence, the *pisteis atechnoi,* which can be used but not invented, i.e. their persuasive presence may conflict with the logic of speech. It is precisely this difference that Aristotle's concept of tragic recognition or discovery (*anagnôrisis*) and the central element of the image (*eikôn*) tries to overcome: in a dramatic fusion of artistic and inartistic means of proof (or persuasion). In fact, as a carefully invented moment within an overall dramatic structure, *anagnôrisis* combines the probabilistic logic of narratives of causation with the production of images as demonstration of proof.

Anagnôrisis — dramatic recognition — as Aristotle defined it in his *Poetics,* describes a crucial moment or scene of discovery, which opens a passage from ignorance to knowledge in regard to crucial aspects of the dramatic plot. In its most powerful form, dramatic discoveries involve a sudden insight into the true or hidden identity of central characters, which above all affects a change in perspective on the action and in turn asks for a revision in judgment. In other words, the concept of *anagnôrisis* connotes a relation between recognition and identification which is essential for dramatic denouement. Dramatic recognition can occur both on the level of the internal action of the play and on the level of interaction between play and audience. The most efficient scenes of discovery are those in combination with *peripeteia* (dramatic reversal) which presents another crucial concept in Aristotle's poetics. Both concepts are usually treated as inseparable aspects of the dramatic plot, but in Aristotle they present two distinct strategies, and from the perspective of forensic rhetoric, the concept of *anagnôrisis* is obviously applicable to legal presentations of proof, which is not so obvious for dramatic reversal — even though it might occur as the result of forensic presentations, it is certainly not their central concern.[33]

The dramatist's challenge in constructing scenes in a manner which Aristotle found most convincing lies in the fact that the insight which is to be accomplished with the help of *anagnôrisis* runs counter to the knowledge which the drama has helped to establish in the course of its events up to this point. The moment of dramatic discovery thus also marks a potential conflict between two narratives of causation which hinges on the recognition or misrecognition of the identity revealed. While there are very different ways of handling such scenes, Aristotle at a later point in the *Poetics* adds a short paragraph with a ranking of successful dramatic recognition:

---

33 See Eden, *Poetic and Legal Fiction,* 10f.; Halliwell, *Aristotle's Poetics*, 213–15.

> The best of Discoveries [...] is that arising from the incidents themselves (*ex auton pragmaton*), when the great surprise comes about through the probable incident (*di'eikton*), like that in the *Oedipus* of Sophoclos; and also in *Iphigenia* [...] These last are the only Discoveries independent of the artifice of signs and necklaces. Next after them come Discoveries through reasoning (*ek sullogismou*).[34]

Aristotle's hierarchy of discoveries is clearly related to his discussion of the various instruments of proof in the *Rhetoric.* In the sense that scenes of discovery in a drama rely as much on the presentation of proofs (or evidence) as do forensic arguments, there is an obvious "similarity between the instruments of rhetorical proof and those of tragic recognition," and the dramatist has to resort to "methods equally fundamental to rhetorical persuasion."[35] Moreover, Aristotle's preference for tragic recognition resulting from *probable* incident, rather than from signs or syllogistic reasoning, coincides with his distinction between artistic versus inartistic proof in the *Rhetoric.*[36] Eden concludes that

> [r]ead, as it must be, in conjunction with the *Rhetoric,* the *Poetics* ... classifies the procedures of tragic discovery according to categories derived from the treatment of legal proof. In keeping with his evaluation of these proofs in the *Rhetoric,* Aristotle also upholds in the *Poetics* the more *entechnic* over the more *atechnic* means, the discovery which emerges as a *consequence of the logical dispositions of events* over the one which relies on the spectacular effect of the simple sign or palpaple proof.

One very crucial instrument in assuring the persuasiveness of both dramatic scenes of discovery and forensic presentations of proof was the deliberate visualization of actions and events as if they were happening before one's eye. This visualization was a necessary, even inevitable means of proof in Athenian courts, since most of the evidence relied on testimony and demonstrative evidence was rarely available. Witnesses and litigants therefore had "to reproduce the vividness of ocular proof through language."[37] But it is not just the vividness of these visualizations that the Aristotelian *eikôn* or image offers to the dramatist (and the forensic orator). Scenes of dramatic discovery, as well as legal presentations of proof, will be most convincing by making them adhere to the 'logical disposition of events,' i.e. by describing (staging, creating) them exactly as they would appear as real events to ordinary experience. In other words, Aristotle puts a check on the persuasive

---

34 Aristotle, *The Rhetoric and Poetics*, 16, 1455a16–21. The Greek terms appear as Eden gives them in her discussion.

35 Eden, *Poetic and Legal Fiction*, 11.

36 Eden, *Poetic and Legal Fiction*, 24, my emphases.

37 Eden, *Poetic and Legal Fiction*, 72.

power of the visual by subsuming its effect *as a function* within the general logic of probable actions and events. Another passage from the *Poetics* shows this close affinity of Aristotle's rhetorical and poetical understanding of ocular proof and its relation to probability:

> when he is constructing his plots … and the diction in which they are worked out, the poet should remember to put the actual scenes as far as possible before his eyes (*pro* ommaton). In this way, seeing everything with the vividness of an eye-witness as it were, he will devise what is appropriate, and be least likely to overlook incongruities.[38]

In light of definitions like these, Eden argues that Aristotle's concept of the poetic image — *eikôn* — should be understood as the merging of logical demonstration and psychological appeal: "Aristotle's *eikôn* possesses both the power of logical demonstration" by its adherence to probability and "the power of … ocular demonstration through its great vividness."[39]

That the image or *eikôn* should be integrated into a logical course of events, thus subsumed to the narrative of probability or causality that the drama presents, does not mean that the dramatic image always appears logical or predictable. In fact, when employed within a scene of discovery, the dramatic presentation of proof assumes a disrupting quality. In these cases the *eikôn* appears unexpectedly, miraculously even; in other words, *anagnôrisis* presents a moment of conflicting probabilities (or narratives of causality) in an image which belongs to both 'stories' — but not in the same way. Discoveries that result from the 'things themselves' are most powerful precisely because they seem to work against the expectations of experience to create a new, more intensive one. In other words, these scenes result from a certain course of events, yet they suddenly reveal a different logic underlying these events which in turn demands a revision of our relation to the plot. As Stephen Halliwell explains, scenes of recognition "because of their involvement with the unexpected, might sometimes *seem* irrational or contrary to probability." Yet they are an "integral part of the unity and order which the audience or reader perceives in the plot-structure (and hence in the causation of the action) and in which, through sympathetic understanding, its emotions are rationally engaged."[40]

The powerful representation of evidence by means of ocular proof is thus not without risks for the rhetorician. Its psychological force may turn out to be greater than the evidentiary effect it is meant to serve. At the very mo-

---

[38] Aristotle, *The Rhetoric and Poetics*, 17, 1455a22–26.

[39] Eden, *Poetic and Legal Fiction*, 74.

[40] Halliwell, *Aristotle's Poetics*, 213.

ment of its revelation, the image of evidence lacks a discursive frame which allows us to translate its effect into meaning. As we will see, the passage from the perception of the truth to an understanding of its meaning as evidence — its identification — is not always easy to achieve, and it may lead to completely different conclusions.

In most trials, if not in all, we will find complex mixtures of verbal argument and visual demonstration, all employed to assure the convincing effect of the respective stories. This is also true for the trial at the center of *To Kill a Mockingbird,* to which I will now turn. Here, the truth depends on the identification of the black body as the central 'piece' of evidence. Moreover, the correct identification of the body as evidence relies on the revision and recontextualization of its images, which is made possible by rhetorical interventions and disruptions. At crucial moments in *To Kill a Mockingbird,* the dramatized body thus serves as the focus of scenes of discovery. These scenes enact the novel's underlying emphatic concept of identification which is expressed in one of the most quoted statements of the lawyer-hero Atticus Finch: "You never really understand a person," he advises his daughter Scout, who is also the novel's narrator, "until you see things from his point of view … until you climb into his skin and walk around in it."[41] The preoccupation with the body and the skin of others clearly resonates with the central theme of race, racial difference, and racism. At the same time it is inherently connected to the visual register and to images, both perceptual and imaginary.

III

In the summer of 2001, the Chicago Public Library prepared a reading list for its project "One book, One Chicago." Following the example of other cities, where similar projects had been run successfully since 1998, the library asked the citizens of Chicago to read the same book at the same time during one week in the fall, in order to "boost community bonding and a love for literature." The optimistic expectation was to unite Chicago's diverse multicultural populace in the act of communal reading. As Library Commissioner Mary Dempsey explained: "This is an opportunity for people to get entranced by a book. We hope the discussions cross cultural, class and racial lines." For some time, the commission in charge of selecting the book had been looking for a book that had "a universal meaning," as one member de-

41 Lee, *To Kill a Mockingbird*, 33 (in the following *TM* with page number).

clared, when it finally settled on Harper Lee's 1960 novel *To Kill a Mockingbird*. The suggestion was accepted unanimously, and Chicago mayor Richard Daley publicly endorsed the book as a "compelling" choice (Reardon/Mills "Book Club Starting Up").

Of course, the film version of *Mockingbird* featured prominently in the planned events for the book week, and in addition there were lectures, exhibitions, and a play presented by members of the Chicago bar association. After the terror attacks of September 11, the organizers worried whether people's minds were too preoccupied with the tragedy to spend time reading a 40-year-old novel about the American South. However, the *Chicago Tribune* insisted that the novel was "still relevant," and even more so after the attacks on the World Trade Center and the Pentagon. Acknowledging the growing suspicion and aggression against Muslims and Arab Americans, staff writer Patrick Reardon recommended the reading of *Mockingbird* as a remedy to xenophobia and racism. The passage deserves a full quotation:

> "To Kill a Mockingbird" is a book about differences — and about the need to accept them. … The point today is that, in pursuing an international war on terrorism, this nation runs the risk of loosing its perspective — of demonizing the enemy and envisioning itself on the side of angels. …
>
> In many ways, Lee's book is the perfect novel for all of us to read at this time. Now more than ever, we need to think about its lessons of tolerance and community. Read on, Chicago! Read on.[42]

Especially among lawyers, Atticus Finch is held in high regard. Law professors like Thomas Shaffer and Timothy Hall use *To Kill a Mockingbird* as moral primers in their introductory lectures on legal ethics, and the civil trial lawyer Mike Papantonio has written a 'motivational book for lawyers' with the title *In Search of Atticus Finch*. In a foreword to Papantonio's book, Morris Dees, arguably one of the most successful trial lawyers engaged in civil rights litigation over the last decades, describes how his encounter with *Mockingbird* changed his professional career and made him want to become a civil rights lawyer:[43]

---

[42] Reardon, "Novel Idea," n.p.

[43] Dees turned to civil rights litigation in the sixties after making a fortune in direct mail publishing. In 1971 he co-founded the Southern Poverty Law Center, which raises money for and launches lawsuits, especially concerning civil rights, hate crimes, and domestic terrorism. Most famously, Dees and the SPLC won several cases against the Klu Klux Klan, which allegedly contributed to the bankruptcy of the organization when the plaintiffs in one case were awarded 38.7 million dollars in damages — the highest award ever won in a civil suit.

> On a warm June night in 1966, I saw *To Kill a Mockingbird* at a local drive-in theatre. The Civil Rights Movement was happening all around me and I was sitting it out. When Atticus Finch walked out of the empty courtroom … and the upper gallery, still packed with black folks, rose in his honor, tears were streaming down my face. Why couldn't I be a lawyer like Mr. Finch?[44]

But the admiration for the book is not unanimous. At the same time, when the Chicago librarians chose Lee's novel as their favorite, their colleagues at the high school in Muskogee, Oklahoma, decided to take *To Kill a Mockingbird* from their reading list because they felt it to be too "uncomfortable" for their freshman classes.[45] Censorship for reasons of obscenity and racial insensitivity has haunted the novel from the day of its publication,[46] but a more thorough attack was launched in 1992, when New York law professor Monroe Freedman accused Atticus Finch of having been a passive supporter of the racist ideology implicit in the legal proceedings of Southern justice. Freedman concluded his critical barrage with the verdict that the gentleman lawyer should no longer be celebrated as an ideal example of legal ethics: "Finch never attempts to change the racism and sexism that permeate the life in Maycomb, Ala. On the contrary, he lives his own life as the passive participant in that pervasive injustice. And that is not my idea of a role model for young lawyers."[47] The uproar that ensued was remarkable. Since Atticus Finch could not defend himself, notable men of the legal profession offered *pro bono* representation, among them the (late) president of the American Bar Association, Talbot D'Alemberte. He insisted that "fictional heroes" like Atticus Finch should "still inspire" their readers since "[c]ontrary to what Professor Freedman asserts, Finch rose above racism and injustice to defend the principle that all men and women deserve their day in court represented by competent counsel, regardless of their ability to pay."[48]

From the perspective of rhetoric, it seems obvious that even after fifty years, many people find *To Kill a Mockingbird* very persuasive, even compelling in its advocacy of tolerance, racial equality, due process, and a colorblind ethics of equal justice for all. And since *Mockingbird* is on almost every high school reading list, one might assume that the rhetorical appeal of the book is especially successful for the teaching of these ideals. Unfortunately, literary scholars have neglected the novel almost completely until very recently, so that there are only very few attempts to understand the book's

---

44 Papantonio, *In Search of Atticus Finch,* 7.

45 Reardon/Mills, "Mockingbird sure to spark," n.p.

46 See Johnson, *Threatening Boundaries,* 14–17.

47 Freedman, "Atticus Finch Esq. R.I.P.," 21.

48 Qtd. in Johnson, *Threatening Boundaries,* 19.

unique status as a cultural icon.[49] My own position is that neither ideological accusation nor blind admiration would do justice to the novel. Within its immediate historical context, *To Kill a Mockingbird* presents above all an ambitious and also ambivalent attempt to find a compelling counter argument against Southern images of blackness and northern images of Southern whiteness. The sustained cultural resonance of the novel and the movie until today, however, may be due less to the presentation of 'nostalgic' images of race and racism. Rather, it has to do with the suggestive way the projection of these images even today allows for the identification of race, as well as of the evidence of racism, in American society.

In her perceptive reading of the novel, Diann Baecker has taken conventional interpretations of *To Kill a Mockingbird* to task for not paying enough attention to the "Africanist presence"[50] in the novel, that is, according to Toni Morrison's definition, the "blackness that African people have come to signify"[51] for a culture that perceives itself as 'white.' For Baecker, the negotiation of racial identity in *To Kill a Mockingbird* must be seen as a dialectic of racial identification and non-identification based on the difference between images of whiteness and of blackness. The "Africanist presence" in *To Kill a Mockingbird,* Baecker writes, "is a necessary (although not sufficient) component of what it means to be an American," since "white America has defined itself as much by that-which-it-is-not as by that-which-it-is."[52] Referring to Kenneth Burke's concept of rhetorical identification as consubstantiality, Baecker argues that rhetoric cannot be successful without identification, which in turn implies that *Mockingbird* may be persuasive only to the degree that readers do not simply identify the images of blackness and whiteness it presents, but moreover identify *with* the differences between those images. Identification in *To Kill a Mockingbird* thus not only "implies shared characteristics," but also "boundaries since it is a way of *defining* and definitions involve not only what something is but what it is not."[53]

---

[49] For a long time, Johnson's work on the novel was the sole example of scholarly criticism. There has been a notable increase in articles during the last five years; however, the two most recent collections of critical essays by Bloom, *Modern Critical Interpretations,* and O'Neill, *Readings,* not only feature the same familiar articles, they unfortunately also neglect some of the more important newer writings, like Sundquist, "Blues for Atticus Finch"; or Baecker, "Telling It in Black and White."

[50] Baecker, "Telling It in Black and White," 124.

[51] Qtd. in Baecker, "Telling It in Black and White," 125.

[52] Baecker, "Telling It in Black and White," 125.

[53] Baecker, "Telling It in Black and White," 125.

Certainly, at the historical moment in which the book appeared, the question of what would positively constitute American identity and what could not was very much contested and embattled. In 1954, the Supreme Court's *Brown v. Board of Education* decision dealt a severe blow to the culture of segregation in the South by declaring segregated schools irreconcilable with the constitutional principle of equality. The South responded with cultural indignation, political resistance, and open violence against blacks and white supporters of desegregation. In order to mobilize resistance among white Southerners, ideologies of racism almost without fail resorted to images and stories in which desegregation was graphically represented as black sexual aggression against white women; in the image of the black rapist the threat of desegregation to white Southern culture found its most visible form.

The image of the black rapist had always been the center piece in the visual foundation of Jim Crow racism in the South. Its fateful career began during the Reconstruction era after the Civil War and helped to legitimize a system of racial repression and violence against black males. Its power rested on the perverse logic that the black male should be invisible as a man in his racial, i.e. black visibility: as long as he was black, he was supposed to be inferior; as soon as he was seen as a man, he became a threat to white males. Thus, the slightest attempt to call attention to the visibility of black masculinity was seen as a transgression aimed at the center of the racist system as a whole. According to the logic of racial identification in the Jim Crow system, Southern whites defined their own whiteness against the racialized visibility of blackness based on and controlled by images of black racial inferiority or sexual aggression.

The paradoxical logic which underlies this racialized perception of self and other has been described by Grace Elizabeth Hale as "the contradictory, simultaneous need for race to be visible — blackness — and invisible — whiteness."[54] Yet the visual foundation of American whiteness was not merely a regional phenomenon whose effects were confined to the Jim Crow system in the American South. The construction of whiteness through the racialization of mass culture and its spectacles must be seen as a symptom of the general modernization of American identity after the Civil War.[55] Since Reconstruction and the beginning of segregation culture, Hale writes,

> Southern whites constructed their racial identities on two interlocking planes: within a regional dynamic of ex-Confederates versus ex-Slaves and within a national dynamics of the South, understood as white, versus the nation. …

---

54 Hale, *Making Whiteness,* 9.

55 For a similar argument, see, for instance, Wiegman, *American Anatomies,* 39–42.

> Grounding the modern whiteness that in turn grounded national reconciliation, the specifically southern culture of segregation became doubly important for the nation, as racial narratives and spectacles utilized southern settings and reworked southern history and as southern blacks in growing numbers began to migrate out of the region.[56]

In the attempt to find "new grounds of difference to mediate the ruptures of modernity," modern American nationalism, according to Hale, largely depended on "a newly narrowed and deepened opposition between Americans and non-Americans."[57] After the Spanish-American War, the defeat of the last Indian nations, and the official closing of the Western frontier, this opposition became internalized, as it were, in the concept of racial identity: "Not self-evidently more meaningful, not more real or natural than other markings, race nevertheless became the crucial means of ordering the newly enlarged meaning of America."[58] In the emerging consumer culture of the late 19th and early 20th centuries, American national and cultural identity more and more relied on visual representation and the identification with images. Within this culture of "emphasized visibility," Hale states, the "desire to mark racial difference as a mass identity, as white versus 'colored,' converged with the means to create and circulate the spectacle." Both in the North and in the South, the modernization of racial identity was made possible by controlling the "geographical and representational mobility of nonwhites,"[59] a general logic which found its most obvious and egregious manifestation in the South's system of segregation.

After the Second World War, however, the institutionalized segregation and open repression of blacks in the South could be less and less regarded as some sort of cultural archaism, which would simply disappear with the general progress of modernization. The identification of American culture and society as the most advanced democracy had served to mobilize Americans in the fight against Nazism and Fascism, and had been further developed as a crucial tool in the ideological battle with communism. In face of what Lawrence Friedman characterized as an "unprecedented American commitment" to international human rights, "American (understood as white) racism" in the fifties "[was proclaimed] the last obstacle to the attainment of a democratic American utopia."[60]

---

56 Hale, *Making Whiteness,* 9.
57 Hale, *Making Whitenesss*, 6.
58 Hale, *Making Whitenesss*, 7.
59 Hale, *Making Whitenesss*, 8.
60 Friedmann, *American Law in the 20th Century,* 286–87.

As a Southern novel about race, *To Kill a Mockingbird* is thus marked by the additional problem of national and cultural identification, which in the course of the civil rights movement of the 1950s and 1960s upset the fundamental dialectic of segregation by introducing new, desegregated concepts of whiteness and blackness. For the first time since the Civil War, the question of race, although it had never been marginal, took center stage again in the American drama of identification: "the meaning of race in America … had once again become a visibly and narrowly political as well as cultural problem."[61] Lee's novel clearly reflects these developments, and its specific historical position between the early formative period of the civil rights movement and the violent radicalization of white Southern resistance during the late 50s and in the following decade deserves special attention. From this transitional perspective, the problem of race in *To Kill a Mockingbird* appears two-fold. It concerns the loss of control both over the visibility of blackness and the invisibility of whiteness and their national interpretations, on the one hand, and, on the other hand, the increasing use of images of blacks as evidence, not for race, but for racism. Indeed, the book is about differences — but not necessarily about the need to accept them. Rather, the seductive power of *Mockingbird* resides in its ability to negotiate and shift the grounds of racial difference and identification by reference to the concept of equality.

The claim of identity as equality is, most prominently, emphasized in the trial of Tom Robinson, in which the problematic negotiation of whiteness and blackness turns into a drama of identification and mis-identification. Again, we have to account for the different versions of this negotiation because the drama of identification is played out differently in the novel and in the movie.

IV

The trial in *To Kill a Mockingbird* confronts its audience with two conflicting accounts or stories of one incident. In one account the incident is described as the beating and the rape of a white woman by a black man, while the other narrative tells about a white woman trying to kiss and to seduce a black man.

The accused, Tom Robinson, is a black farm worker who has been caught in the room of Mayella Ewell by her father, Bob Ewell. In court, both the father and the daughter claim that the defendant "took advantage of"

61 Friedmann, *American Law in the 20th Century*, 287.

Mayella (as the term 'rape' is mostly paraphrased in the novel and the movie during the trial scenes) and tried to flee when the father approached the scene. They also claim that the defendant brutally assaulted the woman, beating her across the face and arms. Tom Robinson denies all these charges during his testimony. According to his narrative, Mayella Ewell asked him inside the house in order to help her with some chores, then embraced him and kissed him, and asked him to kiss her back. Robinson denies that he in any way assaulted, hit, or even attempted to rape Mayella, and that he was merely trying to be helpful, because he "felt right sorry" for her (*TM*, 217). The accusation that the defendant "took advantage" of Mayella calls attention to the all-pervasive yet hidden logic of a general economy which underlies the social hierarchy and interaction in the small town of Maycomb. This logic not only reproduces the actual economic conditions and the status of the various communities and individuals who live in this fictional Southern microcosm. It moreover regulates the public and private relation between the groups and their members, and it is also the foundation of the 'modern' or 'liberal' value system which is represented by Atticus. The Ewells are clearly outside the system, both economically (they live on relief checks, and "none has [ever] done an honest day's work," as Atticus recalls in *TM*, 169) and legally (the law is not enforced even though they regularly break it). That his position is determined by economic parameters beyond his control, which also determine his credit in legal dealings, is acknowledged by Ewell on the stand, when he accuses the cross-examining Atticus of "taking advantage" (*TM* 193) of him.[62]

It is of course impossible to characterize the conflict between the two accounts of the same incidents simply as a "story-telling contest." As a Southerner and trained as a lawyer, Harper Lee knew quite well that if a white woman in the thirties accused a black man of raping and assaulting her, there would have been no contest of stories, in many cases not even a trial, but the

[62] Neither daughter nor father actually use the term 'rape.' The father's testimony "I seen that black nigger yonder ruttin' on my Mayella" (*TM*, 190) causes much excitement in the courtroom, and the witness is reprimanded by the judge to keep his remarks "within the confines of Christian English usage." He then agrees with the prosecution's term "sexual intercourse" (*TM,* 192). His daughter uses the term suggested by her legal interrogators, claiming that Tom "took full advantage" of her — the very term which is then used by her father as an accusation against the legal tactics of the defense. The traversing term not only reveals the common conceptual ground which binds the terms of racial and social transgression and violation to the terms of its legal recognition and acknowledgment. It also identifies the law's evidentiary force (the power to reveal and to prove) with the imaginary threat of black masculinity — both Atticus and Tom Robinson are accused of 'taking advantage.'

swift 'southern justice' of a lynch mob.[63] In fact, even though the practice of lynching in the South had decreased from its high time in the late 19th century to the thirties, it had never stopped completely, and as the notorious Emmett Till case demonstrated, still in the fifties black males could be killed for just looking at a white woman, talking to her, or incidentally touching her.

The lynching of Emmett Till, a 14-year-old African American boy from Chicago, who was kidnapped, tortured, and killed by two white men for allegedly whistling at a white woman, shocked the nation in 1955 and left some obvious traces in *To Kill a Mockingbird.* The Till case is special because it was extensively covered in the news and even on television. Even more outrageous than the killing itself was the subsequent trial where an all-white jury acquitted both defendants after only one hour of jury deliberations, completely ignoring the evidence brought forward by the prosecution. Particularly, the jury refused to acknowledge the identity of the victim's mutilated body, whose image had been publicized widely. They rather followed the argument of the defense that the body was not Till's, but had been deliberately plunged into the river where it had been found as part of a conspiracy against the South; and that in fact Till was still alive.[64] The refusal to acknowledge the black body of the victim *as the victim* is crucial, since this refusal is at the center of the drama of identification in *Mockingbird* as well.

The rape accusation was thus very easily accepted as a true story, regardless of opposing facts or evidence. It presented a 'text' whose interpretation was fixed by the ideology of racism and white supremacy. This story was especially powerful when coupled with the image of black men as sexually aggressive predators, eyeing and stalking the innocent white Southern girl — the modern tradition of this imagery can be traced back to the novels of Thomas Dixon and D. W. Griffith's *Birth of a Nation* and was extensively used in the campaigns against the *Brown* decision by the then Governor of Alabama, George Wallace. Thus, there was any reason for the contemporary reader of *To Kill a Mockingbird* to understand and react to the actuality of the accusation brought against Tom Robinson. But the novel does not simply attempt to reveal the injustice of the accusation and the anachronistic racist assumptions on which it is grounded. The procedural strategy which is almost

---

63 See Tolnay/Beck, *A Festival of Violence;* Hale, *Making Whiteness;* Brundage, *Lynching in the New South*; Gunning, *Race, Rape, and Lynching;* and Wiegman, *American Anatomies.*

64 For comprehensive accounts of the Till case, see Whitfield, *A Death in the Delta;* Hudson-Weems, *Emmett Till.*

painstakingly emphasized during the examination and cross-examination of the various witnesses and of the black defendant himself also serves as a means to probe into the nature and function of racist images and narratives and the way they mutually reinforce each other.

What makes Tom Robinson's case a rather hopeless one is that the defendant acknowledges some of the basic facts. He concedes that he was in the house, alone in the room with the white woman. He also testifies that he ran away — always a sign of guilt — when the father appeared. Yet paradoxically, it is this confession that allows for the confrontation of the two accounts in the first place. Only because the accused indeed took part in the incident does he have a story of his own to tell. If the defendant was accused without evidence of his participation in the event, he could only deny the accusation. The irony is that Tom's testimony, while it weighs heavily against him, also makes it possible for him to speak and present a different version of the action, i.e. a story that may prove his innocence.

Of course, this does not mean that the black defendant can speak freely for himself; he is only allowed to assume the presence of a witness, serving as a piece of evidence within the rhetorical strategy of his lawyer, Atticus Finch. This strategy attempts to stress the conflict between the different stories in order to make it possible for the audience to judge the plausibility of each account. Atticus' attempts are highlighted during the testimony of the alleged victim, Mayella Ewell. After Mayella has told the court about the beating and the rape, the defense lawyer asks her to identify the perpetrator. This is a crucial moment, because without the formal act of identification, the crime cannot be linked to the defendant:

> 'Miss Mayella, not to be tedious, you've testified that the defendant hit you, grabbed you around the neck, choked you, and took advantage of you. I want to be sure you have the right man. Will you identify the man who raped you?'
>
> 'I will, that's him right yonder.'

Yet this is not enough for Atticus. His next move is somewhat surprising, because he counters verbal, i.e. testimonial, evidence and its visual reference with the active presence of the defendant:

> Atticus turned to the defendant. 'Tom, stand up. Let Miss Mayella have a good look at you. Is this the man, Miss Mayella?'

What seems to be redundant is in fact a rhetorical device. By repeating his question for identification and at the same time emphasizing the active visual presence of the person to be identified, the lawyer demands an alignment of the verbal account with the visual impression and thus enforces a comparison of the two. The effect is not lost on the audience:

> Tom Robinson's powerful shoulders rippled under his thin shirt. He rose to his feet and stood with his right hand on the back of his chair. He looked oddly off balance, but it was not from the way he was standing. His left arm was fully twelve inches shorter than his right, and hung dead from his side. It ended in a small shrivelled hand, and from as far away as the balcony I could see that is was no use to him.
>
> 'Scout,' breathed Jem. 'Scout, look! … he's crippled!' (*TM,* 204–05)

The insistence on identification opens a space for the recognition of visual evidence that obviously conflicts with the evidence given by verbal testimony. Atticus' point is not to deny that "this is the right man," but rather that the image of the man does not match the story of the witness. He thus enforces a new perception of the defendant's body that defies the image of the black rapist by which the rape story had appropriated the same body as physically threatening and sexually aggressive. The ground of identification is suddenly shifted from the fixed text of racist ideology to the evidence of the visual image.

The surprised reaction by the children indicates the sudden character of that shift. However, the revised visibility of the black body in *To Kill a Mockingbird* unfolds its persuasive power only for an audience which is unacknowledged by the court of law — a status which is emphasized by the fact that Atticus is unaware of the presence of his kids. Furthermore, the specific position of this audience in relation to the legal process is important: Jem and Scout have sneaked into the crowded court house only with the help of the reverend of Maycomb's black church, and they have been given places in the front row of the balcony reserved for blacks only in the segregated courtroom. According to the logic of segregation, their position as whites in an all-black audience is of course an impossible one, yet it is precisely this impossible position which makes them invisible to their father, i.e. the gaze of the law.[65] Yet in turn, their own gaze is empowered, because from the vantage point on the balcony, as Scout instantly realizes, the children (and the black audience) can "see everything" (*TM,* 181). What the novel thus emphasizes by the placement of the children is a subtle, yet also crucial dialectic which informs the racial vision of the law — in both directions. The unacknowledged audience on the black balcony is invisible to the law because it does not have a voice in the legal process; however, this makes the same

---

[65] When the reverend worries that their father might object to the children's presence, Jem assures him that Atticus "can't see us this far away," which puts them out of Atticus' jurisdiction. As Jem knows — and Scout is about to learn — the law's power focuses only on what it can see (or choses to see). See Goodrich, "Specula laws"; and Haldar, "The Evidencer's Eye."

audience especially and exclusively competent for judging the legal process by its visuality: the black spectators and the children in *To Kill a Mockingbird* put the image of the law on trial. More precisely, the vantage point of the legally disenfranchised community of blacks allows them to see more clearly the contradiction and conflict between the stories the law tells about itself and the images it projects — it is a perspective of racial vision from where stories get cross-examined with the help of images and *vice versa.*

This is exactly what Scott and Jem experience as a sudden insight when they look at the body of Tom Robinson. The conflict between image and story becomes obvious through the defendant's physical disability. The crippled hand and the useless arm clearly undermine the initial impression of barely contained physical strength and power and thus consequently work against the stereotypical image of the black rapist alluded to in the first line of Scout's description: "Tom Robinson's powerful shoulders rippled under his thin shirt." If the conflict between the ideologically framed impression and the sudden realization of its actual visuality produce a disruption of the mythological unity of text and image, this disruption is nevertheless marked from the start as the result of a rhetorical strategy. It is, in fact, the result of a carefully prepared moment of *anagnôrisis,* an instant of the truth which lies in the things themselves, whose recognition, however, would have been impossible without the space for its appearance provided by the rhetorical direction of perception: "take a good look at the man."

That the direct visual perception of certain physical features is informed by assumptions about Tom's guilt or innocence had already been made very clear during the preceding examination of Mayella's father. The identification scene described above indeed presents the defendant's body as the conclusive piece of a chain of circumstantial evidence which Atticus had carefully built up before. The first element had been established by the first witness, Sheriff Heck Tate, who testified that Mayella had been strangled around the neck and that her right eye was heavily bruised. In the following cross-examination of Bob Ewell, Atticus asks the witness to prove that he can read and write — a question that the prosecution immediately objects to on grounds of relevance:

> 'Mr Ewell, can you read and write?'
>
> Mr Gilmer interrupted. 'Objection,' he said. 'Can't *see* what witness' literacy has to do with the case, irrelevant 'n' immaterial.'
>
> Judge Taylor was about to speak but Atticus said, 'Judge, if you'll allow the question plus another one, you'll soon *see.*'
>
> 'All right, let's *see,*' said Judge Taylor, 'but make sure we *see,* Atticus. Overruled.' (*TM,* 195, my emphases)

At first sight, this is simply an example of the strategy of delayed enunciation, one of the oldest tricks of the story-telling trade, both in law and in literature. Beyond that it is yet another moment of shifting the rhetoric of the trial from the verbal to the visual, which is clearly acknowledged, even explicitly announced by the parties involved. The question of reading and writing thus turns into the question of seeing; what is to be proved in the demonstration that follows is less the fact of the witness' literacy but rather the jury's ability to perceive the demonstration of an alleged fact as visual evidence for another fact. If we look at the following scene in terms of identification, it is obvious that the move from word to image again also implies a shift of the grounds of identification:

> 'Would you write your name for us,' [Atticus] asked. 'Clearly now, so the jury can see you do it.'
>
> Mr Ewell wrote on the back of the envelope and looked up complacently to see Judge Taylor staring at him … to see Mr Gilmer half-sitting, half-standing at his table. The jury was watching him, one man was leaning forward with his hands over the railing.
>
> 'What's so interestin?' he asked.
>
> 'You're left-handed, Mr Ewell,' said the Judge Taylor. (*TM,* 195–96)

What started out allegedly as a test of the father's reading and writing abilities was in fact an attempt by Atticus to add yet another piece of evidence to a potential story that would counter the rape narrative of the Ewells. The public demonstration of his being left-handed is deeply resented by Bob Ewell. However, it is rather clear that his rage is not based on a deeper insight into what the defense lawyer is actually doing. Feeling vaguely that he has been duped into helping to make a point for the defendant, he complains that "[t]ricking laywers like Atticus Finch always took advantage of him all the time with their tricking ways." He also perceives that the lawyer's 'trick' somehow poses a threat to his own account of events, and he thus fervently "told [the jury] again and again what happened … [n]othing Atticus asked him after that shook his story" (*TM,* 196). When the prosecution in an attempt to undermine Atticus' strategy asks Ewell, whether he was "ambidextrous," the father replies "I most positively am not!" adding that he could "use one hand as good as the other" (*TM,* 196). He thus not only fails to understand the prosecution's term, but also its strategic function, despite the fact that his final assertion states what the prosecution presumably wanted to hear. Bob Ewell may know how to read and write, yet he obviously does not understand how stories are built in the courtroom.

In contrast, the Finch children on the balcony are well aware of the strategic nature of bringing out conflicting stories during cross-examination, as

Scout's professional reaction demonstrates: "Never, never, never on cross-examination ask a witness a question you don't already know the answer to, was a tenet I absorbed with my baby-food. Do it, and you'll often get … an answer that might wreck your case" (*TM,* 195). Thus the lawyer's daughter immediately recognizes the evidentiary function of Bob Ewell's public signature, and sees its implied connection to other established facts. Yet in contrast to her brother's triumphant assessment that Ewell's left-handedness completely destroys the prosecution's rape story, Scout still has some doubts:

> I didn't think so; Atticus was trying to show … that Mr Ewell could have beaten up Mayella. That much I could follow. If her right eye was blacked and she was beaten mostly on the right side of the face, it would tend to show that a left-handed person did it. Sherlock Holmes and Jem Finch would agree. But Tom Robinson could easily be left-handed, too. … I imagined a person facing me, went through a swift mental pantomime, and concluded that he might have held her with his right hand and pounded her with his left. I looked down at him. His back was to us, but I could see his broad shoulders and bull-thick neck. He could easily have done it. (*TM,* 196–97)

For an eight-year-old this chain of reasoning is certainly remarkable; once again the reader is made aware that Scout is a keen observer and used to the evaluation of probability at the center of the legal trial. What is even more remarkable is how this process of cognition moves from the courtroom demonstration to a series of images projected by Scout's imagination, which the lawyer's daughter deliberately calls upon to test the validity of her father's implied reasoning. What Scout attempts is indeed a positive identification by an imaginary confrontation with the unknown rapist — "a person facing" her — which in turn puts her in the place of the victim. Atticus' dramatization of Bob Ewell's left-handedness moves Scout to investigate alternative narratives of causality. More precisely, she tries to find a probable logic of events in which the images she just saw can be integrated. Scout's reaction to this challenge is a "mental panto*mime*": the production of a mimetic and dramatic scene in the Aristotelian sense. In her attempt to imagine the probable, Scout thus follows Aristotle's advice to the poet to put "actual scenes as far as possible before his eyes (*pro ommaton*)," in order to see "everything with the vividness of an eye-witness."[66] Within the Aristotelian logic that frames both productions, there is an even deeper affinity between Atticus' demonstration of proof and Scout's chain of mental images. The imaginary construction of a logical chain of events with the help of images is a fundamental activity both in Aristotle's *Rhetoric* and his *Poetics.* The Aristotelian *eikôn* un-

---

[66] Aristotle, *The Rhetoric and Poetics*, 17, 1455a26.

folds its rhetorical and its poetical force as an integrated element within a narrative of causality; a narrative which in turn gains in persuasiveness through the psychagogic power of the image. This complementary logic is deeply indebted to Aristotle's ideas about the movements of the soul; i.e., the specific psychological processes involved in human emotion, cognition, and judgment. After he asserts (in *De Anima*) that "the soul never thinks without an image," Aristotle describes how these images serve as a basis for judgment and action in words that resonate with his advice to the poet discussed earlier:

> Perceiving … is like mere assertion and thought; when something is pleasant or painful, (the soul) pursues or avoids it, as it were asserting or denying it. … To the thinking soul images serve as sense perceptions … That which can think, therefore thinks the forms in images, and just as in those what is to be pursued or avoided is determined for it, so … [the soul] is moved … but sometimes you calculate on the basis of images or thoughts in the soul, as if seeing, and plan what is going to happen in relation to present affairs. And when one says, as there, that something is pleasant or painful, so here one avoids or pursues — and so in action generally.[67]

The close connection between imagination and judgment relies on the central function of the image in the working of both faculties.[68] In this respect, the difference between what is perceived and what is imagined is relatively small, however, when it comes to judging past or future actions, the soul can only rely on the *phantasmata* of the imagination. In other words, in the absence of perceptual images, only the imagination can produce images of the probable; therefore any subjective judgment of probability will rely on *phantasmata* in the way its poetic dramatization and its legal demonstration will rely on the *eikôn.* As Eden convincingly shows, the point of convergence of all these various productions of images must be seen once again in the language and the concepts of legal procedure and proof.[69] One of Eden's examples of Aristotle's use of legal terminology is particularly striking in regard to the trial of Tom Robinson in *To Kill a Mockingbird.* In contrast to Plato, who in the *Sophist* had defined imagination as "a mixture of sensation and opinion (*doxa*),"[70] Aristotle in *De Anima* consistently "reidentifies" the Platonic "*doxazein* — coming to an opinion — … as *krinein,* … [which] in the legal sense, denotes making a choice between two parties in a judicial suit

---

67 Aristotle, *The Rhetoric and Poetics*, 431a-431b10.
68 See Eden, *Poetic and Legal Fiction,* 78.
69 See Eden's comments in *Poetic and Legal Fiction,* 81, 84.
70 Eden, *Poetic and Legal Fiction,* 84, note.

based on the evaluation of evidence."[71] From the perspective of the Aristotelian framework, the rhetorical-poetical images produced by Atticus' demonstrations of proof and the psychological *phantasmata* with which Scout reacts to the dramatized evidence can be regarded as re-identifications of the mythological images and doxic knowledge of racism.

According to Aristotle, the imagined perspective of an eye-witness will help the poet to "devise what is appropriate" and prevent him from "overlook[ing] incongruities" in the scenes he creates. Yet Scout's imaginary confrontation with the rapist and her identification of Tom have two severe faults. On the one hand, they project a conclusion based on an imaginary encounter ("I … concluded that he *might* have held her …") onto a real person, while the conclusion itself is still informed by the initial rape story. In this way, Scout's perception, or more precisely her point of view, becomes compromised by her fantasy: "I looked *down* at him." From this tainted point of view, only those aspects of the defendant's body become visible that always already 'prove' what the story of the black rapist wants to make the jury believe. In fact, what is missing from Scout's legal reasoning about probability is a crucial principle of due process which should inform her speculations: the presumption of innocence. The second flaw in Scout's identification again lies in the nature of the process: as a 'pantomime' it consists completely of images (*phantasmata*) without words. Without words, however, there is no critical distance to the story the images appear to 'prove'; Scout becomes a part of the narrative of causation she has imagined. What she does not yet realize, however, is precisely how her own imagined role as a victim in the scenario and her identification of Tom as the rapist are connected.

Commenting on the importance of acts of visual perception in Lee's novel, Laurie Champion has written, "*To Kill a Mockingbird* is primarily a story about perception, the ability to see clearly."[72] Yet even while the visual rhetoric of evidence which is employed in the scenes described might be said to address most of all the children's 'unconquered eye,' the novel does not simply present the truth of its images as revelations. What the children see and what the readers see with them, is already part of a more common knowledge, i.e. an element within another narrative of causation. When Jem gasps "look, he's crippled," the reverend of Robinson's church explains: "[Tom] got it caught in a cotton gin … when he was a boy … like to've bled to death … tore all the muscles lose from his bones —" (*TM,* 205).

---

71 Eden, *Poetic and Legal Fiction,* 83, note.
72 Champion, "The Unconquered Eye," 127.

And with this image of the mutilated, flayed body of a young boy still lingering in the children's (and the reader's) minds, the novel immediately shifts back again to the courtroom stage, where Atticus asks the Mayella for the third time: "Is this the man who raped you?" (*TM,* 205). The novel thus links the discovery of visual evidence to the narrative or memory of a past event. Shifting the perception from story to image, to another story and to yet another image, the black defendant's body is recontextualized and transformed into the mutilated body of a victim. While the visual rhetoric of evidence may open up a space for new perceptions, the novel suggests, these perceptions are no proof in and for themselves. What is also needed is a new story, which gives the evidence its proper meaning. Shifting the ground of identification thus implies revision and re-contextualization. Moreover, on the level of the reader's imagination, the image of the mutilated black boy would most likely have reverberated with the pictures (or the memories thereof) of the flayed body of Emmett Till. The graphic description of the "muscles" torn "lose from his bones" not only charges the identification scene witnessed by Scout in *To Kill a Mockingbird* with considerable emotional impact, it also allows for a reading of Tom's body within a more contemporary cultural history of racism and racist violence. The image of Emmett Till's body may be said to serve as an important subtext for the novel's imaginary identification of the experience of racism as a wounded or vulnerable body — a point I will return to in the course of my discussion.

The complex process of identification during the testimony of Mayella Ewell is interpreted rather differently in the filmic adaptation of the novel, where the basic 'pieces of evidence,' and especially the body of the defendant, are presented in a rather peculiar way. While the movie appears to stay true to the novel in its basic narrative and plot line, it does so mostly on its own visual terms. For instance, there is much more emphasis on the reaction of the audience to the examination of the witnesses. Yet the crucial revision happens when the movie adds an element to the scene of identification which suggests a rather different relation between rhetoric and evidence, between image and story. In fact, the movie trial makes identification exclusively a matter of performance.

Again, Atticus asks Tom Robinson to stand up and have the witness take "a good look" at him. But where the novel at this moment of vision shifts to the perception of the black body by the children, the movie redirects the spectator's gaze to the body of the white attorney. The moment of vision is heightened when Atticus interrupts his questioning and silently looks at some glasses and a water pitcher on the judge's table. Finally, he picks up a glass and asks Tom to catch it when he throws it. While the audience is won-

To Kill a Mockingbird (1962): Atticus Finch (Gregory Peck) asks the alleged rape victim, Mayella Ewell (Collin Wilcox Paxton), to identify the defendant, Tom Robinson (Brock Peters).

dering what the defense counsel is up to, Atticus retrieves the glass from the defendant, goes back to the table and asks Tom to catch it again, this time, however, with his left hand. When the defendant declines, "I can't do that," and Atticus asks him why, Tom explains that he had crippled his left arm in an accident as a boy: "all my muscles were torn lose." This solemn declaration excites so much noise in the courtroom that the judge has to pound his gavel to demand silence.

This is not to blame filmic inaccuracy or distortion, but rather to emphasize the specific rhetorical strategy of the movie trial. Clearly, the throw and catch routine is a very good performance to bring the point across — but what precisely is the point?

I use the term "performance" to call attention to a certain tendency in the filmic rhetoric of evidence which runs counter to that used in the novel. For once, the movie stresses the moment when the lawyer changes from a verbal to a visual strategy. As I said before, the novel enforces a shift of attention from the verbal examination in the courtroom to the perception of the de-

To Kill a Mockingbird (1962): The defendant, Tom Robinson (Brock Peters), stands up for identification.

fendant's body by the children. This perception confronts the reader with an image in the sense of the Aristotelian *eikon:* as a vivid description which also presents the final scene of discovery within a chain of probable evidence. In the movie this visual moment is occupied by the image of the white lawyer looking at the glasses and, in a moment of inspiration, taking the glass and throwing it.

What we see is not a black body inscribed in various stories, but rather a white body getting ready to create a new story — what the film wants to make us see is not the scripted body, but the scripting mind. In short, what the spectators watch is not a scene of recognition, but of cognition. While Atticus decides to change from verbal rhetoric to visual rhetoric in the movie, the courtroom is turned into a stage, with the lawyer as the director. The lawyer puts the body of the defendant on display, makes it a part of his performance. The defendant in turn takes on a role in his lawyer's script and he thus becomes a piece of evidence in Atticus' narrative of truth.

The crucial difference between the evidence of the body in the novel and the body in the movie is that only the latter goes 'into' evidence in the legal

To Kill a Mockingbird (1962): Atticus Finch (Gregory Peck) preparing for the demonstration of crucial evidence.

To Kill a Mockingbird (1962): The defendant (Brock Peters) performing the evidence.

sense. The lawyer thus not only commands the visual dramatization of the body as evidence, he also, and more importantly, forces the defendant to tell his story to the law. Without this act of (self-) textualization, the performance of the body would be insignificant, indeed, non-existent for the law. Ironically, the logic which underlies this procedural demand is only addressed in the novel when the prosecutor during his examination of Mayella asks her to identify the defendant:

> Mayella pointed to Tom Robinson. "I have to ask you to be more specific, please," said Mr Gilmer. "The reporter can't put down gestures very well." (*TM,* 198)

This little incident indicates how the novel contrasts rather than aligns the textualization of evidence by the law and by literature, respectively. Mayella's pointing gesture is already part of the audience's experience when the prosecutor asks the witness to state the already obvious for the sake of the law. This suggests that in the novel legal demonstration is a reconstruction of evidence from prior experience — in contrast to the movie where evidence and experience are collapsed into a performance.

However, that does not mean that the movie could dispense with textualization. Like the novel, the film has to struggle with the fact that visual evidence without a story is only an effect, it has no meaning per se. Thus we learn the sad story about the crippling accident when Tom explains his predicament to the court. Both in the novel and in the movie, the knowledge that can give the evidence its proper place and meaning by giving it a history is localized in a specific space with a specific function. While in the novel the space and source of this knowledge is the black community which shares this knowledge with the white children, in the movie a different source and space are assigned to the story of Tom's accident: the space of the performance of the law. What is more, in the movie the audience reacts with amazement to Tom's testimony, as if this story were unknown to most of the spectators.

At least to the white spectators, with the telling exception of Atticus, the lawyer whose exclusive knowledge about the accident allows him to script his little performance. The accident is never mentioned in the novel's courtroom, which means that legally speaking a very crucial fact is never allowed into evidence — officially that is, because it is rather obvious that this story is known to almost everyone in the town of Maycomb. Truth, the novel suggests, is a story of shared experience. The crucial exception, however, are the jury members, because they are not part of the town's community but rural farmers, some of them even belonging to the mob who tried to lynch Tom Robinson on the night before the trial. The distinction between the members of the jury and the Maycomb community is very obvious in the novel; indeed, the difference between town people and out-of-town people clearly separates those with access to knowledge stored in true stories based on actual events (history) from others whose 'knowledge' is mere opinion based on the text of racist ideology (the myth of white supremacy).

In the movie scene, this distinction gets lost in the very dramatization of evidence on the visual level. That is, the story which presents the true knowledge about the defendant — Tom's accident and his subsequent physical incapacity — is known only to him (and Atticus who presumably learned this information from his client). Nowhere does the film indicate that this information may exist beyond the sphere of personal, subjective history, before the very moment it is brought to light in court. The film thus presents the courtroom as the privileged space where true but hidden knowledge can be turned into collective, i.e. public knowledge. In the novel, such public knowledge is stored in narratives of past experience which build a community's shared history. Different communities may have different narratives of experience and therefore can build collective knowledge only by sharing their respective stories. In this respect, the movie's performance and its element of revelation and surprise suggest a different source for true collective knowledge. This knowledge resides less in stories of experience but rather in the collective experience of images. This experience is both heightened and intensified by the performance of the body — by the *living image* of a body. By implication, the truth is always already there, hidden in the very visibility of the body as image. Only when the image is brought to life by an act of performance can its truth become identified by all who experience it.

There are several reasons why the distinct way in which the movie presents the crucial evidence of the case in comparison to its literary source deserves to be discussed less as an error than as a deliberate rhetorical strategy. First of all, as we have seen, the evidence at stake exists in two forms. On the one hand, there is the image of the crippled (or mutilated) body of Tom Robinson; a direct, demonstrative proof, as it were, which immediately addresses the senses of the audience — and which is easily recognized by the children. On the other hand, there is also the story of the event behind the image, a 'proof' which exists as discursive information and communal knowledge. Both the novel and the film separate these two dimensions of evidence, only to bring them together again in a scene of recognition. And, as I have tried to show, in the novel, the synthesis of visual and discursive proof remains outside the court, and emphatically so, since it is neither pointed out and shown nor related verbally during the trial, and it thus does not go on record. In contrast, the film does not simply show or describe the evidence; it stages it as a visual performance. The movie insists that the verbal explanation of the visual demonstration stays *within* the courtroom, i.e. within the room of its own performance. What is important beyond the different concepts of common knowledge and individual experience discussed above is the way in which the movie and the novel suggest a different relation between legal evidence and the kind of truth presented in film and literature, respectively. Thus the film completely aligns its own evidence with that moment of truth at the center of the trial: its ideal of legal evidence resembles its own mode of production as the planned organization and composition of images, i.e. as the visual dramatization of a script. In the novel, there is no such legal moment of truth within the confines of the law, and it appears obvious that legal evidence and literary evidence are very different in kind. Yet precisely because they are different, one can complement the other: although legal rhetoric and literary rhetoric of evidence are not surrogates or substitutes, they depend on each other in order to establish and secure true and just identification

To Kill a Mockingbird thus presents two trials of the same case in two different media; their strategies may be different, but they also complement each other so successfully that the audience may hardly notice the subtle yet crucial revisions of the novel's verbal rhetoric by the visual rhetoric of the film text.

These differences are not just artistic choices in order to optimize the effect of the respective mode of representation. I would in fact argue that the distinct performative strategy of the filmic version strongly enhances one central objective of the novel precisely by providing a more immediate visuality for the latter's verbal images and projections. In other words, the comparison between the two versions of *Mockingbird* should not lead to the all-too-simple conclusion that the novel favors words (stories, textuality) over images, while the film favors images (performances, visuality) over words.

As I have tried to argue earlier, identification depends on a specific relation between the visual and the verbal, and it is precisely this relation that is at stake when identification fails or turns into misidentification. The passages discussed above suggest that *To Kill a Mockingbird* is a rather 'visual' novel to begin with — a point which has already been stated in other interpretations. Carolyn Jones, for example, writes that the novel's underlying ethic, expressed by Atticus Finch, is "cast[] in visual terms, and in the metaphor of vision, the function and the content of the novel merge."[73] Laura Champion's reading of the novel in terms of the Emersonian "unconquered eye" is likewise based on the observation that just moral judgment in the novel "is not mental but visual," and that for Lee only a vision unhampered by "predisposed discrimination" and one that "cyclically leads to a cleansed eye, that again and again remains unconquered" may put an end to racist perceptions and images.[74] Finally, Patrick Chura has observed how the novel uses "visual images" to communicate "moments of deepest insight" which are "central to our understanding of the novel"[75] — an observation that is clearly congruent with the discussion of the novel in terms of *anagnorisis* and *eikôn*. All these are pertinent findings because they show how *To Kill a Mockingbird* carefully attempts to draw the attention of its readers to the crucial function of images and of visual perception. Noting some very telling chronological lapses in the novel, Chura concludes that Lee's major concern was not the historically accurate or authentic representation of racism in the thirties but the presentation of "an amalgam or cross-historical montage" whose "'historical present' is diluted by the influence of events and ideology concurrent with its period of construction."[76] Using Stephen Greenblatt and Jacques Lacan as his theoretical framework, Chura interprets the novel's particular blending of retrospective and contemporary perspectives on the

---

73 Jones, "Atticus Finch," 62.
74 Champion, "Unconquered Eye," 135.
75 Chura, "Prolepsis and Anachronism," 19.
76 Chura, "Prolepsis and Anachronism," 1.

problem of race as an attempt to contain its own criticism of Southern racism within a liberal-conservative narrative and ideology. In Chura's analysis, this attempt at containment is demonstrated by the central strategy employed in *To Kill a Mockingbird,* where crucial insights into the racist structures and ideology that dominate everyday life in the South are presented as dream-like images, whose presence is both powerful and somehow inexplicable, since the novel resists to give them a more recognizable discursive form. In other words, the mediating consciousness of Scout, in whose narration the perspectives of adult retrospection and participation as a child are merged, does not confront the reader with adult insights but rather with unconscious 'sights' of racism, i.e. "visual images and metaphors" that synthesize "pre-discursive" knowledge in "an unconscious or dream state"[77] and that contain the evidence of racism without ever making it explicit. Again, this assessment turns on the difference between the perspective of Scout as the narrator (retrospective) and as the spectator (participant) of past events which somehow taints the novel's representation of racism and race. There are, however, different ways to explain the strategic function of these images within the dialectic of experience and cognition that in my view is the concern of the novel.

Here I part ways with the readings just mentioned, for at the same time the novel leaves no doubt that the conspicuous prominence of the visual results from its destabilized, disturbed, or disrupted relation to a text. In other words, the two central concepts which govern *Mockingbird's* mimetic and narrative logic — experience and evidence — are both to be secured only by a delicately balanced relation between text and image, between visualization and textualization. The Aristotelian logic of the novel — its narrative of causation, its demonstrations of proof and dramatic discoveries — is indeed a rather fragile one.

V

One of the major reasons for the lasting success of *To Kill a Mockingbird* is often seen in its apparent regression into legal nostalgia and the heroic image of the lawyer, which makes the figure of Atticus Finch so attractive for lawyers in the first place. While this is certainly the case, *Mockingbird's* most effective performance may not be the nostalgic heroism of the law, but rather

77 Chura, "Prolepsis and Anachronism," 22.

its equally nostalgic image of a public and private sphere completely free from any intrusion by the rhetoric and the images of mass media.

As has been recognized in the critical discussion of *To Kill a Mockingbird*, the novel's representation of the trial of Tom Robinson bears more than superficial resemblance to one of the most famous cases of racial injustice in American legal history, the series of trials of the so-called Scottsboro Boys between 1931–37. Claudia Johnson observes some "striking parallels" between the Scottsboro case and the case of Tom Robinson which go beyond the obvious similarities in regard to time (the 1930s), place (Alabama), and the charge of rape. These include "the threat of lynching," the "similarity between … Atticus Finch and the real-life Judge James E. Horton," and the fact that the accusing women in both cases are "very poor, working-class women who had secrets that the charges of rape were intended to cover up," which made "the veracity or believability of the accusers … an issue" in both cases.[78] The other famous incident in American legal history, which, as Patrick Chura states, "unquestionably [seems] to have provided a workable model for … Lee's fictional Tom Robinson trial,"[79] is the already mentioned 1955 lynching of Emmett Till. Since Lee's novel is set in the 1930s, however, the references to the Till case have not been given the same attention as the more obvious one to the Scottsboro trials. Yet the commonalities and connections between the Till trial and the trial of Tom Robinson in *To Kill a Mockingbird*, which Chura describes in great detail, also suggest that the novel's author was quite aware of the more immediate contemporary references of her fictional case, even while she chose to present them in a rather oblique manner.

There can be no doubt that the legal and cultural significance of both the Scottsboro trials and the Emmett Till case relied very much on the public attention and resonance they affected with the help of the mass media. In fact, modern criminal procedure in American courts, as Michael Klarman has argued, is very much a result of the Supreme Court's reaction to racially motivated injustice in Southern criminal trials — a reaction that was backed by public opinion in the North, but much less so in the South. Even before the Warren court in the fifties decided to put an end to segregation in Southern schools, the Supreme Court moved to federalize state regulations of due process. Of the six landmark cases regarding criminal procedure which the Supreme Court decided between WWI and II, four involved black defendants

---

[78] Johnson, *Understanding*, 19.
[79] Chura, "Prolepsis and Anachronism," 1.

from Southern states, and two of them, *Powell v. Alabama* (1932)[80] and *Norris v. Alabama* (1935),[81] were the result of the Scottsboro trials. Both decisions reversed convictions by Southern courts on the grounds that due process requirements had been violated; in *Powell* the defendants had been denied the right to counsel, and in *Norris* the defendants had not been tried by a jury of their peers since blacks had been intentionally excluded from the juries that indicted and convicted them.[82] However, these decisions hardly had any impact in Southern courts. Especially in capital cases like rape and murder, Klarman observes, "the Court's criminal-procedure rulings had only the slightest impact on the southern criminal justice system." Nevertheless, he concludes that

> the fact that some high court decisions had little direct effect … does not mean that the litigation producing those decisions was inconsequential. With alternative forms of protest generally unavailable to southern blacks, litigation may have played an important role in mobilizing civil rights consciousness, organizing black communities, and educating white northerners and judges about the evils of the Jim Crow system.[83]

These effects, however, would have been much less explicit without the public attention these cases received through their extensive coverage by the mass media. In light of Klarman's observations about the difference between the cultural effects of civil rights litigation and its legal consequences, the strategic historicity of *To Kill a Mockingbird* links its representation of legal procedure in the thirties to a strong concern with the more current cultural reactions to Southern racism in the late fifties and early sixties. In fact, the role of the mass media since the 1930s in creating and sustaining a public debate about racism and racial injustice irritated the South much more than the decisions of the Supreme Court in regard to legal procedure. In the media representations of these cases, racial injustice was not merely a failure of the Southern legal system, but it was also portrayed as a result of a way of life; racism in America was thus presented as a regional and a cultural defect. But while the image and rhetoric of the Scottsboro case in the media was still informed by reformist impulses based on the trust in legalism, this trust declined rapidly after the South reacted with 'massive resistance,' both politically and culturally, to the Supreme Court's decision on desegregation in *Brown v. Board of Education,* and open violence against blacks and white sup-

---

80 287 U.S. 45 (1932).
81 294 U.S. 587 (1935).
82 Klarman, "The Racial Origin," 48–49.
83 Klarman, "Is the Supreme Court Sometimes Irrelevant?," 131.

porters of desegregation increased dramatically. The Emmett Till case became a key event for the shift within the Civil Rights movement from litigation to activism.

The tremendous resonance of both the Scottsboro and the Till cases in the public sphere was the result of their intense coverage in the media. Surprisingly, it is precisely this dimension of larger cultural and public interest and significance which the novel, despite its obvious references to both cases, completely ignores. When the trial of Tom Robinson opens at the Maycomb court house, we learn that it has attracted a considerable audience — even people from rather remote places, turning the small county seat into a "Roman carnival" (*TM*, 176). The amount of public attention is both worrisome for the Sheriff of Maycomb and outright despicable for respectable citizens like Miss Maudie Atkinson, the Finches' neighbour, who finds it simply "morbid" to watch "a poor devil on trial for his life" (*TM*, 175–76). In this respect, the trial in Maycomb resembles the Scottsboro and the Till cases, with their huge crowd of spectators and the atmosphere of sensationalism and public excitement. However, both actual cases also featured the overwhelming presence of the media; newspaper journalists from around the country (and the world), a huge crowd of photographers, the use of film and — in the Till case — of television turned the trials of the Scottsboro boys and of the Till murderers into national (even international) spectacles.

There is nothing like this in Maycomb. Except for Mr. Underwood, the "sole owner, editor, and printer" of the *Maycomb Tribune* (*TM,* 162), there are no journalists, no photographers, and certainly no film or TV cameras inside or outside the Maycomb courthouse. If at first glance this might appear as some minor insignificant detail, one only has to compare *Mockingbird's* blind spot in this respect with Theodore Dreiser's *An American Tragedy* (1925) or Richard Wright's *Native Son* (1940), which are extremely aware of the media — or, as far as movies are concerned, one could point to *Inherit the Wind* (1960), the film about the famous Scopes' trial of 1925, which likewise highlights the cultural presence of the media in the twenties.

Why then this conspicuous absence of the media in the novel and the movie? I would argue that *To Kill a Mockingbird* tries to project an ideal of legal procedure as a model for a cultural rhetoric on race and racism. This is why both in the novel and in the movie, the dramatization of images of race and of racism is carefully scripted and staged. The novel's concern with real and imagined images, as well as its emphasis on visual perception and discrimination in the production of legal and cultural evidence, are strangely at odds with its obvious neglect of the changing visuality of race and racism and their rhetorical function in the public sphere between the thirties and the fifties. This is especially notable in regard to the center piece of racist 'justice' in the South: the practice of lynching. In the early twentieth century Southern lynch 'parties' had become public spectacles which drew audiences of thousands of spectators. While there were arguably fewer lynchings than in the late 19th century, their gain in publicity and therefore public resonance with the help of mass media, mass communication, and mass transportation was enormous. Local newspapers would announce lynchings in advance, while the use of telephone and telegraph could extend the reach of prospective spectators, who would use trains and trucks to arrive at the scene in time for the spectacle.

The perverse increase in interest also changed the nature of these acts of racial violence: modern lynchings developed a procedural structure, emphasizing their ritualistic character and function. Newspaper reports from early twentieth-century public lynchings in the South often stressed the orderly fashion in which the determined citizenry went about to 'see justice done.' One important feature of the 'procedure' was the identification of the black 'defendants' by the professed white victims or their relatives, often demanding especially cruel punishment in public places. In the modern culture of segregation, the spectacle of lynching also began to reach beyond those who were present to include a much larger audience on the level of symbolic participation. The cultural effect of these public dramatizations of white supremacy and racial violence was greatly enhanced by their reproduction and dissemination through photographs and picture postcards. Until the mid-thirties, images of the corpses of African Americans mutilated by a Southern lynch party, publicly displayed in front of white men, women, and even children, became a central element of the visuality of racial violence, emphasizing white supremacy and, at the same, effectively instilling fear in the collective imagination of African Americans.[84]

Between the thirties and fifties, however, anti-lynching activism by the National Association for the Advancement of Colored People (NAACP) effectively started to use the same images of Southern lynchings to undermine the powerful grip of the visuality of race and gain political support among white liberals. As Elisabeth Hale notes, the 1934 lynching of Claude Neal in Marianna, Florida, not only "signalled the end of the gruesome southern practice of spectacle lynchings,"[85] it also differed in the fact that it was turned into a spectacle not by white Southerners but by black activists of the

---

84 See Allen, *Without Sanctuary*.
85 Hale, *Making Whiteness*, 222.

NAACP (National Asssociation for the Advancement of Colored People). Even though the lynching of Neal was not one of the carefully staged spectacles that had attracted white crowds, but had happened in the backwoods of Northern Florida, Hale writes,

> the NAACP made the torture and murder of Claude Neal into a spectacle. It uncovered the details, constructed the story, and provided the meaning, telling the nation a tale of white southern injustice rather than of the still-persuasive black beast rapist. And they told it well.[86]

While the white press, as was usual practice, had announced the lynching way in advance as an invitation to the "lynch party," it refrained from reporting details of Neal's ten-hour torture by hundreds of white men, who took their turn in beating the alleged black rapist to death. The NAACP then sent Howard Kester, a white Southern liberal who supported the organization's objectives, to conduct an undercover investigation, and Kester turned the reports of the lynching, gleefully told to him by the members of the lynching mob, into an illustrated pamphlet which sold more than 15,000 copies. One notable feature of the story which Kester told was the unusual attention given to the mutilation of the black man's body. Describing in glaring detail Neal's castration as related to him by an eye-witness, Kester not only reverted the focus of identification from the alleged white victim to the real black victim, but he also centered the meaning of the event in the confrontation between white and black bodies, thus "transforming the eye-to-eye narrative structure in which one violated body demanded another more violated one, a black man's body for a white woman's contaminated soul, into a tale of competing bodies for competing truths."[87]

Pamphlets and reports by eye-witnesses distributed by the NAACP not only stressed the suffering of the victims and the atrocious violence inflicted on them, they often also commented on the disturbing psychological effects of public lynchings on the white audience, especially women and children. One of these pamphlets confronted its readers with an image of the mutilated corpse of a black man hanging from a tree. Yet the accompanying text shifts the attention of the beholder to the little white girls in the onlooking crowd, who were completely engrossed by the horrific spectacle, asking whether such an image must not inevitably lead to the corruption of their innocence. In this way, the white Southern anxiety that was both instrumentalized and realized in the lynching spectacles was reverted by a counter inter-

---

86 Hale, *Making Whiteness,* 223.
87 Hale, *Making Whiteness,* 224.

pretation and a counter use of images: white Southern innocence is 'raped' by the spectacle of lynching.

In its use of the Scottsboro and Till cases, *To Kill a Mockingbird* makes some very selective choices, which must be interpreted as a careful attempt to negotiate the disruptive visuality of images of race as evidence of racism with the help of legal rhetoric. Thus the novel's rhetorical and legal references to the Scottsboro case serve to recontextualize the visual or imaginary references to the Till case and its disturbing visuality of racist violence. While the Scottsboro case was certainly a media event, it was still dominated by verbal rhetoric, that is, its cultural presence and significance rested to a great part on the detailed textualization of the cases in legal documents and papers, trial records, numerous briefs, appeals, opinions, and, finally, in the Supreme Court's decisions on due process already mentioned. Through the intense activism by the NAACP, the ACLU (American Civil Liberties Union), the ILD (International Labour Defense), and other groups that later formed the Scottsboro Defense Committee, the Scottsboro defendants could be represented in court by a very courageous and competent defense lawyer from New York, Samuel S. Leibowitz, and their case was closely monitored by the press. And even though every trial ended with verdicts against the Scottsboro boys, the fact that their initial convictions were overturned and that all were saved from the death penalty — in addition to the Supreme Court interventions — marked a victory for civil rights litigation in the thirties.

More importantly, the Scottsboro cases publicly exposed the extreme racial bias of Southern criminal procedure, which more than often appeared to be nothing more than the 'lynching' of a black defendant in the form of a trial. Nowhere was this exposure more obvious than in the widely distributed opinion of Alabama circuit court judge James E. Horton in which he granted a motion for a new trial for Haywood Paterson, one of the Scottsboro defendants. In his carefully crafted statement which took over an hour in reading (more than the jury took in deliberating), Judge Horton painstakingly refuted the state's evidence point for point, especially the evidence based on the testimony of the state's star witness and one of the alleged victims of the gang rape, Victoria Price.[88] The judge's statement is a rather unique document in American legal history and one of the few texts or records whose cultural significance by far exceeded its legal consequences. The

88 The second victim, Ruby Bates, recanted her initial testimony and became a surprise witness for the defense in the subsequent trial. Bates also became active in the defense committee and participated in public demonstrations against the verdicts in Washington and in other northern cities. See Carter, *Scottsboro.*

latter exclusively concerned Judge Horton himself, since he was not only taken from the case, but he also lost his reelection — his reasoning about the evidence of the case, however, was completely ignored. In *To Kill a Mockingbird*, the Scottsboro case serves as the model for the fundamental conflict between the mythical rape story and the story told by the real evidence, which in both cases is initially brought to light during the cross-examination of the alleged victim by the defense counsel. Atticus Finch's rhetorical moves in the courtroom appear like a mixture of Leibowitz's aggressive defensive strategy and Judge Horton's more solemn reasoning on the basis of factual and probable evidence — the novel's narrative logic is clearly indebted to both.

In sharp contrast to the Scottsboro affair, the Emmett Till case does not exist in legal documents — all transcripts of the trial have been destroyed — and it did not lead to any influential decisions by higher courts. And yet, its impact on the civil rights movement was tremendous. The widespread public reaction to the "first great media event of the civil rights movement," as David Halberstam called the Emmett Till case, was achieved above all with the help of images and public performances which centered around the visuality of the victim's corpse. When Till's body was dicovered, the local officials tried to bury it immediately, but when a court order from Chicago, Till's home town, forced them to send the boy's remains to Illinois, they issued strict orders not to open the sealed casket. When the casket arrived in Chicago, it was received by Till's mother, Mamie Bradley, several family members, and also NAACP activists and journalists at the train station. Nearly collapsing, Mamie Bradley insisted on opening the casket right there and then. When she saw what was in the box, she decided to leave it open for everyone to witness. The traumatic scenes at the train station were being photographed and the images published immediately, first by Chicago papers and later nationwide. The public display of the body and funeral during the three-day Labor Day weekend were "strategically planned," as Clenora Hudson-Weems states in her book on the Till case, in order "to let the public witness this atrocity." Photographs of the dead boy in the open casket, which were reproduced on magazine covers, turned into icons in the collective memory of the event because they "represent[ed] the embodiment of brutal racism and death."[89] The disruptive visuality of this evidence of racist violence is completely absent from *To Kill a Mockingbird,* even though the Till case is clearly present as a sub-text — a *visual* script — for the novel's attempt to visualize the black defendant as a victim of racism.

---

89 Hudson-Weems, *Emmett Till*, 46.

VI

One could of course attribute the novel's neglect of the significant visuality of the public debate on racism to its fundamentally nostalgic perspective, which would also explain its refusal to acknowledge the important role of the press in this regard in shaping and reshaping the public image of race and racism in the South. Yet, as the book's conclusion makes evident, this neglect is strategic, in fact, it amounts to an inevitable denial that is bound up with the evidentiary desire of the novel to present a true identification of race and racism.

Just when it seems that Tom Robinson's body has been effectively written out of the story, the problem of misrecognition, which had been identified with the racial body, returns to Maycomb with a vengeance: "Mr Ewell found himself as forgotten as Tom Robinson. … If Mr Ewell was as forgotten as Tom Robinson, Tom Robinson was as forgotten as Boo Radley" (*TM,* 273, 274). The last sentence aligns the three bodies in the composite image of race the novel is set to identify. Since Robinson was shot shortly after the trial, the novel's conclusion, set a few months later, is only concerned with those bodies that have survived.

After a school pageant on Halloween, where Scout had to wear a costume made of paper and wire, turning her into a ham in the parade of Maycomb's agricultural products, she walks home with her brother Jem. Since she has forgotten her clothes, she still has to wear the ham costume — a detail which already combines a comical reversal of identity: Scout becomes a walking ham; with a tragic reversal of identification: the descendants of Ham are said to be black and cursed, according to the Bible; and Scout effectually takes on the skin of another race. Noah's three sons, Japteh, Seth, and Ham, were said to be the forefathers of different populaces and races of the ancient world.[90] Ham, who was said to be of dark complexion, became the father of the African and Egyptian races. According to Scripture, Ham once looked at Noah when the latter was in a drunken stupor and lying naked in his tent. When Noah found out about Ham's knowledge, he cursed Ham's youngest son, Canaan, to become 'a servant of all servant to his brothers.' White supremacist theologians and racist Christian fundamentalists have often used this scriptural evidence (which in itself is rather vague, as one would expect) to claim the inferiority of African Americans and their 'natural' or 'moral' disposition for being slaves. This is by no means the only incident in the novel that refers to this background and the theories that sprung from it. There is

[90] Genesis 9:18–28, 10.

a lengthy discussion about the Egyptians and the roots of black civilization, and the theme of indecent exposure, incest, violence, and drunkenness is obvious in the behavior of Bob Ewell. Clad as a ham, Scout thus unwittingly fulfills precisely the condition which her father had demanded for true identification: "You never really know a person … until you climb into his skin and walk around in it" (TM, 33).

While this cross-racial identification might go completely unnoticed, the misidentification that ensues from it is rather serious. When on the way home from school the children are attacked by some unknown assailant, Scout is hit to the ground, while she tries desperately to find out what is happening to Jem, but her sight is blocked by the ham-costume. While she thus has to assume that Jem is trying to defend them against the assault, she also feels the presence of yet another person, but she cannot make out who the person is and does not realize the identity of the attacker. When she finally reaches the house, Atticus and his sister come to their help. Soon Jem is found to be unconscious with a broken arm, while the sheriff later discovers Bob Ewell's dead body in the woods.

What ensues from this experience of violence is yet another scene of identification where Scout herself has to take the witness stand. As the Sheriff asks her about what happened, she recounts the strange attack on her and Jem, staggering through her recollection at first, but slowly beginning to differentiate between the attacker, herself, and Jem, and, finally, the other person:

> "Then all of a sudden something grabbed me an' mashed my costume … think I ducked on the ground … heard a tusslin' under the tree sort of … they were bammin' against the trunk, sounded like. Jem found me and started pullin' me towards the road. Some — Mr Ewell yanked him down, I reckon. They tussled some more and then there was this funny noise — Jem hollered …" I stopped. That was Jem's arm. … "And then?" Mr Tate was looking at me sharply.
>
> "Somebody was staggerin' around and pantin' and — coughing fit to die. I thought it was Jem at first, but it didn't sound like him, so I went lookin' for Jem on the ground. I thought Atticus had come to help us and had got worn out —"
>
> "Who was it?"
>
> "Why there he is, Mr Tate, he can tell you his name." (*TM*, 297, original ellipses)

Scout's testimony reflects both the loss and the gradual regaining of those structures of difference which make identification possible. It is, however, not only the violent attack which helped to disturb these structures, but also the fact that Scout was forced to assume a point of view different from the one that informs her own perception of difference. Again, the scene shows how strong the ties are between visual perception and identification: since

Scout's vision is obstructed by the costume (as is her ability to move), she is unable to correctly distinguish and thus identify anyone at first. Since the attacker's identity had in the meantime turned out to be Bob Ewell's, Scout can start to redraw the lines of difference with the help of naming. What she cannot do, however, is to give a name to the fourth person, the one who presumably killed Bob Ewell and saved the children from harm.

The identification thus remains incomplete, and the missing part has to be provided by the unidentified person himself. In contrast to the central identification in the trial, where Tom Robinson is pointed out and named as the assailant, this equally significant disclosure of identity at the end of the novel is emphatically staged as an act of self-identification. Nevertheless, as in Scout's sudden realization of the real identity of the victimized black body in the courtroom, we are confronted again with an image of a body, only this time, as an image of victimized whiteness:

> He was still leaning against the wall. He had been leaning against the wall when I came into the room, his arms folded across his chest. As I pointed he brought his arms down and pressed the palms of his hands against the wall. They were white hands, sickly white hands that had never seen the sun, so white they stood out garishly against the dull cream wall in the dim light of Jem's room. … His hair was dead and thin, almost feathery on top of his head. … A strange small spasm shook him … but as I gazed at him in wonder the tension slowly drained from his face. His lips parted into a timid smile, and our neighbour's image blurred with my sudden tears.
>
> "Hey, Boo," I said. (*TM,* 297–98)

This time the recognition signals less the emergence of new truth through the cognitive synthesis of word and image, as was the case in Scout's 'new image' of Tom Robinson. The identification of Boo Radley, the mentally disturbed son of the Finches' neighbors, is clearly a scene of restoration or recognition of an identity that one had forgotten, but which gradually returns in an image of mutual acknowledgment.

Locked up during the day by his parents, Boo had managed more than once to escape at night and deposit little gifts for Jem and Scout in the knothole of an old tree. The children did not know this, and for them it had become a game of daring to enter the neighbor's house in order to get a glimpse of what they imagined was a madman locked up in chains. That Boo's identity had been unknown or misconstrued due to his enforced invisibility suggests that Scout's identification does not so much restore a lost or forgotten memory, but rather reveals a repressed knowledge.

At first sight, the novel seems to suggest a structure that would allow a reading of the two scenes of identification in which they complement each other to emphasize to the reader how much the evidence of social knowledge and of 'true' identity rely on the 'ability to see clearly.' The final recognition of Boo's humanity and physical fragility would then offer the novel's readers an insight into the potential reasons for the repressed identification (or enforced misidentification) of Tom Robinson as the inhuman rapist: just as Scout had imagined Boo as a monster out of fearful ignorance and filled with the fables of doxic knowledge, the racist construction of the black rapist, so the novel seems to imply, is likewise grounded in a mixture of fear, ignorance, and the doxic fictions of racism. There can be no doubt that the novel encourages its readers to invest in such a reading in order to support a universal perspective of identification. From this perspective, Atticus' impassioned plea for equality in his closing statement in the courtroom can be aligned with Scout's recognition of Tom's and Boo's shared humanity. In other words, from the universalist perspective, legal and literary evidence and identification would be one. Arguably, the universalist interpretation was and still is the strongest source for the novel's cultural standing and enduring success.

Yet, in order to allow for such a view on racial identity, the novel has to make one last realignment in redefining the difference between legal and literary evidence. As a consequence, the respective modes of identification on which the similar claims to equality in law and literature rest are in the end declared to be irreconcilable. In the final struggle over correct identification, Boo's identity is both acknowledged by the perception of literature and misrecognized or repressed by the gaze of the law. While Scout is able to recognize and identify Boo as the one who saved her life and that of her brother, it is Atticus, the champion of equality and color blindness, who falls victim to a misidentification. His failure to see clearly is even more disturbing since he mistakes his own son for Ewell's killer. When he consequently decides to present Jem to the law, the sheriff intervenes:

> For once, if you don't see it my way, there is not much you can do about it, if you wanta try; I'll call you a liar to your face. Your boy never stabbed Bob Ewell … I'm not a very good man, sir, but I am sheriff of Maycomb County. Lived in this town all my life … Know everything that's happened here since before I was born. There's a black boy dead for no reason, and the man responsible for it is dead. Let the dead bury the dead this time, Mr. Finch. Let the dead bury the dead. (*TM*, 303–04)

Through his investigation of the evidence and with the help of Scout's testimony, Sheriff Tate was able to establish the true identity of the person who saved Atticus' children and killed Bob Ewell. He thus can see through Atticus' misunderstanding and tries to prevent the lawyer from delivering his innocent son to the law. Yet Tate also refuses to disclose Boo Radley's identity to the law; on the contrary, he even creates a new story from the factual evidence, in which Bob Ewell attacked the kids, stumbled over a tree trunk, fell onto his own knife, and died. When Atticus at last apprehends, yet still appears to be insisting on due process and the rule of law, the sheriff offers a justification for the repression of identification and evidence that finally convinces the lawyer:

> 'I never heard tell it's against the law for *a citizen* to do his utmost to prevent a crime from being committed, which is exactly what *he* did, but maybe you'll say it's my duty to tell the town all about it and hush it up. Know what'd happen then? All the ladies in Maycomb includin' my wife'd be knocking on *his* door bringing angel food cakes. To my way of thinkin', Mr Finch, taking *the one man* who has done you and this town a great service an' draggin' him with his shy ways into the limelight — to me that's a sin. It's a sin and I'm not about to have it on my head. If it was *any other man* it'd be different. But not *this man*, Mr Finch.' (*TM,* 304; my emphases)

In this explanation, the novel's refusal to acknowledge the public sphere is not a nostalgic detail but justified as a strategy. Publicity, the sheriff suggests, would be a sin: the sin of exposing innocent whiteness not only to the law, but to a more general discrimination. What Boo Radley, the fragile, hidden representative of Southern, male whiteness, has done was not a crime, but an act of self-defense: not only did he protect the kids from harm, but he also removed the threat of white racism from the community of Maycomb — a great service, indeed.

The sheriff's appeal not to drag Boo into the limelight is characterized by the simultaneous acknowledgment and denial of identity. While his references to the shy neighbor carefully avoid any names and remain generic ("a citizen," or "he"), they also insist on the uniqueness of the very identity they are meant to circumscribe without exposing it ("the one man," or "this man"). The passage is crucial in order to understand the specific correlation between literary and legal identification and evidence the novel seeks to establish. On the one hand, it is obvious that Boo's identity can only be acknowledged in full from the perspective of literature; Scout's narrating voice is not only the first, but the only agency that simultaneously recognizes and addresses Boo Radley and thereby establishes a ground of mutual acknowledgment. Neither her father nor the sheriff address and acknowledge Boo in the same way. In fact, as the exchange between Atticus and Tate demonstrates, the law either mistakes (or neglects) Boo's identity, or it attempts to conceal or repress it. When Atticus expresses his gratitude to Boo, he addresses him with his formal name: "Thank you, Arthur, for my children."

(*TM,* 305) — formality may represent sincerity here but nevertheless it is in utter contrast to the fact that Arthur Radley is far from being a normal, accepted member of the Maycomb community.

Boo Radley's identity must be concealed before the public and before the law because his identity is at once like and unlike that of all other (white) men or citizens. In fact, his identity, which is so clearly marked as white and male, represents the ideal of individuality as a *shared* feature of white identity. Since Boo's uniqueness, however, is grounded not in his own individuality but in his exceptional whiteness, he represents whiteness as the very foundation of individuality *and* equality. Sheriff Tate's emphatic statement at the end — "[I]f it was any other man, it'd be different. But not with this man, Mr Finch" — clearly expresses the dialectic of identification which the novel tries to negotiate. From the perspective of the law, all men are equal, that is all 'any other man' except 'this man': Boo Radley. Boo's uniqueness apparently cancels out equality before the law for himself, yet, paradoxically, it is in this way that equality before the law is established for any other man in the first place.

This concept of equality, as we have seen, is universal in more than one sense. It transcends not only racial difference but also the difference between legal and literary identification and evidence. However, the fact that Boo's existence, already more a rumor than a reality for most people in Maycomb, must be forcibly denied after he has become an important agent in the novel's plot against white racism, reveals that both the literary and the legal notion of equality are based on a fundamental difference. The fundamental difference which Boo Radley in his "shy ways" and solitary existence represents is precisely the difference that whiteness makes for racial equality. Treating Boo differently makes possible equality before the law for all other men; yet this fact can only be acknowledged by literature, while it must be repressed by the law. While the law therefore is forced to conceal true identity and its evidence, literature can represent both its true manifestation and its repression. The novel thus institutes itself as the repository of a racial identity — Southern whiteness — which the law must hide, yet which it nevertheless needs for its own fictions of equality. Moreover, the novel also institutes itself as a form of public discourse where whiteness can be saved from its exposure in other media. It is certainly a proof of the success of the strategic repression of Boo's legal identification that most readers still assess the novel's legal ethics as impeccable. In an almost uncanny, yet also predictable way, *To Kill a Mockingbird* feeds into an understanding of ethical privilege that is still racialized. While the law's unfair treatment of the innocent African American and his execution by the prison guards are rightly perceived as both illegal and immoral, the law's reaction to the white Boo Radley is mostly regarded as an act of equity that, while it is not covered by the law, is justified nevertheless for its moral value.

The safety of whiteness from legal acknowledgment and public exposure, however, is also a literary necessity. Saving Boo Radley from the law and from the public and making his true identification the exclusive office of literature finally amounts to transforming racial identification from a question of legal ethics into one of literary aesthetics. Thus, when Atticus asks his daughter to accept the story concocted by the sheriff — "Mr Ewell fell on his knife. Can you possibly understand?" — Scout, the perceptual and narrating agent of the novel, answers with assurance:

> "Yes sir, I understand," I reassured him. "Mr Tate was right."
> Atticus disengaged himself and looked at me. "What do you mean?"
> "Well, it'd be sort of like shootin a mockingbird, wouldn't it?" (*TM,* 304)

The explanation given by Scout is also the novel's own position, as the allusion to its title indicates. Moreover, the ethical motivation for concealing Boo's identity emphasized by the sheriff ("that's a sin") is substituted by an aesthetic motivation: Atticus had admonished the children earlier that it would be a sin to shoot and kill mockingbirds because all they did was imitating other birds with their song for the enjoyment of their human audience. The novel's final position on the problem of racial justice and equality thus turns out to be an appeal for the development of an aesthetic and ethical sensibility — the education of empathy — which stands for the essentially humanizing function of mimetic literature. Likewise, the identification of Boo Radley with the mockingbird (and thus with the novel itself), which Scout and the novel's readers are asked to accept in the end, turns the image into the last, precarious refuge for Southern whiteness.

Chapter 6

Dissenting Opinions: William Gaddis, Alan Dershowitz, and the Spectacles of Media Justice

This chapter attempts a comparative interpretation of two rather dissimilar novels, William Gaddis' *A Frolic of His Own* and Alan Dershowitz's *The Advocate's Devil.* Despite their obvious differences in terms of motivation and genre, however, the fact that both novels were published in the same year (1994) makes them interesting as comparable, if contrastive, reactions to a specific moment in the changing history of the correlation of American law and literature. Although they do not refer directly to the crucial dialectics of rhetoric and evidence which informed the central positional texts of the law-and-literature movement discussed in the initial chapters of this book, both Gaddis' and Dershowitz's novels arguably could be read as literary commentaries on specific theoretical positions which characterize the various efforts to invigorate the critical relation between the legal and the literary in postmodern American culture.

Moreover, the comparative discussion of the specific correlations of law and literature in Gaddis' and Dershowitz's narratives will pick up and tie together the central arguments made in the foregoing chapters. Charles Brockden Brown's initial attempt, for example, to problematize the tension between the subjectivity of witnessing and the power of language to form consent through public testimony is also a major issue in Gaddis' and Dershowitz's negotiations of the tension between private experience and public rhetoric. They also share Cooper's apprehensiveness about the essential role of the news media for the formation of opinions and beliefs about justice and legal procedure. Finally, as I will attempt to show, Gaddis and Dershowitz present two diverging solutions to the central problem outlined in Lee's *To Kill a Mockingbird,* i. e. the diminishing role of literary fiction as the most significant and influential extra-legal forum for the cultural representation and critique of the law. In other words, both novels are driven by the same concern about the status of literary evidence in the face of the powerful rhetoric of the law which formed the major motivation for the literary engagement with the law throughout American cultural history. The obvious difference of the contemporary cultural conditions informing the potential correlations of the legal and the literary lies in the fact that the cultural presence of the law has become almost completely dominated and defined by the mass media and popular culture. Both novels have to face these conditions — but even though they use the literary representation of the law's rhetoric in similar ways to criticize its deteriorating cultural effects they do so in radical dissimilar ways.

I

At first sight, the differences between the novels are more than obvious, especially when looking at their authors' position within the field of law and literature. Steven Weisenburger has called William Gaddis' novels "the most daunting satirical fictions of postmodern America," and his characterization of Gaddis' first two novels also holds true for *A Frolic of His Own:* [R]ising out of paradox and contradiction, they envision postwar society as a thousand-plateaued landscape of 'plots,' detailed in all the exhaustive, erudite minutiae of its own subterranean erosion."[1] In contrast, Alan M. Dershowitz is arguably one of the best known lawyers in the United States today. Dershowitz, who also teaches at Harvard Law School, has been involved in some of the most spectacular, if not to say notorious cases in recent American legal history. His clients have included Mike Tyson, Claus von Bulow, O. J. Simpson, and Michael Milken. Even though he always was a prolific writer, *The Advocate's Devil* was Dershowitz's first work of fiction, followed in 1999 by another novel, *Just Revenge.*

Using the term in its most literal meaning, both texts could be described as 'legal fictions,' yet it is obvious that they differ remarkably in their perspective on law and on literature. The first question, then, is whether or not we have two cases that have to be argued separately or whether both can be put on the stand in a single court, as it were.

Although I am tempted to argue for the second option, I will restrain myself at the onset as far as possible from comparing the two novels directly. Rather, by way of indirection, I will start with a discussion of what I think is their common concern, then make some short remarks about the definition of legal and literary authorship and authority in relation to the inherent tendency of modern media for visual representation and the dramatization of evidence. In a subsequent step, I will look at the two novels separately to highlight some of their interesting and significant similarities. In conclusion, the focus of my attention will turn to the question in what way the contrast between the two novels reflects on the contemporary relation between law and literature, between the literary and the legal.

---

1 Weisenburger, *Fables of Subversion*, 199.

The comparative strategy I will follow is based on the observation that Gaddis and Dershowitz are above all in surprisingly similar ways at once inspired and troubled by the current conditions that affect the central *cultural* function of both law and literature: the meditation on and mediation of a common sense of justice. The guiding notion of a common or shared sense of justice which I will use here is based on the writings of Robert Cover on the relation between '*nomos* and narrative,' that is, on the way our ideas about law and justice are grounded in and negotiated through certain stories or narratives. According to Cover, the ability to point out what is right or wrong, just or unjust, within or outside the law, is essentially bound to our tendencies towards narrative orientation and justification. Law and literature both answer to this need in their own ways — another point of convergence which assures their inevitable contest. As Cover writes: we "inhabit a *nomos* — a normative universe," because we "constantly create and maintain a world of right and wrong, of lawful and unlawful, of valid and void."[2] This sense of justice relies less on the rules and regulations, the "principles and formal institutions of the law," and more on locating the law within certain "narratives that give [the law its] meaning."[3] Only through its being embedded in these narratives does the law turn into something more than just an ensemble of rules; as a *nomos* the law becomes a narrative we inhabit. Or, as Cover writes: "[t]o inhabit a *nomos* is to know how to *live* in it."[4]

Cover's concept of the *nomos* — the common sense of justice — and its narrative foundations offers itself as an explanation for the complex question of how the law can become a concept, a force, or a dimension of our everyday life even while most of us rarely have contact with the law, hardly read the law, and even less practice the law professionally. Given our normal distance to its practice and its theory, it is by no means natural why most members of a certain culture should have a common sense of justice in which the law plays a central role. Thus, for instance, Jerold Auerbach has shown how certain traditional structures of arriving at justice without litigation or reference to the 'official' legal institutions were gradually given up or even deemed 'illegal' during the professionalization and institutionalization of American law from the 17th century onward.[5] As Cover insists, the central role of law in establishing the *nomos* is not simply the result of the

2 Cover, *Narrative*, 95.
3 Cover, *Narrative*, 96.
4 Cover, *Narrative*, 97.
5 The *nomos* which Cover describes has a history as well; there is nothing natural about a normative universe in which the law as we know it serves as a crucial component. Cf. Auerbach, *Justice Without Law?,* esp. 4–17, 115–37.

power of the state and the institutional force of law. What we believe to be "normative behavior," in the sense that includes moral, ethic and legal 'norms' must be inscribed into narrative codes before it can become effective as a behavioral norm, as Cover explains:

> The codes that relate our normative system to our social constructions of reality and to our visions of what the world might be are narrative. The very imposition of a normative force upon a state of affairs, real or imagined, is the act of creating narrative. … To live in a legal world requires that one know not only the precepts, but also their connections to possible and plausible states of affairs. It requires that one integrate not only the 'is' and the 'ought,' but the 'is,' the 'ought,' and the 'what might be.' Narrative so integrates these domains. Narratives are models through which we study and experience transformations that result when a given simplified state of affairs is made to pass through the force field of a similarly simplified set of norms.[6]

Given the crucial role of narrative in the creation and the maintenance of the normative universe in which a common sense of justice may emerge and sustain itself, Cover concludes, that "the creation of legal meaning … always takes place through a cultural medium." What Cover calls "jurigenesis" is not simply a matter of legislative semantics or juridical interpretation: the meaning of the law is always determined by a "creative process" that is "collective and social" — in other words, legal meaning is a cultural creation.[7]

At first sight, this characterization may appear rather obvious. Nevertheless it demands some clarification. The functional equation outlined by Cover places the *nomos* as a system of norms and values on par with the creation of narrative constructions and explanations, on the one hand, and with the creation of legal meaning as a collective cultural process, on the other. This not only suggests that the creation of legal meaning in the cultural realm translates the laws into an inhabitable *nomos* in the first place — by giving it or embedding it into a system of narratives. It also reveals that social behavior as it appears to be guided or informed by the law in fact already follows a cultural interpretation of the laws or of the legal system. Only in its cultural meaning, then, does the law become an effective force of social control.[8] But this also means that the cultural interpretation of the law, because it can never be fully anticipated nor regulated by the law as it is, may yield effects that run counter to the law's intended meaning.

---

6 Cover, *Narrative*, 102.

7 Cover, *Narrative*, 103.

8 See Cover, *Narrative,* 102–03; and on the tension between social and cultural "jurisgenesis" and the "autism" of the law, see Cover, *Narrative,* 138.

The most obvious example of such a paradoxical development today can be seen in the ongoing debate on excessive litigiousness in contemporary American law and culture. The central question which fuels this debate is whether Americans are a fundamentally litigious people and therefore take recourse to the law more often than people from other countries; or whether, on the contrary, Americans are driven to excessive litigation against their better nature by the peculiar adversarial character of their law and the profit-driven litigiousness of their lawyers. Critics of the U.S. legal system like Paul F. Campos, for instance, have denounced the "jurismania" of American legal culture and the "madness of American law," which has led to the "collapse of the common good" and the "death of common sense," as Philip K. Howard wrote.[9] For Campos, Howard and others, the *nomos* of American law has become increasingly uninhabitable because today litigation at all costs has become its master narrative.[10]

In one of the first assessments of the litigious society of the eighties, the legal critic Jethro Lieberman wrote that the "United States was not founded on revelation or ancient custom or noble conquest. It was founded on law and on a legal system that centered on litigation."[11] The tragic irony is that American litigiousness more and more erodes the integrating function of the legitimating narrative that American law used to weave around itself. The ideal of 'justice for all' must turn into a farce, and finally collapse into its opposite, if it is to be pursued merely as an individual search for legal restitution.

In regard to Cover's concept of *nomos* as narrative, William Gaddis and Alan Dershowitz offer rather unique assessments of the ambivalent character and the deteriorating effects of contemporary narratives about and by the law. One major consequence is that the common sense of justice in both novels appears to disintegrate into distinct competing stories of individual law and subjective justice. The common sense of justice is thus subverted by a universal desire for litigation; the tacit consensus of shared behavioral norms is replaced by the 'norm' of 'adversarial legalism' — what Robert A. Kagan has described as the American way of law.[12] For Kagan, American ad-

---

9 See Campos' *Jurismania*; and Howard, *The Collapse of the Common Good*; and *The Death of Common Sense.*

10 Examples include Crier, *The Case Against Lawyers*; Glendon, *Nation Under Lawyers;* Nader/Smith, *No Contest.*

11 Lieberman, *The Litigious Society*, 15.

12 See Kagan, *Adversarial Legalism,* 12. For an interpretation of adversarial legalism from the perspective of legal and cultural history, see Friedman, "Are We A Litigious People," esp. 60–64.

versarial legalism cannot be considered as a purely cultural or purely legal phenomenon. What he calls the distinctive legal style unique to American legal culture is above all informed by the highly active roles litigants and lawyers play in the decision process and the implementation of rules and policies. Or, as Gaddis puts it: "This free enterprise society is an adversarial society so the law emerges from that adversarial attitude. So here we are, all adversaries."[13]

As we will see, law and literature may offer rather different reactions to this state of affairs. The most interesting aspect in this respect, however, is how this reaction must take recourse to and rely on the narrative norms of its respective counterpart. If the crisis of normative behavior is also the crisis of narrative norms, then law and literature may share a common concern and interest: the revision and reconstruction of narrative forms that would connect the legal and the literary, i.e. *nomos* and narrative, in a meaningful way.

Yet beyond Dershowitz's and Gaddis' shared concerns about the sense of justice in contemporary American culture and society, there are other important aspects which encourage a comparative examination of their works. For one, despite the differences between the works and their authors, both novels are the result of a similar transgressive impulse: Gaddis and Dershowitz make a bold step beyond the field of their respective legitimate discursive authority. If the authority to speak in public and for the public is a claim that the authors share, these claims nevertheless are legitimized only by their distinct positions in two separate fields of social and cultural practice. As Pierre Bourdieu has argued,[14] authority is granted to individuals according to the specific power structure of a given partition of the entire field of social practices. Bourdieu calls these partitions *fields* and insists that while any field may assume to be autonomous from other fields, its objective autonomy is always relative to the hierarchy of power between all fields.[15]

From this perspective, what separates literature from law most fundamentally, especially in regard to their respective cultural significance, are precisely the different categories and assumptions according to which they are granted their legitimacy. Principally, the authority of a respected literary writer and that of a respected lawyer are based on the high level of performance in their respective fields, which is recognized and thus legitimized by such forms of public acknowledgment as the award of literary prizes or the

---

13 Qtd. in Knight, *Hints and Guesses*, 203.

14 Bourdieu, *Language and Symbolic Power*, 230.

15 Bourdieu, *Language and Symbolic Power*, 239–40.

award of law degrees and titles. In the cases at hand, the two authors use their authority to make inroads into the neighboring field: Gaddis acts as a lawyer in writing (albeit fictitious) summaries and opinions, while Dershowitz assumes the role of an author of literary fiction that conforms to the laws of a specific genre — the courtroom drama. In face of Gaddis' professed inclinations for a career in the law,[16] it seems rather consequential that he would immerse himself completely in legal writings when preparing for his fourth novel, researching tort law decisions, especially those involving negligence, and reading through eighty volumes of *American Jurisprudence*.[17] Even though Dershowitz has insisted that "life is not a narrative,"[18] he obviously believes that the most controversial legal issues do find their most adequate representation in form of fictional literature.

The terms 'acting' and 'role' deliberately point to the performing, yet also *performative* nature of both transgressions. This means that neither author sheds his legitimate cloak of authority, he merely assumes another: both in law and literature, it is hard to separate the nature of their performance from the performative nature of literary and legal speech acts. If the ultimate power of the performative speech act is to "bring into existence what it utters,"[19] this power is always linked to the specific conditions of performance that define law and literature as professions in similar ways centered around linguistic practices of persuasion, or more precisely, rhetorical power. Both novels thus meet in the most important area where law and literature as distinct modes of performing (and performative) discourse overlap: the realm of public speech or rhetoric. Comparing the two novels and their perspectives on the contemporary conditions of public speech will arguably reveal a great deal about how their authors see their own professions affected by these conditions.

Both Gaddis and Dershowitz obviously share an intense interest in the *language* of the law as a public form of rhetoric and its relation to justice. In a certain sense, rhetoric traditionally signified a mode of oral address which would elevate private, subjective utterances to the status of objective, i.e. commonly acceptable meaning. Speaking rhetorically thus meant to address less a concrete audience of individuals but rather an abstract congregation of collective categories of understanding and communication, that is, a com-

---

16 Moore, *William Gaddis*, 142.
17 Moore, *Gaddis,* 153 n15.
18 Brooks/Gewirtz, *Law's Stories*, 67.
19 Bourdieu, *Language and Symbolic Power,* 42.

mon *sense*.[20] And no matter whether rhetoric achieves its power by means of manipulation or persuasion or by reference to facts and truth, it always depends on the right — the just, the legitimate, the appropriate — choice of words.

Since the advent of modern mass media, however, the realm of public meaning and therefore of common sense has become less and less governed by language, that is, by verbal utterances and signs, and more and more by images, that is, by visual signs.[21] The transgressive impulse of both Gaddis' and Dershowitz's assumptions of authority thus must be seen as a reaction to the equally transgressive, or even aggressive, takeover of the public arena by the images of the media. This takeover affects both literature and the law because their authority and legitimacy are deeply rooted in a specific understanding of the cultural relation — the symbolic hierarchy — that governs the opposition between words and images, between the verbal and the visual mediation of justice.

The opposition between words and images which dominates Western cultural history, as W. J. T. Mitchell has convincingly argued, stands as the bedrock of common-sense distinctions between idea and fact, between argument and evidence, and between objective reality and subjective imagination. "The gulf between words and images," Mitchell states, is still seen to be "as wide as the one between words and things, between (in the largest sense) culture and nature," because:

> [t]he image is the sign that pretends not to be a sign, masquerading as (or, for the believer, actually achieving) natural immediacy and presence. The word is its "other," the artificial, arbitrary production of human will that disrupts the natural presence by introducing unnatural elements into the world — time, consciousness, history, and the alienating intervention of symbolic mediation.[22]

In the preceding chapter I have already discussed the enormous impact of images in American culture on the perception of racial identity and racial identification. I tried to show how the legal concept of identification tacitly relates to and interacts with cultural codes of identity, both discursive and visual. I argued among other things that the central cultural mode of identification always came to rest on an image the identifying subject could iden-

---

20 The term *common sense* has been emphasized because it will be used in the following discussion in both its main connotations: as a lesser and more vague term for 'meaning' or 'significance,' and as referring to a perceptual competence, meaning both 'being attentive or sensitive to' and 'being aware of,' 'having a sense' for something.

21 See Crary, *Techniques of the Observer;* and Lowe, *Bourgeois Perception*.

22 Mitchell, *Iconology*, 43.

tify with. In this respect, the interplay of word and image could be regarded as a specific rhetoric of identification which differed according to the perspective of the spectator and his or her cultural position.

Yet the relation between image and word presents more than just a difference or the interplay between two distinct modes of identification and signification. Given the complex history of mediating technologies — technologies of telling and showing in public — the word-image opposition always was (and still is) a constant point of struggle between different media which in any specific historical situation characterizes the conditions of public rhetoric and common sense. And it is precisely the specific hierarchical order of the media *as a system* that essentially grounds the legitimacy of public speech in any given case. Moreover, in a situation where the public sphere is both an arena of discursive contestation and of economic competition, the rhetorical struggle between different media more often than not becomes charged with a strong tendency for dramatic excess — that is, the media spectacle emerges as a basic mode of cultural representation.

For better or for worse, both law and literature are faced with and challenged by the cultural power of the media. Thus a central concern within debates about the changing nature of the cultural presence and effect of the law is that the media have somehow captured the *nomos* of American legal culture and that the meaning of justice is constructed above all in and by the media. The reason for the incalculable dominance of 'media law' is that it has successfully introduced the dramatization of evidence and the dramatic staging of evidence as the established standard for the cultural burden of proof. In their distinct ways, Gaddis and Dershowitz show the close interrelation and mutual reinforcement of U.S. America's culture of litigiousness and the dramatization of legal struggle and contest by the media. The authority of law and literature as verbal professions, and thus as authoritative representations of the law, today has become threatened by the effects media like television have on the public perception of the law. The public image of the law in contemporary American culture has become dominated by new forms of representation and dramatization, especially by the genre of the spectacular or notorious trial. In the age of the media trial, law and literature as professional rhetorics are more and more troubled by the suggestive force of media performance.

II

Under the conditions of mass media culture, the professions of law and literature can no longer rely on words alone. The contemporary demands of high visibility and the incessant drive towards drama and spectacle has set certain standards of audience expectations and of public self-presentation. Moreover, the increasing desire for 'truth' as resulting from adversarial struggle has also established a certain standard of proof in the eye of the public jury. What counts as and what does not count as evidence (and what is used as evidence in the struggle for truth) has increasingly come to rest on its dramatic potential, its versatility for dramatization. Evidence in its dramatic form is understood as a performance, as a staging of the truth of the matter. Of course, there is nothing new to the inherent theatrical nature of the courtroom trial in Anglo-American legal procedure. Today, however, as numerous critics have argued, theatre and drama have become the standard forms of the presentation of evidence which guide our expectations of the truth in legal processes. The solemn profession of the law has turned into a public performance in which lawyers and judges become professional actors.

This reorientation of the legal profession must not involve a denigration or a perversion of justice, as legal scholar Robert Burns has argued. In fact, his emphatic understanding of the trial as a professional performance has led Burns to develop a particular theory of the trial which recognizes that "[j]udgment as it occurs at trial is a kind of skillful performance of a particular complex kind." The various "linguistic practices and performances that the trial comprises … come together to achieve the minor miracle of a convergence on and display of the practical truth of a human situation." Yet, as Burns indicates, this convergence of legal performances in the service of truth is only perceived and understood by those who participate in the "minor miracle" as professional performers. For what is needed to gain a "position to know"[23] is a professional competence which allows one actor to see through the other's acting. While such competence may appear easy for those who already belong to the profession, the lay jury in and outside the courtroom may find it hard or even impossible to unravel the complex interplay between act and fact, between dramatic evidence and practical truth.

In contrast to the optimism of professionals like Burns, the most poignant, if ironic description of this disturbing cultural situation has been offered not by a lawyer or a legal scholar but by Thomas Pynchon in his novel

---

23 Burns, *Theory of the Trial,* 3.

The Crying of Lot 49, where the lawyer-actor Metzger points out the postmodern condition of legal performance:

> '… our beauty lies,' explained Metzger, 'in this extended capacity for convolution. A lawyer in a courtroom, in front of a jury becomes an actor, right? Raymond Burr is an actor, impersonating a lawyer, who in front of a jury becomes an actor. Me, I'm a former actor who became a lawyer. They've done the pilot film of a TV series … based loosely on my career, starring my friend Manny Di Presso, a one-time lawyer who quit his firm to become an actor. Who in this pilot plays me, an actor become a lawyer reverting periodically to being an actor. The film is in an air-conditioned vault at one of the Hollywood studios, light can't fatigue it, it can be repeated endlessly.'[24]

The extended capacity for convolution which Metzger finds so enjoyable characterizes the image of the law in the "age of the television trial," as Paul Thaler has called the contemporary cultural situation of media convoluted legal procedure. Thaler describes the essential logic underlying this situation in terms very similar to Pynchon's:

> Inevitably, the camera compels each court member to confront his courtroom 'image' as it is electronically bounced off a television audience. Participants can suddenly find themselves as part of the audience, since televised proceedings allow them to interact with their own performances. They can scrutinize their remarks, body language, and nuances of their performance as broadcast on television, As the distinction between actor and audience is blurred, so, too is the fine line between impartiality and self-conscious performance.[25]

To understand more fully how the logic of postmodern performance culture ties in with the important role of the mass media in contemporary American legal culture, and how the presentation of legal trials in the mass media today in turn feeds on and further enhances the adversarial tendencies in American law and culture, it is necessary to take a short look at the emergence of the media trial as a genre of public rhetoric.

The authority of both law and literature as modes of public speech is based on the specific construction of audiences and the regulation of authorship. The audience that the literary and the legal text address must possess a certain degree of competence in reading and interpreting such texts. However, the *common* sense of justice goes beyond the limits of literacy; it must also be made manifest as an experience. In other words, the idea of justice cannot be divorced from the concept of the public arena as a space of collective experience. Lance Bennett and Marta Feldman, for instance, in their seminal study on the 'reconstruction of reality in the courtroom,' stated that

---

[24] Pynchon, *Crying*, 21.
[25] Thaler, *The Watchful Eye*, 16.

> even though justice procedures may vary, they have the common function of enabling members of society to understand … the grounds for fair and just settlements of disputes. This implies that if the terms of justice are to make sense to the average members of society, the formal procedures of justice must somehow incorporate everyday means of communication and judgement.[26]

Unfortunately, Bennett and Feldman's important investigation of the crucial function of storytelling strategies in the courtroom almost exclusively relied on a concept of story-telling, i.e. a legal or cultural narratology.[27] Written before the advent of televised courtroom proceedings, the book can offer only implicit suggestions as to how much 'everyday means of communication and judgement' have changed under the growing influence of aggressive strategies of visualization. As the conditions or modes of collective experience change so do the modes of cultural representation and in effect the common sense of justice may change accordingly.

The disturbing fact for both American law and literature since the advent of modern mass media was and still is the impending loss of control over the public sphere in the face of the enormous power of competing agencies of public discourse such as the newspapers and tabloid press, radio, television and, most recently, the internet. In one way, as the preceding chapters have continuously argued, the relation between law, literature and the media in the U.S. has always been characterized by cultural interference and competition at least since the times of Brown and Cooper. Since the introduction of television in the 1940s and the gradual emergence of a postmodern public sphere since the 1960s, however, the complex interplay between these forces has taken on a new quality. The television format presents a distinct mixture or convergence of the local and the global, projecting and transforming the public sphere into a 'private' space while at the same time translating private events into public spectacle.[28] This state of affairs had some troubling consequences for American legal culture and the cultural perception of the law as well. At the heart of the complex matter is the ambivalent function of television as a means of objective documentation and as an expression of popular judgment and opinion.

Thus the Warren Commission, for instance, after its investigation of President John F. Kennedy's assassination and the subsequent shooting of

---

26 Bennett/Feldman, *Reconstructing Reality in the Courtroom*, 20.

27 See Chapter 2.

28 See, for instance, Morley/Robins, *Spaces of Identity*. For television as a postmodern medium, see Thorburn, "Television." For the influence of mass audience television on legal culture, see Thaler, *The Watchful Eye*; and Sherwin, *When Law Goes Pop*, esp. 14–39.

Lee Harvey Oswald in front of television cameras, stated that "part of the responsibility for the unfortunate circumstances … must be borne by the news media." The Commission asserted that the media had completely upset the delicate balance between public judgment and judgment by the law, since the "experience in Dallas [was] a dramatic affirmation of the need for steps to bring about a proper balance between the right of the public to be kept informed and the right of the individual to a fair and impartial trial."

Although the press claims that it only serves the strong public interest in the law and in justice, its "imperatives for newsworthiness, saleability, speed, and excitement" work against the "solemn, dispassionate, calculated rules of evidence and the punctilious rules of court."[29] But television differs from written news in that the camera appears to be a much more impartial instrument of recording than the subjective descriptions of an individual observer. Television can document the rules of evidence and of the court with much more persuasiveness and truth than any other verbal medium. At least, that is what Albert Friendly and Ronald L. Goldfarb could still assert in 1967:

> [T]he dignity and integrity of trials depends on the participants, and not on television's portrayal of them. The performance of some attorneys at some trials is obnoxious, even without cameras; cameras would merely show it for what it is. … It is hardly an argument against the medium to assert that television may show a performance, good or bad, more vividly to more people.[30]

The idea of the transparency of the medium has always been the major argument for the defense of courtroom television by its proponents, even though it has developed from its early, experimental phase into a full blown commercial enterprise. Celebrating television's "glass eye," Anna Quindlen of the *New York Times* enthusiastically remarked in 1991: "The raw material from which we reporters build stories on — most of it was there on screen. It was the first time … that I could cover a story just as well from my living room as I could on the scene."[31] The problem however, as Paul Thaler puts it, is that "television is hardly a glass eye, a benign and remote technology; rather, it is a powerful and active observer … that narrowly frames the world … to dictate 'meaning.'"[32] For Thaler, the television trial "has added an entirely new dimension to the process [of justice]: a vast, mediated public, emotionally involved with the issues and controversy attached to a particular case."[33]

---

29 Qtd. in Friendly/Goldfarb, *Crime and Publicity*, 10.
30 Friendly/Goldfarb, *Crime and Publicity*, 239.
31 Qtd. in Thaler, *The Watchful Eye,* xxii.
32 Thaler, *The Watchful Eye,* xxii.
33 Thaler, *The Watchful Eye,* 12.

But Quindlen's assessment of the function of the TV camera suggests yet another predicament of legal rhetoric in the "age of the television trial."[34] With the advent of courtroom TV, the image has entered the inner sanctum of the word — of law and justice as a story or a text — and turned it into yet another public spectacle. And this spectacle threatens to become the transparent, the ideal, and indeed, the visible source of legal authority in a postmodern culture of performance. As Peter Goodrich has stated, what we are witnessing today is "the emergence of law in the videosphere" where the legal process itself becomes subject to "media constraints, the genres of spectacle or viewing" and the "performative demands of screen acting."[35]

Yet the peculiar nature of heightened public visibility that has come to govern the perception of American justice at the turn of the 21st century is less that it is so obviously the result of a rather conscious effort at staging, acting, and dramatizing the representation of legal evidence and the struggle for truth. Rather what makes contemporary public performances of the law so different from their predecessors in earlier centuries, is that a good performance is expected by the audience. The legal process, especially in its form as a courtroom trial, has become a public drama. With the help of media resonance and obsessive media coverage from within the legal arena, the inherent theatricality of courtroom proceedings has successfully been transformed into a TV format. While the American film industry had of course always used the courtroom drama to exploit the epic and tragic dimensions of Anglo-American legal struggle, only the televisionary appropriation of the legal drama on a large scale could effectively turn the exceptional into the ordinary. Constant TV coverage of legal trials thus encouraged certain expectations about the inherently dramatic nature of the process itself; the law turned into generic spectacle.

As Cornelia Vismann has suggested, the radical transformation of the public image of American law and its proceedings began in the 1950s, during the McCarthy hearings and their national presence on TV. In contrast to the

---

34 Thaler, *The Watchful Eye,* xix.

35 Goodrich, "Europe in America," 2075, 2076. Goodrich's assessment of the situation is not altogether negative, though. He seems to believe that the increased public visibility of courtroom proceedings and trials may also increase the transparency of the legal process itself, preventing the law from "hiding behind occult writs and prior judgments" and turning the trial into "a self-consious and transparent rite" (Goodrich, "Europe in America," 2076). For a salient critique of Goodrich's vision, see Vismann, "Tele-Tribunals."

traditional courtroom trial, Vismann writes, "hearings belong to the genre of tribunals"[36] and though they often assume the status of a trial, tribunals differ essentially in certain aspects from ordinary trials:

> The orderly and hermetic world of the court, with its specifically dedicated architectural environment, stands in contrast to the tribunal, a kind of road show that can be held anywhere. Without the rules and precedent of proper trial procedure, it works not only with cameras, bright lights, and noise, but also with unscrupulous tricks and lies; greedily borrowing procedural forms and strategies from sports as much as from the law. This permeability eats away at the distinction between inside and outside, the very distinction that is most essential to judicial performance. It is not so much that the cameras transmit the proceedings to the outside, but rather that the great mass audience, glued to the TV-screen, becomes part of the tribunal.[37]

For Vismann, the increasing presence of the television camera in American courtrooms has more and more impressed the logic of the medium on the procedural strategies of the trial and the employment of these strategies by the prosecution and the defense. This effect has been enforced even more by the "tendency within the justice system itself, a move towards *tribunalization*"; and finally, the "lines between real court trials and fictional courtroom dramas are additionally blurred when television series re-create courtroom scenes and TV stations report live from the courts."[38] Vismann concluded: "If television cameras are present in court proceedings, elements that have their origins in the disorder of the tribunal will of necessity seep into the court trial. The ritual of legal search for justice will give way to the logic of the duel."[39]

The redefinition of the logic of the legal trial as a kind of duel, that is, as a highly dramatized and individualized form of struggle must resonate in rather particular ways with the inherent adversarial tendencies of American culture. The move towards tribunalization turns the legal trial into a site for ritual contest; a dramatic conflict where more is at stake than truth and justice as the result of rational and objective procedure. In its dramatized media version, American adversarial legalism has found its archetypical cultural representation.[40]

---

36 Vismann, "Tele-Tribunals," 8.

37 Vismann, "Tele-Tribunals," 9.

38 Vismann, "Tele-Tribunals," 16.

39 Vismann, "Tele-Tribunals," 18.

40 William Haltom, in his study on characteristic media coverage of judicial actions observed a strong tendency to dramatize normality when he stated that the "news media dramatize abnormal cases until, over time, they have normalized dramatic cases" (Haltom, *Reporting on the Courts,* 186).

Thus, Robert Hariman has argued that the "popular trial" has become a central "genre of public discourse"[41] or rhetoric during the second half of the 20th century. Likewise, Robert Sherwin has described the increasing dominance of the "notorious case" in the cultural imagination and perception of the law. These cases, Sherwin points out, "infuse the particular facts of a specific legal controversy with larger meanings. The trial is no longer about factual truths only; its truths have become symbolic."[42] Neither the popular nor the notorious trial are singular events, rather they have become the generic standard of the public representation of the law. Thus the media falsely encourage, as Fox and van Sickel note, "the impression that the majority of the defendants actually *have* trials and that they are either found guilty or acquitted after a jury has considered all relevant evidence."[43] That the majority of cases in real life never goes to trial but instead is worked out through plea bargaining is a fact that finds no adequate representation in the *nomos* of American media. Consequently, cultural historians Richard Fox and Robert van Sickel speak of "tabloid justice" to describe a general atmosphere or cultural environment:

> When [the] three dynamics — a legal proceeding presented largely as entertainment, an obsessive media establishment, and an intensely attentive public — converge, the environment of tabloid justice emerges. Within this context, the idealized priorities of the criminal justice system, such as justice and fairness, have become secondary to the press' interest in attracting large audiences by presenting shocking images. This is the atmosphere of the tabloid justice era ….[44]

One point that deserves special notice is the fact that tabloid justice is characterized by an emphasis on cultural and social confrontation, controversy and antagonism. The "polarizing manner in which the media now cover criminal trials," Fox and van Sickel criticize, "has potentially aggravated some of the most troubling social divisions in U.S. society."[45] In the same vein, Sherwin comments that "one of the hallmarks of the notorious case is its staging of competing world views," a dramatic struggle at whose conclusion "some meanings will reign triumphant"[46] while others will be defeated.

It requires no great feat of imagination to suggest that there is an inherent relation between the media's interest in staging legal conflicts as antagonistic battles, on the one hand, and the thriving litigiousness characteristic of con-

41 Hariman, *Popular Trials, 18.*
42 Sherwin, *When Law Goes Pop*, 73–74.
43 Fox/Sickel, *Tabloid Justice*, 12.
44 Fox/Sickel, *Tabloid Justice*, 5.
45 Fox/Sickel, *Tabloid Justice*, 5.
46 Sherwin, *When Law Goes Pop*, 77.

temporary American legal culture on the other.[47] Both aspects are in a way complementary tendencies that enhance each other by the narrative logic they share and pursue in their own ways. Which brings us back to Robert Cover's concept of the *nomos,* and the question how the compulsory logic of adversarial narratives shapes the cultural understanding of law in contemporary America. For it appears obvious that the law may be less and less seen as an agent for the neutral regulation of conflict for the greater good of common justice. On the contrary, the law is used increasingly as an instrument for the incitement and perpetuation of conflicts between groups in the search for individual justice. In the novels by William Gaddis and Alan Dershowitz, the two conflicting views, or *nomoi*, describe the same basic antagonism each fiction tries to negotiate and solve on its own terms.

III

Rhetoric is the source of the language of legal argument. The attempt of ancient lawyers to increase the effectiveness of litigation claims before the public in democratic courts, also gave birth to a concept of language as a medium of persuasion and argument.[48] The rhetoric of the Anglo-American common law, as Peter Goodrich has noted, is characterized by its "antirrhetical" structure or logic. Due to its roots in religious discourse and argument, common law rhetoric "complies with the adversarial form of all doctrinal discourse and is best understood as a form of antirrhetic or discourse of defense and denunciation."[49] The deep structure of legal reasoning grounding in the common law tradition, Goodrich concludes, is thus already rhetorical in the sense of an "agonistic practice."[50] In other words, the reasoning of Anglo-American common law is inevitably bound to the structure of litigation, its rhetoric is inherently adversarial, contesting, and conflict driven.

---

47 As Olson writes: "Like other savvy publicists, lawyers … learned ways of getting 'free media.' The old ethical code had frowned on contacts with the press except in the fairly narrow range of circumstances, mostly involving comments on behalf of particular clients who needed their affairs explained in public. … Nowadays lawyers and law offices employ publicists and media advisers" (*The Litigation Explosion*, 25).

48 See, for instance, Kennedy, *Art of Persuasion,* 26–29; and Kennedy, *Classical Rhetoric,* 18–21.

49 Goodrich, "Antirrhesis," 59.

50 Goodrich, "Antirrhesis," 60.

In William Gaddis' *A Frolic of His Own*, the rhetoric of litigation has spread far beyond American courts of law to become the universal mode of social intercourse. As Jonathan Raban aptly remarked: "almost everyone in the novel is suing almost everyone in sight for damages. … For every suit there is a countersuit, for every judgement an appeal."[51] It is no accident that the novel's main protagonist, the untenured college teacher, part-time historian and amateur playwright Oscar L. Crease at one point ends up suing himself because he managed to run himself over with his own car.

Ironically, Oscar is the son and grandson of distinguished judges, and allegedly he "only wants justice, after all," but there is both a self-assertive and self-destructive dimension to his claims. As one of the many lawyers in the novel observes: "this is a suit between who you are and who you think you are."[52] This points at the irreconcilable antagonism between the ideal of justice and its reality — the system of the law. Obviously Oscar inherited the system but not the common wisdom of the judges who formed it. The system has become so intricate and complex that it leaves no room for justice, as Oscar's brother-in-law Harry, also a lawyer, exclaims in the novel's opening sentence: "Justice? — You get justice in the next world, in this world you have the law" (*FO,* 13). If at all, the idea of justice and the authority of the law exist only in and as a (rather bad) piece of historical fiction: Oscar's ill-fated Civil War drama, *Once at Antietam*. Yet even this attempt to reclaim the lost authority of the law with the help of literature fails, because the play is shamelessly plagiarized by a Hollywood producer and turned into a gory spectacle, aptly called "The Blood in the Red, White and Blue."

Oscar's rather pathetic troubles with the law are contrasted with the highly publicized and controversial lawsuits his father, a distinguished federal judge, has to decide. One case involves a massive steel sculpture called 'Cyclone Seven' erected in the remote southern town of Tatamount. When an unfortunate dog of indistinct breed named 'Spot' gets trapped in the intricate artwork, and the town people are about to liberate the animal with oxyacetylene torches, the enraged artist successfully gets Judge Crease to issue an imposition, thus effectively preventing the good folks of Tatamount from forcefully dismantling the menacing sculpture in time to save the hapless dog. While this decision enrages both the citizens of Tatamount and the juvenile owner of the dog a good deal (which does not prevent the owner of the pet from suing the city officials when Spot the dog gets electrocuted by

---

51 Raban, "At Home in Babel," 3.
52 Gaddis, *A Frolic of His Own*, 474 (in the following *FO* with page number).

a bolt of lightning that hits 'Cyclone Seven'), Oscar's father manages to increase the wrath of the common people even further. In the case of a boy accidentally drowned by a fundamental minister during baptism the old judge rules that God must ultimately be held responsible — which also means that no damages can be awarded. In reaction to what they perceive as outrageous miscarriages of justice, those who feel outraged (almost everybody) form instant protest movements, variously demanding 'free Spot' or 'Impeach Judge Crease.' The press and the media, of course, have a field day.

As in his other novels, Gaddis displays an almost obsessive interest in the way spoken and written language form more and more complex networks of antagonistic meanings in which the characters almost inevitably get entangled by their own incessant linguistic activities. As Patrick O'Donnell has cogently observed, the overarching "project" of Gaddis' novels is to "denature" the linguistic processes and practices that "allow us to construct the identities of speakers and hearers as deliverers and recipients of speech." The aim of Gaddis' fictions, whether they focus on art and forgery (*The Recognitions*), on money and the stock market (*JR*), or on religion (*Carpenter's Gothic)*, is thus to reveal how "the 'orders' of speech and identity partake of the larger contexts — the wordly and cultural regimes — that frame them."

More precisely, in *A Frolic of His Own,* Gaddis shows how the law as a discursive system increasingly comes to shape and control the American sense of reality and identity. Law becomes the dominant "medium of speech"[53] and thus of communication and self-assertion; it becomes, finally, the essential medium through which reality is assessed and represented. In *A Frolic of His Own* American culture and society have become legal fictions. The novel thus presents a dystopian version of Cover's *nomos;* a universe of excessive jurisgenesis that has turned completely jurispathic.

As the law in Gaddis' novel has become the dominant medium of speech, it has also clearly infused everyday conversation with an intense adversarial spirit. In the social universe of *A Frolic of His Own*, language serves as the basic weapon in what Deborah Tannen has called America's "argument culture," based on the "assumption that truth emerges when two polarized, warring extremes are set against each other."[54] People in the novel do not converse or communicate in the conventional sense of these terms; there is no orderly traffic of ideas or exchange of meanings. Instead, opinions and statements are regularly hurled against the opponent and hardly does anyone listen to anyone else. Misunderstandings abound and meanings collide and

---

53 O'Donnell, "The Reader's *Frolic*," 162.
54 Tannen, *The Argument Culture,* 131.

crash almost constantly. This points to an understanding of language in which verbal discourse is less a medium of communication but rather the means to encourage and realize the self-asserting performance of the individual.

The persuasive force of verbal rhetoric and performance, as Marie Maclean writes, relies on a common frame of reference for both the speaker and the listeners: "[A] base of shared expectations, whereby power is granted to others, to the hearers as well as the teller."[55] For Maclean, performance usually functions as a "metatext"[56] for the audience, but in *A Frolic of His Own* the metatext threatens to become the only text. More precisely, the novel represents a mode of discourse whose message *is* its performance without the power of persuasion and without meaning. As Oscar notes in utter despair: "it's all just more words and more words until everything gets buried under words" (*FO,* 160).

What is indeed buried under all those words is the common frame of reference which would allow for a meaningful performance of rhetorical exchanges. Obviously the law has seeped into the most intimate dialogues between the characters; thus at one point Oscar's sister Christina exasperatedly yells at her husband Harry: "My God … can't you say anything without writing a whole legal brief to go with it?" (*FO,* 348).

Yet the omnipresence of legal discourse in no way provides a common source of meaning. The law's meaning is always already adversarial, contested, and therefore unstable; legal language in its degraded, unprofessional everyday form is simply a medium of opposing claims and dissenting opinions. O'Donnell aptly concludes: "all 'talk' in the novel self-reflexively circles around the twinned issues of the point or 'end' and the legitimacy of talking in the first place."[57] The result is a complete loss of discursive order: "Everyone talks in a novel replete with legal briefs, newspaper clippings, depositions, case studies, judgments, citations, passages from Oscar's play — there is, in short, no end to language here, no sense that the talking will stop."[58]

The novel, however, does not simply describe the disturbing aspects of a deeply adversarial culture and its fragmented, warring discourses. The text rather incorporates the logic of endless claim and counter claim and turns it into its own central principle of construction. Gaddis' formal strategies in

---

55 Maclean, *Narrative as Performance*, 7.
56 Maclean, *Narrative as Performance*, 7–8.
57 O'Donnell, "The Reader's *Frolic*," 164.
58 O'Donnell, "The Reader's *Frolic*," 165.

this way not only work against most of the conventional expectations of a reading audience. More importantly, they also highlight the crucial function of performance in and for his own text. Sentences flow into each other without punctuation, are left without closure, or taken up by other speakers but with a very different meaning — there is an almost complete absence of formal order on the level of grammar and syntax in the dialogues which make up the most part of the novel. As Raban comments: "Gaddis really listens to the way we speak now. The talk is brilliantly rendered, with a wicked fidelity to its flimsy grammar, its elusions and hiatuses, its rush-and-stumble rhythms."[59]

This state of linguistic anarchy is complemented by the disturbing lack of personal naming and address. Often the identity of the speaker remains uncertain while the dialogue relentlessly rushes on, switching between its different sources and also between different locations and time frames without warning or prior notice. In other words, Gaddis denies the marks of authorship and thus of authority to his characters — a crucial gesture which is reflected in the story itself where the protagonists have to cope with the loss of authority in many different ways. What characterizes this loss most pertinently is the lack of control over language; language itself appears to be independent of its sources, freed from authorship and its control. Common frames of reference become increasingly unstable, and thus there can be no mutual recognition of meaning, no satisfaction of shared expectations. As Oscar's half-sister Christina suggests, this may well be the reason why the rhetoric of litigation has become so central: "[i]t's the only common reference people have for making other people take them as seriously as they take themselves … that's all they're asking for, isn't it?" (*FO,* 13). Thus the law becomes the last resort for any claim of personal identity and authority. Yet even this last resort turns out to be an illusory one — at least for the characters in the novel. Christina's additional remark that "money's just the yardstick, isn't it" (*FO*, 13) reveals that at the source of litigation is the drive towards compensation where social and psychological losses are set up against monetary gain and profit. Oscar both wins his lawsuit (on appeal) but also loses it, since the sum he is awarded in the end does not even cover his costs for legal representation. As Robert Weisberg writes: "Gaddis' characters turn to law to find the deep justifying structure for their lives and find instead a house of cards."[60]

---

59 Raban, "At Home in Babel," 3.
60 Weisberg, "Taking Law Seriously," 453.

If we move from the tale to the telling, we get an altogether different picture. While the radical strategies Gaddis employs may leave his characters (and a number of his readers, to be sure) helplessly entangled in the Gordian knots of (spoken) language, the medium itself — the written text of the novel — gains considerable weight as a means of authentic representation. It is an authoritative voice in its own right — a metavoice. Joseph Tabbi, for instance, states that, whereas "Gaddis surpresses his own personality and 'literate voice' to become a medium for other voices, a recorder of … multiple cultural quotations," the author nevertheless "remains very much alive in the formal arrangement of the narrative."[61]

From the perspective of literary agency, it is obvious how the formal structure of the novel, with its technical control and stylistic mastery, becomes the foundation of literary authority. Less obvious yet probably more significant for the successful effect of this performance is the sharp contrast of the anarchy of spoken language with other modes of written discourse and with the images of television and film. Paradoxically then, the authenticity of spoken language as well as the loss of its authority and persuasive power come to rest on its formal characteristics — the lack of order and structure which in turn points to the absence of a controlling source — and its inferior position in an entire system of different media of representation.

This paradox is due to the two-fold perspective the novel projects on the very language it represents. On the one hand, the reader readily recognizes in the dialogues and monologues an authentic reproduction of everyday speech, its chaotic and unordered structure, as well as its powerlessness and lack of significance. On the other hand, however, the reader is also forced to acknowledge the authority and significance of the satirical performance of authenticity: Gaddis clearly imitates, and even radicalizes and ridicules legal rhetoric without diminishing its power and authority — at least in the written judgements of Judge Crease.

The question for now is how the lack of authority of everyday speech relates to the spectacular images of the media and the professional discourse of the law.

61 Tabbi, *Postmodern Sublime*, 180.

IV

Where everyday language has lost its authority, even the most simple commonsensical acts of discrimination must fail. A point that is made obvious, for instance, in the burlesque conversations between Oscar and the insurance lawyer Frank Gribble, who is completely — and quite literally — deaf to the finer points of spoken language because he speaks and thinks only in legalese:

> — Yes, it might be a little difficult, if we could dig up some similar cases and we need to examine the car, wouldn't we.
> — Examine the car of course, I only want justice after all.
> — It's garaged at your, at the place of the accident I can't find the, what kind of car is it.
> — Sosumi.
> — I'm being quite serious Mister Crease.
> — So am I! It's a Japanese car, a Sosumi.
> — Oh. Oh dear, yes I'm sorry, it's so hard to keep track of them all nowdays. We had a whole family killed in an Isuyu and I made a similar error. (*FO,* 27–28)

The fine irony is that Gribble, who gets confused by words so easily, like all the other lawyers in the novel appears to be obsessed with linguistic discriminations — yet only according to the *letter* of the law. That is, the law as a formal structure of signification is tied to a written system of differences and discrimination of meaning, a system that is meant precisely to isolate legal meaning from the constantly shifting, unstable meanings of everyday language. No wonder then, that for Gribble, "words always cause … problems don't they when it becomes less a matter of their *actual meaning* than their interpretation" (*FO,* 473, my emphasis). Yet there is obviously a world of meaning between Gribble's 'actual meaning' of words and Oscar's belief in the expressive function of words: "Isn't that what language is for? To say what you mean? That's why man invented language, isn't it? So we can say what we mean?" (*FO,* 266). Oscar's predicament is that he expects the law to follow his ideas about language in general while Gribble's notion of 'actual meaning' exclusively refers to the legal definition of words and things.

The essential motive for the law's linguistic rigidity and formality as a professional discourse, however, is explained by Harry, Oscar's brother-in-law, in his response to Christina:

> — But damn it Christina, that's what we're talking about. What do you think the law is, that's all it is, language.
> — Legal language, I mean who can understand legal language but another lawyer, it's like a, I mean it's all a conspiracy, think about it Harry. It's a conspiracy.

— Of course it is. I don't have to think about it. Every profession is a conspiracy against the public, every profession protects itself with a language of its own ... till it all evaporates into language confronted by language turning language into theory till it's not about what it's about it's only about itself ... (*FO,* 251)

Harry's cynical theory of professional discourse ironically supports Christina's observation that the all-pervasive adversarial structure of language is ultimately a means of self-assertion and self-protection. Legal discourse in this respect comes to resemble every-day speech since in the final analysis they are both completely self-centered, empty practices — what Gaddis calls language turned into 'theory.' Indeed, from this perspective, the struggles over such abstract issues as the 'form' and the 'idea' of a work of art that dominate Oscar's copyright suit, are rather apt to illustrate the clash between law and literature as the conflict between different models of language.

Counselor Gribble's search for the actual meaning of words must appear almost nostalgic when compared to the linguistic zest of his colleague, Jawaharlal Madhar Pai, Esq. In a deposition where Pai acts as the attorney for the film producer Jonathan Keister, who allegedly plagiarized Oscar's play, he completely upsets Oscar's conventional belief in both the formal difference between idea and expression and their integrity in a work of art. Oscar stubbornly believes that "[t]he idea executed is the idea expressed, transformed into a play, in other words it's definitely bound to the execution. So there are two things there to talk about" (*FO,* 183). Yet he also insists that "you can't divide a work of art, the idea from the technique that expresses it." This is not the perspective of the law, Pai tells him, because to separate the idea from the execution is "exactly what you're going to have to do in a court of law. The idea is an abstract form and that's not what we're here to talk about" (*FO,* 200).

The law cannot talk about ideas because ideas, especially in literature, are not "actual thing[s]," that is, they cannot be defined according to form and so cannot be copyrighted. The basic *form* that allows the law to define the authorship as well as the identity of a work of literature is precisely the written, printed word. Ironically, most of the deposition record is taken up by the objections of Oscar's attorney, Harold Basie, whose statements are only allowed to "go on record" if they are concerned with the form of the deposition, but not if they refer to the substance or content of Pai's relentless questions.

Gaddis' masterful exploitation of the very format of the deposition also demonstrates that the legal idea of 'form' is utterly shallow owing to the rigid formalization of its own language. The deposition stands as an obvious example of the law's obsession with the literal as against the literary use of language; an obsession clearly aimed at the regulation of public speech exclusively in terms of property rights. In a culture obsessed with the law, language, Gaddis implies, only achieves power if it is allowed to go on record; everyday language, because it is always by nature “off the record,” cannot claim any public authority. If there is no linguistic authority apart from the law’s definition of form and authorship based on writing and print, spoken discourse is also reduced to an irrelevant form of rhetoric. In fact, one could argue that in *A Frolic of His Own* the rhetorical function of everyday language is reduced to an endless performance of rhetoricity — of which the rigid formality and the corrupt language games of legal speech then present only a more professional and more powerful version. This emphasis on the constructive (and deconstructive) nature of language is certainly an aspect that makes Gaddis’ novel so attractive for postmodernist readings of its conscious textuality. Yet as Robert Weisberg warns, the novel should not be “demeaned as a postmodernist critique of the authenticity of the literary voice” or “the reducibility of the law to language.”[62] My own argument here is that the opposition between Oscar’s literature and Harry’s law cannot be resolved by reference to linguistic skepticism or even rhetoricity as the general condition of all fictions, legal or literary. Rather, this opposition has to be read in relation to the entire field of cultural rhetoric. Law and literature, or more precisely, legal discourse and everyday speech in Gaddis’ novel must be understood as two different, and indeed antagonistic reactions to the pervasive logic of the spectacle which dominates the public sphere. Despite their obvious differences, Oscar’s literature and Harry’s law still look at justice as a form of conflict resolution that has to be actively brought about. In other words, whatever it is to Harry or to Oscar, justice for both is neither irrelevant nor accidental, it is not the product of chance but rather of competence. At least that is the ideal. Yet precisely this ideal is completely missing from the media narratives that govern the American *nomos* of law and justice. Nor only are the narratives of the media more effective and persuasive, they also lack any will for order or regulation. They do not tell, they simply show American adversarial culture as a natural con-

---

62 Weisberg, “Taking Law Seriously,” 447, 445. For a similar perspective which rejects purely postmodernist readings of Gaddis’ novels, see Knight, *Hints and Guesses,* 3–15. I would agree with both Knight and Weisberg that any interpretation that sticks too closely to the framework of postmodern theory would do scant justice to Gaddis’ awareness of these theories — and his professed distance from them. Yet this profession is also an indication that Gaddis’ texts are always engaged in arguments and negotiations with contemporary theory without merely illustrating it.

dition whose guiding logic is not the search for justice but the struggle for survival.

Compared to the law's obsessive language of discrimination and literal definition, and the powerless chaos and ambivalence of everyday speech, the images of television and film represent two other modes of rhetoric that seem to move across the boundaries between the private and the public realm with uncanny ease. In the novel, the images of television present the only access to the world and its reality outside of the run-down family estate where most of the action takes place. Oscar particularly seems to be as much addicted to the TV screen as he is to his Pinot Grigio, yet the 'reality' presented by the TV images increases the chaos of indiscrimination beyond recognition, which common language desperately struggles to keep at bay:

> Scenes of mayhem from Londonderry to Chandigarh, an overweight family rowing down a main street in a freak flood in Ohio, a molasses truck overturned at the Jersey Turnpike, gunfire stabbings, flaming police cars and blazing ambulances celebrating a league basketball championship in Detroit interspersed with a decrepit grinning couple on a bed that warped and heaved at the touch of a button. (*FO,* 237)

Television serves as a powerful source of dispersive images, a world without differences where any distinction between real and symbolic violence, between advertisement, info- and edutainment collapses into the overwhelming power of immediate emotional address — and distress.

In a similar fashion, the detested movie spectacle, when it finally makes its appearance in the novel after more than 400 pages of spoken and written discourse, unfolds with such sweeping immediacy and intensity of visible performance that even Oscar cannot resist its power:

> suddenly the room shook with the sound of cannon fire, the screen with a tumult of plunging horses, flaring rockets and the Stars and Bars and men, men — look! as
>
> **The Blood in the Red White and Blue**
>
> unfurled
>
> before them, going up in flames … till the smoke cleared, the music died and now the room echoed with the clop, clop of a horse … (*FO,* 411, text setting in original).[63]

---

[63] The change in typography is from the original print version. Gaddis uses this technique to mark different genres of writing or of written documentation: For instance, the depositions and the opinions have their own distinct typographical form, and even baking recipes are highlighted in this way.

Just as the deposition reduced Oscar's play to its mere form and thus deprived it of its authority by the definitions of the law, the movie transforms the text of the play into a spectacle, thereby reducing it to the performative power of the sensual — of sounds and images. Oscar's idea of justice embodied in a literary text is defeated on all fronts; while his authorial control over his own text is denied by the legal reduction to form, its emotional impact and public performance are superseded by the images of television and the movies. Oscar becomes the tragic figure of lost authorship, a living anachronism who still subscribes to an idea of authorial power and poetic justice magically emanating from the printed word:

> because it's on the page! he suddenly erupted, — it's always been that way, the *silent beautiful* words coming off the page together to *stop and listen* to them to, to savour them without some vain fool in a costume prancing around up there just getting in their way, any of them. … (*FO,* 472; my emphases)

The idea of justice is lost in its translation from text into image, from verbal rhetoric to visual performance: "Look at it it's a travesty, they make a movie that's a vulgar travesty and now they make a travesty of the whole judicial process" (*FO,* 465).

For Gaddis, language in the form of speech and writing has reached the zero point of its public and cultural authority. The logic of litigation, as the secret driving source of rhetorical argument and cultural self-assertion, has completely given over to the latter and as a consequence public speech is reduced to a meaningless spectacle — a spectacle where justice will not and cannot prevail. Oscar's stubborn and ultimately devastating litigation suits against himself and against the movie industry, which form the central thread of the novel's various storylines, exemplify the struggle for cultural authority between the 'silent, beautiful' words (in literature and in law) and the spectacular images of film and television. This struggle is also at the heart of Alan Dershowitz's *The Advocate's Devil,* although it is clearly represented from a rather different perspective.

V

Abe Ringel, the protagonist of Alan Dershowitz's first novel *The Advocate's Devil*, resembles his creator in obvious ways. Both are defense lawyers from a Jewish, urban background who are highly self-conscious and successful professionals and also highly media savvy. In fact, one of the novel's central concerns is that the media have become a decisive force within the legal system that no one involved can escape. Dershowitz describes Ringel's relation to the media in terms that most likely match his own:

> Abe was accessible to the media — most of the time. He had spent years building these relationships because that was how the legal system worked — for better or for worse, press coverage was part of the game, and spin was the first rule.[64]

In a book about the O.J. Simpson trial, Dershowitz explains why the lawyer has to observe the rules of the media game:

> Why should lawyers care about public relations? Their job is to persuade judges and jurors, not the public or the pundits. But the jurors come from the same public that would be watching [the case] on television: And judges, too, are human beings, who are influenced by public opinion.[65]

However, in the same book, he notes that "many observers … derived the wrong lessons from this case, largely because of the way much of the press, radio, and television treated it."[66] Despite the intense media coverage of the trial, Dershowitz warns, crucial facts about it still remained invisible and therefore unintelligible to the larger public:

> Even those who watched the trial's live coverage saw only what went on in the courtroom itself, and not in the field, where investigation took place, or in the lawyers' offices, where many of the crucial decisions were made.[67]

The lawyer plays to two audiences at once, in two different courts: that of the law and that of the media public. Both games have rules that, even though they may be similar in some respects, have to be distinguished carefully lest the difference between justice according to the law and justice according to public opinion will break down. The major difference, as Dershowitz persistingly points out, is that while the public's judgment is mostly and almost inevitably based on *belief* — because people rely on "secondary sources" — any juror's judgment and his or her decision must be based on *doubt* — that is, reasonable doubt:

> The jurors in the Simpson case were not asked to vote on whether they believed 'he did it.' They were asked *whether the prosecution's evidence proved beyond a reasonable doubt that he did it.*[68]

---

64 Dershowitz, *The Advocate's Devil*, 88 (subsequently quoted as *AD* and page number).
65 Dershowitz, *Reasonable Doubts,* 17.
66 Dershowitz, *Reasonable Doubts,* 17.
67 Dershowitz, *Reasonable Doubts,* 17.
68 Dershowitz, *Reasonable Doubts,* 38, original emphasis.

The confusion of the rules and the delicate relation between belief and doubt are at the center of *The Advocate's Devil.* When the famous basketball player Joe Campbell asks Ringel to defend him against the charge of date rape, the lawyer accepts the case as a welcomed opportunity to boost his public image with the successful defense of a celebrity client because "a victory in the Campbell case would propel him into that small circle of lawyers whose names were immediately recognized around the country" (*AD,* 184). The problem is that Ringel wants to be both publicly known and professionally recognized, he wants to be on "the popular TV talk shows" as well as in "the casebooks that law students read" (*AD,* 183). In other words, the media savvy lawyer's dream is to reconcile the image of justice with its exemplary text(s). What Ringel fails to recognize, however, is that the public image of the law is already governed by the demand for, and expectation of, *dramatic* evidence, that is, 'truth' in the public court takes on the form of a visible spectacle unfettered by linguistic reasoning or argument.

Consequently, the Campbell case turns into a lawyer's nightmare. The basketball star emerges as a pathological liar whose proclaimed innocence appears more and more doubtful. His competence in handling the media, however, is clearly of a superior order. Moreover, Campbell turns out to be something like a student of the law himself, since the famous ball player checks out his potential victims by making his own little studies of the law's casebooks. Searching through electronic databases like CompuLaw on the internet, Campbell specifically looks for women who have claimed to be rape victims and whose claims have been denied in court and the perpetrators acquitted. Campbell then sets up chance meetings with his victims, first to seduce and then to rape them. As Campbell well knows, the women's credibility will prove severely damaged in the event of a trial. Campbell thus uses the media to play off the law against itself, a cunning strategy that leads to the near-rape of Ringel's daughter, who is saved only in the very last minute. As a computer illiterate, Ringel for a long time remains blind to the immense power of this criminal use of information; his desire to get Campbell acquitted for his own public profit proves stronger than his growing awareness of his client's guilt.

Campbell is the 'advocate's devil' precisely because he is able to use the power of the image against the text of the law and its rules in and out of court. In this way he upsets the hierarchy that guarantees the authority of word over image, and in the trial he successfully introduces his own silent evidence, bypassing the rules of testifying under oath. Because it is silent, Campbell's testimony cannot be recorded and compared to the 'stories,' that is, the recorded testimony, of the prosecution witnesses. This is exactly the point where the authority of the law and its understanding of verbal 'truth' clashes with Campbell's dramatization of evidence — his own 'image' of truth.

When Ringel first meets Campbell, he is very careful about the story which his client tells him. Because he knows that any changes in the story may shatter his defense:

> Don't let the client tell you his story before he understands the implications of what he is saying … if a client told one story at the outset and then changed it, this created big problems both for the lawyer and client. Most criminal defense lawyers had become … cautious about letting their clients ramble on without some structure. (*AD*, 36–37)

Ringel's focus on ordered narratives and linguistic control resembles that of Gaddis' lawyers and their obsession with form. For Ringel, words also might cause problems when their semantic potential threatens to transgress the limits of narrative constructions. The facts of the case, from the defense lawyer's perspective, present a 'story' that must appear structured, orderly and consistent. Only then can the story, told by the client, be used for the defense by his attorney. Defendant and attorney are thus both 'authors,' albeit in a very different sense. The structured story allows for the authorization and control of the truth (or the lie) of the client's innocence by his or her lawyer, which is as much a means of power as of self-protection. Narrative consistency not only is the sign of truth, for the lawyer it is the basis for the belief in the defendant's innocence. Ringel therefore is afraid of hearing his client's "untutored version of the facts"(*AD*, 37) because the "Supreme Court had recently ruled that if a lawyer knows his client is lying, he is not permitted to put him on the witness stand" (*AD*, 36). Even when he finds out that Campbell has been lying to him, Ringel sticks to his legal logic of narrative truth, unaware that his client tells his 'story' by very different means. The problem is that Ringel's legal definition of knowledge (of the truth) is so completely tied to words that everything that escapes verbal description and definition cannot be accounted for. When his colleague argues that "[y]ou can't call Campbell as a witness if you *know* he's going to lie about *anything*" (*AD*, 195), Ringel replies that his duty as a defense lawyer "is to separate the part of the truth that helps the client from the part that hurts" (*AD*, 197). This separation, however, exists only through and for verbal discourse, in short, it is made possible solely by the law's decision about what is being uttered and what has to remain silent. What does not get into the record, does not exist as fact. To control the story is to control the facts.

Yet, despite Ringel's efforts to control the testimony of his client and to refuse him to take the stand, Joe Campbell manages to eloquently testify to his innocence:

> Jennifer [the rape victim] began to weep softly. Several of the jurors were looking at her as she sobbed. Ms. Scuba Diver's eyes [the forewoman of the jury, thought to be highly critical of Campbell] were firmly on Campbell's head, which was shaking gently back and forth. He must have been aware that the forewoman was observing him as he squinted slightly and formed a silent *tsk, tsk* sound. The effect of these subtle movements by Campbell was to send a pained message of disappointment in Jennifer for finally crossing the line from truth to falsehood. (*AD,* 227)

Nonverbal communication turns into an eloquent and devastating commentary on verbal testimony: The performance of the visual image of "pained disappointment" renders the story of the witness false; the image literally pushes the word across "the line from truth to falsehood." Campbell thus uses the techniques of the public image — evoking belief, aiming at emotional response — to overturn the authority of verbal testimony and witnessing. Ringel only slowly becomes aware of what is actually happening:

> At first Abe didn't understand what Campbell was trying to do. Then it hit him: Campbell was *testifying* without taking the witness stand. He was having a … private conversation with … the most important and dangerous member of the jury. … And from the look on [her] face, Joe Campbell seemed to be scoring, as usual. (*AD,* 228)

What is so scandalous and upsetting for Ringel about Campbell's behavior is that it turns the legal court into a public court, dominated by strategies of the image and of dramatization. The way he singles out the forewoman through "eye-contact" to make her believe his show of disappointment and innocence is exactly the way Campbell picks out one-night-stands from his audience at the basketball game, as Ringel realizes. Even though Campbell "used lust" (*AD,* 250) to communicate his innocence, the basketball player is merely employing the excess of performative power deriving from his physical, visual presence — an excess which both addresses and satisfies the public's *desire to believe* in innocence or in guilt. The decisive gesture is the transformation of the courtroom and of the witness stand from spaces of the word and its professions into spaces, or better, *screens* for the image and its projections. This is where the image (of true innocence) escapes the rules of legal discourse, where it successfully bypasses the control of the visual by the verbal in order to become an eloquent though silent proof, a piece of hard evidence always off the record.

Yet, it is not simply Campbell's charisma as a public person or his suggestive presence that seduces "Ms Scuba Diver" into believing him. The silent testimony of the rapist is completely integrated within the overall logic of the trial as a dramatic presentation or play itself. That is, the jury forewoman already reacts to the testimony of the victim as if it was a potential performance. Only in this way can Campbell's silent reaction assume the form of a commentary: one actor seeing through another actor's play. The play in this case extends far beyond the boundaries set by the rules of (verbal, i.e. spoken or written) evidence because it always engages all parties in a dramatic struggle for truth. Moreover, its dramatic structure more easily and naturally adapts to the adversarial expectations of its prime audience, the jury. Truth ascertained in this way is not arrived at through linguistic reasoning that follows the 'letter' of the law. Rather, the truth at this very moment is a dramatic discovery, a revelation which takes not a verbal but a visual form: an image of truth.

Ringel, the media-conscious lawyer, thus becomes haunted by what Paul Thaler has called the "Faustian Bargain": once the image is allowed into the court room, which after all still is a space dominated by verbal and written discourse, the rules of the game are changed forever. Campbell, in a way, is Ringel's Mephistopheles. The promise of public recognition and professional acclaim has a sinister downside, as Ringel "had to worry about how to defend his client without losing his bar certificate — or his soul" (*AD,* 179).

VI

Despite their obvious differences, both novels give us as a central figure a man of the law who is also a man of letters. Both the older Judge Crease in Gaddis' *Frolic* and Ringel's teacher Haskel Levine in *The Advocate's Devil* live in the world of the word; they are shut off from the public and the media, and both die in the course of the novel. The two respected lawyers thus stand for an older order of legal and literary rhetoric completely independent of public opinion and media justice. Crease and Levine present "learned elders who chose the law, long ago, because it was a place where a love not for money but for justice and language could be entertained."[69]

---

69 Knight, *Hints and Guesses,* 229. Jonathan Raban's observation that in *A Frolic of His Own* "lawyers are … honored as the last surviving instruments … of order in this disorderly world" (Raban, "At Home in Babel," 4.) must be restricted to Judges Crease and Bone and their opinions, which Gaddis presents as masterful legal arguments. Other representatives of the legal profession in the novel are treated rather differently and with decidedly less admiration.

For Ringel, Haskel represents a "bygone era" when it was possible "to emerge as the greatest and most respected lawyer in Boston without ever seeing the inside of a television or radio station." Haskel "never comment[s] about a legal matter outside of the courtroom" (*AD,* 185) and unlike his favorite pupil, never had any difficulty in finding the right balance between the desire for public recognition and the autonomy of the law. Haskel thus embodies Dershowitz's own criticism of the increasing impact of court television and public trials, while Ringel's acknowledgment of the important role of the media well reflects Dershowitz's own practices and appearances in TV and radio stations. Ringel relies heavily on the wisdom of his teacher. Whenever he has a problem, he visits Haskel, hoping the old feeble man will give him advice. This advice usually takes an obscure form — riddles, anecdotes, or fables, and rather condensed quotes from the shared past of both law and literature, i.e. the past of oral and written tradition, the verbal past. The authority of Haskel's peculiar 'precedents' — the cases from Jewish sources he uses as examples — relies exclusively on words or, more precisely, on 'stories' without authors that have already acquired the status of common wisdom, of a common sense of justice.

The same could be said of Judge Crease, Oscar's father, who peppers his opinions with literary allusions and proverbs taken from literary and legal sources from the vast repertoire of traditional lore. The old Judge's texts stand in stark contrast to the sophistry of his younger colleagues, the indiscriminate dispersive images of television, and the desperate and mindless Babel of everyday speech. In his opinions, the authority of the person and that of the text (of the words) converge and thus profess to each other's power. In fact, these are the only instances in the novel where the text acquires a body, where words are not merely uttered but embodied in a distinct and highly original style and voice.

Both Haskel and Judge Crease represent an almost archaic authority of legal and literary discourse that is indeed 'bygone' and about to be replaced by the authority of the image and the law as spectacle. They are the defenders of the dying word, who strictly separate the public from the court of the law. Their rhetoric is informed by rules, rules which come from language and are observed by language; a strictness of form which guards the word from the image and at the same time regulates it, controls it. Gaddis and Dershowitz seem to agree about the devastating effect of a totally commercialized production of images, yet Gaddis appears to be much more pessimistic about the possible resistance of legal and literary discourse. How can either survive their transformation into a travesty? Dershowitz, in contrast, still believes in the power of the word, or, more precisely, in the authority of the author over the text. In the end, Ringel reads a letter to be sent to the American Bar Association aloud at his mentor's grave, arguing against the introduction of blanket rules and instead insisting that "[e]very lawyer will have to continue to struggle with the dilemma" (*AD,* 372) that there is no absolute security, no absolute justice in language.

The most troubling aspect, however, is that today the dilemma has created a desire for justice as a dramatic spectacle reigned by images. Both novels appear to describe the dilemma most basically as a lack of evidence or truthfulness in linguistic exchanges about the world. It is this evidentiary lack which the image appears to fill with its own eloquence and dramatic intensity. More precisely, the drive towards dramatization which appears to pervade the adversarial process in American law, and more generally and more obviously, the adversarial rhetorics of American culture make words appear the weaker form of evidentiary rhetoric. In an understanding where the struggle for truth can only be dramatic, linguistic reasoning, i.e. the logic and the logos of the word, become subservient to the staging power of the spectacles of justice.

From this perspective, the respective endings which Dershowitz and Gaddis give to their novels offer some interesting contrasts. Abe Ringel's letter read at Haskel's grave is literally addressed to the dead. Thus, ironically, the novel's most important statement about legal ethics and truth in the age of tabloid justice and media trials is presented not to the public, but to a rather intimate audience, as if Dershowitz did only trust his readers to share and understand the plea which Ringel voices. The court of literature seems to be the only place left where a media-conscious lawyer like Ringel (or Dershowitz) could escape the drive towards publicity and visual self-dramatization. But of course, the novel's final scene, presented in the form of an epilogue set in italics, is itself an act of staging as well, created precisely for an effect of dramatic intimacy that only literary fiction allows. It is certainly no accident that Dershowitz's alter ego, Ringel, presents his own opinion in the debate on the limits of client-lawyer privileges as a letter — a written document — to be read aloud. Always a lawyer, and a very contemporary one to boot, Ringel opts for a mode of representation and rhetorical address which follows the forms of the courtroom.[70] The letter to Haskel is thus turned from a medium of private communication into a pronouncement of judgment: the classical form of dramatized legal discourse. For Dershowitz, literature is no longer a space of intimate communication; rather, like every

70 Dershowitz is careful to point out that the document is read aloud at Haskel's grave *before* Ringel sends it in to the American Bar Association.

other mode of verbal representation it is always already addressed to the public, and as public rhetoric literary fiction serves to dramatize the law.

This fateful tendency is clearly acknowledged by Gaddis in *A Frolic of His Own.* When Oscar's father dies, his son learns the news through the images on television. What is represented, however, is not a standard obituary but the replay of earlier violent protests in the wake of one of the judge's most controversial opinions, in which he had ruled that "God has no place in [a] court of law" (*FO,* 259):[71]

> — Look! The flaming effigy swung closer in the floodlit melee of flying rocks and beer cans, Stars, Bars, and Stripes asunder, signs and placards brandished and trampled, GOD IS JUDGE aloft and IMPEACH smoldering on the judicial robes — what do they, look!
> — It had to happen sooner or later, Oscar, I mean he was almost …
> — What did! What are they doing all this again for! they …
> — What the media's all about Oscar, pictures make the news, no fun showing an old judge writing a landmark legal opinion but they get an excuse to show their old file tape full of rum and riot, burning crosses, burning flags stir the pot … any excuse to stir up the flames of hatred and …
> — But what excuse, I didn't hear the …
> — He died, Oscar. (*FO,* 406)

Harry's explanation exposes the logic of adversarial dramatization inherent in the image rhetoric of the media. Judge Crease is not interesting as a legal author who wrote landmark opinions; for the media he is only interesting, he only exists, in fact, as a figure of public controversy.

Gaddis' novel ends not with the creation but with the destruction of a central text, the civil war drama "Once Upon Antietam", Oscar's dramatized letter to his dead father, and a discussion of "the possibility or impossibility of justice in America."[72] This accident could be read almost as an act of defiance. When Oscar's half-sister Christina burns her brother's piles of unanswered letters and papers, she also seizes a manila folder which contains the last act of the play and throws it into the fire. Both father and son are thus burned *in effigy*; yet while the burning of the old judge is turned into a public spectacle, and into an image on the TV screen, his unhappy son leaves no legacy of his writing, neither public nor private. Though the act is highly symbolic, the way Gaddis presents it makes the destruction of Oscar's dramatic representation of justice appear almost as an accident, apparently un-

---

71 In the second of the two opinions written by Judge Crease which involved the outdoor steel sculpture "Cyclone Seven," recounted in *FO,* 252–59.
72 Thielemans, "*Once in Antietam,*" 178.

acknowledged by Christina — certainly not by her brother who does not even witness the scene:

> She stood there for a moment still till shaken by a cough, eyes watering from the smoke looking for something, anything to prod the smoldering heaps into flames, seizing the manila folder rolled like a stave bent down to thrust it at the embers raising a blue flame that crept along the margin and leaped to yellow life as she stood away from the blaze empty handed in the smoke and the stillness … (*FO,* 509)

Even careful readers might actually miss the significance of Christina's fatal misuse of the enveloped documents since Gaddis only mentions the very folder in passing a few pages before the final flames, lying unobtrusively "on the floor under the sideboard."

After all the talk in *A Frolic of His Own* is exhausted, and all documents have been read, the novel thus ends, if only temporarily, with a moment of stillness. Nevertheless, the gesture of withdrawal, the open denial even of disclosure (which is also a denial of closure), differs markedly from Ringel's speech at Haskel's grave. In contrast to Dershowitz, Gaddis finally dispenses with the dramatization of rhetoric and evidence even to the point of self-destruction, since "Once in Antietam" is in fact a play written *in realiter* by Gaddis in the early stages of his career, a project he had aborted in mid-creation.[73] Letters are burned, not sent, or read aloud — certainly this is a carefully staged moment as well. A moment, however, where drama is completely devoid of any dramatization; the effect of a literary rhetoric that opens access to an intimate tragedy without turning it into a public spectacle.

VII

At the outset of this chapter I noted that one motivation for the comparison of the two novels by William Gaddis and Alan Dershowitz was that they may offer certain insights into the peculiar relation between law and literature at the end of the 20th century. One rather obvious indication for the symptomatic character of both works, I argued, should be seen in the transgressive move by their authors of using the resources of the respective other to elucidate the limits and the conditions of their own professional discourse. Acts of professional transgression are also at the very center of the plot of each

---

73 "Once at Antietam" was begun very early in Gaddis' career (1957), yet never finished. See Moore, *William Gaddis;* and especially Thielemans for the relation between Gaddis' play and its role in the later novel.

novel. As a conclusion to the preceding discussion I will therefore take a short look at what could be called the anxiety of imitation inscribed in both Gaddis' and Dershowitz's legal fictions. This anxiety has always been characteristic of the relation between law and literature understood as competing rhetorics of evidence, yet it has taken on a new urgency during the last century with the rise of modern media.

Throughout my discussions of the various texts and contexts in which American law and letters have constituted themselves (as practices and as professional discourses) precisely through the relation they assumed to one another, there was a common emphasis on the attempt of the law to legitimate itself by controlling or regulating its own literariness on the one hand, and the lawfulness of literature (as public rhetoric, as property, as lawful speech, etc.) on the other. Similarly, I have tried to show repeatedly how literary fictions use the representation of legal practice and the strategic imitation of legal discourse in order to demonstrate the latter's shortcomings and illegitimacy as a rhetoric of evidence and a representation of truth and justice. In my initial chapters I also argued that the concept of just representation in legal and literary rhetoric cannot be divorced from the concept of mimesis, or imitation. In fact, one central argument of this investigation was that the fundamental demand for truth in language was intensified and turned into a professional undertaking by the desire (and the necessity) to distinguish between true and false representations of real events in court and on stage.

One tenet of the law-and-literature movement's criticism of the law was that the legal discourse aims to repress or disavow its own literariness or rhetoricity.[74] Hence, as has been discussed at various points, legal authorship and legal interpretation always attempt to maintain their difference from literary authorship and interpretation by insisting on the objectivity and rule-bound nature of its own textual practices over and against its literary counterpart and the latter's dependence on fictionality and rhetorical persuasion. As a dominated discourse (in comparison to the law as a discourse of power and dominance), literature reacted to its legal definition and regulation by claiming a special status for its own rhetoric of evidence; literary or poetic truth came to be seen as truly autonomous and thus closer to disinterested verity, bound only to the higher laws of nature, divine or spiritual laws, or the superior principles of universal ethics and morals.

In this respect, the relation between law and literature does not describe an opposition, but rather reveals their interdependence as complementary

---

74 See my discussion of the rhetoricity thesis in chapter 2.

rhetorics of evidence. This understanding also guided the respective professionalization of law and literature from the 17th century onward, which also meant that both professions attempted to guard their field of practice by denouncing what they saw as especially transgressive moves by their counterpart. The debates surrounding the problem of testimony and the narratives of witnesses, as well as those concerned with 'libelous' or 'obscene' writing, are examples for specific areas of conflict between law and literature where concepts of lawful writing and literary legality are constantly contested by both sides. These debates particularly included the ongoing revision and regulation of mimesis or imitation from the perspective of literature and from that of the law, respectively. Again, even these conflicts still operated within the complementary logic of the law and literature relation.

The particular problem of transgression which is at the center of Gaddis' and Dershowitz's novels, however, is different. The precarious correlation between law and literature is threatened in both *A Frolic of His Own* and *The Advocate's Devil* by the dramatization of evidence and the adversarial rhetoric of the media. If we take the media as a system which constructs and disseminates symbolic meaning within a culture with unprecedented force and speed, it certainly must affect the conventional regulation of mimesis and imitation expressed by the law and literature correlation. This is exactly what Gaddis and Dershowitz in their own distinctive way react to; and this reaction can be detected within the novels as both the threat and the anxiety resulting from the emergence of the "culture of the copy."[75] Moreover, the mediagenic understanding of truth as drama, especially visual drama, disrupts the correlation and interaction of law and literature as *textual* practices, effectively establishing a third field or source for the generation of a cultural *nomos*. Both novels respond to the challenge implied by this rupture of the law and literature relation, yet their conclusions are rather different.

In *The Advocate's Devil*, the new mediagenic rhetoric of evidence is represented by Joe Campbell. Campbell is in fact a product of the media and he has completely incorporated their specific mode of representation and self-representation. Yet the player made famous by the media is also a media player. Not only does he use his public personality to satisfy his sexual appetites, he also uses another medium, the computer, to plan and set up his date

[75] According to Hillel Schwartz, there is a particular obsession with copy, doubling, illusion, forgery, etc. in Western culture as a whole — an obsession which obviously has increased after the development of new media technologies in the last century, especially visual and later digital media (Schwartz, *The Culture of the Copy*).

rapes. The latter aspect presents the more dangerous transgression into the field of the law. On the one hand, Campbell uses the legal database to find his own 'precedents': cases which offer precisely the kind of story which Campbell then copies. He thus effectively turns the legal precedent against the law itself; and since the law in the first case has established the truth of a certain fact — the story told by the rape victims was false — it will not turn against its own decision in the second instance. Legal precedents are not based on fictions, which means they are not based on constructions of fictitious events but on reconstructions of real events. The threat of Campbell's criminal perversions lies in the complete subversion of the law's logic which enables it to discriminate between fiction and fact in the first place. By copying the events of the precedent, Campbell reconstructs the legally established rape 'fiction' as a real event, yet since his victims are already discredited in the eyes of the law, the real event is regarded as a fiction. The law thus remains blind to the reality of its own fictions.

It is hard to establish whether Dershowitz was aware of how much he made Campbell resemble a professional lawyer in his search for precedents. Yet all the details of Campbell's representation underscore the danger which resides in an unlawful imitation both of the law's stories and of its professional practices. After all, one of the main tasks of a lawyer is to find the cases which could serve as a precedent for the specific narrative she wants to present to the judge and to the jury. The precedent serves as a frame of reference which allows a legal judgment of the alleged facts of the present case on the basis of a prior judgment of another, similar case. Since two cases are hardly completely alike, no matter how many similarities one could find, the challenge for each side is to present the facts of the case at hand in such a way as to make them appear analogous to the facts established in those precedents which would be most favorable for their respective goal — i.e. successful defense or conviction. The choice of precedent is of course not completely arbitrary, yet it is even within limits always a strategic choice — and the strategy almost always aims at the acceptance of a particular story as the most probable representation of factual events. The precedent thus serves as something like an already established genre or model for the conflicting narratives presented in each new case.

Campbell's acts of illegitimate imitation seriously disturb the order of mimesis which the law struggles to uphold to keep its own fictions stable. While Campbell's lawyer tries hard to control his client's stories, he fails to notice that it is Campbell who is actually controlling the narratives of the law. As we have seen, this control includes even the performance in the court room, again calling attention to Campbell's superior media competence. The basketball player has indeed turned himself into the director of the legal spectacle, forming a new dramatic synthesis out of legal precedent and literary invention — a deceitful play, to be sure, but one that is both persuasive as a fiction and moreover sanctioned by the law. Ringel of course knows — and one has to presume Dershowitz does as well — that such duplicity cannot be completely avoided. The law is not an airtight, flawless narrative operation whose outcomes would be impeccable and always true. In fact, Dershowitz more than once has Ringel resort to the famous legal dictum that it was better that ten guilty men would go free than to convict one innocent man of a crime he never committed. This saying readily acknowledges the fallibility of legal storytelling, at the same time as it defends this fallibility because it protects the innocent. In Campbell's case, however, the benign blindness of the law in regard to its own shortcomings is turned against the process itself; Campbell in fact uses the professional stories of the law to unhinge their power to 'narrate' truth and justice — he makes the law speak his own fictions.

Dershowitz's solution to the inherent dilemma of copying the law and the resulting disturbance of the mimetic order of the law as narrative is professional but also ambivalent. It is professional because it leaves the responsibility for judgment in the hands of the lawyers: the professional lawyer has to be aware of the ethical implications of the privileges granted to the stories told by his clients. This solution is clearly compatible with Dershowitz's explicit perspective on the law and storytelling movement and its claims that a deeper understanding of narrative fiction and narrativization would help professional lawyers and judges in their practice and make the process of adjudication more just. In Dershowitz's view, such an understanding would not be helpful, on the contrary. Reality, Dershowitz insists, is not a 'story' or a 'narrative' and it does not follow any narrative logic. To presume so would not only be a distortion of the incalculable contingency of factual events but, what is worse, it would make it all too easy to trap the innocent in the narrative expectations of the jurors.[76] This is why the law must guard its narratives and fictions, why it must aim to contain the transgressive potential of storytelling within the boundaries of its own professions. For Dershowitz, the answer to the dilemma of copying and the dramatization of evidence is some sort of internal control or self-disciplining of law and literature; his own transgression into the field of professional literature is ultimately meant to demonstrate how easily fictions may lead to fatal illusions if they are

[76] Cf. Dershowitz, "Life is Not a Dramatic Narrative," 104–05. For the storytelling and the law see Papke, *Narrative and Legal Discourse.*

handled professionally, yet unethically. To the last point Gaddis would have most likely agreed. Nevertheless, Gaddis' own ethics are, as Christopher Knight has shown at length, much more bound to the specifics of literary fiction and moreover fully aware of the complexity and ambivalence of professional disciplines and their own illusions.[77]

The disruption of the mimetic order is at the center of Gaddis' *A Frolic of His Own* as well. This is certainly not a new topic for Gaddis, who has been obsessed with copying, imitation, forgery and counterfeiting from the very beginning of his career. Starting with *The Recognition* — a novel whose main concern is the problematic relation of copy and original or, more precisely, the substitution of the latter by the former — Gaddis never stopped following up his initial concern to a point where it would be no exaggeration to state that his entire work presents an ongoing reflection on the contemporary proliferation of the fake.

It should come as no surprise that Gaddis should eventually turn to the law in his investigation of the 'culture of the copy.' In his own words, the fascinating thing about the law is that it is "always trying to anticipate contingencies."[78] The attempt by legal discourse to regulate the imitation of verbal art by defining originality and the difference between lawful imitation (like parody, for instance) and unlawful imitation (like plagiarism), comes of course very close to the concepts and theories of literary criticism — and in the confrontation between Oscar and counselor Pai, for instance, Gaddis stages an interesting (and very entertaining) debate between law and literature on the very topic of copying, imitation, and truth in art. Despite the comic overtones, however, Gaddis' concern with the problem of falsification through imitation is essential and fundamental. One can sense his intense engagement with this question so central in our culture, in a remark Gaddis made in an essay on religion, belief and truth — one of Gaddis' very rare public statements. There he writes about the denial of the holocaust by certain pseudo-historians:

> Once upon a time, fiction was a way of getting at some kind of truth: we concocted fictions to get us through the night or, nostalgic for absolutes, we embraced revelation as ultimate truth. Now fiction is used to bring on the darkest night of all, in which historical reality in its most monstrous epiphany is dismissed as a mischievous, fictive concoction by the so-called Holocaust revisionists … This denial, made in the face of all the tangible evidence and all the witnesses, living and dead, of the systematic murder of six million human beings of different

---

77 In his "Conclusion" Knight emphasizes the ambivalence inscribed into Gaddis' ethic of the artist: see Knight, *Hints and Guesses,* 242.

78 Qtd. in Knight, *Hints and Guesses,* 229.

> race and religion, is a lie of such enormous proportions that it will live on and reemerge to taint history forever. It offers the worst-case scenario of the willing suspension of disbelief.[79]

The main point in this statement is that for Gaddis, there is a necessary and inevitable interdependence between fiction and truth, history and justice; and that the denial of the holocaust presents only the most spectacular and obvious form of the denigration or deterioration of the precarious balance between these different, but nevertheless interdependent concepts. The denial of the holocaust is a fiction that presents itself as true historiography. It pretends to do justice to historical facts while, in fact, it amounts to a perversion of both historical and fictional evidence. In a way, the holocaust deniers, especially those who take on the garb of professionals dedicated to historical truth, are for Gaddis what Campbell presents for Dershowitz: the most dangerous form of copyists, whose imitation of form completely subverts the latter's function. The function in both cases is the subservience of form, i.e. of regulated discourse to truth and evidence, a claim that is undermined by the performative versatility and prowess of imitation contemporary counterfeiters within the realm of law, history and fiction are capable of.

Yet despite these affinities, there is a marked difference in Gaddis' negotiation of the problem of postmodern imitation and its status for the relation between law and literature. This is most obvious in Oscar's reactions to the various interpretations or appropriations of his play "Once in Antietam." Neither the law, nor the movie industry, Oscar exclaims, are capable of understanding the true essence and meaning of his play. Their presentations of the drama — as a film or in a legal opinion — thus present denigrated 'copies' which Oscar in both cases denounces as 'travesties.' Readers are confronted with the original (exclusive the final act, burned in the end) at length, followed by various versions in the opinions of the judges involved in Oscar's cases, culminating in Judge Bone's extended summary of the plot and, finally, the first sequences of the movie. At the same time, Oscar remains completely blind to his own 'rewriting' of texts ranging from Plato to Augustine. Moreover, for most readers aware of American literary history, Oscar's Civil War drama at many turns appears like an unconscious parody of William Faulkner or Eugene O'Neill. In this way, Gaddis obviously suggests that on the one hand, copying is inevitable when it comes to literature — like the law, literature is bound to its precedents. On the other hand, he insists that there is also a difference between a copy which perverts what it imitates

---

[79] Gaddis, "Old Foes With New Faces," 15.

and another which actualizes, realizes, and even elevates what it copies to the status of revised evidence and truth.

The play, which is written almost as a parody of O'Neill's *Mourning Becomes Electra*, tells the story of Oscar's grandfather, Thomas Crease (though called only Thomas in the play), during the time of the Civil War. Thomas is both a slaveholder and plantation owner in the American South, and an industrial entrepreneur with monetary interests in the North. When the war breaks out, he pays substitutes on both sides to avoid participation in military action. Accidentally, the two substitutes meet and kill each other in the battle of Antietam. The play thus foreshadows Oscar's own dilemma when he sues himself in his obsessive search for justice. For Oscar, the play presents an attempt to come to terms with the complex history of his family; and since it is indeed based on documentary evidence found in old letters among his grandfather's papers, the drama becomes a fictional doubling of factual history. Unwittingly, the play also turns into the script for Oscar's own fateful doublings and problematic acts of self-imitation. Like the main protagonist in *Once in Antietam,* Oscar remains completely blind to the destructive aspect of his actions and thus feels no responsibility towards the effects these actions result in. Moreover, like Thomas in the play, who worries more about his pension and what he considers his unjust treatment by the state after the war, Oscar's search for justice is similarly self-centered and strongly interested in monetary compensation — despite his claims to the contrary. In the following conversation between Oscar and Christina, Gaddis demonstrates how Oscar's attempts to follow a high ideal of original, immortal art on the one hand, and his drive for personal vindication on the other, split him into two halves or copies of himself that will ultimately defeat each other and himself:

> — That's what I mean! My work, it would never be heard of, it would just disappear as though it had never existed, as though I'd never lived.
> — Would it matter? I mean you'd be sitting over there on the other side happy as a clam wouldn't you? …
> — That's not it he said … but it is, isn't it. Because my work it would exist wouldn't it, its only claim to existence would be this fraudulent counterfeit this vulgar distorted forgery and the thing itself, the original immortal thing itself would never be … That's it yes! … the artist is working on his immortality every minute, everything he creates, that's what his work is, his immortality and that's why having it stolen and corrupted and turned into some profane worthless counterfeit is the most, why it's sacrilege, that's what sacrilege really is isn't it? Isn't that really why I got into all of this?
> — Frankly Oscar, the way you've been waving that court decree around waiting to hear about your damages I thought it might have something to do with money.

> — Well of course it does! Because that's the only language they understand. I've said it a thousand times haven't I? that that's the only way I can be vindicated? (*FO,* 369–70)

There is no doubt that the notion of imitation presents the key to art as well as to its destruction in Gaddis' novel. Oscar's pathetic struggle for the originality of his art thus also has to be read in contrast to his creator's efforts to make the faithful and meticulous imitation of everyday discourse the foundation of his own literary voice.

Like his sister Christina, most readers will soon look through Oscar's antics as the "gentleman poet" and "last civilized man" to discover that its all just a "desperate pose" (*FO,* 348). Yet ultimately, Oscar's real tragedy results from his unbroken trust in the law to defend his originality against its appropriation and vulgar imitation by the media. In a culture of the copy, Oscar sees the law as the final sanctuary for the notion of originality — and finds his hopes utterly shattered and betrayed. The law, Gaddis suggests, no longer protects the literary profession of ideas and their artistic value because the law itself, as a form of writing and speaking, has lost its own originality. The proliferation of legal discourse as the main medium of cultural exchange and communication has driven literature out of circulation, as it were. From this perspective, Christina's sensible observation about the artistic value of Oscar's foolishness seems perfectly justified: "where it's all laws, and laws, and everything's laws … he's done something nobody's told him to, nobody hired him to and gone off on a frolic of his own I mean think about it Harry. Isn't that really what the artist is all about?" (*FO,* 349).[80] Oscar, of course, is blind to such an aesthetic of individual resistance and autonomy since he still believes in the original integrity of 'high' art and demands that the law should acknowledge his play as such. What makes Oscar blind to his own work is in fact his inability or unwillingness to judge it critically by himself; instead, he leaves it to the law — in vain, as it turns out.

Literary art, Gaddis suggests, even one that appears so desperate as Oscar's legal and literary frolics, can only exist for itself and can only be acknowledged as such outside of the law; it must resist the law and the lure of adversarial legal culture even while it finds itself strangely fascinated by and entangled in it.

---

80 Christina's phrase and Gaddis' title refer to a well-known legal phrase from the law of torts: "a master is not liable for the torts of his servant who is not at all on his master's business, but is 'going on a frolic of his own'" (Prosser, *Handbook,* 477, quoting Baron Parke).

Bibliography

Abraham, Henry J. *Freedom and the Court: Civil Rights and Liberties in the United States.* 5th ed. New York: Oxford UP, 1988.

Adams, Charles Hansford. *'The Guardian of the Law': Authority and Identity in James Fenimore Cooper.* University Park & London: Pennsylvania State UP, 1990.

Allen, James, ed. *Without Sanctuary: Lynching Photography in America.* Santa Fé: Twin Palms, 2000.

Altman, Andrew. *Critical Legal Studies: A Liberal Critique.* Princeton: Princeton UP, 1990.

"An Account of a Murder Committed By Mr J____ Y____, Upon This Family, in December A.D. 1781." *The New York Weekly Magazine* 1796: 20 (No. 55); 28 (No. 56).

Aristotle. *On Rhetoric.* Trans. George A. Kennedy. New York: Oxford UP, 1991.

Aristotle. *The Rhetoric and Poetics of Aristotle.* Trans. W. Rhys Roberts and Ingram Bywater. Ed. Friedrich Solmsen. New York: Oxford UP, 1954.

Asimov, Michael. "When Lawyers Were Heroes." *U of San Francisco Law Review* 30.4 (1996): 1131–38.

Auerbach, Jerold S. *Justice Without Law? Resolving Disputes Without Lawyers.* New York: Oxford UP, 1983.

Bakhtin, Mikhail M. *The Dialogic Imagination.* Austin: U of Texas P, 1981.

Balkin, J. M. "The Domestication of Law and Literature." *Law and Social Inquiry* 14 (1989): 787–822.

Baecker, Diann L. "Telling It in Black and White: The Importance of the Africanist Presence in *To Kill a Mockingbird.*" *Southern Quarterly* 36.3 (1998): 124–32.

Ball, Milner S. "The Play's the Thing: An Unscientific Reflection on Courts Under the Rubric of Theatre." *Stanford Law Review* 28 (1975): 83.

Banton, Michael. *Racial Theories.* 1987. Cambridge: Cambridge UP, 1998.

Bardes, Barbara Ann, and Suzanne Gossett. "Cooper and the 'Cup and Saucer' Law: A New Reading of *The Ways of the Hour.*" *American Quarterly* 32.5 (1980): 499–518.

Barnard, Philip, Mark L. Kamrath, and Stephen Shapiro, eds. *Revising Charles Brockden Brown: Culture, Politics and Sexuality in the Early Republic.* Knoxville: U of Tennessee P, 2004.

Bauman, Richard W. *Critical Legal Studies: A Guide to the Literature.* Boulder: Westview, 1996.

Baym, Nina. "A Minority Reading of Wieland." *Critical Essays on Charles Brockden Brown.* Ed. Bernard Rosenthal. Boston: Hall, 1981. 87–103.

Beaujour, Michel. "Some Paradoxes of Description." *Yale French Studies.* 61 (1981): 27–59.

Beer, John. "William Gaddis." *Review of Contemporary Fiction* (2002): 69–110.

Belknap, Michael R. *Federal Law and Southern Order.* Athens: U of Georgia P, 1987.

Bell, Derrick A. *Race, Racism, and American Law.* Boston: Little, Brown and Co., 1973.

Bell, Michael Davitt. "'The Double-Tongued Deceiver': Sincerity and Duplicity in the Novels of Charles Brockden Brown." *Early American Literature: A Collection of Critical Essays.* Ed. Michael T. Gilmore. Englewood Cliffs: Prentice Hall, 1980. 133–57.

Bennett, W. Lance, and Marta S Feldman. *Reconstructing Reality in the Courtroom: Justice and Judgment in American Culture.* New Brunswick: Rutgers UP, 1981.
Bentham, Jeremy. *'Legislator of the World': Writings on Codification, Law, and Education.* Eds. Philip Schofield and Jonathan Harris. Oxford: Clarendon, 1998.
Bercovitch, Sacvan. *Rites of Assent.* New York: Routledge, 1993.
Berry, Mary Francis. *Black Resistance, White Law.* New York: Penguin, 1994.
Binder, Guyora, and Robert Weisberg. *Literary Criticisms of Law.* Princeton: Princeton UP, 2000.
Bloom, Harold, ed. *Modern Critical Interpretations of 'To Kill a Mockingbird.'* Philadelphia: Chelsea House, 1999.
Blumenberg, Hans. "Anthropologische Annäherung an die Aktualität der Rhetorik." *Wirklichkeiten in denen wir leben.* Stuttgart: Reclam, 1986. 104–36.
–. "Wirklichkeitsbegriff und Möglichkeit des Romans." Ed. Hans Robert Jauß. *Nachahmung und Illusion.* Vol. 1. München: Fink, 1964. 9–27.
Bosco, Ronald A. "Lectures at the Pillory: The Early American Execution Sermon." *American Quarterly* 30.2 (1978): 156–76.
Bourdieu, Pierre. *The Logic of Practice.* 1980. Trans. Richard Nice. Stanford: Stanford UP, 1990.
–. *In Other Words.* Trans. Matthew Adamson. Cambridge: Polity Press, 1990.
–. *Language and Symbolic Power.* Ed. John B. Thompson. Cambridge: Polity Press, 1991.
Brazil, John R. "Murder Trials, Murder, and Twenties America." *American Quarterly* 33.2 (1981): 163–84.
Brooks, Peter, and Paul Gewirtz, eds. *Law's Stories: Narrative and Rhetoric in the Law.* New Haven: Yale UP, 1996.
Brown, Charles Brockden. *Edgar Huntly, or, Memoirs of a Sleepwalker.* 1799. *The Novels and Related Works of Charles Brockden Brown.* Eds. Sidney J. Krause and S.W. Reid. Vol. 2. Kent: Kent State UP, 1977.
–. *Literary Essays and Reviews.* Eds. Alfred Weber and Wolfgang Schäfer. Frankfurt a.M.: Lang, 1992.
–. *The Rhapsodist and Other Uncollected Writings.* Ed. Harry R. Warfel. New York: Scholar's Facsimiles and Reprints, 1943.
–. *Wieland or The Transformation, An American Tale.* 1798. *The Novels and Related Works of Charles Brockden Brown.* Eds. Sidney J. Krause and S.W. Reid. Vol. 1. Kent: Kent State UP, 1977.
Browne, Irving. *Law and Lawyers in Literature.* Holmes Beach, Fla.: W.W. Gaunt, 1982.
Brundage, Fitzhugh W. *Lynching in the New South.* Urbana: U of Illinois P, 1993.
Burns, Robert P. *A Theory of the Trial.* Princeton: Princeton UP, 2001.
Cahill, Edward. "An Adventurous and Lawless Fancy. Charles Brockden Brown's Aesthetic State." *Early American Literature* 36.1 (2001): 31–70.
Campbell, George. *The Philosophy of Rhetoric.* 1776. Ed. Lloyd Bitzer. Carbondale: Southern Illinois UP, 1963.
Campe, Rüdiger. *Affekt und Ausdruck.* Tübingen: Niemeyer, 1990.
Campos, Paul F. *Jurismania: The Madness of American Law.* New York: Oxford UP, 1998.
Carter, Dan T. *The Politics of Rage: George Wallace, the Origins of the New Conservativism, and the Transformation of American Politics.* New York: Simon & Schuster, 1995.
–. *Scottsboro: A Tragedy of the American South.* Chapel Hill: U of North Carolina P, 1991.

Champion, Laurie. "'When You Finally See Them': The Unconquered Eye in *To Kill a Mockingbird.*" *Southern Quarterly* 37.2 (1999): 127–36.

Chandler, James, Arnold I. Davidson, and Harry Harootunian, eds. *Questions of Evidence: Proof, Practice, and Persuasion Across the Disciplines.* Chicago: U of Chicago P, 1994.

Charvat, William. "Cooper as Professional Author." *James Fenimore Cooper: A Reappraisal.* Eds. Mary E. Cunningham and Howard Mumford Jones. Cooperstown: New York State Historical Society, 1954. 128–43.

Chase, Richard. *The American Novel and Its Tradtion.* Garden City: Doubleday, 1957.

Cheyfitz, Eric. "Literally White, Figuratively Red: The Frontier of Translation in *The Pioneers.*" *James Fenimore Cooper: New Critical Essays.* Ed. Robert Clark. London: Barnes & Noble, 1986. 55–95.

Chielens. Edward E. "Periodicals and Development of An American Literature." *Making America/Making American Literature: Franklin to Cooper.* Eds. A. Robert Lee and W. M. Verhoeven. Amsterdam: Rodopi, 1996. 93–103.

Chura, Patrick. "Prolepsis and Anachronism: Emmett Till and the Historicity of *To Kill a Mockingbird.*" *Southern Literary Journal* 32.2 (2000): 1–26.

Clanchy, M. T. *From Memory to Written Record.* London: Edward Arnold, 1979.

Clark, David Lee. *Charles Brockden Brown: Pioneer Voice of America.* Durham: Duke UP, 1952.

Clark, E. Culpepper. *The Schoolhouse Door: Segregation's Last Stand at the University of Alabama.* New York: Oxford UP, 1993.

Clark, Robert. *James Fenimore Cooper: New Critical Essays.* London: Barnes & Noble, 1986.

Coady, C.A.J. *Testimony: A Philosophical Study.* Oxford: Oxford UP, 1992.

Cody, Michael. *Charles Brockden Brown and the* Literary Magazine*: Cultural Journalism in the Early Republic.* Jefferson: MacFarland, 2004.

Cook, Charles M. *The American Codification Movement.* Westport: Greenwood, 1981.

Comnes, Gregory. *The Ethics of Indeterminacy in the Novels of William Gaddis.* Gainesville: U of Florida P, 1994.

–. "The Law of the Excluded Muddle: The Ethics of Improvisation in William Gaddis' *A Frolic of His Own.*" *Critique* 39.4 (1998): 353–66.

Conley, John M., and William O'Barr. *Just Words: Law, Language and Power.* 2nd ed. Chicago: U of Chicago P, 2005.

Constable, Marianne. *The Law of the Other: The Mixed Jury and Changing Conceptions of Citzenship.* Chicago: U of Chicago P, 1994.

–. "The Modern American Jury: Fact and Law in Law and Society." *Journal of American Culture* 15.1 (1992): 25–36.

Cooper, James Fenimore. *Early Critical Essays.* Ed. James F. Beard. Gainesville: Scholar's Facsimiles, 1955.

–. *A Letter to His Countrymen.* New York: John Wiley, 1834.

–. *Notions of the Americans: Picked Up by a Travelling Bachelor.* 1828. *The Writings of James Fenimore Cooper.* Ed. James F. Beard. Albany: State U of New York P, 1991.

–. *The Pioneers, or, The Sources of the Susquehanna.* 1823. New York: Penguin, 1988.

–. *The Ways of the Hour.* 1850. Phoenix Mill: Sutton, 1996.

Corcos, Christine Alice. *An International Guide to Law and Literature Studies.* 2 vols. Buffalo: William S. Hein, 2000.

Cornell, Drucilla, Michel Rosenfeld, and David Gray Carlson, eds. *Deconstruction and the Possibility of Justice.* New York: Routledge, 1992.

Cover, Robert. *Narrative, Violence, and the Law: The Essays of Robert Cover.* Eds. Martha Minow, Michael Ryan, and Austin Sarat. Ann Arbor: U of Michigan P, 1992.

Crary, Jonathan. *Techniques of the Observer: On Vision and Modernity in the Nineteenth Century.* Cambridge: MIT Press, 1990.

Crenshaw, Kimberlé, et al., eds. *Critical Race Theory: The Key Writings That Formed the Movement.* New York: The New Press, 1995.

Crier, Catherine. *The Case Against Lawyers.* New York: Broadway Books, 2002.

Culler, Jonathan. "Deconstruction and the Law." *Framing the Sign.* Cambridge: Blackwell, 1988. 139–51.

Dalton, Clare. "An Essay in the Deconstruction of Contract Doctrine." *Yale Law Journal* 94.5 (1985): 977–1114.

Daston, Lorraine. *Classical Probability in the Enlightenment.* Princeton: Princeton UP, 1988.

–. "Marvelous Facts and Miraculous Evidence in Early Modern Europe." *Questions of Evidence.* Eds. James Chandler, Arnold I. Davidson, and Harry Harootunian. Chicago: Chicago UP, 1994. 243–74.

Davidson, Cathy. *Revolution and the Word: The Rise of the Novel in America.* New York: Oxford UP, 1986.

Davis, Adrienne D. "Identity Notes Part One: Playing in the Light." *American University Law Review* 45 (1996): 695–720.

Davis, Lennard J. *Factual Fictions: The Origin of the English Novel.* 1983. Philadelphia: U of Pennsylvania P, 1997.

Debord, Guy. *The Society of the Spectacle.* New York, 1994.

Dekker, George. *The American Historical Romance.* New York: Cambridge UP, 1987.

–. *James Fenimore Cooper: The American Scott.* New York: Barnes & Noble, 1967.

Delgado, Richard. *Critical Race Theory: The Cutting Edge.* Philadelphia: Temple UP, 1995.

Derrida, Jacques. "Before the Law." 1982. Ed. Derek Attridge. *Acts of Literature.* New York: Routledge, 1992. 181–220.

–. "Différance." Trans. Alan Bass. *Margins of Philosophy.* Chicago: U of Chicago P, 1982. 1–27.

–. "Force of Law: The 'Mystical Foundation of Authority.'" *Deconstruction and the Possibility of Justice.* Eds. David Gray Carlson, Drucilla Cornell and Michel Rosenfeld. New York: Routledge, 1992. 3–67.

–. "The Law of Genre." 1980. Ed. Derek Attridge. *Acts of Literature.* New York: Routledge, 1992. 221–52.

Dershowitz, Alan M. *The Advocate's Devil.* New York: Warner Books, 1994.

–. *Contrary to Public Opinion.* New York: Pharos, 1992.

–. "Life is Not a Dramatic Narrative." Eds. Peter Brooks and Paul Gewirtz. *Law's Stories: Narrative and Rhetoric in the Law.* New Haven: Yale UP, 1996. 99–105.

–. *Reasonable Doubts: The O. J. Simpson Case and the Criminal Justice System.* New York: Simon and Schuster, 1996.

Dimock, Wai-Chee. *Residues of Justice: Literature, Law, Philosophy.* Berkeley: U of California P, 1996.

Dolin, Kieran. *A Critical Introduction to Law and Literature.* Cambridge: Cambridge UP, 2007.

Dray, Philip. *At the Hands of Persons Unknown: The Lynching of Black America.* New York: Random House, 2002.

Dubrow, Heather. "The Status of Evidence." *PMLA* 111.1 (1996): 7–20.
Dudensing, Beatrix. *Die Symbolik von Mündlichkeit und Schriftlichkeit in James Fenimore Cooper's* "Leatherstocking Tales." Frankfurt a. M.: Lang, 1993.
Dunne, Dominick. *Justice: Crimes, Trials, and Punishments.* New York: Three Rivers Press, 2001.
Eden, Kathy. *Poetic and Legal Fiction in the Aristotelean Tradition.* Princeton: Princeton UP, 1986.
Ely, James W., Jr. "The South, the Supreme Court, and Race Relations, 1890–1965." *The South as an American Problem.* Eds. Larry J. Griffin and Don H. Doyle. Athens: U of Georgia P, 1995. 126–44.
Fair, Bryan K. "Using Parrots to Kill Mockingbirds." *Alabama Law Review* 45.2 (1994): 403–71.
Ferguson, Robert A. *Law and Letters in American Culture.* Cambridge, Mass.: Harvard UP, 1984.
Fine, Laura. "Gender Conflicts and Their 'Dark' Projections in Coming of Age White Female Southern Novels." *Southern Quarterly* 36.4 (1998): 121–29.
Fish, Stanley. *Doing What Comes Naturally: Change, Rhetoric, and the Practice of Theory in Literary and Legal Studies.* Durham: Duke UP, 1989.
–. "The Law Wishes to Have a Formal Existence." *The Stanley Fish Reader.* Ed. H. Aram Veeser. Oxford: Blackwell, 1999. 165–206.
–. "Rhetoric." *The Stanley Fish Reader.* Ed. H. Aram Veeser. Oxford: Blackwell, 1999. 114–44.
Fiss, Owen. "The Challenge Ahead." *Yale Journal of Law and Humanities* 1 (1980): viii-xi.
Fliegelman, Jay. *Declaring Independence: Jefferson, Natural Language, and the Culture of Performance.* Stanford: Stanford UP, 1993.
–. "Introduction." *Wieland and Memoirs of Carwin the Biloquist.* New York: Penguin, 1991. vii–xiii.
Fluck, Winfried. *Das kulturelle Imaginäre: Eine Funktionsgeschichte des amerikanischen Romans.* Frankfurt: Suhrkamp, 1997.
Foote, Horton, and Harper Lee. *The Screenplay of 'To Kill a Mockingbird.'* 1st ed. New York: Harcourt Brace & World, 1964.
Fox, Richard L., and Robert W. Van Sickel. *Tabloid Justice: Criminal Justice in the Age of Media Frenzy.* Boulder: Lynne Rienner, 2001.
Freedman, Monroe H. "Atticus Finch — Right and Wrong." *Alabama Law Review* 45.2 (1994): 473–81.
–. "Atticus Finch Esq. R.I.P." *Legal Times* Feb. 24, 1992: 20–21.
Freeman, Michael, and Andrew D. E. Lewis, eds. *Law and Literature.* Vol. 2. Oxford: Oxford UP, 1999.
Friedman, Lawrence M. *American Law in the 20th Century.* New Haven: Yale UP, 2002.
–. "Are We a Litigious People?" *Legal Culture and the Legal Profession.* Eds. Lawrence M. Friedman and Harry N. Scheiber. Boulder: Westview, 1996. 53–77.
–. *A History of American Law.* 1973. 2nd ed. New York: Simon and Schuster, 1985.
Fremon, David K. *The Jim Crow Laws and Racism in American History.* Berkeley Heights: Enslow, 2000.
Friendly, Alfred, and Ronald L. Goldfarb. *Crime and Publicity: The Impact of News on the Administration of Justice.* New York: The Twentieth Century Fund, 1967.

Gaakeer, Jeanne. *Hope Springs Eternal: An Introduction to the Work of James Boyd White.* Madison: U of Michigan P, 1998.
Gaddis, William. *A Frolic of His Own.* New York: Simon and Schuster, 1995.
–. "Old Foes With New Faces." *Yale Review* 83.4 (1995): 1–16.
Gemmette, Elizabeth V., ed. *Law in Literature: Legal Themes in Short Stories.* New York: Praeger, 1992.
Gilbert, Geoffrey. "The Late Lord Chief Baron." *The Law of Evidence.* 1754. 5th ed. Philadelphia: Crushank, 1788.
Ginzburg, Carlo. "Checking the Evidence: The Judge and the Historian." *Questions of Evidence. Proof, Practice, and Persuasion across the Disciplines.* Eds. James Chandler, Arnold I. Davidson, and Harry Harootunian. Chicago: U of Chicago P, 1994. 290–303.
Glendon, Mary Ann. *One Nation Under Lawyers.* New York: Farrar, Straus and Giroux, 1994.
Goodman, James. *Stories of Scottsboro.* New York: Pantheon, 1994.
Goodrich, Peter. "Antirrhesis: Polemical Structures of Common Law Thought." *The Rhetoric of Law.* Eds. Austin Sarat and Thomas R. Kearns. Ann Arbor: U of Michigan P, 1994. 57–102.
–. "Europe in America: Grammatology, Legal Studies, and the Politics of Transmission." *Columbia Law Review* 101 (2001): 2033–80.
–. *Languages of the Law: From the Logics of Memory to Nomadic Masks.* London: Weidenfeld and Nicolson, 1990.
–. *Law in the Courts of Love: Literature and other Minor Jurisprudences.* London: Routledge, 1996.
–. *Legal Discourse: Studies in Linguistics, Rhetoric, and Legal Analysis.* New York: St. Martin's Press, 1987.
–. *Oedipus Lex: Psychoanalysis, History, Law.* Berkeley: U of California P, 1995.
–. "Specula Laws: Image, Aesthetic, and Common Law." *Law and Critique* 2.2 (1991): 233–54.
Goody, Jack. "The Letter of the Law." *The Logic of Writing and the Organization of Society.* New York: Cambridge UP, 1986. 127–70.
Gossman, Lionel. "History and Literature: Reproduction or Signification." Eds. Robert H. Canary and Henry Kozicki. *The Writing of History.* Madison: U of Wisconsin P, 1978. 3–40.
Gotanda, Neil. "A Critique of 'Our Constitution is Color-Blind'." Ed. Kimberlé Crenshaw, Neil Gotanda, Gary Peller, and Kendall Thomas. *Critical Race Theory: The Key Writings That Formed the Movement.* New York: The New Press, 1995. 257–275.
Greiner, Donald J. "Brown's Use of the Narrator in Wieland: An Indirect Plea for the Acceptance of Fiction." *CLA Journal* 13 (December 1969): 131–36.
Grimké, Thomas Smith. *An Oration, on the Practicability and Expediency of Reducing the Whole Body of the Law to the Simplicity and Order of a Code.* Charleston: A. E. Miller, 1827.
Grossman, James. "Cooper and the Responsibility of the Press." *James Fenimore Cooper: A Reappraisal.* Eds. Mary E. Cunningham and Howard Mumford Jones. Cooperstown: New York State Historical Society, 1954. 144–53.
–. *James Fenimore Cooper.* Stanford: Stanford UP, 1949.
Gunning, Sandra. *Race, Rape, and Lynching.* New York: Oxford UP, 1996.

Gustafson, Thomas. *Representative Words: Politics, Literature, and the American Language, 1776–1865*. New York: Cambridge UP, 1992.

Habermas, Jürgen. *The Structural Transformation of the Public Sphere*. Cambridge: Harvard, 1989.

Hacking, Ian. *The Emergence of Probability*. Cambridge: Cambridge UP, 1975.

Hagenbüchle, Roland. "American Literature and the Nineteenth-Century Crisis in Epistemology: The Example of Charles Brockden Brown." *Early American Literature* 23 (1988): 121–51.

Hagstrum, Jean. *The Sister Arts*. Chicago: U of Chicago P, 1958.

Haldar, Piyel. "The Evidencer's Eye: Representations of Truth in the Laws of Evidence." *Law and Critique* 2.2 (1991): 171–89.

Hale, Grace Elizabeth. *Making Whiteness: The Culture of Segregation in the South, 1890–1940*. New York: Random House, 1998.

Hale, Matthew. *The Primitive Origination of Mankind*. London, 1677.

Hall, Kermit L., William M. Wiecek, and Paul Finkelman. *American Legal History: Cases and Materials*. 1991. 2nd ed. New York: Oxford UP, 1996.

Halliwell, Stephen. *Aristotle's Poetics*. 1986. Chicago: U of Chicago P, 1998.

Haltom, William. *Reporting on the Courts: How the Mass Media Covers Judicial Actions*. Chicago: Nelson-Hall, 1998.

Halttunen, Karen. "Early American Murder Narratives: The Birth of Horror." *The Power of Culture: Critical Essays in American History*. Eds. T. J. Jackson Lears and Richard Wightman Fox. Chicago: U of Chicago P, 1993. 67–101.

Haney López, Ian F. *White by Law: The Legal Construction of Race*. New York: New York UP, 1996.

Hariman, Robert, ed. *Popular Trials: Rhetoric, Mass Media, and the Law*. Tuscaloosa/London: U of Alabama P, 1990.

Harris, Cheryl I. "Whiteness as Property." *Harvard Law Review* 106 (1993): 1709–89.

Haskins, James. *The Scottsboro Boys*. 1st ed. New York: H. Holt and Co., 1994.

Hathorn, Richmond Y. "Rhetoric." *Encyclopedia Americana*. Danbury, 1992. 466.

Heilbrun, Carolyn, and Judith Resnick. "Convergences: Law, Literature, and Feminism." *Yale Law Journal* 99 (1990): 1913–56.

Herman, Shael. "The Fate and Future of Codification in America." *American Journal of Legal History* 40.4 (1996): 407–37.

Hesford, Walter. "'Do You Know the Author?': The Question of Authorship in *Wieland*." *Early American Literature* 17 (1982): 239–48.

Hibbitts, Bernhard J. "'Coming to Our Senses': Communication and Legal Expression in Performance Cultures." *Emory Law Journal* 41.4 (1992): 874–960.

Higginbotham, A. Leon, Jr. *Shades of Freedom: Racial Politics and Presumptions of the American Legal Process*. New York: Oxford UP, 1996.

Hoff, Timothy. "Influences on Harper Lee: An Introduction to the Symposium." *Alabama Law Review* 45.2 (1994): 389–401.

Horwitz, Morton J. *The Transformation of American Law, 1780–1860*. Cambridge: Harvard UP, 1977.

Howard, John R. *The Shifting Wind: The Surpreme Court and Civil Rights from Reconstruction to* Brown. Albany: State U of New York P, 1999.

Howard, Philip K. *The Collapse of the Common Good: How America's Lawsuit Culture Undermines Our Freedom*. New York: Oxford UP, 2001.

–. *The Death of Common Sense: How Law is Suffocating America.* New York: Random House, 1994.

Howells, Christina. *Derrida: Deconstruction from Phenomenology to Ethics.* Cambridge: Polity, 1999.

Hudson-Weems, Clenora. *Emmett Till: The Sacrificial Lamb of the Civil Rights Movement.* Troy: Bedford, 1994.

Hughes, Rowland. "'Wonderfully Cruel Proceedings': The Murderous Case of James Yates." *Canadian Review of American Studies* 38.1 (2008): 43–62.

Huie, William Bradford. "The Shocking Story of Approved Killing in Mississippi." *Look* Jan. 24, 1956: 46–50.

–. "What's Happened to the Emmett Till Killers?" *Look* Jan. 22, 1957: 64.

Hurst, James Willard. *Law and the Conditions of Freedom.* Madison: U of Wisconsin P, 1956.

Hutchinson, Allan C., ed. *Critical Legal Studies.* Totowa: Rowman & Littlefield, 1989.

Ickstadt, Heinz. "Instructing the American Democrat: Cooper and the Concept of Popular Fiction in Jacksonian America." *James Fenimore Cooper: New Critical Essays.* Ed. Robert Clark. London: Vision and Barnes and Noble, 1986. 15–37.

Iser, Wolfgang. *Das Fiktive und das Imaginäre.* Frankfurt/Main: Suhrkamp, 1993.

James, Henry. *Letters of Henry James.* Ed. Percy Lubbock. Vol. 2. New York: Scribner's, 1920.

Johnson, Claudia Durst. *Understanding 'To Kill a Mockingbird'.* Westport: Greenwood, 1994.

–. *'To Kill a Mockingbird': Threatening Boundaries.* New York: Twayne, 1994.

–. "Without Tradition and Within Reason: Judge Horton and Atticus Finch in Court." *Alabama Law Review* 45.2 (1994): 483–509.

Johnson, Nan. *Nineteenth-Century Rhetoric in North America.* Carbondale: Southern Illinois UP, 1991.

Johnson, John W. *American Legal Culture, 1908–1940.* Westport: Greenwood, 1981.

Johnson, Sheri Lynn. "Cross-Racial Identification Errors in Criminal Cases." *Cornell Law Review* 69 (1984): 934–87.

Johnston, John. *Carnival of Repetition.* Philadelphia: U of Pennsylvania P, 1990.

Jones, Carolyn. "Atticus Finch and the Mad Dog: Harper Lee's *To Kill a Mockingbird.*" *Southern Quarterly* 34.4 (1996): 53–63.

Jordan, Cynthia S. "On Rereading *Wieland*: The Folly of Precipitate Conclusions." *Early American Literature* 16 (1981): 154–74.

Kadish, Sanford H. *David Dudley Field and His Criminal Code.* Berkeley: Boalt Hall Alumni Association, 1979.

Kafer, Peter. *Charles Brockden Brown's Revolution and the Birth of American Gothic.* Philadelphia: U of Pennsylvania P, 2004.

Kafka, Franz. *Der Prozeß.* 1925. Frankfurt a. M.: Fischer, 1960.

–. "Vor dem Gesetz." *Sämtliche Erzählungen.* Frankfurt a. M.: Fischer, 1970. 131–32.

Kagan, Robert A. *Adversarial Legalism: The American Way of Law.* Cambridge: Harvard UP, 2001.

Kahn, Victoria. "Rhetoric and the Law." *Diacritics* 15 (1989): 21–34.

Kamrath, Mark. "Charles Brockden Brown and Contemporary Theory: A Review of Recent Critical Trends in Brown Scholarship." *Profils Américains: Charles Brockden Brown.* Vol. 11. Montpellier: Université Paul Valery Montpellier, 1999. 213–77.

Kayman, Martin A. "Lawful Writing: Common Law, Statute and the Properties of Literature." *New Literary History* 27 (1996): 761–83.

–. "Law-and-Literature: Questions of Jurisdiction." Ed. Brook Thomas. *Law and Literature.* Vol. 18. *REAL. Yearbook of Research in English and American Literature.* Tübingen: Narr, 2002. 1–20.

Kelly, William P. *Plotting America's Past: Fenimore Cooper and the* Leatherstocking Tales. Carbondale: Southern Illinois UP, 1983.

Kelman, Martin. *A Guide to Critical Legal Studies.* Cambridge: Harvard UP, 1987.

Kennedy, Duncan. "The Structure of Blackstone's *Commentaries.*" *Buffalo Law Review* 28 (1979): 211–12.

Kennedy, George. *The Art of Persuasion in Greece.* Princeton: Princeton UP, 1963.

–. *Classical Rhetoric and Its Christian and Secular Tradition from Ancient to Modern Times.* London: Croom Helm, 1980.

Kindermann, Wolf. *Man Unknown to Himself: Kritische Reflexion der amerikanischen Aufklärung: Crèvecœur — Benjamin Rush — Charles Brockden Brown.* Tübingen: Narr, 1993.

Klarman, Michael J. "Brown, Racial Change, and the Civil Rights Movement." *Virginia Law Review* 80 (Feb. 1994): 7–150.

–. "How Brown Changed Race Relations: The Backlash Thesis." *Journal of American History* 81 (June 1994): 81–118.

–. "The Racial Origin of Modern Criminal Procedure." *Michigan Law Review* 99 (Oct. 2000): 48–97.

Knapp, Steven, and Walter Benn Michaels. "Against Theory: Literary Studies and the New Pragmatism." *Critical Inquiry* 8.4 (1982): 723–42.

Knight, Christopher J. *Hints and Guesses: William Gaddis' Fiction of Longing.* Madison: U of Wisconsin P, 1997.

Koffler, Judith. "Assimilation of Law and Literature: An Approach to Metanoia." *ASLA* 3.1 (1978): 5–11.

Kopperschmidt, Josef. "Zur Anthropologie des forensischen Menschen." *Rhetorische Anthropologie: Studien zum Homo rhetoricus.* Ed. Josef Kopperschmidt. Munich: Fink, 2000. 205–43.

Korobkin, Laura. "Murder by Madman: Criminal Responsibility, Law, and Judgment in *Wieland.*" *American Literature* 72.4 (2000): 721–50.

–. "Narrative Battles in the Court Room." Ed. Marjorie Garber. *Field Work: Sites in Literary and Cultural Studies.* New York: Oxford UP, 1996. 225–36.

Krauss, Elissa, and Martha Schulman. "Symposium: Juries: Arbiters or Arbitrary? Redefining the Role of the Jury: The Myth of Black Juror Nullification: Racism Dressed Up in Jurisprudential Clothing." *Cornell Journal of Law and Public Policy* 7 (Fall 1997): 57–84.

Kreyling, Michael. "Construing Brown's *Wieland*: Ambiguity and Derridean 'Freeplay.'" *Studies in the Novel* 14 (1982): 43–54.

Landsman, Stephan. "From Gilbert to Bentham: The Reconceptualization of Evidence Theory." *Wayne Law Review* 36 (1990): 1149–68.

Langbein, John H. "Historical Foundations of the Law of Evidence: A View from the Ryder Sources." *Columbia Law Review* 96 (1996): 1168–202.

Lanham, Richard. *The Motives of Eloquence.* New Haven: Yale UP, 1976.

Lausberg, Heinrich. *Handbook of Literary Rhetoric: A Foundation for Literary Study.* Trans. Matthew T. Bliss, Annemiek Jansen, and David E. Orton. Leiden: Brill, 1998.

Ledwon, Lenora, ed. *Law and Literature.* New York/London: Garland Publishing, 1996.

Levine, George. *Realism and Representation: Essays on the Problem of Realism in Relation to Science, Literature and Culture.* Madison: U of Wisconsin P, 1993.

Levinson, Sanford, and Steven Mailloux, eds. *Interpreting Law and Literature.* Evanston: Northwestern UP, 1988.

Lewis, R. W. B. *The American Adam.* Chicago: U of Chicago P, 1955.

Lewis, William Draper, ed. *Great American Lawyers.* 1907. Vol. 1. South Hackensack: Rothman Reprints, 1971.

Lieberman, Jethro K. *The Litigious Society.* New York: Basic, 1981.

Limon, John. *The Place of Fiction in the Time of Science.* Cambridge: Cambridge UP, 1990.

Litton, Alfred G. "The Failure of Rhetoric in Charles Brockden Brown's *Wieland.*" *Lamar Journal of the Humanities* 16.2 (1990): 23–40.

Locke, John. *An Essay Concerning Human Understanding.* 1690. Ed. Peter H. Nidditch. Oxford: Clarendon, 1975.

Looby, Christopher. *Voicing America: Language, Literary Form and the Origins of the United States.* Chicago: U of Chicago P, 1996.

Lowe, Donald. *The History of Bourgeois Perception.* Chicago: U of Chicago P, 1982.

Luck, Chad. "Re-Walking the Purchase: Edgar Huntly, David Hume, and the Origins of Ownership." *Early American Literature* 44.2 (2009): 271–306.

Maclean, Marie. *Narrative as Performance: The Baudelairian Experiment.* London: Routledge, 1988.

Marks, Marlene Adler. *The Suing of America: Why and How We Take Each Other to Court.* New York: Seaview, 1981.

McCoubry, H. *The Development of Naturalist Legal Theory.* London: Croom Helm, 1987.

McCurdy, Charles. *The Anti-Rent Era in New York Law and Politics, 1839–1865.* Chapel Hill: U of North Carolina P, 2001.

McWilliams, John P. "Innocent Criminal and Criminal Innocence: The Trial in American Fiction." Ed. Carl S. Smith. *Law and American Literature.* New York: Knopf, 1983. 45–123.

–. *Political Justice in the Republic.* Berkeley: U of California P, 1972.

Meyler, Bernadette A. "Book Review: The Myth of Law and Literature." *Cornell Law Faculty Publications* 44 (2005): 1–10. <http://scholarship.law.cornell.edu/lsrp_papers/44>.

Mellinkoff, David. *The Language of the Law.* Boston: Little, Brown and Company, 1963.

Michaels, Walter Benn. "Against Formalism: The Autonomous Text in Legal and Literary Interpretation." *Poetics Today* 1.1–2 (1979): 23–34.

–. *The Gold Standard and the Logic of Naturalism.* Berkeley: U of California P, 1987.

Miller, Charles A. "The Forest of Due Process of Law: The American Constitutional Tradition." Eds. Roland J. Pennock and John W. Chapman. *Due Process.* New York: New York UP, 1977. 3–68.

Miller, Perry. *The Legal Mind in America.* New York: Doubleday, 1962.

–. *The Life of the Mind in America.* New York: Hartcourt, 1965.

Minda, Gary. *Postmodern Legal Movements.* New York: New York UP, 1995.

Mitchell, W. T. J. Ed. *Against Theory: Literary Studies and the New Pragmatism.* Chicago: U of Chicago P, 1985.

–. *Iconology: Image, Text, Ideology.* Chicago: U of Chiacago P, 1986.

Moran, Michael G. Ed. *Eighteenth-Century British and American Rhetorics and Rhetoricians.* New York: Greenwood, 1994.

Morisson, Toni. *Playing in the Dark: Whiteness and the Literary Imagination*. Cambridge: Harvard UP, 1992.

Morley, David, and Kevin Robins. *Spaces of Identity: Global Media, Electronic Landscapes and Cultural Boundaries*. London: Routledge, 1995.

Moore, Steven. *William Gaddis*. Twayne's United States Authors Series. Boston: Twayne, 1989.

Mukherji, Subha. "'Understood Relations': Law and Literature in Early Modern Studies." *Literature Compass* 6.3 (2009): 706–25.

Murphy, Peter. *A Practical Approach to Evidence*. London: Blackstone, 1980.

Myrsiades, Kostas, and Linda Myrsiades, eds. *Un-Disciplining Literature: Literature, Law, and Culture*. New York: Peter Lang, 1999.

Nedelsky, Jennifer. *Property and the Limits of American Constitutionalism*. Chicago: U of Chicago P, 1990.

Nelson, William E. *Americanization of the Common Law: The Impact of Legal Change in Massachusetts Society, 1760–1830*. Cambridge: Harvard UP, 1975.

Newmyer, R. Kent. "Harvard Law School, New England Legal Culture, and the Antebellum Origins of American Jurisprudence." *Journal of American History* 74.3 (1987): 814–35.

Nichols, Marcia. "Cicero's *Pro Cluentio* and the 'Mazy' Rhetorical Strategies of *Wieland*." *Law and Literature* 20.3 (2008): 459–76.

O'Barr, William. *Linguistic Evidence: Language, Power, and Strategy in the Courtroom*. San Diego: Academic Press, 1982.

O'Donnell, Patrick. "The Reader's *Frolic*." Eds. Jean-Louis Brunel and Michel Gresset. *Profils Americains: William Gaddis*. Vol. 6. Montpellier: Université Paul-Valery Montpellier, 1994. 161–71.

O'Leary, Kevin. "Masters of the Legal Universe." *OC Metro* May 16, 2002: 32–43.

Oliver, Mary Beth, and Dana Fonash. "Race and Crime in the News: Whites' Identification and Misidentification of Violent and Nonviolent Criminal Suspects." *Media Psychology* 4 (2002): 137–56.

Olson, Walter K. *The Litigation Explosion*. New York: Truman Talley, 1991.

O'Neill, Terry, ed. *Readings on To Kill a Mockingbird*. San Diego: Greenhaven, 2000.

O'Shaughnessy, Toni. "'An Imperfect Tale': Interpretive Accountability in *Wieland*." *Studies in American Fiction* 18.1 (1990): 41–54.

Osborn, John Jay, Jr. "Atticus Finch — The End of Honor." *U of San Francisco Law Review* 30.4 (1996): 1139–43.

Outland, Ethel Rose. *The "Effingham" Libels on Cooper*. Studies in Language and Literature 28. Madison: U of Wisconsin, 1929.

Papantonio, Mike. *In Search of Atticus Finch: A Motivational Book for Lawyers*. Pensacola: Seville, 1996.

Papke, David R. *Narrative and the Legal Discourse: A Reader in Storytelling and the Law.* Liverpool: Deborah Charles, 1990.

–. "Neo-Marxists, Nietzscheans and New Critics: The Voices of the Contemporary Law and Literature Discourse." *American Bar Foundation Research Journal* (Fall 1985): 883–97.

–. "Law in American Culture: An Overview." *Journal of American Culture* 15.1 (1992): 3–14.

Pascal, Blaise. *Thoughts* [*Pensées,* 1670]. Trans. W. F. Trotter. Ed. Charles W. Eliot. The Harvard Classics 48. New York: Collier, 1909–1914. Frag. 294.

Patey, Douglas Lane. *Probability and Literary Form.* Cambridge: Cambridge UP, 1984.

Peck, H. Daniel. *A World by Itself: The Pastoral Moment in Cooper's Fiction.* New Haven: Yale UP, 1977.

Person, Leland S. "Cooper's *The Pioneers* and Leatherstocking's Historical Function." *ESQ* 25.1 (1979): 1–10.

Phelps, Theresa Godwin. "The Margins of Maycomb." *Alabama Law Review* 45.2 (1994): 511–29.

Plato. *Laws.* Trans. R.G. Bury. Plato in Twelve Volumes. Vol. 10, 11. Cambridge: Harvard UP, 1967–68.

Porsdam, Helle. *From Civil to Human Rights: Dialogues on Law and the Humanities.* London: Edgar Elgar, 2010.

–, ed. *Lawways and Folkways.* Odense: Odense UP, 2001.

–. *Legally Speaking: Contemporary American Culture and the Law.* Amherst: Massachusetts UP, 1999.

Posner, Richard A. *Cardozo: A Study in Reputation.* Chicago: U of Chicago P, 1990.

–. "The Ethical Significance of Free Choice: A Reply to Professor West." *Harvard Law Review* 99 (1985): 1431–48.

–. *Law and Literature.* Cambridge: Harvard UP, 1988.

–. "Law and Literature: A Relation Reargued." *Law and Literature: Text and Theory.* Ed. Lenora Ledown. New York: Garland, 1996. 61–73.

Potkay, Adam S. "Theorizing Civic Eloquence in the Early Republic: The Road from David Hume to John Quincy Adams." *Early American Literature* 34 (1999): 147–70.

Pound, Roscoe. *The Formative Era of American Law.* New York: Pete Smith, 1950.

Prosser, William. *Handbook of the Law of Torts.* St. Paul: West, 1941.

Pynchon, Thomas. *The Crying of Lot 49.* 1965. London: Picador, 1979.

Raban, Jonathan. "At Home in Babel." *New York Review of Books* Feb. 17, 1994: 3–6.

Railton, Stephen. *Fenimore Cooper: A Study of His Life and Imagination.* Princeton: Princeton UP, 1978.

Reardon, Patrick T "'Mockingbird' Sure to Spark Talk on Race and Alienation." *Chicago Tribune.* Aug. 6, 2001.

–. "Mockingbird Takes Wings." *Chicago Tribune* Oct. 12, 2001.

–. "Novel Idea Still Relevant." *Chicago Tribune* Sept. 29, 2001.

–, and Marja Mills. "Book Club Starting Up, and Whole City is Invited." *Chicago Tribune* Aug. 3, 2001.

Reid, Thomas. *Essays on the Intellectual Powers of Man.* 1785. London: Macmillan, 1941.

–. *An Inquiry into the Human Mind on the Principles of Common Sense.* 1764. Ed. Derek R. Brookes. Edinburgh: Edinburgh UP, 1997.

Rescher, Nicholas, and Carey B. Joynt. "Evidence in History and in the Law." *Journal of Philosophy* 56.13 (1959): 561–78.

Reutlinger, Mark. *Evidence: Essential Terms and Concepts.* Aspen: Aspen Law and Business, 1996.

Ricœur, Paul. *The Rule of Metaphor.* Toronto: U of Toronto P, 1977.

Ringe, Donald A. *James Fenimore Cooper.* Twayne's United States Authors Series 11. Updated ed. Boston: Twayne, 1988.

Rockwood, Bruce L., ed. *Law and Literature Perspectives.* Vol. 9. New York: Peter Lang, 1996.

Rorty, Richard. *The Linguistic Turn*. Chicago: U of Chicago P, 1967.

Rose, Mark. "The Author as Proprietor: *Donaldson v. Becket* and the Genealogy of Modern Authorship." *Representations* 23 (1988): 51–85.

Ross, John Frederic. *The Social Criticism of Fenimore Cooper.* Folcroft, Pa.: Folcroft P, 1969.

Ross, Trevor. "Copyright and the Invention of Tradition." *Eighteenth-Century Studies* 26.1 (1992): 1–27.

Rushdy, Ashraf. "Exquisite Corpse." *Transition* 9.3 (2000): 70–77.

Russo, James R. "'The Chimeras of the Brain': Clara's Narrative in *Wieland*." *Early American Literature* 16 (1981): 60–88.

Samuels, Shirley. "Wieland: Alien and Infidel." *Early American Literature* 25 (1990): 46–66.

Sampson, William. *An Anniversary Discourse Delivered Before the Historical Society of New York, on Saturday, December 6, 1823; Showing the Origin, Progress, Antiquities, Curiosities, and Nature of the Common Law.* Washington D.C.: Thompson, 1826.

Sarat, Austin, ed. *Race, Law, and Culture: Reflections of* Brown v. Board of Education. New York: Oxford UP, 1997.

–. "Rhetoric and Remembrance: Trials, Transcription, and the Politics of Critical Thinking." *Legal Studies Forum* 23.4 (1999): 355–78.

Sarat, Austin, and Thomas R. Kearns, eds. *The Rhetoric of Law.* Ann Arbor: U of Michigan P, 1994.

Saunders, David. "Approaches to the Historical Relations of the Legal and the Aesthetic." *New Literary History* 23 (1992): 505–21.

Scheppele, Kim Lane. "Facing Facts in Legal Interpretation." *Representations* 30 (1990): 42–77.

Schmidgen, Wolfram. *Eighteenth-Century Fiction and the Law of Property.* Cambridge: Cambridge UP, 2006.

Schmidt, Leigh Eric. *From Demon Possession to Magic Show: Ventriloquism, Religion, and the Enlightenment.* 2000. <http://www.materialreligion.org/journal/magic.html>.

Schneck, Peter. "Pictorial Desires and Textual Anxieties: Modes of Ekphrastic Discourse in Nineteenth-Century American Culture." *Word and Image* 15:5 (1999): 54–63.

Schramm, Jan-Melissa. *Testimony and Advocacy in Victorian Law, Literature, and Theology.* Cambridge Studies in Nineteenth-Century Literature and Culture 27. Cambridge: Cambridge UP, 2000.

Schwartz, Bernhard. *Main Currents in American Legal Thought.* Durham: Carolina Academic P, 1993.

Schwartz, Hillel. *The Culture of the Copy.* Cambridge: MIT Press, 1998.

Seed, David. "The Mind Set Free: Charles Brockden Brown's *Wieland*." *Making America/Making American Literature.* Eds. A. Robert Lee and W. M. Verhoeven. Amsterdam: Rodopi, 1996. 105–22.

Seltzer, Mark. "Saying Makes It So: Language and Event in Brown's *Wieland*." *Early American Literature* 13 (1978): 81–91.

Shaffer, Thomas L. "Growing Up Good in Maycomb." *Alabama Law Review* 45.2 (1994): 531–61.

Shakelford, Dean. "The Female Voice in *To Kill a Mockingbird*: Narrative Strategies in Film and Novel." *Mississippi Quarterly* 50.1 (1997): 101–13.

Shapin, Steven. *A Social History of Truth: Civility and Society in Seventeenth-Century England.* Chicago: U of Chicago P, 1994.

Shapiro, Barbara J. *"Beyond Reasonable Doubt" and "Probable Cause": Historical Perspectives on the Anglo-American Law of Evidence.* Berkeley: U of California P, 1991.

–. "Classical Rhetoric and the English Law of Evidence." *Rhetoric and Law in Early Modern Europe.* Eds. Victoria Kuhn and Lorna Hutson. New Haven: Yale UP, 2001. 54–72.

–. *Probability and Certainty in Seventeenth-Century England: A Study of the Relationship between Natural Science, Religion, History, Law and Literature.* Princeton: Princeton UP, 1983.

–. "To a Moral Certainty: Theories of Knowledge and Anglo-American Juries 1600–1850." *Hastings Law Journal* 38 (1986): 153–93.

Sharpe, Tony. "(Per)Versions of Law in Literature." *Law and Literature.* Eds. Michael Freeman and Andrew D. E. Lewis, 1999. 91–115.

Shelley, Percy Bysshe. *The Complete Works of Percy Bysshe Shelley.* Eds. R. Ingpen and W. E. Peck. New York: Gordian P, 1965.

Sheridan, Thomas. *A Course of Lectures on Elocution.* 1762. Hildesheim: Georg Olms, 1970.

Sherwin, Richard K. "Picturing Justice: Images of Law and Lawyers in the Visual Media." *U of San Francisco Law Review* 30.4 (1996): 891–901.

–. *When Law Goes Pop: The Vanishing Line Between Law and Popular Culture.* Chicago: U of Chicago P, 2000.

Shulenberger, Arvid. *Cooper's Theory of Fiction: His Prefaces and Their Relation to His Novels.* New York: Octagon Books, 1972.

Simpson, William M. "Reflections on a Murder: The Emmett Till Case." *Southern Miscellany: Essays in History in Honor of Clover Moore.* Ed. Frank Allen Dennis. Jackson: U of Mississippi P, 1981. 177–200.

Slaughter, Joseph R. *Human Rights, Inc.: The World Novel, Narrative Form, and International Law.* New York: Fordham UP, 2007.

Slawinski, Scott. *Validating Brotherhood: Audience, Patriarchy, and Charles Brockden Brown's Editorship of the* Monthly Magazine *and* American Review. New York: Routledge, 2005.

Slotkin, Richard. *Regeneration Through Violence.* Middletown: Wesleyan UP, 1973.

Smelser, Marshall. "The Federalist Period as an Age of Passion." *American Quarterly* 10.4 (1958): 391–419.

Smith, Carl S., Jr., John P. MacWilliams, and Maxwell Bloomfield. *Law and American Literature: A Collection of Essays.* New York: Alfred A. Knopf, 1983.

Smith, Gary, and Matthias Kroß, ed. *Die ungewisse Evidenz: Für eine Kulturgeschichte des Beweises.* Berlin: Akademie Verlag, 1999.

Smith, Henry Nash. *Virgin Land: The American West as Symbol and Myth.* 1950. Cambridge: Harvard U P, 1970.

Snedaker, Kathryn Holmes. "Storytelling in Opening Statements: Framing the Argumentation of the Trial." *American Journal of Trial Advocacy* 10 (1986): 15–45.

Solbach, Andreas. *Evidentia und Erzähltheorie: Die Rhetorik anschaulichen Erzählens in der Frühmoderne und ihre antiken Quellen.* München: Fink, 1994.

Spiller, Robert E. *Fenimore Cooper, Critic of His Times.* New York: Russell & Russell, 1963.

Stachenfeld, Avi J., and Christopher M. Nicholson. "Blurred Boundaries: An Analysis of the Close Relationship between Popular Culture and the Practice of the Law." *U of San Francisco Law Review* 30.4 (1996): 903–16.

Steiner, Wendy. *The Colors of Rhetoric.* Chicago: U of Chicago P, 1982.

Stieglitz, Uwe. *George Campbells Philosophie der Rhetorik.* Rhetorik Forschungen. Vol. 12. Tübingen: Niemeyer, 1998.

Stolzenberg, Nomi Maya. "Bentham's Theory of Fiction — A Curious Double Language." *Cardozo Studies in Law and Literature* 11.2 (1999): 223–61.

Stone, I. F. "The Murder of Emmett Till." *The Haunted Fifties.* New York: Random House, 1963. 107–09.

Suggs, Jon-Christian. "Epistemology and the Law in Four African American Fictions." *Legal Studies Forum* 14.2 (1990): 141–62.

–. *Whispered Consolations: Law and Narrative in African American Life.* Ann Arbor: U of Michigan Press, 2000.

Summers, David. *The Judgment of Sense: Renaissance Naturalism and the Rise of Aesthetics.* Cambridge: Cambridge UP, 1987.

Sundquist, Eric J. "Blues for Atticus Finch: Scottsboro, Brown and Harper Lee." *The South as an American Problem.* Eds. Larry J. Griffin and Don H. Doyle. Athens: U of Georgia P, 1995. 181–209.

Swearingen, James E., and Joanne Cutting-Gray. "Cooper's *Pathfinder:* Revising Historical Understanding." *New Literary History* 23.2 (1992): 267–80.

Swift, Zephaniah. *A Digest of the Law of Evidence, in Civil and in Criminal Cases.* Hartford: Oliver D. Cooke, 1810.

Tabbi, Joseph. *Postmodern Sublime.* Ithaca, 1995.

Tannen, Deborah. *The Argument Culture: Stopping America's War of Words.* New York: Ballantine, 1998.

Thaler, Paul. *The Watchful Eye: American Justice in the Age of the Television Trial.* Westport, Conn.: Praeger Publishers, 1994.

The early life and complete trial of Mary, alias Polly Bodine, for the murder of Emeline Houseman and her child ... New York: n.p., 1846.

Thielemans, J. "*Once in Antietam,* a lost Play Recovered. On *A Frolic of His Own.*" Eds. Jean-Louis Brunel and Michel Gresset. *Profils Américains: William Gaddis.* Vol. 6. Montpellier: Université Paul-Valery Montpellier, 1994. 173–84.

Thomas, Brook. *American Literary Realism and the Failed Promise of Contract.* Berkeley: U of California P, 1997.

–. *Cross-Examinations of Law and Literature.* Cambridge: Cambridge UP, 1987.

–. *Law and Literature.* REAL. Yearbook of Research in English and American Literature. Vol. 18. Tübingen: Narr, 2002.

–. *The New Historicism and Other Old Fashioned Topics.* Princeton: Princeton UP, 1991.

–. *Plessy v. Ferguson: A Brief History with Documents.* New York: Bedford, 1996.

–. "Reflections on the Law and Literature Revival." *Critical Inquiry* 17 (1991): 510–39.

Thorburn, David. "Television as an Aesthetic Medium." *Critical Studies in Mass Communication* 4.2 (1987): 161–73.

Thurschwell, Adam. "Reading the Law." *The Rhetoric of Law.* Eds. Austin Sarat and Thomas R. Kearns. Ann Arbor: U of Michigan P, 1994. 275–332.

To Kill a Mockingbird. 1962. Universal International Pictures (UI). Dir. Robert Mulligan. Script by Horton Foote, based on the novel by Harper Lee. 129 min.; black and white.

Tolnay, Stewart Emory, and E. M. Beck. *A Festival of Violence: An Analysis of Southern Lynchings, 1882–1930.* Urbana: U of Illinois P, 1995.

Tompkins, Jane. *Sensational Designs: The Cultural Work of American Fiction, 1790–1860.* New York: Oxford UP, 1985.
Tushnet, Mark. "Critical Legal Studies: An Introduction to its Origins and Underpinnings." *Journal of Legal Education* 36 (1986): 505–17.
Tushnet, Mark C. *Making Civil Rights Law.* New York: Oxford UP, 1994.
Twining, William. *Theories of Evidence: Bentham and Wigmore.* London: Weidenfeld and Nicolson, 1985.
Twining, William L. *Rethinking Evidence: Exploratory Essays.* Cambridge: Blackwell, 1990.
Unger, Roberto Mangabeira. *The Critical Legal Studies Movements.* Cambridge: Harvard UP, 1986.
Vandevelde, Kenneth J. "The New Property of the Nineteenth Century: The Development of the Modern Concept of Property." *Buffalo Law Review* 29 (1980): 325–67.
Vining, Joseph. "Generalization in Interpretive Theory." *Representations* 30 (Spring 1990): 1–12.
Vismann, Cornelia. "Tele-Tribunals: Anatomy of a Medium." *Grey Room* 10 (2003): 5–21.
Voloshin, Berverly R. "Wieland: 'Accounting for Appearances.'" *New England Quarterly* 59.3 (1986): 341–57.
Wallace, Karl R. Ed. *History of Speech Education in America: Background Studies.* New York: Appleton, Century, Crofts, 1954.
Waples, Dorothy. *The Whig Myth of James Fenimore Cooper.* Hamden, Conn.: Archon Books, 1968.
Ward, Ian. *Law and Literature: Possibilities and Perspectives.* Cambridge: Cambridge UP, 1995.
Warner, Michael. *The Letters of the Republic.* Cambridge: Harvard UP, 1990.
Warren, James Perrin. *Culture of Eloquence: Oratory and Reform in Antebellum America.* University Park: Pennsylvania State UP, 1999.
Watt, Ian. *The Rise of the Novel.* Berkeley: California UP, 1957.
Webster's Third New International Dictionary of the English Language. Springfield, Mass.: Merriam, 1971. 1811.
Weisenburger, Steven. *Fables of Subversion: Satire and the American Novel.* Athens: U of Georgia P, 1995.
Weiss, Gunther A. "The Enchantment of Codification in the Common-Law World." *Yale Journal of International Law* 25 (2000): 435–540.
Weisberg, Richard. *The Failure of the Word: The Lawyer as Protagonist in Modern Fiction.* New Haven: Yale UP, 1984.
–. "Law in and as Literature: Self-Generated Meaning in the 'Procedural Novel.'" *The Comparative Perspective on Literature: Approaches to Theory and Practice.* Eds. Clayton Koelb and Susan Noakes. Ithaca and London: Cornell UP, 1988. 224–32.
–. *Poethics and Other Strategies of Law and Literature.* New York: Columbia UP, 1992.
Weisberg, Robert. "The Law-Literature Enterprise." *Yale Journal of Law and the Humanities* 1 (1988): 1–67.
–. "Taking Law Seriously." *Yale Journal of Law and the Humanities* 7 (1995): 445–55.
Weitin, Thomas. *Zeugenschaft: Das Recht der Literatur.* München: Fink, 2009.
Weldon, Roberta F. "Charles Brockden Brown's *Wieland*: A Family Tragedy." *Studies in American Fiction* 12.1 (1984): 1–11.

Welsh, Alexander. "The Evidence of Things Not Seen: Justice Stephen and Bishop Butler." *Representations* 24 (1988): 60–88.

–. *Strong Representations: Narrative and Circumstancial Evidence in England.* Baltimore: Johns Hopkins UP, 1992.

West, Robin. *Narrative, Authority, and Law.* Ann Arbor: U of Michigan P, 1993.

Wetlaufer, Gerald B. "Rhetoric and its Denial in Legal Discourse." *Virginia Law Review* 76 (1990): 1545–97.

White, James Boyd. *Heracles' Bow: Essays in the Rhetoric and the Poetics of the Law.* Madison: U of Wisconsin P, 1985.

–. "Law as Rhetoric, Rhetoric as Law: The Arts of Cultural and Communal Life." *University of Chicago Law Review,* 52.3 (1985): 684–702.

–. *The Legal Imagination: Studies in the Nature of Legal Thought and Expression.* Boston: Little, Brown, 1973.

Whitfield, Steven J. *A Death in the Delta: The Story of Emmett Till.* Baltimore, Md.: Johns Hopkins UP, 1988.

Wiegman, Robyn. *American Anatomies: Theorizing Race and Gender.* Durham: Duke UP, 1995.

Wilf, Steven. "The First Republican Revival: Virtue, Judging, and Rhetoric in the Early Republic." *Connecticut Law Review* 32 (2000): 1675–98.

Williams, Juan. *Eyes on the Prize.* New York: Viking, 1987.

Williams, Patricia. *Alchemy of Race and Rights.* Cambridge: Harvard UP, 1991.

Wilson, James. *The Works of James Wilson.* Ed. Robert Green McCloskey. 2 vols. Cambridge: Belknap, 1967.

Wiltenburg, Joy. "True Crime: The Origins of Modern Sensationalism." *The American Historical Review* 109.5 (2004): 1–56.

Woodmansee, Martha. "The Genius and the Copyright. Economic and Legal Conditions of the Emergence of the Author." *Eighteenth-Century Studies* 17.4 (1984): 425–48.

Woodward, Calvin. "Listening to the Mockingbird." *Alabama Law Review* 45.2 (1994): 563–83.

Woodward, C. Vann. *The Strange Career of Jim Crow.* New York: Oxford UP, 1974.

Wright. Edward T. *How to Use Courtroom Drama to Win Cases.* Englewood Cliffs: Prentice-Hall, 1987.